# POLITICAL CHANGE IN THE THIRD WORLD

## CHARLES F. ANDRAIN

## Volume 79

Routledge
Taylor & Francis Group

LONDON AND NEW YORK

First published in 1988

This edition first published in 2011
by Routledge
2 Park Square, Milton Park, Abingdon, Oxon, OX14 4RN

Simultaneously published in the USA and Canada
by Routledge

711 Third Avenue, New York, NY 10017

*Routledge is an imprint of the Taylor & Francis Group, an informa business*

First issued in paperback 2013

© 1988 Allen & Unwin, Inc

*British Library Cataloguing in Publication Data*
A catalogue record for this book is available from the British Library

ISBN 13: 978-0-415-58414-2 (Set)
eISBN 13: 978-0-203-84035-1 (Set)
ISBN 13: 978-0-415-60129-0 (hbk Volume 79)
eISBN 13: 978-0-203-83578-4 (Volume 79)
ISBN 13: 978-0-415-84997-5 (pbk Volume 79)

**Publisher's Note**
The publisher has gone to great lengths to ensure the quality of this reprint but
points out that some imperfections in the original copies may be apparent.

**Disclaimer**
The publisher has made every effort to trace copyright holders and welcomes
correspondence from those they have been unable to contact.

Y EDITIONS:
NT

# POLITICAL CHANGE IN THE THIRD WORLD

# POLITICAL CHANGE
# IN THE THIRD WORLD

**Charles F. Andrain**

Boston
UNWIN HYMAN
London    Sydney    Wellington

**Allen & Unwin, Inc.**
8 Winchester Place, Winchester, Mass. 01890, USA

Published by the Academic Division of
**Unwin Hyman Ltd**
15/17 Broadwick Street, London W1V 1FB, UK

Allen & Unwin Australia Pty Ltd,
8 Napier Street, North Sydney, NSW 2060, Australia

Allen & Unwin (New Zealand) Ltd, in association with the Port
Nicholson Press Ltd
60 Cambridge Terrace, Wellington, New Zealand

**Library of Congress Cataloging-in-Publication Data**

Andrain, Charles F.
  Political change in the Third World/Charles F. Andrain.
      p.    cm.
Includes index.
ISBN 0-04-497029-3      ISBN 0-04-497030-7 (pbk.)
  1. Developing countries—Politics and government.
2. Developing countries—Economic policy.    3. Revolutions—
Developing countries.    4. Decolonization—Developing countries.
I. Title.
JF60.A535  1988
320.9172'4—dc19

**British Library Cataloguing in Publication Data**

Andrain, Charles F.
  Political change in the third world.
  1. Developing countries—Politics and
  government
  I. Title
  320.9172'4      JF60
  ISBN 0-04-497029-3
  ISBN 0-04-497030-7 Pbk

# CONTENTS

Preface

| | |
|---|---|
| 1 Models and Political Change | 1 |
| 2 Models of Third World Political Systems | 13 |
| 3 A Theoretical Explanation of Political Change | 52 |
| 4 Political Change in Vietnam | 76 |
| 5 Political Change in Cuba | 119 |
| 6 Political Change in Chile | 151 |
| 7 Political Change in Nigeria | 215 |
| 8 Political Change in Iran | 252 |
| Conclusion | 284 |
| About the Author | 290 |
| Index | 291 |

# PREFACE

This book explores three types of political change in the Third World: (1) alterations in political leaders and in the content of public policies, (2) more fundamental transformations of political structures, policy priorities, and ways of processing basic policy issues, and (3) impacts that economic, education, and health policies exert on societies, such as changes in unemployment, inflation, growth rates, income equality, literacy, infant mortality, and life expectancy.

In this volume, I analyze the ways that sociopolitical structures, beliefs, and public policies cause Third World political change. Chapters 1 and 2 present an overview of political changes in the Third World, with a focus on how different models of political systems—folk, bureaucratic-authoritarian, reconciliation, and mobilization—explain the dynamics of political events. Chapter 3 formulates a theory of political change and elaborates the features that distinguish "within-system" from "between-system" change. The next five chapters use these theoretical models to explain political changes in Vietnam, Cuba, Chile, Nigeria, and Iran.

Three distinctive features characterize this book. First, it relies on theoretical models to understand the process of systemic change in diverse Third World nations. During the last decade most comparative works on the developing areas either sketched abstract models or made detailed descriptions of specific cases. Few analyses applied general structural theories to historical changes in specific situations. Second, this book adopts an explicit policy focus often missing from other structural interpretations of political change. It probes beliefs about public policies, the role of government organizations and political parties in the policy process, the ways of handling policy issues, the content of economic, education, and health policies, and the impact of these three government programs on the society, especially on diverse social groups. Third, particularly since World War II the United States, the Soviet Union, multinational corporations, and intergovernmental agencies such as the World Bank and the International Monetary Fund have influenced policy performance in Third World nations. The book stresses the interaction between these foreign institutions and the domestic situation as they jointly affect political change.

Over the past thirty years several individuals have contributed to the ideas and findings presented in this book. David E. Apter of Yale University originally formulated the different models of political systems. My analyses constitute revisions and elaborations of his systemic typologies. During the early 1960s Carl G. Rosberg applied models of government decision-making to the African situation. As director of the Institute of International Studies at the University of California, Berkeley, he facilitated my research on the Berkeley campus. Since the early 1960s Virginia Thompson Adloff has encouraged me to pursue the reasons for historical political changes in Asia and Africa. The late Ben G. Burnett of Whittier College initially stimulated my interest in Latin American politics, especially Chile. At San Diego State University I received a sabbatical grant that enabled me to complete this book during the 1986–1987 academic year. Several SDSU colleagues who offered intellectual encouragement include David Johns, Richard Gripp, Brian Loveman, L. Vincent Padgett, D. Richard Little, Tae Jin Kahng, William A. Schultze, C. Richard Hofstetter, Betty Nesvold, and Ivo Feierabend. Professor Stanley Michalak of Franklin and Marshall College provided a detailed, insightful, and constructive review of the manuscript. I also appreciate the assistance of the editorial staff at Allen and Unwin, Inc., including Lisa Freeman-Miller, editor; Peggy McMahon, editorial assistant; and Lois Smith and Christina Moose, copy editors. Anne L. Leu efficiently typed the final draft of the manuscript. Michele Wenzel and Peggy McCroskey helped with the typing of earlier versions.

# 1

## MODELS AND POLITICAL CHANGE

In the old days, graduate students may have gone into the field as barefoot empiricists. Today they go equipped with elaborate systems models. . . . The barefoot empiricists didn't know where they might step; the recent students have trouble getting their feet on the ground.

— Sidney Verba

The term "Third World" originated during the post–World War II era to describe the cleavages fragmenting the world system. The cold war separated East from West—the Warsaw Pact nations from the NATO alliance. The economic cleavage divided North from South— the industrialized nations from the nonindustrial societies. As coined by the French demographer Alfred Sauvy, "Third World" referred to nations that favored a third, nonaligned path outside the Western industrialized capitalist countries (the First World) and East European state socialist societies (the Second World). Located in the southern part of the globe, nations in Asia, Africa, and Latin America also sought economic independence from the more developed states in Western Europe, Eastern Europe, and North America.[1] Today many Asian, African, and Latin American countries have failed to attain nonaligned status, economic independence, or growth. Most align with the Soviet Union or the United States—the two superpowers. Few have engineered high rates of industrial growth. Nevertheless, these aspirations retain a powerful attraction for most non-European leaders. Despite the extensive diversity throughout the less developed territories, the Third World concept provides a useful term for

1

generalizing about political changes in Asia, Africa, the Middle East, and Latin America.

To explain political changes in the Third World, social scientists have used models that focus on the key aspects of a political system. Through these models the observer can better understand the significance of political beliefs, the performance of political structures, the behavior of political leadership, and the operation of the public policy process. Without becoming either "barefoot empiricists" who miss the forest for the trees or theoretical sky pilots whose aerial view obscures their vision of specific trees, analysts seek to explain how the components of a political system affect one another, the whole system, and the degree of sociopolitical change that results from these interactions.

Among the early Greek philosophers, Plato offered the most convincing justification of models as theoretical guides for understanding dynamic political reality. In his famous allegory of the cave, Plato portrayed the tensions between the ideal world of systemic models and the actual empirical world. He imagined the empirical world as a cave, where people live as prisoners chained by their legs and necks. Under these darkened conditions, they can see only the shadows cast by the firelight on the wall of the cave that faces them. If one of the prisoners becomes free and leaves the cave, the freed prisoner perceives more clearly the nature of political reality. From this enlightened position, he can gain theoretical insight into the empirical world. What had formerly appeared as shadows or meaningless illusions now becomes intelligible. According to Plato, after gaining this theoretical understanding, the political theorist must return to the cave to enlighten his fellows about the meaning of political reality and to guide them toward a reconstructed political system freed of ignorance and impurity.[2]

In *The Republic*, Plato contrasted the theoretical world with the actual political world. Whereas models of political systems represent enlightenment—the pure Forms of Truth—the actual political world resembles a darkened cave. Models are pure; the empirical world is messier. As a simplified picture of reality, a model contains a few variables; the theoretician constructs a *system* that illustrates the linkages among these variables. The parts of a model are abstract rather than concrete. A few general, abstract variables such as structure and belief are isolated for detailed analysis. Thus a model downplays the nuances, differences, and complexities of concrete societies but concentrates instead on the general, simplified tendencies of systemic performance and change. By contrast, the actual political world is more complex than a model. Many variables, not only a few, produce political outcomes. Rather than fitting closely together in systemic interdependencies, the

2

parts of the actual world behave more randomly. Instead of viewing the political universe from an abstract perspective, participants in concrete political situations focus on more particular, immediate, and empirical objects. Perhaps for this reason, the meaning of concrete political events becomes murky. A model is needed to enlighten political reality.

## Purposes of Models

From the Platonic perspective, both the political leader and the political analyst need models. For the leader, a model represents a vision of the world reconstructed according to pure principles. For instance, the Ayatollah Khomeini, who led the overthrow of Shah Mohammed Reza Pahlavi and established the Islamic Republic, organized the new political system based on principles derived from the Koran. According to him, the ayatollahs—the "sign" or "light of God"—and the *fuqaha*, the Islamic scholars, should constitute the vanguard force that transforms society and educates the people in Islamic virtues. Because these clergy know Islamic law and practice justice, they must assume the responsibility for directing the government, guiding the people, and enlightening the masses—all tasks performed by Plato's philosopher-kings.[3] After the 1973 military coup, Chilean political leaders stressed the primacy of economic development over socialist values; however, they still upheld the need for a rational central authority to guide the unenlightened masses toward a capitalist economy. According to the monetarist technocrats, people act irrationally. Voting with imperfect information, they elect governments that adopt paternalistic, welfare-state policies; economic ruin results. Only an enlightened, authoritarian government led by the rational technocrats can educate the masses and steer the society toward free-market principles.[4] The leaders of the Vietnamese Communist party scarcely show any commitment to a free-market economy. Yet, like the Chilean technocrats, they want their society governed by an enlightened elite that blends Leninist principles of party organization with Vietnamese traditions of rule by the mandarins. Indeed, the main revolutionary leader in twentieth-century Vietnam was Ho Chi Minh, which means "Ho who enlightens."

For the theorist less actively involved in public policymaking than the Vietnamese communists, Iranian ayatollahs, or Chilean technocrats, models become the most theoretically useful ways to understand the political world. Why do some political systems persist and others undergo drastic changes? How do economic, education, and health policies secure changes in society? Models provide some answers to these questions. More specifically, they serve five purposes for the comparative analyst.[5]

First, by delineating theoretically significant variables, models organize information. This book concentrates on three basic variables of a political system: the political regime, political leadership, and the contents of public policies. We conceive of a political system as a mode of policy production, that is, a way of making and carrying out public decisions affecting the society. The political regime comprises the *beliefs* that guide decision-making, the power of *structures* (social groups, national governments, parties, foreign institutions) in the policy process, and the *behavioral ways of processing policy issues*. The policymakers include those individual leaders who formulate and implement public decisions. This book explores the contents of three specific policies—economic, education, health—and their impact on society and the political system.

Second, besides organizing information around basic descriptive categories, models help us explain political phenomena. They pose questions about certain effects—for example, political system changes—that puzzle the investigator. This book probes the reasons behind three types of political change in the Third World: (1) changes within a political system—that is, changes in leadership and policy contents, (2) fundamental changes from one political system to another, such as the transformation from a reconciliation to a bureaucratic-authoritarian type, and (3) changes in society caused by economic, education, and health policies. Theoretical explanations for these changes involve specifying the general propositions and the specific historical conditions that lead to certain outcomes, such as a between-system change.[6] For example, what general propositions explain the transformation of one political system to a different system type? To understand this change, we need to analyze the structures and beliefs of both the government in power and the opposition. An incumbent regime faces greater instability if the political cohesion of social groups supporting the existent government is weak, if government leaders have neither the will nor the ability to exercise effective coercion and to form a coalition, and if the ruling political elites demonstrate a waning commitment to an ideological cause. By contrast, if organizations opposed to the incumbent regime develop stronger cohesion, wield more effective coercive and consensual power, and become more fervently committed to an ideological cause, then these opposition forces may successfully seize government power and perhaps organize a different system type. Only by applying these general propositions to specific historical circumstances can we fully understand the reasons for between-system changes in such societies as Vietnam, Cuba, Chile, Nigeria, and Iran.

4

Third, some investigators view models as useful tools to predict or forecast future events. This book, however, remains skeptical about the predictive power of theoretical models. Social scientists can make the most accurate causal predictions in a laboratory experiment, where the investigator can fix the time order of variables and through randomization procedures control for extraneous variables that produce spurious relationships. Although simplified models posit relationships among a few variables, the actual political world features several complex factors, rapid social change, and unanticipated events unforeseen by the theoretical model. For this reason, the comparative analyst cannot accurately forecast the future outcomes of present actions.

Fourth, since the time of Plato, some political theorists have regarded theoretical models as guides to action. According to this perspective, the model-builder has the responsibility to design public policies that will control events in the actual political world. For instance, Plato believed that the political philosopher must reshape the existing, impure, corrupt world in light of the theoretical principles found in the perfect model of an ideal political system. Having attained a vision of justice and goodness, the philosopher who becomes political ruler can exercise the power to reconstruct society according to these ideal principles.[7]

During the twentieth century, leaders who have sought fundamental changes in a political system have tried to transform existing arrangements according to an ideal model. Although most folk systems have now become extinct, the folk ideals of piety, faith, and purity still remain alive. In Iran the Ayatollah Khomeini attempted to create an Islamic republic based on his interpretations of the principles of the Koran. After overthrowing the bureaucratic-authoritarian regime of the Shah, the Moslem mullahs set out to purify Iran of the contaminating influences from industrial societies, whether the atheistic Marxism–Leninism in the Soviet Union or the secular interest-group pluralism associated with the United States. For Khomeini and his followers, the Shiite Islamic faith and the Koranic laws supplied the model for reconstituting the sociopolitical order.

By contrast, leaders of reconciliation systems want governments, political parties, and social groups to accommodate conflicting interests so that freedom is preserved; constitutional principles serve as the guide to political action. Based on the legitimacy of political conflict, models of constitutional, representative government specify the formal rules and legal institutions that most satisfactorily reconcile conflicts and guarantee individual freedom, justice, and equity. In the contemporary Third World, few national leaders have shown a strong commitment to constitutional government; Costa Rica (1950–1987), Lebanon (1944–1975), and

Nigeria (1960–1966, 1979–1983) represent important exceptions. Between 1932 and 1973, the year of the military coup, most Chilean leaders upheld the need for a reconciliation system. Even Salvador Allende, the Marxist Chilean president from 1970 through 1973, perceived that his administration exemplified a peaceful transition to socialism via the pluralist path, a different ideological route from that taken by Chinese, Vietnamese, or Cuban leaders.

Blocking this transition to a socialist society, the armed forces that toppled Allende from presidential power established a bureaucratic-authoritarian system ruled by the professional military, civilian technocrats, and corporate executives. For these industrial bureaucratic officials, the short-lived Unidad Popular administration represented a perverted vision, a Marxist nightmare. The army officers declared their intention to excise the "cancer of Marxism" from Chilean society and to transform Chile into an antisocialist model for the rest of Latin America. Under their bureaucratic command, coercive power replaced consensual power based on interest accommodation.

The leaders of elitist mobilization systems like Cuba and Vietnam have used Marxist–Leninist principles as their guide to action. According to the mobilizers, a powerful party, state, and army must organize active mass participation to create a socialist society. These structures put the abstract ideological model into concrete practice. For Fidel Castro, the Cuban mobilizing activities offer hope to other Latin Americans who want to build a more equalitarian society less dependent on United States influence. The Vietnamese Communist revolutionaries saw their armed struggle against the United States and the South Vietnamese military government as an object lesson for other societies seeking freedom from "American imperialism."

Fifth, analysts use models to evaluate systemic performance according to explicit criteria. From this evaluative perspective, models designate the desirable and undesirable features of political systems. For example, Marxist-Leninist leaders in Vietnam, North Korea, and Cuba have sketched models of capitalism and socialism that justify the superiority of the socialist path to development. Following Lenin's interpretations, they perceive capitalism as associated with colonialism (France, Japan) or neocolonialism (United States); it brought enslavement and inequality to the proletariat and peasantry. For these leaders, socialism—a planned economy with public ownership of the means of production—will bring freedom and equality to the manual workers, peasants, and working intellectuals. By contrast, policymakers in Western Europe and North America assume that constitutional government, not state socialism, will secure civil liberties and equality before the law. Taking a crossnational view of the Third World, constitutionalists equate political development with legal restraints on the exercise of arbitrary, monopolistic power. From the historical perspective, political development involves the decline of the absolutist state and the evolutionary emergence of civil liberties, competitive elections, parliamentary supremacy, and limitations on executive power. Models of constitutionalism thus specify the structures (decentralized, pluralistic government and competitive parties) and the beliefs (rules guaranteeing freedom) that form the basis for evaluating the relative worth of different Third World political systems.[8]

## Types of Political Systems

David E. Apter has formulated a useful typology of Third World political systems: folk, bureaucratic-authoritarian, reconciliation, and mobilization.[9] The next chapter elaborates on his classifications. Rather than empirical descriptions of concrete governments, these four models represent simplified pictures that portray the dominant modes of political decision-making, that is, distinctive ways of formulating and implementing public policies.

Often within a single society different models compete for supremacy; the conflicting tendencies serve as a source of change in the mode of political production. For example, in precolonial Vietnam, agrarian folk systems at the village level coexisted with an agrarian bureaucratic-authoritarian regime governing the central government. During the first half of the twentieth century, bureaucratic-authoritarian and reconciliation modes struggled for dominance in Cuba. The failure of Batista's faction-ridden bureaucratic-authoritarian government to resolve the problems of high unemployment, income inequalities, and economic dependence on the United States partly explains the emergence of Castro's elitist mobilization system in the late 1950s. From 1970 through 1973, Chile experienced a conflict among three systems. The Unidad Popular (UP) national government tried to rule through a reconciliation system. The left-Socialists and MIRistas (Movement of the Revolutionary Left) mobilized the factory workers and peasants at the local level. Opposed to these populist mobilization activities and the reformist policies implemented by the UP government, the more conservative groups in Chile supported a military coup and the establishment of an industrial bureaucratic-authoritarian state. In late 1973, a military bureaucratic dictatorship suppressed not only the short-lived populist mobilization movement but also the reconciliation system that had governed Chile for more than a century. Thus conflicts among the three systemic tendencies led to a fundamental change in the Chilean political system.

Because these four models of political systems are abstract types, we need more specific subtypes to understand the complexities of sociopolitical change throughout the diverse Third World. For this purpose, the degree of role specialization in a society offers one criterion for expanding the classifications of political systems. Role diffuseness implies that one structure carries out diverse activities, such as political, economic, religious, educational, and familial. For example, where diffuse roles predominate, family structures perform general activities. The head of the family is chief political decision-maker, allocator of land, leader of worship, and teacher of wisdom. Role specialization, however, brings into operation a complex network of different organizations to handle these divergent activities. In highly specialized societies, the father and mother concentrate on rearing their children. Institutions outside the family handle the other functions. Various government agencies—bureaucracies, legislatures, courts, police forces, military institutions—make and carry out political decisions. Factories and firms located outside the home setting produce goods and services. Religious institutions conduct worship services. Specialized schools educate the population in technical skills.[10]

As Table 1.1 indicates, each general system type includes two specific subtypes. Among folk systems, hunting-gathering societies reveal less role specialization than do agricultural societies. Industrial bureaucratic-authoritarian systems are more specialized than agrarian bureaucracies. Of the two types of reconciliation systems—competitive oligarchies and pluralist democracies—the latter feature more complex, specialized political roles. Compared with populist mobilization systems, the elitist subtype has a greater variety of specialized organizations linked to the dominant party.

We assume that systems with higher role specialization secure greater political changes. They have the resources (technical staff, finances, complex organizational networks), especially the more powerful political structures, needed to spearhead sociopolitical changes. (See Table 1.1.) Thus, the agricultural folk system, the industrial bureaucratic-authoritarian systems, the pluralist democracies, and the elitist mobilization systems have realized more extensive, permanent changes than have their less specialized subtypes, which have neither the structures nor the value orientations conducive to fundamental change.

## TABLE 1.1
### MODELS OF POLITICAL SYSTEMS

| TYPE | SUBTYPE | DOMINANT BELIEFS | POWER OF CENTRAL GOVERNMENT | KEY DECISION MAKERS | ROLE SPECIAL-IZATION | DEGREE OF POLICY-INDUCED SOCIAL CHANGE |
|---|---|---|---|---|---|---|
| Folk | Hunting-gathering | Spiritual values | Weak | Family: elders, headmen | Lower | Limited |
| | Agricultural | Spiritual values | Weak | Councils of elders, age grades, title societies, secret societies | Higher | More extensive |
| Bureaucratic-authoritar-ian | Agrarian | Spiritual values | Weak | King, royal court, royal staff, army, local notables | Lower | Limited |
| | Industrial | Material interests | Strong | President, armed forces, civil service, technocrats | Higher | More extensive |
| Reconcilia-tion | Competitive oligarchy | Material interests | Weak | National cabinet, local notables | Lower | Limited |
| | Pluralist democracy | Material interests | Weak | President, prime minister, cabinet, legisla-ture, parties | Higher | More extensive |
| Mobilization | Populist | Ideological values | Weak | Councils, mass parties | Lower | Limited over long term |
| | Elitist | Ideological values | Strong | Party political bureau, charis-matic leader | Higher | More exten-sive over long term |

## Process of Political Change

When referring to changes in political systems, we mean that the mode of political production has altered — that is, the policy process has experienced changes in the structural basis of political rule, the cultural beliefs that become priorities of political decision-makers, and the ways of handling basic issues in the policy process. The structural relationships between the rulers and the ruled may undergo transformation as domestic social groups, government agencies, political parties, and foreign institutions contend for dominance. The purposes of rule may change. Political elites may process basic policy issues in different ways.

The most fundamental changes involve transformations in all three parts of the political regime: structures, beliefs, and ways of processing basic policy issues. I shall call these *between-system* changes. Notable examples include the shift from a folk system to a bureaucratic-authoritarian system or from a reconciliation to a mobilization system. Both revolutionaries and reactionaries have supported fundamental between-system changes. Revolutionaries seek greater leveling, expanded opportunities for group mobility, an exchange of group positions to ensure more benefits for the disadvantaged, and a change in the value bases for ranking people so that political achievements and ideological awareness replace inherited personal qualities. Reactionaries want to restore a rigid, elitist stratification system that has disintegrated. Aiming for a restoration of the displaced political elites to government power, reactionaries also struggle to ensure that the values associated with the *ancien régime* become the dominant legitimating beliefs.

Changes in the political process that bring about modifications of the three systemic parts are *within-system* alterations. In these cases, beliefs, structures, and ways of handling policy issues remain fairly stable, even though specific political leaders and the content of public policies may change. In contrast to revolutionaries and reactionaries, reformists and conservatives prefer more evolutionary, within-system changes. Pledging to narrow the gap between rich and poor, reformists formulate policies intended to expand mobility opportunities. From their perspective, every individual, whatever his or her social origin, should be evaluated according to personal achievements and should secure representation in the government decision process. Conservatives desire limited modifications in the social stratification system. Only minor adjustments should be made in the process by which political leaders represent group interests. According to the conservatives, spiritual equality before God assumes greater importance than secular government efforts to establish more egalitarian conditions on earth.[11]

A third type of political change derives from the effects that economic, education, and health policies wield on society, especially on its social stratification pattern. *Revolutionary* transformations of the social stratification system occur under the following conditions: (1) Economic policies actually secure low unemployment, low inflation, a high growth rate, and expanded income equality. (2) Education policies produce high literacy, a cognitively mobilized citizenry, and a technically trained labor force. (3) Health policies reduce infant mortality and raise life expectancy. The gradual, partial realization of these economic, education, and health-care objectives indicates a *reformist* type of policy change. If political leaders attain these goals at an even more glacial, fragmentary pace, the policy process operates in a *conservative* way. *Reactionary* changes signify that public policy impacts have retrogressed; that is, under reactionary rule,

10

the society experiences greater unemployment, higher inflation, lower income equality, less literacy, higher infant mortality rates, and a shorter life expectancy than prevailed under the displaced system.

Whether exploring between-system changes, within-system changes, or policy-induced changes in society, we theoretically assume that political change stems from conflict; the severity of these conflicts explains the degree of systemic change. Mild conflicts or "tensions" lead to within-system changes and moderate policy impacts. The political elites secure a blend of opposing elements so that the basic mode of political production—the political regime—remains stable. As the classical conservative Edmund Burke asserted, "A state without the means of some change is without the means of its conservation."[12] Hence, within-system change requires an adaptable strategy for handling disturbances to a system's equilibrium. More severe conflicts or "contradictions" undermine the equilibrium of a political system. As a new mode of decision-making comes into being, the nation undergoes a between-system political change and fundamental policy-induced changes in its society.

# Notes

1 See Peter Worsley, *The Three Worlds: Culture and World Development* (Chicago: University of Chicago Press, 1984), 296–332.

2 *The Republic of Plato*, trans. Francis MacDonald Cornford (New York: Oxford University Press, 1945), 227–237.

3 According to Cheryl Benard and Zalmay Khalilzad, *"The Government of God"—Iran's Islamic Republic* (New York: Columbia University Press, 1984), 111, Khomeini "referred to Plato's *Republic*, saying that in the Islamic Republic power would have to be exercised by those who knew Islamic law, the clerics." See also Imam Khomeini, *Islam and Revolution*, trans. Hamid Algar (Berkeley, Calif.: Mizan Press, 1981), 127, 341; D. Ray Heisey and J. David Trebing, "A Comparison of the Rhetorical Visions and Strategies of the Shah's White Revolution and the Ayatollah's Islamic Revolution," *Communication Monographs* 50 (June 1983): 158–174; Amir H. Ferdows, "Khomaini and Fadayan's Society and Politics," *International Journal of Middle Eastern Studies* 15 (May 1983): 241–257.

4 Alejandro Foxley, *Latin American Experiments in Neoconservative Economics* (Berkeley: University of California Press, 1983), 101–102.

5 Lester C. Thurow, "Economics 1977," *Daedalus* 106 (Fall 1977): 86–88; Kenneth N. Waltz, *Theory of International Politics* (Reading, Mass.: Addison-Wesley, 1979), 1–17.

6 George C. Homans, "The Present State of Sociological Theory," *Sociological Quarterly* 23 (Summer 1982): 285–299.

7 *The Republic of Plato*, 234; *Plato's Statesman*, ed. Martin Ostwald, trans. J. B. Skemp (New York: The Liberal Arts Press, 1957), 64–71; Sheldon S. Wolin, *Politics and Vision* (Boston: Little, Brown, 1960), 34–50.

8  See Charles F. Andrain, *Foundations of Comparative Politics: A Policy Perspective* (Monterey, Calif.: Brooks/Cole, 1983), 5–6, 103–156; Robert H. Jackson and Carl G. Rosberg, *Personal Rule in Black Africa* (Berkeley: University of California Press, 1982).

9  For analyses of systems types, see the following works of David E. Apter: *Choice and the Politics of Allocation* (New Haven, Conn.: Yale University Press, 1971), 30–35, 113–118, 140–165; *Introduction to Political Analysis* (Cambridge, Mass.: Winthrop Publishers, 1977), 430–448; *Political Change: Collected Essays* (London: Frank Cass, 1973), 23–60, 73–117; *The Politics of Modernization* (Chicago: University of Chicago Press, 1965), 22–42, 357–431. Apter bases his classifications on political norms (sacred-secular, consummatory-instrumental) and structures of authority (centralized-decentralized, hierarchical-pyramidal). Accordingly, theocratic systems have sacred norms and decentralized authority. Mobilization systems combine sacred norms with centralized authority patterns. Bureaucratic systems feature secular norms and centralized authority. Reconciliation systems blend secular norms with decentralized structures. I have substituted the term "folk" for Apter's "theocratic system," mainly because a theocracy refers to a system where religious officials exercise dominant political power. Even before the twentieth century, few such systems existed. Political anthropologists, however, have located numerous folk societies. See Robert Redfield, "The Folk Society," *American Journal of Sociology* 52 (January 1947): 293–308; Gideon Sjoberg, "Folk and 'Feudal' Societies," in *Political Development and Social Change*, eds. Jason L. Finkle and Richard W. Gable (New York: Wiley, 1966), 45–53.

10  See Neil J. Smelser, *The Sociology of Economic Life*, 2d ed. (Englewood Cliffs, N.J.: Prentice-Hall, 1976), 150–163; Gabriel A. Almond and G. Bingham Powell, Jr., *Comparative Politics: System, Process, and Policy*, 2d ed. (Boston: Little, Brown, 1978), 20, 136–140.

11  Andrain, *Foundations of Comparative Politics*, 89–98.

12  Edmund Burke, *Reflections on the Revolution in France*, quoted in Philip W. Buck, ed., *How Conservatives Think* (Baltimore, Md.: Penguin Books, 1975), 48.

# 2

## MODELS OF THIRD WORLD POLITICAL SYSTEMS

> The structural issues which arise at the level of history or comparative system change pertain to the politics of change in its broadest sense: transformation, the formation of new societies. . . . When we focus on government in structural terms we must ask, what types of systems are represented and what consequences for society do different political systems have?
>
> — David E. Apter

By using general models of political systems, we can explain the political changes in specific countries, such as Vietnam, Cuba, Chile, Nigeria, and Iran. This chapter analyzes four models that illustrate the diversity of Third World political systems: folk, bureaucratic-authoritarian, reconciliation, and mobilization. It first discusses the stages of political and economic development where the four systemic types predominate and then examines the distinctive mode of political decision-making found in each type. This classification is based on three key dimensions of a political regime: (1) the ranking and interpretation of political beliefs that shape policy priorities, (2) the power that structures such governments, political parties, social groups, and foreign institutions wield over the policy process, (3) the strategies for handling crucial policy issues.

The interpretations and priorities given to political beliefs influence the policy process. Beliefs specify the purposes of rule, priorities of political action, perceptions of the world, and justifications of the right to rule. Interpretations of freedom and equality, along with concepts of legitimacy—the emphasis on moral/spiritual values versus material interests, individualism versus collectivism—affect political decision-making.

Sociopolitical structures also shape the degree of change that occurs throughout the Third World. When exploring political change, analysts probe the power of governments, political parties, social groups, foreign states, and transnational organizations over the policy process. Specifically, what is the power of primordial groups (kinship, ethnic, age, gender), religious associations, and economic organizations to press their policy preferences on government officials? What is the power of governments and political parties vis-à-vis social groups? What is the power of foreign states and transnational organizations (multinational corporations, the International Monetary Fund, the Roman Catholic church, the Arab League) over governments and social groups in the Third World?

Because government institutions have the most direct responsibility for making and carrying out binding public policies for a society, they wield a crucial impact on political change in the Third World. Following the interpretation of Richard Rose, we view government as a formal institution (administrative structure) that organizes laws, finances, and personnel to produce public policies.[1] Comparisons of the power exercised by different Third World governments focus on five structural dimensions: (1) the balance between coercion and consensus, (2) the degree of centralized government power, (3) the extent to which a single political agency—whether a specific officeholder, government institution, or political party—coordinates (unifies) the policy process, (4) the degree of social pluralism, that is, the relative independence of social groups from direct government control, and (5) the scope of government power—the range of activities that governments perform.[2] According to these five structural dimensions, the weakest governments wield the least coercion, operate the most decentralized institutions, exercise the lowest coordination over the policy process, allow the greatest group pluralism, and perform the fewest activities. At the opposite extreme, the most powerful Third World governments show the greatest coercion, centralization, coordination, scope of activities, and independence from social groups.

Each political system features a distinctive way of processing policy issues. The policy process centers on the dynamic interaction between sociopolitical structures and political beliefs. Influenced by dominant beliefs and the structural conditions under which they operate, policymakers choose diverse ways to handle basic issues: voluntarism versus determinism, political organization versus social spontaneity, consensus versus conflict, and change versus continuity. First, to attain policy goals, what interaction occurs between the subjective will of the political leader and the objective conditions? The issue of voluntarism versus determinism highlights the linkages between individual purpose to overcome obstacles, on the one hand, and the existing political, economic, and cultural conditions that limit individual choices, on the other. A second issue in political life revolves around the conflict between social spontaneity and political organization. In the struggle to attain policy objectives, which exercise the dominant power, spontaneous social groups or political organizations such as government and party bureaucracies? Third, policymakers confront the issue about conflict and consensus. In the policy process, to what extent do structures and beliefs come into conflict? What degree of harmony is needed to make and carry out effective public policies? Fourth, when formulating and implementing public policies, Third World political leaders must choose the priority given to change and continuity in beliefs as well as structures.

In sum, political change in the Third World involves changes in the three components of a political regime: beliefs, structures, and ways of processing policy issues. Yet no uniform pattern applies to the Third World in general, a specific geographic area, or even a large country such as Nigeria, India, or Iran. To capture this diversity within the Third World, we need explicit models of political systems: folk, bureaucratic-authoritarian, reconciliation, mobilization. By using the basic components to formulate systemic types, we can best understand the complex processes of sociopolitical change in different developing nations.

## Folk System

The French sociologist, Émile Durkheim, drew a striking contrast between the folk system and more complex societies where greater role specialization prevailed. The folk system revealed more cultural and structural homogeneity. Social integration rested on shared moral-spiritual values. Communal ties predominated over the pursuit of individual interests. Although people valued social equality, conformity to group norms downgraded any commitment to individual freedom, which held little meaning or importance. From a structural perspective, the folk system featured minimal role specialization. No powerful state—a specialized, centralized administrative structure composed of bureaucrats, military officers, and police who made binding decisions over a territory—punished deviant behavior. Instead, the pervasive face-to-face group interactions in a homogeneous setting meant that social control occurred by peer-group pressures: gossip, disapproval, taunts, and ostracism. By contrast, more complex societies operated under greater role

15

specialization. The state became stronger and society more differentiated. Solidarity sprang from an interdependence of the heterogeneous groups. Those who violated the communal solidarity faced punishment by state institutions, such as the police, army, and judicial courts. In these heterogeneous societies, conflict revolved around divergent interests. Material interests began to vie with moral-spiritual values for dominance. Individualism—the pursuit of self-interest—clashed with the communal attachment to sacred values. Although people showed weaker support for egalitarian beliefs, they expressed a higher regard for individual freedom than in the simple folk system. As a result of this greater role specialization, heterogeneity, and secular values, complex societies seemed more responsive to sociopolitical change.[3]

The contrast that Durkheim sketched between simple and complex societies also applies to the differences that separate the hunting-gathering folk system from the more agrarian subtype. (See Table 2.1.) Although hunting-gathering systems have largely disappeared today, for most of human history they remained the dominant economic type. As illustrated by the Kung San of southern Africa, people hunted wild game, gathered berries, dug roots from the ground, and collected plants and fruits. Largely isolated from the rest of the world, these societies were politically self-sufficient. No formal government institutions—permanent, stable collections of roles—guided political decision-making. Rather, in these segmentary, decentralized, equalitarian systems, most policies binding on the whole community took place in the family setting. Sociopolitical life revolved around family relationships. Often the headman represented the only distinctive "political" role that carried the authority to make public decisions. The family, not the state, political party, church, or market, supplied integration to the hunting-gathering systems.[4]

The social stratification systems of the hunting-gathering systems were rather flat; few social cleavages divided the homogeneous people. Certainly, no class distinctions split the society into conflicts between rich and poor. The low level of technology impeded the development of an economic surplus beyond subsistence needs. Other than the two roles of hunter and gatherer, no other economic roles existed. Since the hunters and gatherers shared their food with other members of their communities, a relatively equal distribution of wealth minimized economic distinctions. Furthermore, no diverse religious sects disturbed the spiritual solidarity. The most important group cleavages focused on age and sex. Although women and youth enjoyed extensive opportunities to participate in political decision-making, older men played the key political roles.

In the hunting-gathering folk system, political decisions were made

16

## TABLE 2.1
### Folk System

| Variables | Hunting-Gathering System | Agricultural System |
| --- | --- | --- |
| **A. Political beliefs** | | |
| 1. Interpretation and ranking of equality | High stress on equality of solidary believers, lower stress on sexual and age equality | Lower stress on equality, some emphasis on economic stratification |
| 2. Interpretation and ranking of individual political freedom | Individual political freedom has low importance; leaders stress the need to conform to small group authority | Individual political freedom has higher importance. Leaders place greater stress on individual competition in political life |
| 3. Relationship between pursuit of material benefits and of moral-spiritual values | Moral values dominate material ends | Leaders place greater stress on material benefits, although moral-spiritual values still assume primacy |
| 4. Relationship between individualism and collectivism | Stress on collectivism of kin ties | Blend of collectivist and individualist values, stress on individual success in group setting |
| **B. Power of social groups** | | |
| 1. Power of primordial groups in policy process | Strong: Family, kin, clan, age, and gender groups play key political roles; political system is the family writ large | Weaker: Although kith and kin groups play dominant political role, some achieved groups, like title societies and knowledge societies, participate in policy process |
| 2. Power of religious groups in policy process | Strong: Diviners perform ritual activities, uphold public morality, sanctify political authority, and help maintain communal solidarity | Strong: Religious authorities perform ritual functions, uphold public morality, sanctify political authority, and help maintain communal solidarity |
| 3. Power of economic groups in policy process | Weak: Although most individuals perform similar economic roles, such as fishing, hunting wild game, and gathering plants, they are not organized into powerful organizations that shape public policies | Stronger: Individuals plant gardens, farm the land, herd cattle, produce handicrafts, and trade goods. They often form associations to protect their economic interests at public meetings |

*Continued on next page*

TABLE 2.1 *continued*

| VARIABLES | HUNTING-GATHERING SYSTEM | AGRICULTURAL SYSTEM |
| --- | --- | --- |
| **C. Power of political organizations** | | |
| 1. Government | | |
| a. Degree of coercive and consensual power | Consensus prevails over coercion; peer-group presses for conformity, but splitting from group occurs | Although consensus prevails over coercion, a rudimentary police force operates to wield coercive power; dissident individuals can separate and form a new system |
| b. Degree of centralized power | Low: Power is decentralized in family groups, assemblies, and ad hoc gatherings | Higher: Councils and age grades wield greater power in larger-scale systems |
| c. Degree of institutional coordination | High: Elders (heads of families) coordinate policy activities | High: Councils of elders coordinate policy activities |
| d. Independence of social groups from government control (strength of social pluralism) | Low: Family members, elders, and diviners are key groups exercising political authority; factions are based on family ties, age and descent, for example | Higher: Age grades, title societies, secret societies, and cooperative work groups exert more influence over policy process |
| e. Scope of government power | Limited | More extensive |
| 2. Political parties | Not present: There are few diverse or antagonistic interests to articulate and aggregate | Not present: There are few diverse or antagonistic interests to articulate and aggregate |
| **D. Ways of processing basic policy issues** | | |
| 1. What interaction occurs between personal will and social conditions? | Determinism: Structural and cultural conditions overwhelm individual will | More voluntarism: Individuals assert their will to change some aspects of structure and culture |
| 2. Do spontaneous social groups or political organizations wield dominant power? | Social group spontaneity: Natural, ascriptive groups play key policy role | Greater political organization: Although ascriptive groups dominate policy process, achievement-based organizations and voluntary associations play greater role |
| 3. What is the relationship between conflict and consensus? | High on spontaneous consensus based on moral-spiritual values: Limited conflict leads to slow rate of change | Greater social stratification means less consensus and more conflict, which leads to faster rate of change |
| 4. What is the relationship between change and continuity? | Political system remains self-contained; leaders uphold continuity of basic values and sociopolitical structures | Political system has greater contact with outside world; its leaders show greater adaptability and willingness to introduce change |

through informal, nonspecialized mechanisms, rather than through political parties or formal government institutions like a professionalized bureaucracy, military, police force, legislature, and court. Small-scale and self-sufficient, these societies practiced decentralized policymaking. If people failed to reconcile their conflicts or to satisfy their needs through familial institutions, the heads of different families met informally to settle disputes that arose over access to waterholes, distribution of meat, sexual jealousies, and family quarrels. Elders and ad hoc gatherings handled political coordination. Political decentralization did not coincide with strong group pluralism; no powerful voluntary associations separated from the family pressed their competing claims on the headmen and elders. Instead, as in a harmonious family, consensus prevailed over coercive power as the primary way to resolve disagreements. Persuasion and discussion represented the ideal ways to settle conflicts. If individuals violated communal harmony, they lost peer-group respect. When members of a family felt aggrieved about the lack of access to a resource, they often split from their band and formed a new band. Thus informal group pressures and fission represented the main ways to maintain social peace.

Political beliefs in the hunting-gathering system reflected the high structural homogeneity and low role specialization; people shared similar beliefs about equality, freedom, and political legitimacy. Sociopolitical equality took precedence over individual freedom. Individuals found their identity in the wider family community, where shared beliefs upheld equality and solidarity. Legitimacy rested on moral-spiritual and communal ties, rather than on the satisfaction of individual interests. All members affirmed the same religious values. Most often, people held animistic beliefs—the pantheistic notions that gods or spirits indwell the whole natural universe, including the land, sea, mountains, and sky. They worshipped not only the guardian deities of each band but also the spirits of their family ancestors. Political leaders like headmen claimed to embody certain personal moral qualities such as generosity, courage, and kindness toward others. Expression of these moral values justified their right to make binding decisions on the community.

Headmen in the hunting-gathering folk system stressed determinism, social spontaneity, consensus, and continuity with past traditions as the way to handle basic policy issues. Determinism prevailed over individual voluntarism. Structural conditions (the low level of technological development) and cultural beliefs (the attachment of sacred significance to material objects) overwhelmed the individual will to realize significant social changes. Social group spontaneity also triumphed over political organization. No formal-legal institutions operated as distinct organizations separate from the family group. Because people shared similar beliefs about sacred objects and held common economic interests, few conflicts pervaded the policy process. On the contrary, consensus arose spontaneously from agreement on moral-spiritual values. Given the structural-cultural determinism, the high social spontaneity, and the limited group conflicts, change occurred slowly. The major changes took place as an individual progressed through the life cycle from birth, puberty, marriage, and death. In other respects, members of the hunting-gathering folk system retained continuity with past customs, traditions, values, and the minimally differentiated social stratification patterns that had existed for centuries.

Compared with the hunting-gathering folk system, the agrarian folk system, such as the Igbo of nineteenth-century southeastern Nigeria, featured greater role specialization, heterogeneity, diversity, and more favorable prospects for sociopolitical change. Under the agrarian folk system, people lived in more sedentary, densely populated, and spacious environments. The economic structures grew more complex. Rather than hunting wild game, fishing, and gathering plants, individuals herded cattle, cultivated gardens, tilled the land, constructed handicrafts (pottery, textiles, carpets), and traded goods. Religious roles also grew more specialized, as religious officials conducted worship services for ancestral spirits, guardian deities, and the greater gods. Although as in the hunting-gathering folk system inherited ties based on age and sex remained the most important bases of social stratification, the kinship structure increased in complexity; not only the nuclear and extended family but also lineages and clans (groups of lineages) performed important tasks. Non-kin associations such as age grades, title groups, knowledge societies, and secret societies united people on the basis of achieved, not inherited, criteria.

Political organizations in the agrarian folk system showed more specialization than in the hunting-gathering subtype. Whereas the hunters and gatherers secured obedience mainly through consensual means—peer-group persuasion—a rudimentary police agency with coercive power began to emerge in the agrarian folk system. Yet splitting from the political system still remained a feasible option for those who objected to public policies enacted by councils of elders, the main decision-making body. Instead of leading a nomadic life, people in the agrarian folk system often inhabited small villages; hence, their political systems became a bit more centralized than those among the hunter-gatherers. Chiefs wielded more authority; councils of elders coordinated the policy process. Voluntary associations—age grades, title societies, cooperatives, secret societies—reflected the greater social pluralism found in the agrarian folk system. As the role structure grew more specialized, the political organizations increased their scope of power, making decisions about education, healing, access to land, settlement of family disputes, and interactions with neighboring villages.

The political beliefs in an agrarian folk system reflected the higher role specialization. Although members still placed a high value on social equality, justifications for economic elitism developed as a few individuals gained greater wealth from hearding cattle, farming land, and trading goods. Rather than conforming to small group pressures, some people stressed the need for greater individual freedom, competition, and personal achievement; yet the society still valued individual success in a communal setting. Even though moral-spiritual values continued to predominate and people invested material objects with moral significance, a greater emphasis on material interests began to emerge.

More open to the outside world, the agrarian folk systems operated a policy process that showed greater responsiveness to sociopolitical change. Less deterministic than the hunters and gatherers, the political leaders within the agrarian folk system expressed a stronger willingness to organize individuals and groups behind some social changes. Achievement-oriented voluntary associations, which played a key role in the policy process, asserted the need for organized mechanisms, not just spontaneity, as a way to produce change. As the political system became more complex, differentiated, and heterogeneous, conflict over tactics divided the policy participants. Hence, the agrarian folk system retained less continuity with past customs than did the hunting-gathering folk society; adaptability to internal and external changes became more widespread.[5]

Even though folk systems have largely disappeared from the contemporary Third World, they remain important for understanding modern processes of political change. During the nineteenth and twentieth centuries, remnants of folk systems continued operating at the local level, often coexisting with agrarian bureaucratic systems that controlled the national government. More significant, during a time of increasing secularization, centralization, and bureaucratization, the folk values retain a powerful attraction to those who feel alienated from so-called modern institutions now dominant throughout the Third World. Disenchanted by the growing power of the centralized state and the emergence of capitalist industrialization, many people in the developing nations seek a restored emphasis on moral-spiritual values, social equality, communal solidarity, decentralization, widespread mass participation in political decision-making, and an integration between the sacred and secular domains. Often, leaders articulating these values organize protest movements that demand changes in the bureaucratic-authoritarian systems dominating their societies.

## Bureaucratic-Authoritarian System

Whereas most folk systems have disintegrated under the onslaught of centralizing and industrializing forces, bureaucratic-authoritarian (BA) systems have shown a remarkable resiliency. Among the four major types of political systems, the bureaucratic-authoritarian system has been the most pervasive.[6] It has dominated the agrarian, industrializing, and industrial stages of economic development throughout the Third World. Before the twentieth century, agrarian bureaucracies ruled such empires as the Egyptian, Syrian, Han Chinese, Ottoman, Manchu, Spanish, French, and British. During this century the European colonial powers governed their Asian and African colonies through bureaucratic officials. After winning political independence, these territories often experienced bureaucratic rule by the armed forces, police, and their civilian agents in the central government. Military bureaucracies shape the policies of most Latin American governments. Throughout the Third World, either state capitalism or state socialism has become the major strategy for spearheading economic development. Under state capitalism, government technocrats, along with administrators in large-scale domestic private industries and multinational corporations, wield decisive influence. Under state socialism, government officials act as planners and managers who direct economic decision-making.

What variables explain the pervasiveness of bureaucratic-authoritarian systems? First, all Third World political leaders must cope with the problems of domestic disorder. Historically, societies have faced disturbances that stem from severe internal group conflicts and from such external stimuli as war, foreign pressures for modernization, and international economic dislocations (depressions, recessions). To the ruling elites, bureaucratic control has often seemed the most efficient way to lessen the chaos wracking Third World societies.

Second, from the economic perspective, bureaucratic regimes can supply the integrated administrative framework that enables the ruling elites to maintain their economic power or possibly expand economic growth. In agrarian societies, landowners who dominate the central government rely on a BA system to crush peasant revolts and retain the economic status quo. As the industrialization process begins, bureaucratic controls dampen consumer demands that arise from increased education, greater urbanization, and extended mass media penetration. By curtailing popular consumption, the military, police, and technocrats try to expand investment, so that capital accumulation becomes possible. Even at the higher levels of industrial development—for example, in Argentina, Uruguay, Brazil, South Korea, Taiwan—military and civilian bureaucrats have established repressive governments that quash the independent power of trade unions, peasant leagues, liberal media, and competitive, reformist political parties. Through these authoritarian tactics, the state decreases popular consumption, curtails wage increases, limits severe inflationary surges, and expands capital investment. Even though an industrial bureaucratic-authoritarian regime may use rational, technically superior techniques to guide the society toward rapid economic growth, the ruling elite operates in secret, remains unaccountable to representative institutions, and by stressing uniformity squelches the independent initiative needed in a change-oriented environment.

Third, during the last century certain external agencies have facilitated the dominance of bureaucratic-authoritarian systems. European colonialism represented rule by bureaucratic officials—governors-general, governors, district officers, and administrators of large-scale European enterprises. The penetration of the more industrialized Third World nations by multinational corporations has brought technocratic decision-making in bureaucratic organizations. Although claiming to favor democratic regimes in the Third World, most U.S. government officials since World War II have actually supported military rule by professional soldiers, particularly when left-wing leaders espouse egalitarian economic policies that threaten capitalist interests. Dedicated to state socialist economic policies, the Soviet Union has preferred that a bureaucratic-authoritarian state composed of political party professionals, civilian administrators, military officials, and technocratic managers of state enterprises govern Third World societies.

The model of a bureaucratic institution sketched by Max Weber sensitizes us to the contrasts between the industrial and agrarian bureaucratic-authoritarian systems. (See Table 2.2.) According to Weber, a bureaucracy brings rule by the *bureau*—that is, an official position. Thus a bureaucratic system features a sharp distinction between the official and the office (position). Officials make decisions according to impersonal ties—the rights and responsibilities delegated to their office—not according to their personal preferences. This delegation of authority means a centralized, hierarchical style of decision-making. Professional qualifications, as demonstrated by educational credentials, examination performance, and technical expertise, form the basis for recruitment to bureaucratic offices and for promotion to higher positions.[7] Certainly, the industrial, BA systems more fully embody the Weberian model.

## TABLE 2.2
### BUREAUCRATIC-AUTHORITARIAN SYSTEM

| VARIABLES | AGRARIAN BUREAUCRATIC SYSTEM | INDUSTRIAL BUREAUCRATIC SYSTEM |
|---|---|---|
| **A. Political beliefs** | | |
| 1. Interpretation and ranking of equality | Low emphasis on equality, stress on elitist and hierarchical values | Low emphasis on equality, stress on elitist and hierarchical values |
| 2. Interpretation and ranking of individual political freedom | Elites downplay individual civil liberties; instead, they stress the need for the state to control the expression of political ideas | Elites downplay individual civil liberties; instead, they stress the need for the state to control the expression of political ideas |
| 3. Relationship between pursuit of material benefits and of moral-spiritual values | Moral values and material benefits legitimate political authority | Concrete payoffs take precedence over moral values |
| 4. Relationship between individualism and collectivism | Stress on collectivism, especially values of ascribed groups: kin, clan, royal lineage, caste | Stress on collectivism, especially statism and nationalism |
| **B. Power of social groups** | | |
| 1. Power of primordial groups in policy process | Strong: Royal family and nobles wield dominant power | Weaker: Military officers and civil servants secure political power mainly on basis of achievement, not ascription |
| 2. Power of religious groups in policy process | Strong: Religious officials legitimate political authority | Weaker: Religious groups are subordinate to state control |
| 3. Power of economic groups in policy process | State officials rule with large landowners; merchants and peasants exercise little political power | Poor farmers, factory workers, and small businessmen exercise little power; large business corporations exercise greater influence, but the state regulates private business firms to strengthen the military and other government agencies against internal disorder and foreign attack |
| **C. Power of political organizations** | | |
| 1. Government | | |
| a. Degree of coercive and consensual power | Coercion prevails over consensus | Coercion prevails over consensus |

*Continued on next page*

TABLE 2.2 *continued*

| VARIABLES | AGRARIAN BUREAUCRATIC SYSTEM | INDUSTRIAL BUREAUCRATIC SYSTEM |
|---|---|---|
| b. Degree of centralized power | Low: Regions and villages retain some independence from central government | Moderately high: Military, police, and government civilian servants wield centralized power |
| c. Degree of institutional coordination | High: Personal ruler (king, emperor, sultan) coordinates policy activities | High: Military and civilian bureaucracies coordinate policy activities |
| d. Independence of social groups from government control (strength of social pluralism) | Medium: Landowners are politically dominant over merchants and peasants; established churches retain some autonomy | Medium: Private business corporations maintain some independence; other social groups have little political autonomy |
| e. Scope of government power | Limited: stress on defense, foreign affairs, internal order, raising of revenues | More extensive: stress on system maintenance and construction of economic infrastructure |
| 2. Political parties | Not present | Weak: Government either bans competitive political parties or organizes weak party that holds seats in legislature but has limited contacts with the citizens |

**D. Ways of processing basic policy issues**

| VARIABLES | AGRARIAN BUREAUCRATIC SYSTEM | INDUSTRIAL BUREAUCRATIC SYSTEM |
|---|---|---|
| 1. What interaction occurs between personal will and social conditions? | Determinism: Elites fatalistically resign themselves to natural conditions and make few efforts to transform environment | Greater voluntarism: Elites stress their organizational will to command, direct, and overcome obstacles; yet from the deterministic view, individual will is subordinated to organizational demands |
| 2. Do spontaneous social groups or political organizations wield dominant power? | Administrative organization: Rudimentary civil service and army dominate the policy process | Administrative organization: Military, police, civil service, technocracy, and private corporations dominate policy process |
| 3. What is the relationship between conflict and consensus? | High on forced consensus based on institutional control: Elites demand that subordinates submit to their orders; limited conflict leads to rigid policy-making | High on forced consensus based on institutional control: Elites demand that subordinates submit to their orders; limited conflict leads to rigid policy-making |
| 4. What is the relationship between change and continuity? | Elites want to maintain continuity of existing stratification system | Elites have conservative intentions (they want to maintain present stratification system) yet may secure radical effects (they support changes in the power of the state, military, and industrial sector) |

Compared with agrarian bureaucracies, the industrial subtype features more impersonal ties; bureaucratic personnel base their decisions on impersonal rules (rights and duties) associated with a specific office. A more centralized state dominates the policy process; the civil service, armed forces, and police wield greater power. Technical expertise possessed by engineers, economists, and planners determines recruitment to office and advancement through the hierarchy. By contrast, in the agrarian BA systems, personal connections with the king or leading families often influenced decisions made by bureaucrats; personal ties hence triumphed over impersonal rules or role requirements. Agrarian bureaucracies generally operated under less centralized conditions than the industrial subtype. Most often, as in China and Vietnam before the nineteenth century, a folk system at the village level coexisted with an agrarian BA system at the central government level. Villages retained considerable autonomy to manage their own affairs. Leading families also maintained extensive policy influence. Although agrarian bureaucrats had to master certain educational requirements, usually only those born to high-status families gained the opportunity to secure a bureaucratic appointment. Rather than basing recruitment on technical achievements, the ruling elite selected officials according to their inherited personal qualities, such as birth in a royal lineage. Promotion also depended on personal contacts with superiors.

In the agrarian BA system, the central state wielded limited control over social groups. At both the central and local village levels, family groups exerted considerable influence. Members of the royal family advised the king about the proper decisions that the central government should pursue. Within each village heads of senior lineages usually dominated local policymaking. Often only members of religious institutions, such as the Confucian scholar-gentry in China, possessed the educational background needed to serve as government bureaucrats. Besides formulating and implementing public policies, these religious officials legitimated the political order and thereby upheld the status quo. Along with leading families and the clergy, wealthy landowners played the key policy roles. All three groups retained some independence from the bureaucratic state.

By contrast, in the industrial bureaucratic-authoritarian system the state dominates primordial, religious, and economic groups. Kinship groups based on family, lineage, and clan ties play a weaker role in political decision-making. Religious institutions also wield limited political power. Although domestic private business enterprises and multinational corporations possess some freedom to press their claims on government officials, bureaucratic regulation of these businesses strengthens the state. In the rigid economic stratification system of an industrial bureaucratic-authoritarian system, the factory working class, small farmers, and small-scale business firms lack any organizational power to translate their group preferences into public policies.

A less powerful state dominated political life in the agrarian bureaucratic system than in the industrial BA system. Both systems feature coercive rule by civil servants, military officers, and police. Although factions within these bureaucratic agencies try to win support for their policy preferences through consensual strategies, coercive power prevails over consensus. In the agrarian bureaucratic regimes, villages who dared resist the king's commands often faced defeat by the imperial army. During the twentieth century, the means for wielding coercive power have become technologically efficient. Dissident students, intellectuals, journalists, farmers, and factory workers who stage protests against the industrial bureaucratic-authoritarian system suffer the brutal punishments—the electric shocks and nontherapeutic drugs—inflicted by the armed forces, prison officials, and police.

The ruling elites of the agrarian bureaucratic-authoritarian system wielded less centralized control over state and society than do their industrial BA counterparts. Under agrarian conditions, families, villages, established churches, and small-scale traders experienced some local autonomy. A personal ruler, usually a king, coordinated government activities at the central government level but not necessarily actions taken by regional and village leaders. The scope of government activities remained limited to defending the territory against foreign attack, preserving internal peace, building some public works (roads, dams), collecting taxes, administering a legal system, and performing ritual ceremonies that helped integrate the society. Given the noninvolvement of the masses in the policy process, no political parties existed to organize the popular participation.

In the industrialized bureaucratic system, however, the state exerts more centralized power. Military and civilian bureaucrats dominate both central and local government; they, along with a personal ruler—often a presidential monarch—try to coordinate the policy process. Although families, churches, universities, newspapers, and especially large-scale domestic private business enterprises and multinational corporations retain some autonomy, the central government regulates their actions. If these groups foment "excessive" conflict or pose too great a challenge to the industrial bureaucratic elite, they may find their independence diminished. Thus state officials allow only limited pluralism. Certainly, their concept of pluralism does not include competitive political parties that retain freedom from central government control. According to the

27

industrial bureaucratic elite, competitive parties fragment needed unity and order. Either the state forbids their operations, or else it strictly limits their power to influence government decision-making. In the latter case, rather than mobilizing the masses or controlling the executive, party representatives passively sit in the legislative chambers and give verbal support to the bureaucrats who dominate the policy process. These civil servants implement extensive government activities, including defense, the construction of an economic infrastructure, the promotion of industrial investment, the expansion of exports, and the regulation of wage rates. Concerned to maximize industrial investment and thereby raise economic growth rates, the central government gives low priority to enacting public policies that expand consumer goods for the poor, increase economic equality, or provide comprehensive social services, such as income maintenance and health care.

Whether in the agrarian or the industrial bureaucratic-authoritarian system, the dominant political beliefs value neither individual freedom nor sociopolitical equality. Rather than stressing individual freedom, the bureaucratic elites uphold the need for the state to control dissent, especially protests launched against state policies. Instead of according priority to socioeconomic or political quality, state bureaucrats emphasize elitist, hierarchical beliefs. According to this notion, either those born into the ruling agrarian elite or those with technical achievements that advance industrial growth should govern their societies.

Compared with the agrarian BA system, the industrial subtype rests on a more materialistic basis of political legitimacy. Kings in agrarian bureaucracies often claimed to rule by the grace of God; yet the achievement of internal order, safety, adequate food supplies, and success in war also justified the right to maintain power. Giving less importance to moral-spiritual values, industrial bureaucrats hope that concrete payoffs like a rapid economic growth rate, lower inflation, and expanded exports will legitimate their rule.

Although both the agrarian and industrial bureaucratic-authoritarian elites stress collectivism over individualism, they express divergent conceptions of the collective foundations of political legitimacy. Whereas the agrarian bureaucrats intended that public policies benefit primordial groups—the leading families, royal lineages, clans, castes, ethnic groups—the industrial bureaucratic elites proclaim that their policies will strengthen the state and nation, the dominant collective entities.

The processing of basic policy issues led to limited social changes in the agrarian bureaucratic-authoritarian system. Determinism usually triumphed over voluntarism, as indicated by the tendency for the agrarian ruling elites to resign themselves fatalistically to both the material and spiritual universes. Individuals mainly participated in ascribed organizations—families, lineages, clans, castes—rather than in achievement-based associations. Forced consensus prevailed over conflict; the allowance for only limited conflict caused rigidity in the policy process. The agrarian ruling elites stressed continuity with the traditional social stratification system and with the previous political regime. The lower degree of role specialization hindered rapid social change. Military and religious institutions constituted the main bureaucratic agencies; army officers, Catholic priests, and Confucian scholar-gentry, along with educated men from the landed aristocracy, usually held bureaucratic positions in the weakly developed government civil service.

By contrast, the industrializing process in the twentieth century has established the basis for a more specialized bureaucratic-authoritarian system that has the power to implement extensive social changes. Although the formulation and implementation of public policies take place under rigid conditions, the outcomes of the policies may lead to greater changes than intended by the elite. Administrative organization overwhelms social group spontaneity. Throughout the semi-industrialized nations of Latin America and Asia, government civil servants, professionalized military officers, police, and technocrats from large-scale domestic private firms and multinational corporations dominate the policy process. Neither ascriptive kin groups nor voluntary associations representing factory workers, small farmers, and small traders exert much political influence. Under these conditions, the bureaucratic elites controlling the dominant organizations try to force a consensus on those with stakes in the policy outcomes. Rather than allowing diverse groups to express their conflicting policy preferences, the ruling industrial elite demands that others submit to state-imposed decrees. The limited conflict in the policy process hence leads to rigidity, as persons low in the bureaucratic hierarchy fear expressing unwanted information or alternative policy options.

Despite this administrative rigidity in an industrial BA system, the effects of bureaucratic rule may bring greater changes than intended by the elites. Particularly during the twentieth century, a clash between determinism and voluntarism has arisen as states have faced foreign threats and internal demands for modernization. On the one hand, determinism appears the dominant orientation, for individual will becomes subordinated to organizational imperatives. Through tight institutional control over pressures for change, elites hope to avoid drastic modifications in the status quo; certainly, they intend to maintain the continuity of the existing social stratification system, allowing neither small farmers nor factory workers to upgrade their positions. On the other hand, a voluntaristic strain also emerges. Elites stress their organizational will to command,

29

steer society, and overcome obstacles. To meet and deter foreign invasions, they strengthen the power of the state, the armed forces, and the industrial sector. Education becomes more widespread as state bureaucrats train young army recruits. All these changes—education, emerging industrialization, a strong military, and a more centralized state—signal a fundamental break with past traditions.[8]

## Reconciliation System

Unlike elites ruling bureaucratic-authoritarian systems, leaders of reconciliation systems accept the legitimacy of interest-group conflicts. Reconciliation systems feature diversity, pluralism, and dispersed power. Different voluntary associations compete for influence on the political market. Decentralized policymaking prevails as countervailing organizations check the power of the central government. Because of this interest-group conflict, every reconciliation system faces the dangers of group polarization, political stagnation, and civil war.

The pluralist reconciliation system needs both rules and institutions that reconcile group conflicts. In the bargaining process, all contending groups must accept certain procedures for mediating the dispute, especially when one group does not gain as many benefits as desired. Particularly important are norms (informal rules) of toleration, compromise, and civility—that is, a shared attachment to impartial legal procedures and to notions of the general welfare that transcend the interests of particular ethnic, linguistic, religious, and economic groups. Not only norms but also political institutions help accommodate group differences. By fairly treating all citizens, regardless of their group memberships, institutions such as legislatures, courts, coalitional political parties, and public schools unify the pluralistic society. In the legislature representatives gain the opportunity to express diverse policy preferences, to compromise with other legislators, and to negotiate a mutually satisfactory agreement. Courts adjudicate differences and formulate binding common rules on conflicting groups. Reconciling particularistic interests, coalitional political parties combine these special interests into general public policies. Public educational institutions teach the importance of civility, civil liberties, and procedural consensus—the rules that integrate the faction-riven society.[9]

Even though reconciliation systems are comparatively rare in the contemporary Third World, the pluralist approach remains important today. From 1870 through 1940, Britain and France ruled Asia and Africa as the dominant Western colonial powers; during this period French and especially English theorists emphasized the ideals of constitutional liberalism associated with a reconciliation system. After World War II the United States became the dominant superpower; American leaders proclaimed the universal relevance of such notions as social pluralism, civil liberties, the rule of law, representative government, competitive elections, and the accountability of government officials to the voters. These ideals draw a favorable response from segments of the Thirld World political elite, especially lawyers, journalists, university professors, and students.

However great the importance of constitutional liberalism in Western Europe and North America, few Third World societies have maintained a reconciliation system for a lengthy period. During the early 1970s Chile and Uruguay, formerly model Latin American democracies, degenerated into repressive military dictatorships. India and Sri Lanka confront severe communal cleavages that threaten their fragile democratic structures. From 1973 through 1986 only Costa Rica and Venezuela, along with a few micro-states in the Caribbean and South Pacific—the Bahamas, Barbados, Belize, Nauru, St. Vincent, Trinidad and Tobago, Tuvalu—maintained a high elite commitment to civil liberties, competitive elections, independent courts, and civilian supremacy over the military.[10]

Certain political and economic conditions facilitate the maintenance of a reconciliation system. First, national integrating institutions—legislatures, courts, coalitional political parties, comprehensive public schools—unify group interests and strengthen civil values. Second, the society attains a high economic growth rate and extensive income equality. Economic growth expands the supply of resources, so that diverse groups can gain a share of the benefits. Economic equality implies flexible class divisions; individuals from one generation have opportunities to attain a higher occupational status than held by their parents. Because economic resources are widely dispersed, each ethnic or religious group contains people of diverse wealth. Hence, the cleavages crosscut, rather than reinforce, each other. Political compromises become easier to negotiate. Third, the society remains isolated from severe external political and economic disturbances, like war, military invasions, and foreign economic pressures. Especially when the economic pie continues to expand and few external challenges threaten the internal equilibrium, political leaders secure both the resources and the peace needed to reconcile diverse interest-group claims.

Most Third World nations lack the economic and political conditions needed for an effective reconciliation system. First, both civil values and national integrating structures are weak throughout Asia, Africa, the Middle East, and Latin America. Neither legislatures nor courts make the crucial decisions. Political parties rarely establish close contact with the masses and seldom aggregate diverse interests. Few comprehensive public schools exist; instead, public educational institutions reach mainly the urban children, with the rural residents denied access to formal schooling. Most Third World leaders show a weak commitment to civility. By controlling government power, they seek to maximize the welfare of their own families, relatives, clans, castes, or ethnic groups, rather than the welfare of the whole society. Ties to these subnational groups seem stronger than loyalties to the national society. Particularly under conditions of economic scarcity and rising expectations about government performance, political leaders cannot readily develop the procedural consensus needed to accommodate conflicting group claims on limited government resources.

Second, few Third World societies have attained simultaneously both a high rate of economic growth and extensive income equality. Those nations that did accomplish such a feat during the post–World War II era used bureaucratic-authoritarian means, as South Korea and Taiwan indicate. Others with high growth rates, such as Brazil, Indonesia, and Iran, relied on a repressive state to forge capital accumulation by denying rights to the workers; hence, rising income inequality ensued. Most Third World countries experienced neither high growth nor economic equality. Particularly in sub-Saharan Africa, the majority of inhabitants practice subsistence agriculture; the nondifferentiated economic structures scarcely contain the diverse interests that stimulate the formation of oppositional organizations needed in a reconciliation system. Elsewhere feudal lords in North Africa, Asia, and especially Latin America oppressed peasant serfs. Except in Costa Rica, where small cash-crop farmers dominated rural production, the agrarian structures strengthened the tendencies toward economic elitism, rather than equality. Thus political democracy could not easily take root.

Reinforcing group cleavages and rigid class structures also have hindered the effective operation of reconciliation systems. Often people divided by one cleavage, such as ethnic membership, share a similar status on another cleavage, such as wealth. Under these conditions, the cleavages reinforce each other. The gap between rich and poor may also divide Moslems and Christians. Particularly when the economic pie expands slowly, the conflicting moral-spiritual values often exacerbate economic cleavages and thereby impede political compromises. Even where communal (ethnic, religious, caste) cleavages remain weak, an inflexible class structure associated with feudalism and state capitalism prevents extensive upward occupational mobility. As a result of these accentuated economic inequalities, political accommodation of group differences becomes difficult.

Third, few Third World nations can today remain isolated from foreign pressures. Since the end of World War II, the United States and the Soviet Union have replaced the European colonial powers as the dominant foreign states in the Third World. Through expanding trade, granting economic assistance, making loans, training Third World students, selling arms, installing military bases, forming alliances, and exercising diplomatic initiatives, the two superpowers try to strengthen their politico-economic control over the developing areas. The United States government has wielded the strongest influence in Central America, the Middle East (Israel, Egypt, Turkey), and Asia (the Philippines, South Korea, Taiwan, Pakistan). By contrast, the Soviet Union's worldwide power has extended to fewer nations, mainly Cuba and Asian societies such as Mongolia, Afghanistan, Vietnam, and North Korea.

Although U.S. and Soviet policymakers articulate divergent objectives, their actions have strengthened the coercive power of Third World states, especially the armed forces. During the early 1980s more than two-thirds of arms exports (measured in dollar value) came from the Soviet Union and the United States. Most weapons went to the Middle East and Africa. These armaments reinforced the military's control over state and society in most Third World countries. A more repressive, centralized, and coordinated national government resulted. By stressing the need for Third World leaders to adopt a monistic Marxist–Leninist ideology, establish a vanguard communist party, and administer a state-owned, state-administered economy, the Soviet Union has promoted powerful nation-states throughout the less industrialized areas. In countries closely allied with the U.S.S.R., social pluralism remains limited. By contrast, U.S. policy officials articulate the need for a more pluralistic society and limited government. The focus on private enterprises and independent churches has encouraged the development of pluralism. Nevertheless, the U.S. government's preoccupation with economic growth, the hostility toward equal income distribution, and the concentration on national security against communist expansion have influenced Third World leaders to establish more repressive states. For example, U.S. administrations supported military coups that overthrew elected governments in Guatemala (1954), Brazil (1964), the Dominican Republic (1965), and Chile (1973).[11]

As the dominant nongovernment foreign agencies in the world today, the multinational corporations (MNCs) headquartered in the United States, West Europe, and Japan affect the degree of civil liberties practiced by Third World political systems. The multinationals' power revolves around their ability to supply resources needed by less industrialized countries. These resources include marketing networks, financial credit, and advanced capital equipment. The MNC emphasis on capital-intensive investment, rather than labor-intensive activities, reinforces income inequalities. Although reliance on capital-intensive technology accelerates industrialization, it widens the income gap between the modern and more traditional economic sectors, such as the handicraft firms producing clothes, shoes, and other consumer goods. As income cleavages widen, greater political conflict results between the urban elites and rural masses, between managers and workers, and between agri-business corporate heads and subsistence farmers. To repress these conflicts, the military and police gain greater power over government administration. These coercive agencies show little enthusiasm for the popular participation and group conflict that lend vitality to the reconciliation system.[12]

The degree of popular political participation and institutionalized group competition provides a basis for analyzing the two main subtypes of the reconciliation system—the competitive oligarchy and pluralist democracy.[13] (See Table 2.3.) Both subtypes feature extensive group competition. By agreeing to uphold the rules of the political game and to work through established institutions (legislatures, courts, coalitional political parties), competing elites institutionalize group conflict, so that a peaceful accommodation of differences takes place. The two types of reconciliation systems differ in their extent of popular political participation. A competitive oligarchy means rule by the few: wealthy men, high church officials, landowners, corporate executives, senior civil servants, and military officers. Groups such as women, youths, poor farmers, factory workers, and small-scale business people (artisans, traders) are excluded from political participation. By contrast, a pluralist democracy includes far more groups in political decision-making. Diverse groups, not merely a privileged few, have the right to participate. Numerous specialized structures emerge to organize popular participation, including mass political parties, comprehensive labor unions, farm associations, peasant leagues, mutual aid societies, cooperatives, and youth groups. In short, compared with a competitive oligarchy, a democracy has greater pluralism, higher role specialization, and more inclusive political partici-pation.

Many political systems in parts of Latin America and Asia during the late nineteenth and early twentieth centuries functioned as competitive oligarchies. For instance, in colonial India the British allowed Indian lawyers, merchants, aristocrats, journalists, and lower-ranking civil ser-vants some freedom to organize political associations, such as the Indian National Congress, and to share in legislative decision-making. In Chile, Argentina, and Uruguay, a few dominant elites—Catholic church

TABLE 2.3
RECONCILIATION SYSTEM

| VARIABLES | COMPETITIVE OLIGARCHY | PLURALIST DEMOCRACY |
|---|---|---|
| **A. Political beliefs** | | |
| 1. Interpretation and ranking of equality | Lower stress on equality of economic opportunity and political equality: Equality of economic conditions takes low priority | Greater stress on equality of economic opportunity and political equality: Equal economic opportunity and political equality before the law take priority over equality of economic condition |
| 2. Interpretation and ranking of individual political freedom | Lower stress on individual civil liberties, especially on the rights of the masses to challenge the existing social stratification system | Higher stress on individual civil liberties; individuals should realize their goals through joining voluntary associations that pressure government officials for desired policy outcomes |
| 3. Relationship between pursuit of material benefits and of moral-spiritual values | Leaders stress spiritual benefits for the masses but material benefits for the elites | Leaders place greater stress on material benefits for the masses; moral and material ends are in tension, but material pursuits often overwhelm moral values |
| 4. Relationship between individualism and collectivism | More collectivistic: Established groups should constrain pursuit of individual self-interests | More individualistic: Individuals should have freedom to pursue their self-interests |
| **B. Power of social groups** | | |
| 1. Power of primordial groups in policy process | Strong: Leading families, ethnic groups, and men play dominant role | Moderate: Primordial groups participate in an associational context; natural ascriptive groups form voluntary associations. Diverse ethnic groups, men and women, and young and old share a role in political life |
| 2. Power of religious groups in policy process | Moderately strong: Established church wields influential power | Moderate: Diverse religious groups have freedom to conduct worship and to pressure government officials |
| 3. Power of economic groups in policy process | Strong: Landowners, merchants, manufacturers, and financiers play the dominant policy role | Strong: Although private business groups wield the dominant influence in the policy process, labor unions that represent industrial blue-collar workers, agricultural wage-laborers, and government employees also wield some influence over policy formulation and implementation |
| **C. Power of political organizations** | | |
| 1. Government | | |
| a. Degree of coercive and consensual power | Although oligarchs rely on consensual power to settle disputes among elites, they use coercion against dissidents, especially those with a mass base | Consensual power prevails over coercive power |

*Continued on next page*

TABLE 2.3 *continued*

| Variables | Competitive Oligarchy | Pluralist Democracy |
|---|---|---|
| b. Degree of centralized power | Moderately low: decentralized among regional governments and local associations | Moderately high: decentralized among fragmented government institutions and voluntary associations |
| c. Degree of institutional coordination | Moderately high: Legislative leaders and appointed civil servants coordinate policy activities | Low: Prime minister or president, along with senior civil servants, coordinate policy activities |
| d. Independence of social groups from government control (strength of social pluralism) | Moderately high: Business firms, landowners' groups, and churches maintain greatest autonomy | High: Economic, civic action, and other voluntary associations retain independence; popular sector groups represent interests of factory workers, small farmers, and small businesspeople. |
| e. Scope of government power | Limited: stress on system maintenance and construction of economic infrastructure | More extensive: stress on system maintenance, construction of economic infrastructure, and provision of social services to individuals |
| 2. Political parties | Weak: Limited electoral participation means that elite parties in the legislature represent oligarchs' interests | Stronger: Universal suffrage and competitive elections mean that several political parties represent diverse interests; these parties maintain a stronger mass base |
| **D. Ways of processing basic policy issues** | | |
| 1. What interaction occurs between personal will and social conditions? | More deterministic: Oligarchs have neither the will nor the power to secure fundamental changes in society | More voluntaristic: Through participation in voluntary associations that pressure government agencies, individuals assert their will to achieve their policy goals |
| 2. Do spontaneous social groups or political organizations wield dominant power? | Oligarchical organizations constrain spontaneous social groups | Social group spontaneity prevails; voluntary associations actively participate in public policymaking |
| 3. What is the relationship between conflict and consensus? | Balance between conflict and consensus, with stress on consensus to abide by rules of political game | Balance between conflict and consensus, with stress on conflict: Interest group conflict leads to marginal, incremental changes |
| 4. What is the relationship between change and continuity? | Greater stress on continuity: Leaders support conservative change, that is, gradual modifications in social stratification system | Greater stress on change: Leaders uphold continuity in rules of political game but support reformist change, that is, policies that promote upward social mobility |

bishops, landowners, mine owners, merchants, lawyers, army officers—competed for political power. Even though oligarchic, these systems held elections, tolerated some political freedoms, and maintained a separation of powers between the legislature and the executive. Yet the mass of the population—the unpropertied, the factory workers, and the poor farmers—lacked the right to participate in the policy process.

Despite the military relinquishment of formal government power to Latin American civilian leaders during the 1980s, the political systems operated as competitive oligarchies, not pluralist democracies. Although in Peru, Bolivia, Argentina, Uruguay, Brazil, Guatemala, and El Salvador the electoral process enabled civilian politicians to replace military officers as heads of government administration, the military elite still defined the rules of the political game and exerted a veto power over elected presidents. Officers of the armed forces made decisions about (1) issues discussed in the election campaigns, (2) those groups, parties, and candidates that could participate in elections, (3) policies implemented by the government, and (4) parts of the country ruled by civilians. (For example, the Guatemalan army, not the civilian leaders, governed the rural areas.) In this semicompetitive political process, military officials, large-scale business executives, and landowners had greater freedom to shape policies than did factory workers, poor farmers, small business-people, dissident journalists, and left-wing students. Often the military oligarchs excluded left-wing parties from participating in elections. Policies that challenged military power or promised land redistribution gained no support from military and civilian elites. Officers of the armed forces retained control over policies that focused on industrial development, defense industries, and internal order. Elected civilian leaders failed to check the political violence wielded by paramilitary forces and "death squads" against political dissidents.[14]

Although both the competitive oligarchy and pluralist democracy uphold freedom, the pluralist democrats place a higher priority on civil liberty and equal opportunities. According to the pluralist democrats, freedom means civil liberties—the right of all individuals and groups to articulate their policy preferences, to join voluntary associations that will help realize policy claims, and to participate in political decision-making. Rather than stressing the need for equal economic conditions, notions of equality involve the opportunity for all individuals to rise in the social stratification system, to gain access to political leaders, and to enjoy equal public liberties. Democratic pluralists assume that decentralized political decision-making and the maintenance of group freedoms will enable all individuals, regardless of social background, to attain their self-interests. Thus individualist values come to full realization in a voluntary group context; under this conception, the individual fulfills his or her goals by joining voluntary associations that pressure government for desired policy outcomes.

By contrast, the dominant political beliefs in a competitive oligarchy express a weaker commitment to freedom, equality, and individualism. Although the oligarchs want the "better classes"—landlords, capitalists, property owners, high clergy—to govern, they still support some civil liberties for a moderate opposition, favor the representation of diverse interests, and back the gradual incorporation of excluded groups into the political system. Despite their support for limited political freedoms, the oligarchs oppose political equality between the upper and the lower classes and reject government policies that would bring more equal economic conditions. Holding more collectivist political orientations than the pluralist democrats, the competitive oligarchs seek to maintain the sociopolitical status of the privileged groups.

Political legitimacy in both subtypes of the reconciliation system rests on moral and material criteria. From the moral perspective, political leaders place a high value on the law. According to the competitive oligarchs, the law originates from the established authorities and guarantees political order. By specifying the need for individual responsibility to the community and by protecting the individual from the conformist pressures of the masses, the law ensures both freedom and order. For the pluralist democrats, adherence to a higher law that regulates interest-group competition helps maintain the pluralist style of political decision-making. The vitality of a reconciliation system also depends on the pursuit of material benefits from government policymakers. Compared with the competitive oligarchs, the pluralist democrats expect government to play a more active role supplying all citizens with tangible benefits such as employment opportunities, comprehensive health care, high-quality public schools, old-age pensions, child allowances, and personal safety.

The state exerts less active power in a competitive oligarchy than in a pluralist democracy. Compared with the agrarian bureaucrats, the competitive oligarchs govern a more open political system; yet they do employ some coercion against dissident groups that pose a fundamental challenge to oligarchical rule—especially movements representing the interests of poor farmers and factory workers. Government structures operate under decentralized conditions; local elites, such as landlords, village notables, and clergy, make key decisions independent of central government control. At the national level a few men, usually appointed civil servants and perhaps leaders elected by restricted suffrage, coordinate government activities. Rather than performing a coordinating role in the policy process, political parties remain confined to the legislative chambers. Lacking a mass electoral base, parties represent the interests of landlords, merchants, and urban professionals. Social pluralism extends mainly to the dominant groups—leading families, landowners, merchants, manufacturers, and established church officials. These groups retain the greatest independence to press their policy preferences on the central government. The state performs limited activities, such as maintaining internal order, protecting the nation from external invasion, building some public works, raising revenues, and perhaps subsidizing economic development. Few government agencies provide comprehensive social services to the citizenry.

In the pluralist democracy, however, the central government strengthens its power and performs more diverse activities; yet political organizations operate in a decentralized, consensual way. Public policymaking is decentralized among fragmented government institutions and voluntary associations. Often at the national government level, separation of power arrangements gives the courts autonomy from the legislature and executive. Most pluralist democracies also decentralize power throughout the territory. Under a federal setup, regional governments act independently of national government officials. Even where a formal federal system does not operate, regional government institutions wield considerable power over taxes, revenue collection, education, and health care. They, along with voluntary associations (unions, business organizations, professional associations, farm cooperatives, churches), help administer national public policies, such as health insurance, job training, and technical education. Within this pluralist framework, central coordination of government institutions remains limited. Usually a prime minister or president, cabinet ministers, and senior civil servants coordinate government activities. Yet lower government institutions and interest groups retain autonomy to check the power of these central decision-makers. Although several moderately strong parties help elect candidates to the national legislature and perhaps the presidency, they lack the power to coordinate the policy process. Rather than mobilize the population for objectives defined by the national government elite, they represent diverse group interests—ethnic, regional, religious, and economic. Party contacts with the masses occur through interest-group leaders. In the legislature the parties concentrate on reconciling these different interests and on achieving a coalition that can pass some laws satisfactory to the constituent groups.

Primordial, religious, and economic groups gain extensive independence from state control in the pluralist democracies. Primordial groups function as voluntary associations pressing their claims on government

39

for greater employment opportunities, education, health care, and housing. Groups representing the interests of women, youth, and ethnic minorities secure greater access to the policy process than in a competitive oligarchy, where men, elders, and members of leading families and ethnic groups wield dominant control. Under a pluralist democracy, government institutions and religious organizations operate as independent, not integrated, structures. Just as churches try to reconcile people with God, so they act as agencies reconciling diverse interests on earth. Religious groups enjoy the freedom not only to conduct worship services but also to pressure the government. They campaign for tangible benefits such as government financial assistance to church schools as well as for certain moral values like humane treatment in prisons and justice for aliens. Within the democratic pluralist framework, private economic organizations function on a competitive market, whether in a liberal capitalist or a democratic socialist economy. Retaining independence from the state, they also compete for influence over the policy process. Although private business groups wield the greatest power, organizations representing the "popular sector" — factory workers, agricultural wage-laborers, small cash-crop farmers, clerks, traders, artisans — also exert some policy influence.

Given the power of voluntary associations representing diverse primordial, religious, and economic interests, public policymaking occurs through consensual, rather than coercive, strategies. Political leaders bargain, negotiate, and accommodate differences; they rely on rewards, not punishment, as the dominant way to make public policies. In exchange for electoral support, political leaders promise comprehensive government benefits to the citizenry: universal education, health care, pensions for the old, family allowances for the young, financial assistance to church schools, jobs for the unemployed, tax credits and subsidies to businesses, and low-interest loans to farmers. This exchange of benefits typifies the consensual nature of the policy process in a pluralist democracy.

Leaders governing reconciliation systems try to maintain a flexible way of handling the four basic policy issues. Compared with the pluralist democrats, the competitive oligarchs place greater emphasis on determinism, organization, consensus, and continuity. Committed to implement only gradual changes, the oligarchs assume a deterministic stance toward the policy process. From their perspective, traditional cultural values and social structures profoundly shape current human behavior; individual leaders cannot easily change these patterns through the exercise of personal will. Elite organizations, such as those linking patrons and clients, take precedence over spontaneous movements formed by the popular sectors at the bottom of the social stratification system. Although competitive oligarchs accept the legitimacy of policy conflicts, they believe that procedural consensus will most effectively secure political order.

The pluralist democrats recognize the need for flexible government decision-making but assume a more voluntaristic, spontaneous, conflict-laden, and reformist orientation toward handling policy issues. Adopting an optimistic view, pluralist democrats believe that through participation in voluntary associations, individuals can exert their will to achieve their goals. Coalitions with like-minded groups become the preferred strategy for overcoming all obstacles that block individual advancement. Reliance on organization, however, does not mean submission to the state or an elitist political party that mobilizes the society toward a radical reconstruction of the status quo. Instead, social-group spontaneity takes priority over bureaucratic state organization. As new problems arise, individuals at the bottom of the social stratification system join voluntary associations that pressure government leaders to implement policies that will help resolve these problems. In this interest-group competition, a balance occurs between conflict and consensus. Consensus derives from market interdependence and on an agreement to abide by the rules of the game that regulate the group struggle. The focus on making "deals" or exchanges benefiting all contenders reflects a commitment to an open politico-economic market, where the trades bring mutually satisfying rewards. Pluralist democracies also depend on a widespread commitment to legal procedures that apply impartially to all groups, restrict the arbitrary exercise of power, and restrain any tendencies for government officials to monopolize power. Under these consensual conditions, legal procedures and institutional arrangements channel interest-group conflicts into peaceful reconciliation, thereby averting group polarization, political stagnation, and civil war. A pluralist democracy also balances the need for change with the need for continuity. Although the institutions for accommodating differences and the rules for regulating the group struggle remain stable, reformist incremental changes occur in society as individuals and groups gain opportunities to improve their positions in the social stratification system.[15]

## Mobilization System

Unlike reconciliation leaders, who have sought gradual, reformist changes in society, political activists who strive for more rapid, fundamental transformations of the socioeconomic system disdain the reconciliation of group differences. To leaders of revolutionary movements in the

41

contemporary Third World, mobilization represents the most effective way to attain rapid sociopolitical change. For them, mobilization implies a heightened sense of mass political involvement. Ideologically, the masses are expected to view events in political terms, that is, to link their individual good with the well-being of the whole society and to focus on general, common concerns. Striving for a public good—national independence, industrialization, creation of a more just, egalitarian society—becomes both a beneficial end in itself and a means to resolve private problems. Structurally, powerful political organizations such as the party, army, militia, and mass associations gain collective control over political resources and actively use these resources to implement fundamental changes.[16]

Despite its hostility to pluralism and interest-group diversity, the mobilization system shares certain features with reconciliation systems. Both stress popular participation in politics, even though reconciliation leaders rely on more voluntary participation. Political parties play an important role in both systems; whereas reconciliation activists use parties to win elections, mobilization cadres rely on parties as an organizational means to change society. In both systems civilian leaders control the armed forces; yet most Third World mobilization systems feature a greater fusion, rather than differentiation, of military and civilian roles than do reconciliation systems. In short, both the mobilization and reconciliation systems diverge from the bureaucratic-authoritarian system, which features rule by the armed forces, weak or nonexistent political parties, and little if any mass political participation.

Mobilization systems have arisen during the twentieth century, when the masses began to participate actively in political life. These systems most often occur in Third World societies where severe economic inequalities divide the population and deep political conflicts split the society. A sharp economic gap usually separates the rural regions from the wealthier urban areas; within the cities as well, the gulf between rich and poor grows. Ethnic, religious, and economic cleavages lead to political polarization. As the gap widens between elites and masses, between the rural and urban sectors, and between rich and poor, violence and general disorder increase. An oppressive regime that used to control these conflicts by coercive force begins to disintegrate, as exemplified by the decline of European colonial empires and independent agrarian bureaucratic-authoritarian states during the twentieth century. Under these explosive conditions, a mobilization movement arises to promise deliverance from the current woes affecting the whole society.

Political leaders who seek fundamental transformations of the society rely on mobilization strategies to realize their objectives. Before gaining control of the state, a mobilization movement often struggles for national independence from a colonial power and for victory in a revolutionary civil war that involves massive class upheavals. After gaining government power, leaders of mobilization systems may wage wars with foreign governments; in these wars, civilians become highly involved in military activities. Often revolutionaries promote a battle of production to industrialize the society and to attain greater economic equality. By decreasing consumption and expanding capital investment, the state mobilizes the masses for a push toward full-scale industrialization. Then the mobilizing elites use the resulting industrial surplus to lessen economic inequalities. They also wage war on social inequalities and low levels of development by promoting mass literacy and mass health campaigns.

During the twentieth century two divergent types of mobilization systems—the populist and elitist—have tried to forge social change. (See Table 2.4.) Populist mobilization systems feature a lower degree of role specialization. Trying to recapture some elements of the folk system in a differentiated society, populist mobilizers assert the need for equality, political decentralization, and social spontaneity. Opposed to role specialization, they strive to create a political system that places a higher value on mass community involvement than on organizational control. According to them, large-scale bureaucratic organizations destroy shared communal values. Organization brings specialization, expertise, complexity, impersonality, and hierarchy. The populist mobilizers want a system that maximizes equality with other human beings and encourages all people to participate in political life. Instead of the technical expert, the humanistic citizen—the one who shows a general concern for affairs affecting the whole community—becomes the ideal person. Hence, populists assume that political life should stress simplicity, not complexity; social spontaneity, not political organization; equality, not hierarchy; and wholeness, not specialized fragmentation.

The distinction between elitist and populist mobilization systems raises four key questions that focus on political beliefs, the political power of social groups, the power of the state, and public policy performance. First, what is the ideological rationale for mobilizing the masses? What ideological cause do the mobilizers seek to attain? Second, what social groups are mobilized? Third, by what organizational means does mobilization take place? What power does the state wield to organize the society? Fourth, how does the policy process operate? How do the mobilizers handle the basic policy issues? In particular, how much change actually ensues from the mobilization efforts?

Compared with elitist mobilizers, populists concentrate on ideological causes that demand fewer sacrifices from the population. They stress

TABLE 2.4
MOBILIZATION SYSTEM

| VARIABLES | POPULIST MOBILIZATION SYSTEM | ELITIST MOBILIZATION SYSTEM |
|---|---|---|
| **A. Political beliefs** | | |
| 1. Interpretation and ranking of equality | Greater stress on political equality and on equality of socioeconomic condition | Greater stress on equality of true believers in the secular political cause: Socioeconomic equality of opportunity takes precedence over political equality |
| 2. Interpretation and ranking of individual political freedom | Stress on freedom from repressive bureaucratic state but also emphasis on populist conformity to majority beliefs | Low stress on individual political freedom and civil liberties to challenge the party-state elite, greater emphasis on national independence and liberation from foreign oppression |
| 3. Relationship between pursuit of material benefits and of moral-spiritual values | Fusion of moral and material ends: Opposed to the corruption of the *ancien régime*, populists seek a purified political system and greater equality of economic rewards | Fusion of moral and material ends: Elitist mobilizers seek ideological transformations among the masses as well as technical abundance; goal is to enhance production, secure greater economic equality, and lessen cleavages between urban industrial and rural agrarian sectors; secular political religion endows material ends with moral sanctification |
| 4. Relationship between individualism and collectivism | Collectivistic: The people should rule | Collectivistic: Individuals should subordinate their interests to the will of the party, state, and nation |
| **B. Power of social groups** | | |
| 1. Power of primordial groups in policy process | Greater autonomy from party-state control: Youths and women play an influential political role | Less autonomy from party-state control: Dominant party organizes participation by ethnic associations, age groups, and gender groups |
| 2. Power of religious groups in policy process | Opposed to ecclesiastical hierarchies, local basic religious communities — churches of the people — may wield significant policy influence | The state and the party dominate established, orthodox churches |
| 3. Power of economic groups in policy process | Unions of peasants and workers gain extensive autonomy from state control and help shape economic policies | A powerful state and dominant party suppress spontaneous economic associations, which retain little influence over policy process |
| **C. Power of political organizations** | | |
| 1. Government | | |
| a. Degree of coercive and consensual power | Consensual power prevails over coercive power | Coercive power, as wielded by strong military and police, prevails over consensual power |

*Continued on next page*

TABLE 2.4 *continued*

| VARIABLES | POPULIST MOBILIZATION SYSTEM | ELITIST MOBILIZATION SYSTEM |
|---|---|---|
| b. Degree of centralized power | Low: decentralized in village and city councils | High: centralized in powerful party and nation-state organizations |
| c. Degree of institutional coordination | Low: Collective leadership and mass-based party try to coordinate policy activities | High: Party elite and Great Leader coordinate policy activities |
| d. Independence of social groups from government control (strength of social pluralism) | Moderately low: Radical pluralism disperses power to rural unions, factory committees, and workers' militias | Low: Powerful party-state organizations dominate social groups. Youth groups, trade unions, farm associations, women's organizations, and professional groups are party auxiliaries that mobilize the masses |
| e. Scope of government power | Extensive: stress on provision of social services to individuals | Very extensive: stress on system maintenance, construction of economic infrastructure, and provision of social services to individuals |
| 2. Political parties | Moderately strong: Populist, decentralized, and mass-based parties try to secure social change; they represent the interests of the popular sector —factory workers, small farmers, and small business-people | Very strong: One powerful dominant party forges social change; it represents a single general will imposed by the ideological elite |
| **D. Ways of processing basic policy issues** | | |
| 1. What interaction occurs between personal will and social conditions? | Voluntarism: Populist mobilizers assert their will to mobilize resources for greater socio-economic equality | Voluntarism: Elitist mobilizers assert their will to mobilize resources for developmental goals |
| 2. Do spontaneous social groups or political organizations wield dominant power? | Greater social spontaneity, especially as demonstrated by popular sector groups | Greater political organization: Professionalized political party, military, police, and civil service dominate policy process |
| 3. What is the relationship between conflict and consensus? | Greater stress on forming a consensus through persuading groups in popular sector: Conflicts occur with landlords, large-scale capitalists, ecclesiastical hierarchies, and state bureaucrats | Greater stress on conflict with people designated as "outgroups" by ideological elite: Consensus is based on commitment to ideological truth and on party's institutional coherence; intense conflict leads to fundamental change |
| 4. What is the relationship between change and continuity? | Populist leaders often secure rapid, extensive social changes; yet these are short-lived | Elitist mobilizers support fundamental changes in basic values and in the social stratification system; yet they want to maintain their dominant power position and ideological message |

greater freedom from a domestically governed bureaucratic-authoritarian state and more equal distribution of wealth so that workers and peasants can enjoy increased consumption. By contrast, for the elitist mobilizers, freedom involves military sacrifices. It means victory in wars against a foreign enemy, a successful struggle for national independence from colonial rule, and the higher growth that results from the battle to industrialize a society rapidly.

According to both populist and elitist mobilizers, political legitimacy rests on collectivism and a fusion of moral with material values. Intolerant toward the expression of individual dissidence, they assert the supremacy of the collective interests over individual self-interests. For the populists, "the people" should rule. The elitists want individuals to subordinate their interests to the party, state, and nation. Both groups of mobilizers fuse moral with material ends. Opposed to the corruption of both the competitive oligarchy and the bureaucratic-authoritarian state, populists seek a purified political system in which all the people, especially workers and small farmers, more equally share economic benefits. Elitists aim to enhance productivity, stimulate rapid industrial growth, secure greater income equality, and thereby lessen the tensions between the urban and rural sectors. All these material goals assume ultimate sacred value. Along with the ideological transformation of the citizenry, the pursuit of technical abundance serves as the collective cause that mobilizes the population.

Despite the term "elitist," mobilization systems dominated by a centralized, professional elite try to organize more of the population than do populists. Wars against foreign powers and domestic battles for expanded capital accumulation require that nearly all the people join the mobilization struggle. Populist mobilizers, however, represent the interests of the "popular sector"—the peasants, factory workers, and small business people—for greater economic equality and for increased freedom from state control.

The elitist mobilization system secures greater party-state control over social groups than does the populist type. Various primordial groups become party auxiliaries. For instance, the Party organizes associations composed of women, youth, and ethnic-linguistic groups. The state also denies autonomy to religious organizations. Often the party, not the church, becomes a charismatic organization with the "gift of grace." Worship of the nation, the state, and the party takes precedence over loyalty to an orthodox church that operates independently from the state. Besides controlling primordial and religious groups, the ruling political organizations dominate economic associations. Rather than a sharp separation between the state and economic firms, a fusion of the political with the economic sector takes place. Party and state either own or strictly regulate the operations of farms, factories, and firms. No economic groups have the power to form interest groups; instead, trade unions, farm organizations, and business associations come under strict party control, functioning as party auxiliaries. In populist mobilization systems, however, primordial, religious, and economic groups gain greater autonomy from bureaucratic state domination. Women and especially youth play a politically powerful role. Opposed to an ecclesiastical hierarchy, populist mobilizers either conduct their political activities in secular organizations uncontrolled by church officials or establish *comunidades eclesiales de base* (basic Christian communities) of poor people who work to create a new society. Independent peasant leagues, agricultural unions, and factory committees give farmers and workers the organized opportunity to participate in political decision-making.

Unlike populist mobilizers, elitists rule through more centralized, coercive organizations. In this hierarchical, monistic political system, a strong state, a professionalized army, a powerful secret police, and a dominant party that controls mass associations wield decisive power over the policy process. The party elite, often guided by a great leader, coordinates the extensive government activities that revolve around external defense, internal order, construction of an economic infrastructure, and provision of social services to individuals. All these organizations and activities exhibit a high degree of role specialization. Populist mobilizers, however, assume that each person can perform a variety of different roles. A factory worker needs no "bourgeois specialists" to teach him how to work. A small farmer requires no party intellectual or urban-educated bureaucrat to direct work in the fields. Opposed to centralized, hierarchical, elitist forms of governance, populists reject the centralized state, the professionalized army, bureaucratic unions, and a professional party led by the intelligentsia and political engineers. In their place, populist mobilizers decentralize political power to local self-governing units such as elected village and city councils. They organize mass parties with democratic decision processes; popularly elected party assemblies formulate general policies. Factory committees establish worker control of factories. Workers' militias, rather than a professionalized army and police force, provide some order and defend the area against attack. Rather than rule by a single man, collective leadership coordinates these political organizations. Because the populist mobilization system decentralizes decision-making to dispersed organizations, the central state performs fewer activities than in an elitist mobilization system.

Compared with populist mobilizers, leaders directing an elitist mobilization system adopt a more monistic strategy for handling basic policy issues. The unification of political organizations parallels the stress on ideological purity, certainty, homogeneity, and singleness of purpose. Voluntarism overwhelms determinism. Dominant political organizations, such as a strong bureaucratic state and powerful party, assert their will to mobilize resources for comprehensive goals: rapid industrialization, expanded economic equality, mass education, and comprehensive public health care. In the policy process, spontaneous social groups relinquish their power to political organizations, especially the party, military, police, and civil service. Conflict takes precedence over consensus. Adopting a militaristic strategy, the political elite foments conflict with designated "outgroups": ethnic groups, religious groups, landlords, capitalists, antiparty people, and so forth. Besides conflicts with these domestic groups, wars with foreign governments mobilize the population behind the elite. Although mobilization leaders often attain a consensus after lengthy control of government power, this consensus hardly emerges spontaneously; instead, through mass education, indoctrination, and propaganda, the elite imposes a consensus based on commitment to ideological Truth and on the coherence of the powerful party-state. Although stressing the need for fundamental changes in society, elitist mobilizers also seek to maintain the continuity of the ideological message and their dominant power position. From their perspective, only by retaining institutional cohesion can the policymakers secure fundamental changes in the basic values and social stratification system that existed under the previous regime.

During the twentieth century the Marxist-Leninist mobilization regimes in China, North Korea, Mongolia, and Cuba have both maintained their political system and implemented extensive changes in their societies. Certainly, they have expanded resources through programs of industrialization, mass education, and comprehensive public health care. Political power has become more centralized in a strong state and powerful army. When the party-state gained control over formerly independent social groups, the vestiges of pluralism remaining from the old regimes largely disappeared. Despite the revolutionary rhetoric, full-scale equality remains unfulfilled. Party leaders have gained special privileges— food, consumer goods, housing, education, health care—unavailable to the mass of the population. Bureaucratic rigidities stifle policy implementation. Equality of opportunity seems more prevalent than equal economic conditions, equal social status, or especially equal participation in political decision-making. As these revolutionary regimes became institutionalized, they lost the ideological morale, mass enthusiasm, singleness of purpose, and organizational cohesion associated with an elitist mobilization system. Technocrats, production managers, and

48

engineers guide the economic policy process, thereby reinforcing bureaucratic-authoritarian tendencies.

Because their power rests on a more dispersed organizational base, popular mobilizers have demonstrated less success in maintaining government control and achieving structural changes. Like the elitist mobilizers the populists emphasize dominance of voluntarism over determinism. Through the active assertion of the people's will, they believe it possible to overwhelm the objective conditions and realize comprehensive policy changes. Populists rely on spontaneous mass movements, rather than bureaucratic organizations, to attain these changes. Conflict pervades the policy process. For example, in Chile during the early 1970s, populist movements that represented poor farmers and factory workers staged strikes, seized landed estates, established workers' control of factories, and either captured control of local governments or organized new local governing agencies such as popularly elected councils. The mobilizing organizations—peasant leagues, unions, factory committees, workers' militias, councils—constituted a movement or a partial system; they failed to govern the whole society. Reconciliation leaders held weak control over the central government, which lacked the power or the will to crush civil liberties and repress social pluralism. Populists gained the freedom to organize mobilization systems in some rural areas and urban zones. Yet the populist mobilizers neither maintained their local power for long nor secured control over the central state. Instead the Chilean armed forces in September 1973 seized government power, repressed the radical populist movements, and established a bureaucratic-authoritarian system.

In conclusion, the analysis of the four general models of political systems helps us understand political changes in specific Third World countries. Using these models, we will explore systemic changes in Vietnam, Cuba, Chile, Nigeria, and Iran. A theory of political change elaborated in Chapter 3 suggests how and why beliefs, structures, and policy performance explain these political transformations.

## Notes

1 Richard Rose, *Understanding Big Government: The Programme Approach* (Beverley Hills, Calif.: Sage Publications, 1984), 4, 13–20.
2 Charles F. Andrain, *Foundations of Comparative Politics: A Policy Perspective* (Monterey, Calif.: Brooks/Cole, 1983), 179–191.
3 See Steve Fenton, *Durkheim and Modern Sociology* (New York: Cambridge University Press, 1984), esp. 48–115.
4 See Jonathan H. Turner, *Societal Stratification: A Theoretical Analysis* (New York:

49

Columbia University Press, 1984); Harold Barclay, *People without Government* (London: Kahn and Averill with Cienfuegos Press, 1982); Gerhard Lenski and Jean Lenski, *Human Societies*, 5th ed. (New York: McGraw-Hill, 1987), 97–129; Talcott Parsons, *Societies: Evolutionary and Comparative Perspectives* (Englewood Cliffs, N.J.: Prentice-Hall, 1966), 30–50; Aidan Southall, "Stateless Society," *International Encyclopedia of the Social Sciences*, vol. 15 (New York: Macmillan, 1968), 157–168; Robert Redfield, "The Folk Society," *American Journal of Sociology* 52 (January 1947): 293–308.

5 Ted C. Lewellen, "Anthropological Typologies of Preindustrial Political Systems," *Micropolitics* 1, no. 4 (1981): 321–344.

6 Guillermo A. O'Donnell coined the term "bureaucratic-authoritarian" rule. See the following works by him: *Modernization and Bureaucratic-Authoritarianism: Studies in South American Politics* (Berkeley: Institute of International Studies, University of California, 1973); "Reflections on the Patterns of Change in the Bureaucratic-Authoritarian State," *Latin American Research Review* 13, no. 1 (1978): 3–38; "Tensions in the Bureaucratic-Authoritarian State and the Question of Democracy," in *The New Authoritarianism in Latin America*, ed. David Collier (Princeton, N.J.: Princeton University Press, 1979), 285–318. See, too, Fernando Henrique Cardoso, "On the Characterization of Authoritarian Regimes in Latin America," in *The New Authoritarianism in Latin America*, 33–57; Juan J. Linz, "Totalitarian and Authoritarian Regimes," in *Handbook of Political Science*, vol. 3, ed. Fred I. Greenstein and Nelson W. Polsby (Reading, Mass.: Addison-Wesley, 1975), 175–357, esp. 264–350; Ernest Kilker, "Weber on Socialism, Bureaucracy, and Freedom," *State, Culture and Society* 1 (Fall 1984): 76–95.

7 Reinhard Bendix, *Max Weber: An Intellectual Portrait* (Garden City, N.Y.: Anchor Books, 1962), 426; *From Max Weber: Essays in Sociology*, trans. and ed. H. H. Gerth and C. Wright Mills (New York: Oxford University Press, 1958), 196–224.

8 See Ellen Kay Trimberger, *Revolution from Above* (New Brunswick, N.J.: Transaction Books, 1978).

9 For analyses of pluralist reconciliation systems, see Robert A. Dahl, *Polyarchy: Participation and Opposition* (New Haven, Conn.: Yale University Press, 1971); Robert A. Dahl, "Governments and Political Oppositions," in *Handbook of Political Science*, vol. 3, ed. Fred I. Greenstein and Nelson W. Polsby (Reading, Mass.: Addison-Wesley, 1975), 115–170; Robert A. Dahl, "Pluralism Revisited," *Comparative Politics* 10 (January 1978): 191–203; Robert A. Dahl, *A Preface to Democratic Theory* (Chicago: University of Chicago Press, 1957); Robert A. Dahl, "Polyarchy, Pluralism, and Scale," *Scandinavian Political Studies* 7, no. 4 (1984): 225–240; Charles F. Andrain, *Political Life and Social Change*, 2d ed. (Belmont, Calif.: Wadsworth, 1975), 62–64, 191–213; Andrain, *Foundations of Comparative Politics*, 172–173, 293–395; David E. Apter, *Introduction to Political Analysis* (Cambridge, Mass.: Winthrop, 1977), 293–375; S. N. Eisenstadt, *Modernization: Protest and Change* (Englewood Cliffs, N.J.: Prentice-Hall, 1966), 129–144.

10 Raymond D. Gastil, *Freedom in the World: Political Rights and Civil Liberties, 1985–1986* (Westport, Conn.: Greenwood Press, 1986), 59–71.

11 Bruce Russett and Harvey Starr, *World Politics: The Menu for Choice*, 2d ed. (New York: W. H. Freeman, 1985), 465–467; Thomas Straubhaar, "The Economics of Third World Arms Imports," *Intereconomics* 21 (May/June 1986): 137–141;

Daniel Chirot, *Social Change in the Modern Era* (San Diego, Calif.: Harcourt Brace Jovanovich, 1986), 194–230; Robert A. Packenham, *Liberal America and the Third World: Political Development Ideas in Foreign Aid and Social Science* (Princeton, N.J.: Princeton University Press, 1973); Richard E. Feinberg, *The Intemperate Zone: The Third World Challenge to U.S. Foreign Policy* (New York: W. W. Norton, 1983); Edward N. Muller, "Dependent Economic Development, Aid Dependence on the United States, and Democratic Breakdown in the Third World," *International Studies Quarterly* 29 (December 1985): 445–469; Stephen White, "What Is a Communist System?" *Studies in Comparative Communism* 16 (Winter 1983): 247–263; Charles F. Andrain, "Capitalism and Democracy Reappraised: A Review Essay," *Western Political Quarterly* 37 (December 1984): 652–664; Lars Schoultz, *Human Rights and United States Policy toward Latin America* (Princeton, N.J.: Princeton University Press, 1981); Lars Schoultz, "U.S. Foreign Policy and Human Rights Violations in Latin America: A Comparative Analysis of Foreign Aid Distributions," *Comparative Politics* 13 (January 1981): 149–170.

12 Chirot, *Social Change in the Modern Era*, 208–222, 247–261; Russett and Starr, *World Politics*, 438–464; Robert H. Bates and Da-Hsiang Donald Lien, "A Note on Taxation, Development, and Representative Government," *Politics and Society* 14, no. 1 (1985): 53–70; Volker Bornschier and Christopher Chase-Dunn, *Transnational Corporations and Underdevelopment* (New York: Praeger, 1985), 117–147; Irma Adelman, "Strategies for Equitable Growth," *Challenge* 17 (May/June 1974): 37–44.

13 Dahl, "Governments and Political Oppositions," 120–122.

14 See Paul W. Drake and Eduardo Silva, eds., *Elections and Democratization in Latin America, 1980–85* (San Diego, Calif.: Center for Iberian and Latin American Studies, Center for U.S.-Mexican Studies, Institute of the Americas, University of California, San Diego, 1986); Paul Cammack, "Democratisation: A Review of the Issues," *Bulletin of Latin American Research* 4, no. 2 (1985): 39–46; Jim Handy, "Resurgent Democracy and the Guatemalan Military," *Journal of Latin American Studies* 18 (November 1986): 383–408; Cecilia Rodriguez, "A Military Menace Hides behind Latin America's New Democracy," *Los Angeles Times*, November 30, 1986, part V, p. 3.

15 See Sheldon S. Wolin, *Politics and Vision* (Boston: Little, Brown, 1960), 429–434; Apter, *Introduction to Political Analysis*, 359–375; David E. Apter, *Choice and the Politics of Allocation* (New Haven, Conn.: Yale University Press, 1971), 162–163; Robert A. Dahl, *Dilemmas of Pluralist Democracy: Autonomy vs. Control* (New Haven, Conn.: Yale University Press, 1982).

16 David E. Apter, *The Politics of Modernization* (Chicago: University of Chicago Press, 1965), 357–390; Charles Tilly, *From Mobilization to Revolution* (Reading, Mass.: Addison-Wesley, 1978), 52–142; Charles Tilly, "Revolutions and Collective Violence," in *Handbook of Political Science*, vol. 3, ed. Fred I. Greenstein and Nelson W. Polsby (Reading, Mass.: Addison-Wesley, 1975), 503–506; Amitai Etzioni, *The Active Society* (New York: The Free Press, 1968), 387–422.

# 3

## A THEORETICAL EXPLANATION OF POLITICAL CHANGE

Men make their own history, but not of their own free will; not under circumstances they themselves have chosen but under the given and inherited circumstances with which they are directly confronted. The tradition of the dead generations weighs like a nightmare on the minds of the living.

— Karl Marx

The crisis consists precisely in the fact that the old is dying and the new cannot be born; in this interregnum a great variety of morbid symptoms appear.

— Antonio Gramsci

Throughout the Third World, changes of political systems alter individual lives. The recent histories of Vietnam, Cuba, Chile, Nigeria, and Iran reveal that political upheavals expanded the opportunities for some persons but brought misery to others. In Vietnam the military dictatorship of General Thieu collapsed during the spring of 1975, when the People's Army of Vietnam seized control of Saigon. Communist party cadres quickly moved to organize a mobilization system that replaced the bureaucratic-authoritarian regime formerly allied with the United States. Supporters of the Thieu government, including soldiers fighting for the Army of the Republic of Vietnam, were sent to "reeducation" camps, where they learned Marxist-Leninist political doctrines and confessed their past sins of collaborating with the Thieu regime. Many urbanites had to leave the cities for "new economic zones." There they repaired roads, built irrigation canals, and planted sweet potatoes. Under these conditions in the Socialist Republic of Vietnam, opportunities for personal advancement seemed limited. The new political system appeared like a nightmare blocking dreams for a better life.

In Cuba Castro and his guerrilla forces seized control of Havana at the end of 1958, toppling the bureaucratic-authoritarian system from power. He started organizing a new mobilization system that promised to purify the Cuban nation of corruption, materialism, economic inequalities, ill health, and illiteracy. To his supporters, Castro embodied the ideal leader—honest, courageous, imaginative, and ideologically committed to a renewed society. Other Cubans remained less enchanted with the mobilizing activities of the socialist government and the economic consequences that stemmed from Castro's policies. Although most people admired the government's success in lowering illiteracy and expanding health care in the rural areas, many resented its failure to raise living standards and to promote civil liberties. Discontented with the economic situation and depressed by the stifling political atmosphere, opponents of Castro's rule sought refuge in Miami.

In Chile and Nigeria as well, popular hopes for a brighter future have been thwarted. The Chilean military coup that overthrew the popularly elected Allende government in September 1973 signaled the change from a reconciliation system to a bureaucratic-authoritarian system dominated by the armed forces and police. They arrested, tortured, imprisoned, and exiled supporters of the overthrown Allende government. Particularly for those Chileans who established workers' participation in the factories, the military takeover transformed their dreams of a liberated, egalitarian country into a nightmare. In Nigeria three military coups, one abortive coup, and a civil war occurred from 1966 through 1976. An elected reconciliation government took office in 1979, only to be overthrown by the armed forces four years later. The military dictatorship seizing power in December 1983 banned political parties, curbed student organizations, abolished the program of universal primary education, and harassed women, especially in the Moslem North. As Gramsci observed in Mussolini's Fascist Italy, so in Chile and Nigeria today the old reconciliation systems died without giving birth to a renewed society.

The Islamic revolution that overthrew the Shah in early 1979 also failed to realize the hopes of its supporters. Even though the urban poor still give their allegiance to the Ayatollah Khomeini, others who initially resisted the Shah have become disillusioned. Whereas under the Shah's bureaucratic-authoritarian rule the Savak suppressed dissidents, under the Islamic Republic several organizations—Pasdarans (revolutionary guards), the Savama, Moslem revolutionary committees—

wield extensive coercion over Iranians' daily lives. Shiite clergy and their agents keep close surveillance over education, the courts, family life, and sexual behavior to ensure that secularizing influences from the capitalist West and the communist East do not contaminate citizens' moral behavior. Committed to restoring the "holy duty" of motherhood, the Islamic theocratic regime has deprived women of employment, education, the right to divorce, and sexual equality with men. For men, sacrificial death in the holy war against Iraq is the way to gain salvation. Morbid symptoms have thus accompanied the drastic change in political systems.[1]

What reasons explain political change in the Third World, both within-system changes and more fundamental between-system transformations of policy priorities, political structures, and ways of processing basic policy issues? I assume that the severity of conflicts accounts for the differences between the two types of systemic change. Whereas within-system change requires an adaptable strategy for handling the tensions that disturb a system's equilibrium, more severe conflicts undermine the equilibrium of a political system and cause the change from one system to a different type.

## Within-System Change

Relatively mild conflicts produce within-system changes—that is, changes in leadership and policy contents. Although tensions occur within each of the three systemic dimensions—beliefs, structures, and ways of handling policy issues—the basic pattern of decision-making remains stable. (See Table 3.1.)

In a stable agrarian folk system, political leaders adapt beliefs, structures, and policy processes to changing situations. Priests and elders reinterpret traditional beliefs to meet new needs. The introduction of a different farming implement, such as a new hoe, often challenges traditional ideas about planting rice; thus, village elders justify the new hoe by invoking traditional religious values—for example, by claiming that it poses no threat to reverence for the earth. Structural change within a folk system occurs through moderate competition among different family-linked organizations, such as groups of elders and age grades. These primordial agencies, along with ad hoc associations, formulate and implement marginal changes. Dealing with the four basic policy issues, folk leaders try to blend conflicting tendencies so that the style of decision-making remains in equilibrium. Although cultural determinism overwhelms the desire to forge a new political system, village elders exert

## TABLE 3.1
### Sources of Change Within a Political System

| | SYSTEMS | | | |
|---|---|---|---|---|
| **Variables** | **Folk** | **Bureaucratic-Authoritarian** | **Reconciliation** | **Mobilization** |
| **A. Beliefs** | Tension between sacred traditional beliefs and more secular ideas emanating from outside sources | Tension between desire for order and perceived disorder | Tensions among diverse ideas for political action voiced by interest groups | Tension between comprehensive, programmatic ideology and the perceived empirical situation |
| **B. Structures** | Moderate competition among ad hoc associations and family-linked organizations | Mild conflicts between bureaucrats (military, police, civil service) and groups that resist bureaucratic directives imposed by ruling elites | Competition and bargaining among self-interested groups | Conflicts between political organizations (party, government) and groups that resist comprehensive changes demanded by mobilizers |
| **C. Ways of processing basic policy issues** | | | | |
| 1. Voluntarism vs. determinism | Leaders have some discretion in reinterpreting traditional values to meet new conditions | Political leaders retain freedom to use administrative organizations that adapt to new conditions | Pluralist leaders remain sensitive to desirability of policy objectives and feasibility of attaining these goals | Leaders blend will to realize fundamental change with sensitivity to objective conditions blocking changes |
| 2. Spontaneity vs. organization | Councils of elders, age grades, and ad hoc associations remain open to popular demands | Bureaucratic agencies adapt to new information from diverse groups at bottom of administrative hierarchy and outside the bureaucracy | Social groups voice demands at policy formation stage, and powerful political organizations implement the policies | System blends political organization with openness to spontaneous demands for change |
| 3. Conflict vs. consensus | Value solidarity minimizes explosive conflicts | Agreement on rational-legal norms helps channel factional conflicts into efficient ways for resolving conflicts | Pluralist leaders balance conflict over policies with consensus on rules of game to regulate conflicts | Leaders blend ideological consensus and conflicts with groups opposed to transformation of social system |
| 4. Change vs. continuity | Priests and elders reinterpret continuing, traditional beliefs to explain changing situation | Procedures continue, but the goals and policy consequences change | Leaders secure a balance between continuity of representative institutions and changes in policies that meet new conditions | Leaders blend will to change status quo with some continuity from the past order that gives meaning to change |

some will in reinterpreting traditional values to meet new conditions. The stress on spontaneity, rather than institutionalized organization, means that ad hoc associations, age grades, and councils of elders remain open to popular demands for more land, new ways to gain food, and greater power to youth. The need to transcend individualism and to avoid anarchy requires the development of at least informal organizations to cope with these demands. Lacking formalized bureaucratic institutions, a folk system relies instead on value solidarity to minimize explosive conflicts. Consensus on traditional religious beliefs facilitates the peaceful settlement of minor conflicts. The moral-spiritual solidarity also supplies the value continuity that legitimates gradual changes in structural arrangements, public policies, and procedures to resolve policy disputes.

Change within a bureaucratic-authoritarian system stems from mild conflicts within the three dimensions of a political system. The tension between a stress on order and the perception of disorder often leads to minor changes in the style of decision-making. From a structural perspective, the bureaucratic elites—military officers, policemen, and civil servants—try to secure social changes by imposing their directives on subordinates. When some resistance occurs to these directives, the bureaucrats may alter their arbitrary, harsh style of rule. Ruling elites who seek to preserve the bureaucratic-authoritarian system develop flexible ways of handling the four policy issues. Voluntarism checks the stifling determinism of the bureaucratic iron cage. Successful within-system change also requires a blend of some spontaneity with organization. Flexible bureaucrats seek new information from diverse groups at the bottom of the formal hierarchy as well as outside the bureaucracy. Political change in a bureaucratic-authoritarian system most effectively occurs when administrators secure a balance between both conflict and consensus and between change and continuity. Procedural consensus helps channel inevitable factional conflicts into efficient ways to resolve problems. Continuity of flexible procedures serves as a stable backdrop for the pursuit of new goals.

In the pluralist reconciliation system political leaders pursue an accommodationist strategy toward changes in public policies; tensions between different beliefs, competing group leaders, and opposing ways of handling political issues lead to incremental changes. Political beliefs of policymakers remain open to a variety of different stimuli. Eclectic and tolerant, the beliefs reflect the plurality of options for political action. As diverse ideas come into conflict, the leadership keeps an open mind to new information that relates to a specific policy issue. From the structural standpoint, a reconciliation system experiences widespread competition among self-interested voluntary associations; bargaining with one another for a share of the economic pie, they help bring about moderate, gradual policy changes. In this bargaining process, ways of resolving the four policy issues come into a creative tension. Reconciliation leaders seek a balance between voluntarism and determinism, spontaneity and organization, conflict and consensus, change and continuity. Although willing to take political actions that will change the status quo, pluralist policymakers remain sensitive to the objective conditions (cultural values, level of economic development, rate of economic growth, distribution of political power) that thwart immediate goal attainment. In the reconciliation policy process, concerns about feasibility (determinism) thus balance a stress on desirability (voluntarism). A balance between social-group spontaneity and political organization also occurs. At the policy formulation stage, a variety of interest groups spontaneously assert their political demands for public policies, such as higher wages, increased land, expanded job opportunities, better educational facilities, and improved health care. Yet these groups realize the need for an efficient administrative organization to implement these policies. At both the policy formulation and implementation stages, diverse groups also must organize effective political coalitions if they are to see their policy objectives translated into desired results. In a reconciliation system the policy process operates most smoothly when the participants reach a balance between conflict over policy options and consensus on the rules of the game to regulate the interest-group conflict. Political stability of the decision-making process most likely occurs when policymakers also balance continuity of the representative structures (legislatures, political parties, interest-group associations) with incremental policy changes that meet new conditions, especially the demands of aspiring groups formerly excluded from political participation.

Although leaders of elitist mobilization systems seek fundamental, drastic, and rapid changes in society, they strive to preserve the mobilization style of political decision-making. A comprehensive ideology sketching a vision of a transformed society and a policy program to reach that vision serves as a guide to political action. Conflict between the unrealized ideological goals and the actual empirical situation mobilizes the people to undergo the sacrifices necessary for realizing a changed society. Powerful political organizations, as embodied in a strong party and centralized government, work toward attaining the comprehensive ideological objectives. In these efforts to secure immediate, comprehensive changes in society, opposition usually breaks out between the dominant mobilizing organizations and groups associated with the previous regime. As the ruling "in-groups" clash with the ideological "out-groups," changes often take place in the social stratification system. The policy process for securing these changes reveals a fusion of opposed ways of handling the four issues. Mobilization leaders blend the will to transform the society with a sensitivity to the objective cultural, economic, and political conditions that prevent immediate goal attainment. Even though political organization triumphs over social spontaneity, mobilization leaders try to blend organizational elitism with some openness to demands of groups at the bottom of the stratification hierarchy, especially poor people's desire for access to employment, education, and health care. Moreover, the mobilization system balances ideological consensus with conflict toward out-groups that oppose transformations of society. Finally, despite their focus on social change, few mobilization elites deny the relevance of past traditions in building a new sociopolitical order. While stressing the exercise of will to transform the social status quo, they retain some continuities from their national histories that give meaning to the changing process. As exemplified by Ho Chi Minh and Fidel Castro, mobilizing leaders reinterpret their traditional national heritage to justify contemporary revolutionary changes.

## Between-System Change

What forces bring about the downfall of one regime and lay the groundwork for a different type of political system? To answer this question, we need to analyze the incumbent government and the opposition, specifically cultural beliefs, structures, policy performance of governing authorities, and policy promises made by opposition leaders. We assume that unlike within-system changes, which stem from mild conflicts, a between-system change emerges when incumbent political leaders face severe conflicts or "contradictions" that they cannot handle within the existing mode of policy production. "Contradictions" refer to conflicts that maintain a political system in the short run but eventually lead to systemic disintegration over the long run.[2] Three such contradictions—cultural, structural, and policy—explain the transformation from one system to a different type. (See Tables 3.2 and 3.3.)

This explanation of between-system change adopts a structural interpretation based on conflicts among sociopolitical organizations, beliefs, and ways of processing policy issues. Other theories postulate that certain cultural or behavioral phenomena—Utopian political ideas, charismatic leaders, or relative deprivations—supply the spark that ignites systemic transformations. Instead, I assume that structural conditions—especially the interactions among the state, domestic social

TABLE 3.2
EXPLANATIONS FOR BETWEEN-SYSTEM POLITICAL CHANGES

| VARIABLES | INCUMBENT GOVERMENT | OPPOSITION |
|---|---|---|
| 1. Beliefs | Government leaders show waning legitimacy and a weakening commitment to an ideological cause | Opposition leaders display a stronger dedication to an ideological cause that rejects incumbent authorities' right to rule |
| 2. Structures | | |
| a. Social groups | Social groups supporting the government show declining cohesion | Social groups opposing the government achieve greater solidarity |
| b. Political organizations | Government is unable to wield efficient coercive and con- sensual power | Opposition organizations have greater ability to build alliances and employ coercive force |
| c. Foreign states and overseas institutions | Foreign structures undermine power of incumbent govern- ment | Foreign structures strengthen power of opposition |
| 3. Policy performance and promises | Incumbent government demon- strates ineffective policy per- formance | Opposition leaders make policy promises that appeal to the disaffected |

groups, and foreign institutions—explain the probability of between-system change. If the incumbent regime becomes fragmented, can no longer either form an effective coalition among its allies or wield coercion against opponents, and loses support from foreign institutions, it will likely disintegrate. An opposition that develops greater organizational solidarity, domestic coalition support, foreign backing, and the power to outmaneuver the incumbent authorities will probably succeed in over-throwing an existing government. The opposition movement's ideological values and structural control over society determine whether it will attempt to institute a different political system. According to this struc-tural interpretation, the likelihood of forging a new type of political system depends on both the subjective will of political leaders and certain objective structural conditions, such as the distribution of power among the state, social groups, and foreign institutions. Combined with a leader's political skills, structural characteristics—the state's cohesive-ness, links with social groups, differentiation, policymaking resources—shape the success in changing the political system and implementing public policies that transform the society. The type of changes that political leaders achieve also depends on their subjective orientations, that is, their political will to realize systemic changes and their conceptions

# TABLE 3.3
## Sources of Change Between Political Systems

| | SYSTEMS | | | |
|---|---|---|---|---|
| Variables | Folk | Bureaucratic-Authoritarian | Reconciliation | Mobilization |
| **A. Beliefs** | Severe conflict between purity of sacred beliefs and external secular values associated with science and technology: Old beliefs no longer have meaning to new situations. Too many outside disturbances (military conquests, floods, famine, mass media infiltration) upset internal value solidarity | Severe conflict between desire for order and actual stress on personal opportunism: Order becomes an end in itself, rather than a means to other ends; rigid, routinized system fails to provide meaning; bureaucratic elites cannot cope with opportunism, corruption, and struggle for group interests | Severe conflict between particularized interests expressed by groups that share no transcendent notions of the common good: Loss of meaning results from pursuit of narrow individual and group interests; group polarization weakens collective value solidarity; result is moral disillusionment and malaise | Severe conflict between ideological goals and perceptions that the system has failed to attain these goals: As gap widens between ideological objectives and perceptions of actual policy performance, ideological message seems irrelevant to concrete needs; elites lose faith in ideological vision |
| **B. Structures** | Severe conflicts between fragile village structures and more powerful external agencies: System has too weak a power base to withstand external disturbances, especially military conquest | Severe conflicts between hierarchy (closed system) and factionalism (system more open to aspiring groups): Growing factionalism undermines centralized, coercive rule; weak process of consensus formation blocks peaceful changes | Severe conflicts between consensus formation and political immobilism (group anarchy): Central leaders lack the coercive power to repress opposition; pluralists lack the time needed to form a consensus | Severe conflicts between centralizing and decentralizing forces: Elites rely on centralized use of coercion to overcome resistance; yet this coercion leads to a breakdown of consensus and to greater resistance at decentralized points in power grid |
| **C. Ways of processing basic policy issues** | | | | |
| 1. Voluntarism vs. determinism | Traditional leaders lack will to change status quo to meet external threats | Rigid bureaucratic controls overwhelm exercise of personal will to enact changes | Exercise of personal will by pluralist leaders underestimates objective conditions | Leaders ignore objective conditions blocking immediate goal attainment |
| 2. Spontaneity vs. organization | System lacks powerful organization to counter outside threats | Stifling organization overwhelms spontaneous initiatives | Interest group spontaneity is not balanced by strong political organizations to implement policies | Political mobilization overorganizes society, which lacks group spontaneity |
| 3. Conflict vs. consensus | Consensus based on shared values disintegrates | Factional conflicts undermine procedural consensus | As groups become polarized, leaders cannot form a consensus | Excessive conflict with domestic and foreign enemies weakens consensus |
| 4. Change vs. continuity | Excessive continuity weakens adaptability to change | Procedural continuity (ultra-legalism) blocks adaptability to change | Change in group positions overwhelms shared commitment to rules that provide continuity | Excessive structural and ideological changes undermine continuity with past that gives meaning to changes |

about the public well-being, salient social problems, causes of these problems, and the most desirable, feasible solutions to them.[3]

## The Decline of Legitimacy

When political legitimacy declines, the prospects for a between-system change become more likely. *If governing elites show a waning commitment to an ideological cause but their opponents are more strongly dedicated to a contradictory cause, the existing system may collapse.* Under these conditions, the ruling elites lose confidence in their right to govern a society, but opposition leaders strengthen their sense of legitimacy, that is, their right to rule. To remain in power the dominant elites must concentrate on retaining legitimacy from government officials, especially the armed forces, as well as from groups that aspire to political power—for example, the urban middle class, unions, and students. When the government can no longer provide either material benefits (employment opportunities, low inflation, education, health care, physical security) or moral values (righteousness, justice, decent human treatment), its legitimacy often plummets. If the opposition appears able to offer desired moral and material benefits, this transference of legitimacy to the opposition may trigger the overthrow of the old regime. The attribution of blame for personal grievances also affects a regime's political stability. If subordinate groups blame God, the devil, fate, luck, or the individual for their deprivations, the political system enjoys greater stability. Only when opposition leaders convince discontented individuals that the political regime bears the blame for personal grievances does a systemic breakdown become probable. In this situation, political legitimacy declines because the existing political regime cannot make policies that resolve the grievances. Opposition leaders convince aggrieved groups that only new cultural beliefs—basic values and fundamental rules for making political decisions—will remedy current problems.[4]

When cultural contradictions become especially severe, the beliefs voiced by the ruling leaders no longer provide meaning to a society undergoing conceptual confusion; a gap arises between opposing values, which signals declining legitimacy. For example, in a folk system conflict emerges between the purity of traditional sacred beliefs and more secular values associated with science and technology. Outside disturbances such as military conquests, floods, famines, and exposure to the mass media upset the internal value solidarity. Contaminated by growing secularization, the society loses its moral purity. Traditional sacred beliefs no longer have relevance to changing structural conditions. In a bureaucratic-authoritarian system, a cultural contradiction often occurs when the perceived need for order clashes with an actual stress on factional struggles for group and personal interests. Dedicated to the pursuit of order as an end in itself, bureaucratic officials cannot cope with pervasive opportunism, corruption, and disorder. Although the reconciliation system rests on the freedom for groups to pursue their self-interests, a loss of meaning may result if no collective value solidarity based on a shared sense of the common good binds the society together. Under these conditions, the pursuit of individual and group interests comes into conflict with the perceived need for a transcendent vision of the public welfare. The resulting group polarization leads to a disintegration of the reconciliation system, which is replaced by a less pluralistic bureaucratic-authoritarian or mobilization style of decision-making. Mobilization systems, which usually last only a brief time, also experience a loss of political vision. In this case, a contradiction develops between the ideological goals and perceptions that the elites have failed to realize their comprehensive objectives. As the gulf between ideological goals and perceived policy performance grows wider, the ideological message seems increasingly irrelevant to concrete needs. Disillusioned with the political cause, both aspiring political elites and the mobilization rulers themselves lose faith in the established ideology. Growing apathy and cynicism result.

The importance of cultural beliefs in explaining between-system change partly depends on the opposition's political leadership. When clergy or intellectuals‧lead the opposition, as occurred in the 1979 Iranian revolution and the Vietnamese revolution against French colonialism, ideology becomes highly important. Both clergy and intellectuals specialize in cultural beliefs, which they use to highlight new policy goals, to discredit the incumbent leadership, and to justify their seizure of government power. A theocratic folk system dominated by the clergy and an elitist mobilization system led by intellectuals both rest on a strong cultural foundation. When the armed forces stage a coup d'état and institute a bureaucratic-authoritarian system, ideology usually assumes less importance as the primary reason for between-system change. The goals of economic growth, national security, and political order take precedence over the need to transmit a comprehensive, systemic ideology to the masses. Similarly, if lawyers and legislators dominate the opposition movement that promises to replace a bureaucratic-authoritarian regime with a new reconciliation system, affirming ideological moral ends takes a subordinate place to institutionalizing rules that regulate the political game.[5]

### The Inefficient Use of
### Coercive and Consensual Power

Structural conflicts also underlie a transformation from one system to a different type. The decision to join an opposition movement seeking a between-system change stems from a commitment to certain political ends and from expectations about the opposition's probable success. When opposition leaders possess powerful organizational capabilities and incumbent government officials inefficiently use their resources, expectations of successful antiregime actions increase. Three structures— domestic social groups, political organizations (governments, parties), and foreign institutions—become crucial to systemic change. First, *if the social groups supporting the incumbent government show a declining cohesion but groups opposing the government achieve greater solidarity, a between-system change is more likely.*

Second, *if opposition leaders wield power more efficiently than do incumbent authorities, the society may undergo a systemic change.* In this situation of "dual power," the civilian government, army, and police can neither use coercion effectively nor form a consensus.[6] Most often, a cruel despot engages in excessive corruption, isolates himself from domestic group allies, and remains too dependent on foreign powers. Under assault from a powerful opposition, the ruler loses control over the society. Particularly when the military and police use of coercion varies over time, political stability becomes endangered. As coercive force waxes and wanes, anger toward the government mounts but the temporary decline of repression reduces fear of punishment. Opposition movements that can form alliances and employ coercion gain the opportunity to seize state power and establish a new political system.[7]

Third, *if foreign states and overseas institutions reinforce the internal structural weaknesses of the existing government but support opposition movements, a between-system change appears probable.* The actions of foreign governments, especially the United States and the Soviet Union, as well as transnational institutions such as multinational corporations, the International Monetary Fund, and the World Bank contribute to ineffective policy performance and thereby weaken a regime's power.[8]

In all four models, a between-system change takes place when the mechanisms of coercive control and consensus formation disintegrate. A folk system collapses if the fragile power structures of a village society come into opposition with a more powerful external agency such as a foreign colonial power or a stronger indigenous state. Under this situation, the folk system has too weak a power base to withstand the external disturbance, especially military conquest. Those groups perceiving a loss of their power may no longer agree to form a consensus.

Although bureaucratic-authoritarian systems retain their stability for a longer time than does the fragile folk system, they, too, break down under severe structural contradictions. Particularly when a sharp conflict divides those elites who prefer a closed hierarchical regime from bureaucrats seeking to open the decision process to more aspiring groups, a change toward a reconciliation system or, less often, toward a mobilization system may result. By relying on coercion and failing to develop processes of consensus formation, bureaucratic elites produce too rigid a system. This rigidity stifles the individual initiative and spontaneity needed for effective policymaking. Personalism and factionalism arise as ways to overcome rigidification; yet these structural tendencies threaten orderly bureaucratic control.

Reconciliation systems often seem plagued by a severe conflict between consensus formation and political immobilism. Faced by group demands for a larger share of scarce economic resources, reconciliation leaders lack the political power to resolve basic problems, such as inequality, corruption, and violence. Pluralist leaders need time to form a consensus; yet time gives opponents opportunity to mobilize against the regime. As group polarization becomes more severe, political stagnation results. That stagnation often leads to the establishment of a more coercive power structure, such as that found in a bureaucratic-authoritarian or mobilization system.

Both elitist and populist mobilization regimes change to a different system type when the forces of centralization and organization come into opposition with decentralizing, spontaneous tendencies. Depending on centralized organization and coercion to overcome resistance, elitist mobilizers develop no effective processes for building a consensus. Thus breakdowns in the policy process occur. Populist mobilizers appear more receptive to spontaneous demands made at decentralized points in the power network. However, if they fail to organize centralized mechanisms that control mass spontaneity, the populist mobilization system will likely collapse, since it becomes especially vulnerable to overthrow by bureaucratic elites who reject the populist demands.

### Ineffective Policy Performance

The prospects for toppling a political regime depend on the effectiveness of policy performance. *If the incumbent government displays ineffective policy performance and the policy promises made by opposition leaders appeal to the disaffected, the likelihood of a systemic breakdown increases.* Ineffective policy performance refers both to failures in the policy process and to a gap between goals and consequences. The policy process revolves around interactions among value priorities, information processing, and the exercise of power. When policymakers hold unclear value priorities, articulate divergent policy goals, or voice objectives strongly opposed by key power centers, the policy process becomes paralyzed. Moreover, difficulties in processing information weaken policy performance, since political leaders receive inaccurate information, cannot interpret the information actually collected, and lack the power to act on this information to attain desired public consequences.[9] Ineffective policy performance also means a gap between policy goals and actual results; certain powerful groups view the policy outcomes as undesirable. For example, if the government fails to lower inflation, decrease unemployment, achieve a higher economic growth, reduce violence, and lessen the inequalities separating the urban areas from the rural sector, aspiring elites may take actions to overthrow the existing government. Depending on the structural capabilities and political beliefs of opposition leaders, a change to a different system may result.

Yet ineffective policy performance by itself does not necessarily lead to fundamental changes in the political regime. Only when policy ineffectiveness combines with a disintegration of state power and a loss of legitimacy can the opposition threaten the regime's stability. As the established leaders lose control over their society, they can less easily formulate and implement policies that will mollify the opposition. When the incumbent government officials make ineffective policies, belief in the regime's legitimacy often declines, thereby weakening its power and increasing the probability of a systemic breakdown.

Ineffective policy performance also occurs when severe conflicts emerge between the ways of resolving the four policy issues: voluntarism versus determinism, spontaneity versus organization, conflict versus consensus, and change versus continuity. Rather than blending these diverse modes, the policymakers stress one style at the expense of the other. As a result, the policy process malfunctions, plagued by excessive rigidity. For example, unstable folk systems seem riven by excessive cultural determinism, spontaneity, consensus, and continuity. By contrast, elitist mobilization systems experience ultra-voluntarism, hierarchical organization, conflict with enemies, and coerced change. The rigid political framework dampens ideological commitment, mass enthusiasm, leadership morale, and popular political participation. Under these conditions, a more bureaucratic-authoritarian style of decision-making usually emerges. Bureaucratic-authoritarian regimes often change to a different system type because they fall prey to structural determinism, organizational routinization, factional conflicts, and continuity based on formal rules. A reconciliation system disintegrates when it faces excessive voluntarism, spontaneity, interest-group conflicts, and change unaccompanied by a widespread commitment to procedures that regulate the group struggle.

## Types of Between-System Change

Although the reasons for the disintegration of a system seem fairly clear, the probability of accurately predicting the particular system type that succeeds the downfall of an old regime remains less certain. For instance, if a bureaucratic military regime collapses, what type of system will then govern the society? Will a reconciliation system emerge, or will the opposition leaders who seize government power establish a mobilization system? Answers to these questions depend on the structural and cultural conditions of the incumbent government and the opposition. If opposition leaders topple a strong bureaucratic state that formerly ruled a society where social groups held weak power vis-à-vis the state, a mobilization system seems more likely than a reconciliation system. Particularly when the counter-elites are ideologically committed to fundamental sociopolitical transformations and have organized a powerful party and army to realize their goals, prospects increase for a mobilization system. However, if a moderate degree of social pluralism prevailed under the former military bureaucracy and the state exercised only weak power, a reconciliation style of political decision-making may replace the overthrown system. In this situation, the former opposition leaders who have gained government power voice more accommodating, pluralist, tolerant beliefs; they also lack the powerful mass party and the disciplined army needed to establish a mobilization system.

Historically, the change from a folk to a bureaucratic-authoritarian system has been the most common occurrence; shifts to a mobilization system have taken place less frequently. During the late nineteenth and early twentieth centuries, the village folk systems lost their political autonomy as the European colonial powers conquered Asian and African territories. Establishing an imperial bureaucratic presence, the French and English colonialists ruled through military officers, district commissioners, and *commandements de cercle*; these bureaucrats wielded the power formerly exercised by village elders, notables, priests, and heads of traditional associations. Vietnam during the last quarter of the nineteenth century illustrates this fundamental transformation from a folk system at the village level to a colonial bureaucratic-authoritarian system. Although the French extinguished village autonomy, some traditional values and structural patterns associated with the folk system remained. When the Vietnamese Communists conquered political power over the thirty-year period between 1945 and 1975, they organized an elitist mobilization system partly based on precolonial village beliefs and structural networks. The army and the Communist party used traditional values and structures to win rural support, especially in the northern and central regions. After gaining government power, however, centralized rule triumphed at the expense of village autonomy; the secular values of Marxism-Leninism superseded the more traditional, sacred values associated with Buddhism, Confucianism, and animism. In this sense, the elitist mobilization system replaced the last vestiges of the rural folk system.

During the twentieth century, bureaucratic-authoritarian systems have transformed into reconciliation and mobilization systems. Military officers and civil servants govern most developing nations today. When the armed forces relinquish power to popularly elected civilian leaders, the policy process shifts from a bureaucratic-authoritarian to a reconciliation mode of decision-making. Such a change occurred in Chile during the early 1930s, when General Carlos Ibañez yielded government office to an elected president, Arturo Alessandri, who gained power one year after the downfall of Ibañez. In Nigeria, elected civilian leaders replaced military personnel as the dominant political officials in 1979. Compared with these changes in Chile and Nigeria, more revolutionary transformations have marked the change from a bureaucratic-authoritarian to an elitist mobilization system in Vietnam and Cuba. During their fifty-year struggle in Vietnam, the Communist party mobilizers first overthrew the Japanese army in 1945, then defeated the French bureaucratic-authoritarian regime in 1954, and finally, in 1975, ousted the southern Vietnamese armed forces from their Saigon power base. In Cuba Fidel Castro and his Rebel Army seized control from the bureaucratic Batista government at the end of 1958 and organized a revolutionary mobilization system that brought fundamental sociopolitical changes to Cuba.

When the Iranian mullahs, ayatollahs, and other Shiite Moslem clergy led a revolution against the Shah during the late 1970s, they converted the bureaucratic-authoritarian state into a theocratic folk system combining sacred values with elitist mobilization structures. Formerly ruled by civilian administrative elites, the army, and the secret police, Iran came under the coercive domination of local mosques, Islamic committees, and revolutionary guards. Attacking the secular values identified with both American capitalism and Soviet communism, the Ayatollah Khomeini struggled to base the new Islamic republic on spiritual values linked to Shiite Islam: idealism, not materialism; simplicity, not ostentation; purity, not corruption; righteousness, not decadence; homogeneous cohesion, not heterogeneous diversity. The new union between church and state represents an unusual restoration of a theocratic folk system amid the more scientific, technological, and secularizing influences animating late twentieth century life.

If a reconciliation system disintegrates, most often bureaucratic-authoritarian modes of political decision-making become dominant, as happens when a military coup d'état causes the downfall of an elected civilian government. Especially in Latin America during the 1970s such changes from a reconciliation to a bureaucratic-authoritarian system frequently occurred. The coups in Argentina, Uruguay, and Chile represented the most notable examples. Whereas the government of President Salvador Allende rested on a pluralistic foundation under-girded by a commitment to civil liberties and a sharing of political power among decentralized agencies, the military leaders who overthrew the Allende regime established a bureaucratic-authoritarian system that centralized state power and extinguished political freedom. Similarly, since gaining political independence from Britain in 1960, Nigerians have lived under alternating reconciliation and bureaucratic-authoritarian regimes. An elected democratic government ruled from 1960 through January 1966, when a military coup overthrew the competitive oligarchy. Elected reconciliation leaders took control again in 1979, stayed in office until December 1983, and fell from power after military dictators staged a coup.

Mobilization systems rarely last for a long period; most often, they change into a bureaucratic-authoritarian system. Over the long run, mobilizing leaders experience difficulties maintaining the high popular enthusiasm, mass involvement, and commitment to fundamental changes associated with a mobilization style of policymaking. When government policies fail to realize ideological goals, popular enthusiasm for the great cause wanes. Political party officials and heads of mass organizations begin to lose their power to state bureaucrats, military officials, the secret police, and technocrats. The pragmatic task of increasing economic productivity takes priority over creating a new equalitarian society and a new person. These changes indicate the transition to a more bureaucratic-authoritarian system. During the early 1970s such changes occurred in Cuba as the revolution became "institutionalized"—that is, more bureaucratized.

## Political Change in Five Nations

Focusing on Vietnam, Cuba, Chile, Nigeria, and Iran, the following chapters explore the reasons for changes between political systems. Why were these five nations chosen for investigation? First, they have undergone diverse types of between-system changes. During the late 1800s, the French conquest of Vietnam brought unparalleled transformations to Vietnamese society. A colonial bureaucratic-authoritarian system replaced the folk system at the village level and the agrarian bureaucratic system at the level of the royal court. Similarly, after World War II Vietnam experienced two between-system changes. In 1945 the Vietnamese Communists established an elitist mobilization system with its strongest base in the north. Thirty years later, the government of the Democratic Republic of Vietnam, along with the National Liberation Front, defeated the military bureaucracy of General Thieu, who ruled southern Vietnam. The Communist party cadres, government officials, and army organized an elitist mobilization system modeled on its northern counterpart.

In Cuba a similar transformation occurred when Fidel Castro overthrew Fulgencio Batista's bureaucratic-authoritarian regime to establish an elitist mobilization system dedicated to revolutionizing the society. During the 1970s, the revolution became "institutionalized": The mobilizing elements receded somewhat and bureaucratic strains became more pronounced.

Most Chilean leaders within the Unidad Popular government (1970–1973) wanted a revolution but without the violence, militarism, and mass mobilization associated with Cuba and Vietnam. However, the military coup in September 1973 blocked the peaceful transition to socialism. The bureaucratic-authoritarian regime that emerged from the ashes of the fallen reconciliation system engineered a sharper break with past conditions than did the Allende pluralist government.

Of the five nations, Nigeria has experienced the least sociopolitical change. Ruled by a colonial bureaucracy from the late nineteenth century through 1960, Nigerians faced far less repression than the Vietnamese suffered under the French. The bureaucratic-authoritarian system remained fairly open to aspiring elites; educated Nigerians, British civil servants, and foreign capitalists shared power in a quasi-competitive oligarchy. After the establishment of a reconciliation system in 1960, these bureaucratic forces still played the key decision-making role. The several military coups that took place between 1966 and 1976 instituted new leaders and established a more bureaucratic-authoritarian mode of policymaking. Yet the military-dominated government remained more open to reconciliation tendencies than did most military regimes in Latin America during the same period. The restoration of elected civilian rule in 1979 failed to end the dominance of government bureaucrats and merchant capitalists over the policy process. Throughout all these systemic changes, new leaders have come into power and policy contents have altered. Yet government policies have brought few fundamental transformations of society, such as rapid industrialization, economic equality, and better personal health conditions.

The 1979 Iranian revolution has secured fundamental changes in society but in a reactionary direction. From 1921 through 1979 the Pahlavi regime ruled Iran as a bureaucratic monarchy. The Shah, aided by a centralized civil service, made the key political decisions. Although modern changes—industrialization, formal education, greater legal equality between men and women—transformed society, the autocratic political system remained stagnant, failing to provide new groups with opportunities for expanded political participation. Various groups—the merchants, the urban dispossessed, students, some professionals, and especially the Muslim mullahs—rallied against the Pahlavi despotism and overthrew the Shah in early 1979. No political party, military clique, or guerrilla band seized government control. Instead, the Shiite clergy dominated the revolutionary forces and established a theocratic folk system. Sacred values reemerged in the educational, legal, and family institutions. Women lost most of the rights they had gained under the Shah. Schools became Islamicized. The industrialization process came to a halt. Government health-care programs disintegrated as professional physicians fled the country. Although the regime gave some attention to the needs of the urban poor, it concentrated on reshaping the political culture around Islamic values.

Second, all five societies experienced some political mobilization as a way to realize sociopolitical change; the type of mobilization, however, differed from one country to another. In Vietnam, a powerful state, party, and army mobilized the people to gain national independence from France, win the war against the United States, defeat the Saigon government, redistribute land, and abolish illiteracy. Organizational mobilization based on military techniques activated the society.

Although Cuban elites also adapted military forms of mobilization, party organization was less powerful than in Vietnam. Maintaining a weaker commitment to Leninism than do Vietnamese leaders, Castro waited until six years after securing government power before he established an official Communist party. Originally mass organizations such as Committees for the Defense of the Revolution played the greatest role in mobilizing the Cuban people against a United States invasion and internal "subversion" by anti-Castro groups. These mass organizations also spearheaded the drive to create a new socialist man and woman who would act according to moral incentives, not bureaucratic directives or materialistic pressures.

More democratic historically than either Vietnam or Cuba, Chile during the early 1970s witnessed mobilization efforts by groups on the left and the right of the Allende government. Rather than instigated by the government, mobilization sprang from below. On the Left, MIR (the Movement of the Revolutionary Left) and the radical wing of the Socialist party organized the factory workers, farm laborers, and landless peasants to stage factory and land seizures. These left-wing mobilizing efforts also stimulated the Right to mobilize, mainly against the Allende government. Middle-class women demonstrated in the streets, as did conservative youths and heads of business associations. Whereas the Left called for a faster transition to socialism, these rightist groups demanded the overthrow of Allende and the elimination of socialist policies. Responding to these rightist demands, the armed forces staged a coup and promptly began to demobilize the leftist organizations.

Mobilization activities never attained such great importance in Nigeria as in the other four nations. At the end of World War II, young people established a Zikist movement that campaigned for revolution and independence from British imperialism. Yet this movement never attracted widespread support among the ethnically diverse population. Poorly organized, insufficiently financed, and repudiated by Nnamdi Azikiwe, it collapsed in 1950 after the British banned the movement. Throughout the 1950s no other mobilization organization emerged to struggle for national independence. Instead, the British government negotiated with Nigerian regional oligarchs about procedures for creating federal institutions. At the end of the decade, it granted political independence to Nigeria.[10]

In Iran the Moslem clergy, not a political party, army, guerrilla band, or youth movement, spearheaded the revolution. Islamic values, rather than nationalism or a secular ideology, rallied the population against the Shah. Local mosques served as the main center for communicating political messages and coordinating the struggle to topple the Pahlavi regime.

Third, the United States and the Soviet Union have influenced the pattern of systemic change in the five nations. The United States government tried to restrain the revolutionary process in Vietnam, Cuba, Chile, and Iran; the U.S.S.R. gave the greatest assistance to the Vietnamese revolutionaries. Soviet aid to Cuba came after Castro gained government power in 1959. From 1954 through 1973 the Eisenhower, Kennedy, Johnson, and Nixon administrations contributed military personnel, weapons, and economic assistance to the Republic of Vietnam in its effort to defeat the National Liberation Front and the North Vietnamese government, which received moral and material support from the U.S.S.R. and China. All U.S. administrations since President Eisenhower's have opposed the Castro government. Although Soviet leaders did not assist Castro's rise to power, they did help him maintain his rule, particularly during the 1970s and 1980s. In Chile, however, the U.S.S.R. offered minimal aid to the Allende government. The U.S. government, especially the Nixon administration, supported those Chilean groups that plotted the overthrow of the Unidad Popular government. After the military seized power, President Nixon and Secretary of State Henry Kissinger backed the military government's drive to immobilize the leftist forces.

In Iran neither the United States nor the Soviet Union encouraged the Islamic revolution against the Shah. The U.S. government strongly supported the Shah and the consolidation of Iranian military power in the Near East. As a neighboring state, the U.S.S.R. occupied Iranian territory during 1920–1921 and again during World War II (1941–1946). Yet the Soviet Union and the pro-Moscow Tudeh party failed to dominate the revolutionary movement that overthrew the Shah. After the Ayatollah Khomeini took government control in 1979, he inveighed against both the United States ("the Great Satan") and the Soviet Union ("the Red Satan").

Nigeria has not faced the superpower rivalries that affected the pace of systemic change in the other four nations. Since 1960 the United States and Nigeria have maintained close economic, educational, and political ties. During the early 1980s Nigeria sold the largest share of its oil exports to the United States. Major U.S. corporations such as Standard Oil and Mobil have invested in Nigeria. More Nigerian youths have studied at universities in the United States than in any other foreign country. The 1979 Nigerian constitution was based on the U.S. federal model. Between 1962 and 1985 the U.S. armed forces trained more than three thousand Nigerian military officers, including Presidents Mohammed Buhari and Ibrahim Babangida. During the Nigerian Civil War (1967–1970), both the United States and the Soviet Union supported Nigeria's central government, rather than the secessionist Biafran government. The U.S.S.R. sent some large weapons, M-16 fighters, bombers, jeeps, torpedo boats, and howitzers. The U.S. administrations relied on Britain to supply military hardware to the Nigerian federal forces. After the war ended, Nigerian foreign policy adopted an independent course from positions taken by the United States government. For example, Nigerian leaders have strongly backed the MPLA regime in Angola and opposed the Afrikaner government ruling the Republic of South Africa—stands that concur with the Soviet orientation toward Africa.[11]

Fourth, each country's specific historical experience illustrates a general theoretical theme that reveals the dilemmas of between-system change. In Vietnam the Communist party revolutionaries have relied on ancient traditional beliefs and structural patterns to win wars and modernize the society. Yet this task of blending precolonial traditions with revolutionary dimensions poses a dilemma: Some aspects of Marxism-Leninism clash with the indigenous culture, but certain traditional practices may be antithetical to rapid modernization. Cuban developments illustrate the tensions between personalism and organization as opposite ways to construct a socialist society. Political mobilization still rests on devotion to the *líder máximo*—Fidel Castro. As a revolutionary Robin Hood, he has been reluctant to institutionalize the organizational base needed to operate a modern, industrialized economy.

The recent history of Chile exemplifies the dilemma of reconciling reformist means with revolutionary ends. President Allende and his supporters wanted to secure the revolutionary transformation of the socioeconomic order but through peaceful, pluralistic means. They never resolved the tensions between the means of a reconciliation system and the goals linked to a mobilization system.

Since attaining political independence the Nigerian political system has alternated between bureaucratic-authoritarian and reconciliation modes of decision-making. The policy process reflects the tensions between bureaucratic organization and social group spontaneity. In this agrarian market economy, merchant capitalists and state bureaucrats contend for influence over government decision-making. Specific policy decisions reveal how the state regulates the market economy and how dominant economic groups shape government actions.

The Iranian Muslim clergy faces a dilemma about choosing the most effective ways to create a sense of folk community in a fractionated, heterogeneous, partially industrialized society. While creating an Islamic theocracy, the Shiite mullahs and ayatollahs have tried to blend the sacred values of a folk system with the centralizing structures associated with an elitist mobilization system. This conflict between simple folk values and complex modern structures has produced unresolved tensions for Shiite policymakers.

# Notes

1 See *The Boat People: An 'Age' Investigation with Bruce Grant* (New York: Penguin Books, 1979); John Korschner and Roberto Fabricio, *The Winds of December* (New York: Coward, McCann, and Geoghegan, 1980); "Terror in Chile," *New York Review of Books* 21 (May 30, 1974): 38–44; Peter Winn, *Weavers of Revolution: The Yarur Workers and Chile's Road to Socialism* (New York: Oxford University Press, 1986), esp. 246–256; Mary Dixon, "Nigeria: Curious Reforms," *AfricAsia*, no. 14 (February 1985): 31–32; Mansour Farhang, "Revolution and Regression in Iran," in *Comparative Politics 85/86*, ed. Christian Soe (Guilford, Conn.:

Duhskin, 1985), 260–262; Bouzid Kouza, "Iran: Why Khomeini Needs the War," *AfricAsia*, no. 4 (April 1984): 20–21; Haleh Afshar, "Women, State and Ideology in Iran," *Third World Quarterly* 7 (April 1985): 256–278.

2  For this interpretation of "contradiction," see Robert L. Heilbroner, *Marxism: For and Against* (New York: W. W. Norton, 1980), 39–40, 77–78.

3  For examples of structural interpretations of political change, see Michael A. Faia, *Dynamic Functionalism: Strategy and Tactics* (New York: Cambridge University Press, 1986); Charles Tilly, *Big Structures, Large Processes, Huge Comparisons* (New York: Russell Sage Foundation, 1984); Michael Mann, *The Sources of Social Power*, vol. 1, *A History of Power from the Beginning to A.D. 1760* (New York: Cambridge University Press, 1986); Eric A. Nordlinger, "Taking the State Seriously," in *Understanding Political Development*, ed. Myron Weiner and Samuel P. Huntington (Boston: Little, Brown, 1987), 353–390. Works that have analyzed revolution, one type of between-system change, include the following: Jack A. Goldstone, "The Comparative and Historical Study of Revolutions," in *Annual Review of Sociology*, vol. 8, ed. Ralph H. Turner and James F. Short, Jr. (Palo Alto, Calif.: Annual Reviews, Inc., 1982), 187–207; Chalmers Johnson, *Revolutionary Change*, 2d ed. (Stanford, Calif.: Stanford University Press, 1982), esp. 169–194; Charles Tilly, *From Mobilization to Revolution* (Reading, Mass.: Addison-Wesley, 1978), esp. 189–222; Theda Skocpol, *States and Social Revolutions: A Comparative Analysis of France, Russia, and China* (New York: Cambridge University Press, 1979), esp. 3–43. My structural explanation of systemic change most closely resembles the approach taken by Skocpol, except that I give greater weight to the beliefs, skills, and policy performance of political leaders—the voluntarist aspects of political change.

4  See Robert H. Dix, "The Breakdown of Authoritarian Regimes," *Western Political Quarterly* 35 (December 1982): 554–573; Robert H. Dix, "Why Revolutions Succeed and Fail," *Polity* 16 (Spring 1984): 423–446; Josef Gugler, "The Urban Character of Contemporary Revolutions," *Studies in Contemporary International Development* 17 (Summer 1982): 60–73; Charles F. Andrain, *Foundations of Comparative Politics: A Policy Perspective* (Monterey, Calif.: Brooks/Cole, 1983), 356–358.

5  Theda Skocpol, "Cultural Idioms and Political Ideologies in the Revolutionary Reconstruction of State Power: A Rejoinder to Sewell," *Journal of Modern History* 57 (March 1985): 86–96.

6  Leon Trotsky, *The Basic Writings of Trotsky*, ed. Irving Howe (New York: Schocken Books, 1976), 101–110.

7  Ivo K. Feierabend, Betty Nesvold, and Rosalind L. Feierabend, "Political Coerciveness and Turmoil: A Cross-National Inquiry," *Law and Society Review* 5 (August 1970): 93–118; Skocpol, *States and Social Revolutions*, 50–51, 80–81, 99; D. E. H. Russell, *Rebellion, Revolution, and Armed Force* (New York: Academic Press, 1974), 87.

8  Harvey Waterman, "Reasons and Reason: Collective Political Activity in Comparative and Historical Perspective," *World Politics* 33 (July 1981): 554–589; Amitai Etzioni, "Toward a Macrosociology," in James S. Coleman, Amitai Etzioni, and John Porter, *Macrosociology: Research and Theory* (Boston: Allyn and Bacon, 1970), 107–143; Dix, "Why Revolutions Succeed and Fail," 423–446.

9  See David E. Apter, *Choice and the Politics of Allocation* (New Haven, Conn.: Yale University Press, 1971), 32–35, 128–154; Etzioni, "Toward a Macrosociology," 121–130; Joan Nelson, "Political Participation," in *Understanding Political*

*Development*, ed. Myron Weiner and Samuel P. Huntington (Boston: Little, Brown, 1987), 142–143.

10 Daniel A. Offiong, "Zik's Tergiversation and the Tenuousness of the Zikist Movement," *Indian Political Science Review* 17 (July 1983): 149–156.

11 Zalmay Khalilzad, "Islamic Iran: Soviet Dilemma," *Problems of Communism* 33 (January/February 1984): 1–20; Bruce D. Porter, *The USSR in Third World Conflicts* (New York: Cambridge University Press, 1984), 90–112; Herbert M. Howe, "US and Nigeria: Twenty-Five Years," *Christian Science Monitor*, October 3, 1985, p. 17.

# 4

## POLITICAL CHANGE IN VIETNAM

> Today, Marxism has replaced Confucianism as a doctrine of political and social action, and a new revolutionary ethic has replaced Confucian morality in Vietnam. . . . But, contrary to what pseudo-revolutionaries believe, Vietnamese Marxists consider Confucianism and the work of the scholars part of their national heritage, to be assimilated by the new society.
> — Nguyen Khac Vien

During the twentieth century Vietnamese revolutionaries have attempted to blend some aspects of their national traditions with more modern demands for extensive changes in society. In their fifty-year battle against the Japanese, French, and United States governments, Vietnamese Communists reinterpreted ancient folk values to suit the contemporary situation. They also mobilized support by relying on certain structures associated with the traditional Vietnamese village. Unlike several other countries of Southeast Asia, Vietnam has experienced a lengthy common identity going back nearly four thousand years. The term "Vietnam" means "south of China"; whereas "Viet" is the national term, "nam" denotes "south." Historically the Vietnamese national identity developed through a continuing military struggle against Chinese domination. Beginning around 200 B.C. the northern segment of Vietnam, the Red River Delta region, came under conquest by the Chinese. Not until 939 did the Vietnamese kingdom first win independence from Chinese rule. Between 1000 and 1800 the northern-based kingdom of Vietnam fought to ward off successive Chinese invasions and also to gain dominance over the southern regions of Vietnam controlled by the Champa and Khmer

(Cambodian) empires. Thus in their twentieth-century drive to liberate themselves from Western powers, Vietnamese revolutionaries stressed the historical relevance of their ancient military struggles against foreign invaders. Now as in the past, although accepting some key Chinese values, the Vietnamese have rejected Chinese structural domination.

## The Traditional Vietnamese Monarchy

Before the French conquered Vietnam in the latter half of the nineteenth century, political life at the imperial court resembled an agrarian bureaucratic system. Politics in the village, which retained extensive autonomy from the central government, followed the folk model. Examining the central and local political systems, let us look first at the social stratification system, then at the dominant political beliefs, and finally at political organizations.[1]

### Social Stratification

Throughout the Vietnamese kingdom social stratification rested on strong primordial ties. Family dynasties ruled the imperial government. Village politics revolved around the nuclear family. Generally, older men made the key decisions; youth and women obeyed.

Although powerful ecclesiastical organizations never played a key part in political life, the Confucian mandarins did have high status. Holding the important government positions at the royal court, province, and district, these scholar-gentry implemented the public policies made by the king. They formed the key link between the imperial government and the village agencies. Rather than inheriting their positions, the mandarins achieved political power by passing a series of examinations based on Confucian religious-philosophical texts. Within each village as well, the mandarins exercised decisive political power. Usually at least one retired ex-mandarin served on the twelve-member council of notables.

Despite some inequalitarian features, the economic stratification system in precolonial Vietnam featured some equality, considerably more than that found in a feudal economy. True, the mandarins usually held more land than did the average peasant; as a result, they had the time and other resources to study for the competitive exams and to give their children more educational opportunities. Compared with landless peasants, landowners also had greater access to the council of notables. Some notables did use their power to appropriate communal land for their private gain. Nevertheless, in other respects economic equality did prevail within the village. Partly because the emperor forbade mandarins to own large plots of land, no landed estates developed until the French conquered the area. Instead, in most regions, each family held a small parcel of land. Both daughters and sons could inherit their parents' property. A widow retained control over a large share of her husband's property. Especially in the northern and central areas, councils of notables allocated some of the communally owned lands to the needy, that is, to the aged, widows, and orphans. Most important, social status did not rest primarily on the possession of wealth but on scholarly achievements. In the social stratification system, the mandarin scholars enjoyed the highest status. Peasants held greater prestige than did small businesspeople such as artisans and merchants, who sold handicrafts. At the bottom of the occupational hierarchy were the soldiers. Significantly, every male, regardless of landed wealth, had the right to become a mandarin. Each village had its teacher, and even poor peasants could become literate and perhaps pass a Confucian exam. These educational opportunities, besides international trade and martial exploits during wars, provided some mobility to the social stratification system.

## Political Beliefs

The cultural values shared by most Vietnamese supplied cohesion to village society and also undergirded the sense of common identity felt by the Vietnamese people. Before the nineteenth century, cultural unity was stronger than structural unity. Even if a powerful central government failed to wield control over all the area of contemporary Vietnam, the Vietnamese did share a commitment to similar beliefs.

Socioeconomic equality took precedence over individual freedom. True, men had higher status than women, the old ruled the young, and mental work such as literary accomplishment took precedence over manual labor. Yet in other respects, equality prevailed. Both men and women, boys and girls, possessed equal rights to join associations that played an important role in village affairs. These mutual aid associations included clubs for students, women, old men, mandarins, and artisans. Neither the imperial court nor the local village prized individual political freedom. Rather than agreeing to disagree, Vietnamese pressed for unanimous decisions after they discussed a political issue.

Within traditional Vietnamese society, communal solidarity rested primarily on a blend of the moral-spiritual domain with the material sector of life. Even though no ecclesiastical priesthood exercised political power, political life fused sacred and secular values. John T. McAlister, Jr., and Paul Mus perceived Vietnam as

> a certain way of growing rice, of living in common on a rice diet, and of asking heaven to protect your harvest just as it did your ancestors. . . . For

the Vietnamese everything is religion down to the simplest acts. . . . Government in traditional Viet Nam was thus inseparable from religion; together they were formed in accordance with the human geography required to cultivate rice. Indeed, government was the spiritualization of this human rhythm of growing rice.[2]

Three religious belief systems have long influenced Vietnamese politics: animism, Confucianism, and Buddhism. According to the animist traditions, each village had its own earth god or spirit. Unrelated to the villagers by family ties, the village deity supplied a spiritual basis for political solidarity. Members of the council of notables took responsibility for organizing worship of the guardian spirit at the local village temple. Both the notables and the peasants suffused primordial values with sacred significance. Reverence for the land and the ancestors rested on a spiritual foundation. The same Vietnamese word *xa* referred to three related but distinct entities: land, people, sacredness. The ancestors were buried in the land where the earth god also dwelled. In the village, peasants grew rice on the land. Rice cultivation represented not only a practical, concrete way to obtain food but also a religious ritual that symbolized the moral-spiritual values of the community, what Émile Durkheim called the *conscience collective*.[3]

At the imperial court and among the mandarins, Confucianism guided political behavior. Around the late fifteenth century, Confucianism became the official religion of the Vietnamese kingdom; all candidates who wanted to join the mandarinate had to pass examinations based on the Confucian classics. As in China, the Vietnamese brand of Confucianism represented a moral way of life stressing rational, not mystical or supernatural, principles. The political elite had the duty to follow the Enlightened Way and govern through moral example. Political education hence rested on moral education. According to these Confucian beliefs, the Emperor was supposed to set a moral example for his followers. He served as the supreme ritual leader, the head of the national family, and the main trustee of the rice fields. According to McAlister and Mus, the Emperor's "ritual acts symbolized the spiritual feelings of the Vietnamese. For example, the Emperor was the prime Plowman who each year used to 'deconsecrate' the precious rice land by opening the first furrow."[4] By performing these ritual acts, the Emperer blended Confucian principles with animist beliefs. He embodied in his person the collective values of the whole Vietnamese society.

Compared with Confucianism, Buddhism was the religion of the masses, rather than the political elite. Introduced into Vietnam around A.D. 200, Buddhism became accepted by most peasants after A.D 1000, at a time when the imperial elites were beginning to accept Confucianism.

Of the three primary belief systems, Buddhism was the most egalitarian. The peasant masses identified Confucianism with hierarchy and the Chinese culture. For them, Buddhism placed greater stress on equality and on opportunities for personal salvation from present conditions; by contrast, Confucianism focused on harmony and the sanctity of the present order. When peasants revolted against the imperial dynasty, they justified their actions by invoking these Buddhist principles of equality. Women also found Buddhism more satisfying than either Confucianism or animism. Stressing patriarchal authority, Confucianism emphasized that men should rule over women. In each village temple, women had few rights to share in rituals that honored the guardian deity. For this reason, they worshiped mainly in the Buddhist temples.

Both the religious and the political beliefs of precolonial Vietnam asserted the primacy of collectivism over individualism. The family and the village, not the individual, constituted the primary sources of attachment. Individuals found personal meaning in life not by struggling to realize their self-interests but by working for the welfare of the family and village. Although ties to the village remained paramount, the Vietnamese identified with the nation too. The distinctive moral-spiritual collective values found throughout Vietnam gave them a shared national identity.

However strong these national attachments, regional value cleavages have historically divided the Vietnamese. These cleavages prevail today, after the structural union of the northern and southern regions. As we have seen, northern Vietnam—the Red River Delta area—is the national heartland. Influenced by Chinese cultural values, the northern Vietnamese express the more austere, Spartan beliefs: group conformity, hard work, deference to authority, organization, and formality. Not surprisingly, the northerners gave greater support to the Vietnamese Communists who also stressed these values. By contrast, the southern Vietnamese have been more influenced by Indian beliefs as well as by French and American values. Less Spartan than their northern comrades, the southerners give greater importance to self-assertiveness, leisure, independence from authority, individual spontaneity, and informality.

*Political Structures*

From a structural perspective, two separate but interacting political systems governed precolonial Vietnam: An agrarian bureaucracy dominated the imperial central government, while a folk system prevailed at the village level. Responsibility for coordinating government affairs lay with the emperor, his council, and the mandarins, who staffed the central ministries as well as the provincial and district administrations. These mandarins constituted the rudimentary buraucracy in traditional Vietnam. Around 1600, only five thousand officials served in the Vietnamese bureaucracy, of whom 75 percent were military officers. At the central level, six ministries formulated public policies dealing with defense, justice, public works, religious rites, finance, and appointments. As in the model of an agrarian bureaucratic-authoritarian system, the central government wielded only a limited scope of power. Its primary activities revolved around levying taxes, building public works (dams, dikes, bridges, roads), maintaining internal order, and recruiting soldiers for external defense against China, the Champa Empire, and the Khmer Empire. The mandarins also provided state assistance (rice, tents, drugs) to the poor, homeless, and sick. Generally, the mandarins, who represented the central government to the village, negotiated with the village notables. However, if the village council refused to comply with imperial directives, imperial troops occasionally burned down the bamboo hedges that isolated each village from the outside world.

Compared with the imperial government, the council of notables wielded greater impact on village life in precolonial Vietnamese society. Political rule was fairly decentralized; surrounded by a bamboo hedge, each village, comprising between three hundred and one thousand persons, retained extensive independence from the central government to manage its own affairs. The village notables ruled mainly through consensual power. True, each council had its own militia to enforce obedience. Small-group pressures for conformity also deterred individual threats to village solidarity. Yet when making political decisions, the notables generally resorted to negotiation, compromise, and accommodation. Appeals to informal village customs, rather than coercion, served as the major way to secure political compliance. The council of notables, composed of twelve members, coordinated political decision-making; it appointed the mayor, the deputy mayor, and the guardian chief to implement the public policies. Of these officials, the mayor acted as an intermediary agent who communicated information between the village council and the mandarin from the imperial government. Since the notables closely supervised the mayor's activities, he could scarcely wield any autocratic power. Villages in traditional Vietnam enjoyed extensive pluralism that checked the council's authority. Based on family connections and occupational ties such as landownership or former mandarin status, factional groups formed on the council. Disputes among these factions weakened the autocratic exercise of power by one man. Furthermore, each village contained several mutual aid groups and clubs. These included age grades, student associations, old men's associations, women's groups, literary associations, economic associations (consumer and mutual credit groups), wedding associations, and burial associations.

81

All these voluntary associations provided essential social services to the villagers. Not only mutual aid groups but, more important, the council of notables performed an extensive range of activities. The council collected head and land taxes, organized the labor force to build public works (canals, rivers, dams, dikes, roads), allocated communal lands, drafted men into the imperial army, and conducted village worship services.

## French Colonial Rule in Vietnam

When the French colonialists conquered Vietnam during the latter part of the nineteenth century, they brought fundamental changes to Vietnamese society. The social stratification system became more rigid as a sharp gap developed between the landed elite and landless peasants. The traditional sense of community disintegrated under the onslaught of alien political beliefs. Structurally, the power of the central state increased; local villages lost their former autonomy. Colonial domination thus meant the emergence of a more powerful bureaucratic-authoritarian system that overwhelmed both the village folk system and the agrarian imperial bureaucracy. All these changes affected southern Vietnamese more severely than the northerners. The French conquered the southern region in 1867, twenty years before they gained control over the central and northern areas. Whereas the French ruled through more centralized, direct mechanisms in the south, precolonial Vietnamese structures retained somewhat greater power in the north.

Why did the folk and agrarian bureaucratic-authoritarian systems collapse, replaced by the French bureaucratic regime? Certainly the superior military and organizational power wielded by the French enabled them easily to defeat the imperial Vietnamese army and the village militias. Culturally, neither animistic nor Confucian beliefs provided an adequate conceptual framework for explaining the unparalleled events that were taking place during the nineteenth century. Village animist principles clashed with the urban lifestyles introduced by the French. Confucianism no longer supplied meaning to the new values based on science, technology, and material progress. Instead, it stressed reverence for past traditions, harmony with physical nature, and the supremacy of collective kin ties over individual rights. As in China, the mandarins governed; they viewed learning the literary classics, poetry, and philosophy as the supreme moral-spiritual end. In contrast, the new French values emphasized scientific learning as a means to achieve greater material development. Unlike Confucianism, they gave greater importance to planning for the future, conquering the physical environment, and securing individual rights. Confronted by the more powerful Western organizations and more dynamic values, the traditional Vietnamese patterns disintegrated under the impact of French bureaucratic rule.[5]

## Changes Brought by the
## French Colonialists

The political beliefs expressed by the French colonialists clashed with traditional Vietnamese values; as a result of the colonial experience, the Vietnamese sense of communal solidarity weakened. Whereas the Vietnamese fused secular with sacred values, the French separated the two realms. Secular values assumed primacy over sacred values. Downgrading village agricultural values that stressed reverence for the land and ancestors, the colonialists showed a higher regard for urban values. Saigon, Haiphong, and Hanoi became the major centers of French cultural influence. In the past, rice cultivation had conveyed a spiritual significance. Under the French, however, the growing of rice for the world export market became a purely secular activity. French colonialism also brought a separation of the spiritual from the secular realms. The Confucian mandarins had always regarded political education as moral-spiritual education. Both pro-Catholic civil servants and anticlerical bureaucrats, however, stressed the need to separate church and state. Colonial bureaucratic rule rested primarily on the effective exercise of power, not on a commitment to provide a moral example. In the past, the Vietnamese emperor had offered moral guidance to the people; embodying the Vietnamese collective solidarity, he united the sacred and secular values. When the French conquered Vietnam, they established direct rule in the south but in the northern-central regions allowed the Vietnamese emperor to keep his post as a powerless figurehead who presided over seasonal festivals and made wine offerings to heaven. Throughout all Vietnam, the French governor-general exercised dominant power as a wholly secular bureaucratic official.

Although the French centralized the power of the state, they fragmented the Vietnamese national identity. Before the colonial conquest, collective ties to family, village, and nation had supplied cultural unity to the Vietnamese people. Under French colonialism, however, the Vietnamese nation became divided into three regions: Tonkin (north), Annam (central), and Cochinchina (south). Along with Laos and Cambodia, these three regions made up the Indochinese Union. The French even forbade the Vietnamese to mention in public the word "Vietnam," the name of their own country. According to the French, Vietnamese now lived in three "countries," not one. Besides devaluing the Vietnamese national identity, the French downgraded the collective ties to family and village. By undermining village autonomy, the colonial power alienated each Vietnamese individual from his collective roots. The stress on individual legal rights to private property and to freedom of religion meant a loss of communal identity.

Although claiming that colonial rule brought greater individual equality and freedom to Vietnam, French officials never interpreted freedom to mean Vietnamese national independence or perceived that a Vietnamese should hold equal status with a Frenchman. Bureaucratic elitism triumphed over individual equality.

Bureaucratic colonial rule also brought fundamental structural changes to Vietnam. As local villages lost their former autonomy, the central state grew stronger. The colonial government wielded greater coercive power than the Vietnamese imperial administration had formerly exercised. Even though only around 12,000 French soldiers, 5000 Vietnamese troops, and numerous security police dominated a society of 24 million Vietnamese, these bureaucratic agents used brutal repression to maintain internal security, especially against educated Vietnamese nationalists, factory workers, and rebellious peasants.[6] Centralized administration replaced the decentralized system under which the villages retained their local independence. Whereas the Vietnamese imperial government had practiced centralized policy formulation but decentralized implementation of policies, the French colonialists no longer merely planned government activities but carried them out as well. Especially in the south, French administrators gained control over the village councils of notables. Qualifications for council membership now depended not on scholarly attainments but on land ownership, wealth, and declared loyalty to French colonialism. To maintain political obedience, the French bureaucrats reserved for themselves the right to disapprove the selection of particular villagers who did not meet these qualifications. The coordination of government decision-making increased under colonialism. Whereas in the past Confucian mandarins representing the emperor had unified the policy process, now French bureaucrats exercised structural coordination. The governor-general in Hanoi, the *résidents supérieurs* in Tonkin and Annam, and the governor in Cochinchina formulated the key political decisions.

The scope of power wielded by the state also expanded. Rather than the council of elders or mutual aid associations performing the key activities, the central government headquartered in Hanoi undertook major responsibilities. Attempting to transform the society from a subsistence economy to a more commercialized economy, the state constructed roads, railways, ports, harbors, canals, and market cities. Economic policies no longer stressed domestic consumption; instead, greater production for the world export market took primacy. Government subsidies to French companies stimulated the expansion of large plantations growing rice, rubber, and coffee, as well as mines that produced coal, zinc, and tin. Thus the colonial state introduced agricultural capitalism to Vietnam and engineered the linkage of its economy to the world capitalist market.

French bureaucratic rule brought a more rigid social stratification system to Vietnam than had prevailed during the precolonial era. In the new class structure, the French and Chinese elites enjoyed the greatest privileges; most Vietnamese were at the bottom of the economic hierarchy. Urban dwellers amassed greater wealth than the rural folk. French civil servants, landlords, and company officials dominated the class structure. Below them came Chinese traders and small industrialists, who concentrated on milling, transporting, and selling rice overseas. Those few Vietnamese who managed to secure elite positions worked as merchants, bankers, office clerks, managers, and lower-ranking civil servants. In the rural areas some ex-mandarins and former employees of the French bureaucracy became wealthy landowners. Especially in the southern Mekong River Delta areas, there arose large landed estates dominated by both French and Vietnamese landlords. On these agricultural plantations, they grew rubber, coffee, sugar, and rice mainly for export to the world market. The mass of rural Vietnamese failed to gain many benefits from increased agricultural production. When the price of grain on the world market fell during the early 1930s, the peasants were devastated. They also suffered from low wages, high rents, high interest rates, high taxes, and high debts. Whereas before the French conquest peasants used to pay taxes in rice, the French bureaucrats demanded monetary tax payments. Lacking money, some poor peasants sold their land to gain cash; others sold their grain at low prices to the wealthy landlords. As a result, around three-fourths of the farmers in the southern region lost ownership of their land; they became either landless agricultural wage laborers or tenant farmers (sharecroppers) who paid high rents and owed huge debts to the landowners.

Under the French colonial system, the peasants lost not only their land but also their access to the political decision process. Particularly in the southern region, village political cohesion declined; the councils of notables fulfilled few functions. Unfortunately for the peasants, the landlords failed to assume responsibility for settling disputes and providing help to the needy in emergencies — activities that the notables used to perform. In the central and northern regions, the notables retained greater power. Unlike the southern area, the north suffered from greater land and water scarcity; floods posed a greater danger. Communal lands constituted a larger proportion of farmland — about 20 to 25 percent, compared with only 2.5 percent in the south. Under these agrarian conditions, the councils of notables retained their power to distribute communal lands, operate the irrigation system, allocate water, and collect taxes. Yet the poorest peasants benefited from neither the communal lands nor the decisions made by the notables. Rather than allocating land to the poor, the notables often appropriated the communal land for themselves. Allied with the French bureaucrats, the notables also enacted high taxes and otherwise oppressed the peasants. Hence, in both the north and south, a rigid class structure based on unequal landownership emerged. Vietnamese landlords and notables linked themselves to French civil servants, landlords, and company officials.

Although urban Vietnamese had greater access to material goods than did the rural folk, they, too, lived at the bottom of the economic stratification system. By 1940 fewer than 1 percent of Vietnamese worked as industrial laborers in mines, textile plants, and match factories. There they endured low wages, long hours, and unhealthy working conditions. Other urban Vietnamese found jobs working as household servants and prostitutes.

In the colonial stratification system, women and youth, along with the poor peasants, suffered the most. Whereas both men and women used to inherit land, under French colonialism only males could inherit land. As we have seen, most of them became landless, especially in the south. In the past all boys, regardless of wealth, had the opportunity to become a mandarin; each village had two or three teachers who prepared students to take the competitive examinations needed for entrance into the mandarinate. During the colonial era, however, educational opportunities actually declined. Few peasant families could afford the high fees demanded by the educational authorities. By 1940 no more than 2 or 3 percent of the Vietnamese attended a school. Even those Vietnamese who had attained a formal education faced bleak employment prospects. Despite their qualifications, few could become even primary school teachers. If they did gain a job, most worked as low-ranking civil servants—for example, as interpreters between the French administrators and the Vietnamese peasants.

Although the French colonialists developed a more differentiated class structure, they hardly governed a pluralist political system. Instead of allowing groups to assert their political demands, the French administrators, military, and police repressed Vietnamese expressions of political discontent. Peasants lacked the freedom to organize for more land, lower rents, lower taxes, and lower interest rates. Factory workers had little opportunity to form labor unions that would gain higher wages and safer working conditions. Except during the popular Front period, which lasted from 1936 through 1939, the colonial government suppressed the nationalist movements led by the urban middle class, such as teachers, students, lawyers, doctors, and lower-ranking civil servants. These educated professionals became the leaders of the Vietnamese movements struggling to overthrow French colonial rule.

### The Victory of the Viet Minh

After an eighty-year period of colonial domination, the French bureaucratic system collapsed during World War II. In late 1940 the Japanese Imperial Army established indirect rule over Vietnam. While the French administrators, allied with the pro-Nazi Vichy regime in France, formally governed the area, the Japanese actually wielded dominant control. They used Vietnam as a transit route and as a source of needed wartime supplies such as rice, machine oil, and cordage. In March 1945, with the Nazi defeat in Europe, the Japanese assumed direct power over the Vietnamese government and expelled the top-ranking French administrators. Five months later, in August 1945, the Viet Minh—the Viet Nam Doc Lap Dong Minh Hoi (Vietnamese Independence League)—overthrew the Japanese and established the Democratic Republic of Vietnam. With a stronger base of support in the northern and central areas, the Viet Minh never gained such a foothold in the south. At the end of World War II the British armed forces took control over Saigon and brought the French back to power. After an eight-year military struggle between the DRV and the French army, the Viet Minh finally conquered French troops at Dien Bien Phu in 1954.

Why did French colonialism disintegrate in Vietnam, and why did the Viet Minh emerge as the dominant nationalist force? The Viet Minh offered to supply those things that the French had taken away from the Vietnamese. Whereas the French had fragmented the Vietnamese national identity, the Viet Minh stressed a new sense of nationalism. Although other Vietnamese leaders had collaborated with the French and Japanese, the Viet Minh more effectively campaigned against Japanese and French imperialism. The French colonialists had created a rigid social stratification system; by contrast, the Viet Minh promised greater equality to women, youth, and poor peasants. Operating a centralized power structure, the French bureaucrats had undermined village autonomy and the power of the mutual aid associations. The Viet Minh developed the centralized organizations needed to defeat the French armed forces. However, the nationalist organizations within the Viet Minh movement were largely based on the mutual aid associations that once played a key role in precolonial Vietnam.

In short, the colonial bureaucratic system disintegrated when the mechanisms of coercive control and consensus formation collapsed under Japanese rule. Ruling by the sword, the French colonialists never bothered to establish their rule on a consensual foundation. When the Japanese army overthrew the weakened colonial regime, the coercive bases of rule deteriorated. By appealing to both nationalist and egalitarian beliefs, the Viet Minh tried to gain the popular legitimacy that undergirded consensual power. A powerful political party and military force provided the coercive power needed to deter internal resistance and defeat the French.[7] Under the leadership of Ho Chi Minh, the Viet Minh thus mobilized the populace to gain national independence.

The dominant political beliefs expressed by the Viet Minh blended nationalist and social revolutionary appeals, with a stress on nationalism. Ho Chi Minh, the founder of the Indochinese Communist party in 1930, the main leader of the Viet Minh, and the first president of the Democratic Republic of Vietnam, never perceived any contradiction between nationalism and communism. For him, national independence from French colonialism served as the means to revolutionize Vietnamese society, install a socialist economy, and ultimately reach the stage of full communism. Son of a Vietnamese administrator whom the French dismissed for anticolonial sentiments, Ho in 1919 attended the Versailles Peace Conference, where he sought more equal rights for the Vietnamese. Disillusioned with the French refusal to acknowledge the legitimacy of Vietnamese nationalist feelings, he became a founding member of the French Communist party during the early 1920s. Later in that decade he went to Moscow, joining the Southeast Asia Bureau of the Comintern (Communist International). In 1930 he founded the Vietnamese Communist party, which later that year was renamed the Indochinese Communist party.[8] Between 1936 and 1953, the Vietnamese Communists asserted the primacy of the nationalist struggle over the class struggle. Political mobilization focused on winning the war against France, abolishing illiteracy, and increasing food production. To accomplish these aims, the Viet Minh rallied a broad social spectrum, including some "patriotic" landlords, wealthy peasants, and urban professionals, as well as factory workers, poor peasants, women, and youths.

By creating a more egalitarian social stratification system in areas controlled by the Viet Minh, its leaders took practical steps to realize their beliefs. The Viet Minh discouraged polygamy, stressed the voluntary choice of marriage partners, distributed land to women, and encouraged them to participate in political organizations. The Viet Minh also extended opportunities to youths. Those who had gained a formal education battled against illiteracy, a campaign that helped solidify the links between the urban educated elite and the uneducated rural masses.

Although extensive land reforms did not begin until 1953, the Viet Minh took earlier actions to secure more economic equality for the poorest farmers. A massive famine struck the Red River Delta during the last years of World War II. After seizing the granaries controlled by the French and Japanese armies, the Viet Minh guerrilla forces distributed the rice to the poor peasants. In rural areas under their control, Viet Minh leaders also enacted a progressive tax system, raised taxes on the landlords, canceled peasant debts, instituted lower rents, improved the irrigation systems, and provided the cotton seeds and cotton cloth needed for packaging rice. By improving the economic well-being of the poor peasants, all these policies helped create greater equality.

The development of a powerful organizational network enabled the Viet Minh to triumph over other nationalist groups, win national independence, and realize a more egalitarian society. Before World War II, French repression effectively crushed the non-Communist nationalist opposition. The war itself weakened French military power. Supplied with weapons and equipment by both the U.S.S.R. and the U.S. Office of Strategic Services, the Viet Minh leaders by 1945 developed a stronger organization than any of their Vietnamese rivals. Compared with the Chinese Communist party, however, the Viet Minh had a weaker rural base. Initially headquartered in the northern mountain areas, where French military control was absent, the Viet Minh first seized control in Hanoi, then conquered Hue, the old imperial capital, and finally took Saigon. With a membership of only 5000 in a country of 24 million, the Viet Minh lacked the power to mobilize the rural population. Only after the war with the French government began in 1946 did the Viet Minh organize a rural base. From 1946 through 1954, it created a massive organizational network throughout the rural areas, especially in the north. Liberation forces, people's revolutionary committees, and national salvation associations mobilized the Vietnamese against the restoration of French colonial rule. The national salvation associations played an especially leading part. Modeled after the mutual aid groups of precolonial Vietnamese villages, associations of women, elderly people, youths, military personnel, peasants, and workers all struggled for "national salvation," a cause uniting secular with sacred values. Under the control of the Viet Minh, these associations helped defeat the French armed forces and thereby win national independence for Vietnam.

## Civil War in Vietnam

With the defeat of the French at Dien Bien Phu in 1954, military conflict in Vietnam did not cease; a new war began that pitted the Democratic Republic of Vietnam (DRV) against the Republic of Vietnam (RVN). According to the Geneva agreement of July 21, 1954, Vietnam was divided into two zones at the seventeenth parallel: "The military demarcation line is provisional and should not in any way be interpreted as constituting a political or territorial boundary."[9] Led by Ho Chi Minh, the Lao Dong (Workers) party governed the Democratic Republic of Vietnam in the north. South of the seventeenth parallel, the U.S. government helped create the Republic of Vietnam, comprising old Cochinchina and the southern areas of Annam. The Geneva accords provided that in July 1956, people in the two zones should vote in a general election by secret ballot for representatives who would decide the terms for reunifying the nation. In 1955, however, Ngo Dinh Diem, installed by the U.S. government as ruler over South Vietnam, canceled these elections and began to suppress opposition to his regime: the Buddhist sects (Cao Dai, Hoa Hao) and the Viet Minh, both of which controlled most villages in the south. Although the Viet Minh temporarily yielded control over the southern areas under terms of the Geneva agreement, Viet Minh leaders remained mobilized to fight the Diem regime. During late 1958 and early 1959 limited guerrilla warfare began in the south with attacks against wealthy landlords and Saigon government bureaucrats.

After the formation in 1960 of the National Front for the Liberation of the Southern Region of Vietnam (NLF), the war escalated. Labeled the "Viet Cong"—the Vietnam Cong San (Communists) by the Diem regime—the NLF stepped up its military campaign during the early 1960s. At that time, American helicopter pilots and military advisers began to arrive. After Vietnamese soldiers assassinated Diem in late 1963, United States involvement increased. U.S. ground combat troops landed in March 1965. Several Vietnamese military officers advised by American officials became rulers over the Republic of Vietnam. Among the best-known officers were Nguyen Cao Ky and Nguyen Van Thieu. They headed a military bureaucratic-authoritarian system that struggled against the elitist mobilization system of the DRV and its southern agency, the NLF. The North Vietnamese government triumphed in spring 1975; the next year the Vietnamese Communist party established the Socialist Republic of Vietnam to govern the whole nation.

Despite extensive U.S. military and economic support, why did the bureaucratic RVN collapse, replaced by a more mobilizing regime? By looking at the political beliefs and power structures of the two opposing sides, we can find some explanations for the systemic transformation.

## The Struggle for Political Legitimacy

Compared with the Saigon government bureaucrats, the North Vietnamese and NLF leaders expressed a stronger commitment to an ideological cause. Mobilizing systems typically seek to overcome severe value cleavages that rack a society. In Vietnam the NLF ideological message tried to surmount the conflict between traditional and modern values. Adapting Marxism-Leninism to the Vietnamese national heritage, NLF spokesmen reinterpreted traditional beliefs for revolutionary purposes. Just as village traditions served the revolutionary cause, so the revolutionary message synchronized with national traditions. In one sense, the NLF was both more traditional and more revolutionary than the Saigon opposition. By appealing to both national traditions and revolutionary Leninist doctrines, the NLF created a more powerful ideological commitment among its supporters than did either President Diem or the military officers.

What traditional values did the NLF leaders reinterpret to meet modern conditions? First, they directed their main appeals to the rural population. Attacking the corruption, decadence, and laxity of Saigon, built first by the French and later controlled by the Americans, the NLF leaders upheld such peasant values as self-denial, heroism, and sacrifice.

Second, like the ancient mandarins, the North Vietnamese party leaders and NLF cadres stressed learning and political virtue as the bases of political legitimacy. Rather than coming from peasant or working-class backgrounds, most Vietnamese Communist leaders were born into educated professional families; they were sons of mandarins, scholar-gentry officials, or intellectuals. For instance, President Ho Chi Minh's father served briefly as a district magistrate in the French colonial administration. Later Ho not only led the revolution against the French but also wrote poetry. His focus on the importance of political education, governance by moral example, and deference to authority figures resembled the mandarin tradition of enlightenment.

Third, like Confucianism, the new political religion articulated by Vietnamese Communists blended secular with sacred values; it united the political and social dimensions of life. Secular political ends — winning the war against the French, defeating the Americans and the Saigon government, abolishing illiteracy, expanding agricultural production, promoting rural health — became endowed with sacred significance. When the NLF cadres helped the peasants with their concrete material tasks, such as building dams, digging ditches, farming, and fishing, they also tried to embody certain moral virtues: selflessness, austerity, modesty, discipline, and courage. By blending secular with sacred values, they sought material and moral legitimacy among the villagers.

Fourth, as in traditional Vietnamese society, collectivism took precedence over individualism. The NLF leaders encouraged their supporters to find meaning not in individual isolation from others but rather in service to their extended family, their village, and especially their nation. Nationalism became the prime collective value. Whereas the French had treated the Vietnamese nation as three countries—Cochinchina, Annam, and Tonkin—the Viet Minh had sought to unify the nation. Similarly, the NLF struggled for the military reunification of the nation against American attempts to split Vietnam into two separate nations. For the NLF, freedom meant not the right of the individual to pursue his self-interests or to oppose the party cause but instead popular liberation from the South Vietnamese and U.S. governmental control. Within the village, party-military cell, and squad, the collective small group asserted its dominance over individual self-expression. Rather than making policies according to majority votes, NLF leaders strove for unanimous decisions; as in the traditional precolonial village, unity was not based on diversity and agreements to disagree. As in the traditional family, group conformity was used to secure unity. Political life became invested with family values. The party-military cell functioned as a substitute family; the party cadre resembled the elder brother who provided a moral example. Throughout the rural areas of South Vietnam the NLF tried to create a sense of national family identity that transcended each village. As head of the national family, President Ho Chi Minh, a bachelor, assumed the title of "uncle" rather than the role of a stern Confucian father.

Although maintaining some continuity with past traditions, the NLF beliefs also expressed a dedication to transforming the society. In adapting Marxism-Leninism to Vietnamese conditions, the Communist party leaders never ignored the revolutionary aspects of their ideology. Whereas the precolonial traditions emphasized harmony, stability, political apathy, and fatalism, the Vietnamese interpretation of Marxism-Leninism asserted the need for conflict, change, active political participation, and mastery over fate. Rather than advocating Confucian humanistic values, the Vietnamese Communists perceived science and technology as the necessary means for expanding economic production. In precolonial Vietnam, the soldier held the lowest status at the bottom of the social stratification system. North Vietnamese and NLF leaders, however, upheld military values. Even though the party dominated the People's Liberation Armed Forces, the guerrilla soldier received high esteem as one who sacrificed for the national cause.

Neither the values sketched by President Diem nor the beliefs voiced by the military officers heading the Saigon government aroused the same dedication as did the NLF ideology. President Diem, a Catholic who had lived in monasteries before coming to power in 1954, tried to blend Catholic doctrines with Confucian principles. Yet only 10 percent of the Vietnamese population was Catholic. Most of the rural dwellers practiced Buddhism rather than Confucianism. Thus the synthesis of Western Catholicism and Chinese Confucianism failed to evoke the widespread popular support that would undergird the legitimacy of his regime. Similarly, the beliefs stressed by General Thieu failed to stimulate the morale, motivation, and commitment needed to win the war against the NLF guerrilla forces and the North Vietnamese army. Whereas the NLF worked toward reuniting the nation, General Thieu stressed not nationalism but regionalism and anticommunism as his main themes. Thieu equated the NLF leaders with foreigners representing an alien presence in the south. Since Thieu and Ky had fought in the French army against the Viet Minh and afterward ruled with U.S. government support, they faced difficulties in attracting nationalist legitimacy. Compared with the NLF cadres, who urged their supporters to play an activist role in the political struggle, the military bureaucrats guiding the Saigon government sought only passive support from their followers. The NLF also represented more achievement-oriented values; performance for the People's Liberation Armed Forces became a source of high status. By contrast, the military officers who headed the Republic of Vietnam placed greater emphasis on personal favoritism and corruption as the ways for the individual to rise through the social stratification system. General Thieu downplayed egalitarian values, focusing instead on the need for the populace to honor military elitism. In contrast, the NLF gave greater importance to equal opportunities for women, youth, and poor peasants to secure an education, gain access to land, and play a role in political organizations.[10]

In sum, whereas the NLF tried to develop a distinctive value system based on nationalism and social revolution, General Thieu and the military bureaucrats failed to create a strong ideological commitment. Legitimacy rested on realizing secular ends such as increased material consumption and protection against Communist attacks. Partly because the NLF merged sacred with secular values in a new political religion based on both modern and traditional values, the NLF developed a stronger value cohesion. As a result, it operated with greater morale, despite the superior military power mounted against it by the Saigon government.

93

*The Struggle for Political Power*

Regardless of the military power, Western technology, and economic assistance given the Saigon government by the United States, it failed to win the war. With fewer resources, the NLF and North Vietnamese government triumphed. The major explanation for this systemic transformation centers on the power structures organized by the two opposing sides. Unable to form a political consensus, the South Vietnamese officials had to rely on coercive power. During the early 1970s, however, the mechanisms of coercive control began to disintegrate. By contrast, the NLF and the North Vietnamese government succeeded in building a stronger power base. As a result, they emerged victorious. Let us examine five structural variables that explain the outcome of this power struggle: (1) the political cohesion of social groups, (2) the unity of the political leadership, (3) the strength of the government, party, and army, (4) the degree of popular political participation, and (5) the dependence on foreign powers.

The Saigon government never developed a cohesive base of group support. Although it dominated the major cities, its control over the rural areas was more limited, especially at night. This urban-rural cleavage naturally hindered its prosecution of the war. Yet even among the villages and within the cities, group cohesion remained fragile. Most peasants living in the Mekong River Delta, the major rice-growing area of the south, supported the NLF or the Buddhist sects, primarily the Hoa Hao. Both the NLF and the Hoa Hao attracted their greatest support in areas characterized by large landed estates, high rents, and the production of rice for export on the world market. There the poor tenant farmers, who made up about 60 percent of the agricultural population, resented the high rents and high interest rates charged by the landed elite. President Diem, who won the support of only Catholic farmers, took steps to suppress both the NLF and the Hoa Hao. Although his army did crush the Hoa Hao, it achieved less success in eliminating the NLF supporters. Since Diem's land reform proposals redistributed only a small amount of land to tenant farmers, his efforts to establish a consensual power base also failed. Thus in the rural areas of the Mekong Delta, the landlords retained their economic power only by relying on the Saigon-based army to repress the peasantry. After Diem was assassinated in 1963, the military rulers who succeeded him also never developed a cohesive power base in the villages. Because of the American air attacks, many villagers fled the rural areas and moved to the safer cities. Yet even in the cities the Saigon military government experienced difficulties in organizing cohesive group support. Diverse groups benefited from military dominance and the continuance of United States assistance to the

Republic of Vietnam. These groups included Vietnamese generals, soldiers, secret police, clerks, translators, hotel managers, real estate salesmen, importers of luxury goods, black marketeers, drug dealers, shoe shine boys, "bar girls," and prostitutes. Most of these groups served as a support staff for either the Vietnamese armed forces or the American military personnel in Vietnam. When the Americans began to leave the country in early 1973 and the power of the South Vietnamese army disintegrated, those groups formerly identified with the Saigon government made few sacrifices to uphold its power.[11]

Although ruling dictatorially, the South Vietnamese army officials allowed some group pluralism; no powerful political party controlled group behavior. So long as a group did not challenge government leaders, it had the freedom to carry on its own affairs. Thus churches, unions, newspapers, universities, small businessmen, lawyers, and opposition parties retained some political autonomy.

A more monistic power network governed North Vietnam and the rural areas controlled by NLF. In the north, the party-state elite dominated the social stratification system, allowing little group autonomy. Neither Catholics nor Buddhists had the independent power to oppose government policy. From 1953 through 1956, the DRV land redistribution program allocated land to the poor peasants who supported the Lao Dong party; this policy destroyed the influence formerly exerted by the landlord and wealthy peasant classes. Rather than allow social groups any autonomy, the Lao Dong party organized economic and religious groups into mass associations, including the National Liaison Committee of Patriotic and Peace-Loving Catholics, the United Buddhist Association, and the National Liaison Committee of Farmers. In the south, the People's Revolutionary Party, which directed the NLF under the guidance of the North Vietnamese Communists, also organized the rural population in a network of "liberation associations": farmers, workers, students, women, and writers. The NLF recruited doctors, engineers, lawyers, businessmen, writers, and professors into the Alliance of National, Democratic, and Peace Forces, a front group that attacked the Saigon government for its repression and dependence on U.S. military power.[12] In short, by organizing social groups, the Lao Dong, the People's Revolutionary party, and the National Liberation Front constructed a power base that enabled them to defeat the Saigon government.

Compared with the military bureaucracy governing the south, the North Vietnamese and NLF mobilization system produced a more united leadership. Most of the North Vietnamese leaders had joined the Indochinese Communist party during the early 1930s. Until the end of the civil war in 1975, few purges fragmented the party leadership. Although

Ho Chi Minh acted as the major figure until his death in 1969, collective leadership, rather than one-man rule, dominated party affairs. Some conflicts did divide the NLF southern leadership from the North Vietnamese party cadres. Whereas the northerners supported rule by the Lao Dong party, the dictatorship of the proletariat, a class struggle against the "national bourgeoisie," and the establishment of an elitist mobilization system in the south, some NLF and Alliance leaders such as Truong Nhu Tang, Provisional Revolutionary Government Minister of Justice, favored a reconciliation system—that is, a system based on a coalition government, compromise with the neutralists, support from the bourgeois professionals, rule by southern leaders in the Alliance, and a "national, democratic," rather than a Marxist-Leninist, revolution. Yet these regional differences between northerners and southerners remained muted until the civil war ended in 1975. By contrast, the Saigon military elite never achieved the same unified leadership. Factional conflicts divided both the army and civil bureaucracy. One group of military officers contended against other segments for greater power and privilege. Each faction sought to consolidate its power with the U.S. government officials. Except for opposition to Communist control, these factions shared little in common. The divisions within the Saigon government obviously hindered its struggle against the NLF.

Despite the extensive U.S. assistance, the power of the Saigon military forces was weaker than the Communist opposition. True, from a numerical standpoint the strength of the South Vietnamese army seemed impressive. More than two million men, including regular troops, local defense forces, and paramilitary personnel, served in the Army of the Republic of Vietnam (ARVN). From the U.S. government, ARVN secured such military equipment as M-16 automatic rifles, machine guns, grenade launchers, and tanks. Yet ARVN proved unable to defeat the North Vietnamese army and the NLF. Corruption and lack of discipline plagued the military. Morale suffered. Especially after the U.S. military forces withdrew in 1973, defections of both officers and rank-and-file troops escalated. Although the NLF and the North Vietnamese army had fewer troops and more primitive weapons, they used their resources more skillfully to defeat the Saigon army. During the late 1960s and early 1970s, Communist troops numbered less than one-half million: about 350,000 combat forces from the North and 100,000 NLF guerrilla forces. They lacked the air power and the technically proficient weapons possessed by the South Vietnamese military. Yet morale, cohesion, and discipline remained higher. Within the military cells, party cadres reinforced group solidarity, supervised performance of troops, made group norms congruent with party goals, and used rewards and punishments to maintain control. Soldiers who performed well on the front received group praise and promotions. Those troops fighting less admirably faced public shaming, reeducation, demotion, and expulsion. Through these small-group control tactics, the People's Liberation Armed Forces (PLAF) obtained fairly high solidarity, despite the malnutrition, malaria, snakebites, homesickness, and death that faced them. Because of this group solidarity, cohesion, and discipline, they proved effective fighters on the battlefields.[13]

The Communist victory also did not stem from the more centralized power wielded by the DRV government, compared with the Saigon administration. True, both elitist mobilization and bureaucratic-authoritarian systems govern through centralized mechanisms. However, the B-52 air strikes directed against the north by the United States forced the DRV leaders to decentralize government administration. Although the central party leaders coordinated, planned, and supervised government activities, local village leaders retained considerable initiative to implement central directives.

In the south, the NLF leaders blended centralized direction with decentralized administration; they used both coercive and consensual tactics. In precolonial Vietnam, centralized policy formation combined with decentralized implementation of these policies at the village level. Similarly, in the areas controlled by the NLF the central elite formulated the policies but the village leaders carried them out, adapting the general decisions to local conditions. The People's Revolutionary Party officials directed the military struggle, guided political education, and settled some disputes that village leaders could not resolve. In turn, the NLF cadres in the villages supervised guerrilla training, conducted literacy drives, organized sports activities, reduced rents, built canals, enacted progressive taxes, and provided health care and other social services. To secure compliance, the NLF leaders exercised both consensual and coercive power. Particularly when taking over a village controlled by the Saigon government, they used coercion against South Vietnamese bureaucrats, security police, and soldiers. Unpopular civilian officials underwent public trials, assassinations, kidnappings, forced labor, and reeducation sessions. To overcome the Saigon-based armed forces, the NLF mined roads, destroyed bridges, and planted booby traps, besides practicing conventional military tactics. Yet like traditional Vietnamese, the NLF also wielded consensual power. Lacking the military equipment possessed by the Saigon army and needing a hiding place during the day, the NLF required support of local villagers. To gain rice, other food, and daytime safety, it stressed such consensual strategies as alliance formation, persuasion, and political education, especially before 1963.

By contrast, the Saigon government employed higher centralization and greater coercion than did the NLF. Financed by the U.S. government, the Thieu regime constructed a military-police bureaucratic state. Rather than govern through a strong political party and a mass-linked organizational infrastructure, the military bureaucracy ruled through the army, secret police, and civil service. With few roots in the villages, the Saigon bureaucrats and soldiers operated a centralized administration. Unable and reluctant to form a consensus, the military elite relied on coercive power. To fulfill their quotas, secret policemen killed old enemies even if they had no connections with NLF cadres. Even neutralists and non-Communists who opposed General Thieu were imprisoned, tortured, and killed. The U.S. military personnel used air strikes, napalm, white phosphorus, chemical defoliants, and search-and-destroy operations in an attempt to defeat the NLF. American pilots dropped in Vietnam three times the weight of bombs used in World War II. From one perspective, these coercive tactics proved effective. Especially between 1968 and 1972, southern guerrilla forces and NLF cadres were decimated. As a result of the abortive Tet offensive, U.S. air bombings, and the Phoenix search-and-destroy program, thousands of NLF supporters lost their lives. Hence northern troops and party cadres played the dominant role in seizing control over the south in 1975. From another perspective, however, the extensive coercion employed by the Thieu regime and the U.S. government stimulated rural discontent. Some peasants joined the NLF because B-52 air raids destroyed their kin, the Saigon army killed their relatives, or American pilots bombed ancestral burial plots, the embodiment of Vietnamese sacred values.[14] Thus, in some cases at least, the application of military coercion boomeranged, weakening rural support for the Saigon government.

Whereas the Communists relied on powerful party organizations to direct government activities, supervise military performance, and mobilize the farmers, the Saigon bureaucrats never organized a powerful party or organizational infrastructure that would rally popular support to their cause. In the north, the Lao Dong party dominated the government, army, and the people. Party cadres supervised the performance of military officers, who also held party membership. Although party cadres constituted only about 4 percent of the population, numerous mass associations channeled the activities of factory workers, peasants, writers, journalists, artists, women, and youths behind the party. In the south as well, the NLF and the People's Revolutionary Party organized associations based on the mutual aid clubs of precolonial Vietnamese villages. These "liberation associations" of women, workers, farmers, students, and youths provided opportunities for political activism organized by the party. Communist cadres relied on youths to win the war against the Saigon government. Most rank-and-file soldiers fighting for the PLAF were between sixteen and twenty-five years old. Through plays, stories, dances, and songs, young NLF leaders imparted political messages that mobilized the peasantry. In contrast, the Saigon military bureaucracy left the people apathetic. Candidates from diverse political parties did partici- pate in elections to the National Assembly, but General Thieu repressed those parties opposed to his rule. Neither General Thieu nor other high-ranking military officers established a powerful organizational net- work that would cement popular loyalty to their regime. Instead, they depended on the bureaucracy, armed forces, and U.S. government assistance to maintain their power.[15]

Finally, the Saigon government lost the civil war because it became too dependent on the United States for psychological support, military equipment, and economic assistance. During 1968 and 1969, over 500,000 American armed forces fought in Vietnam. The South Vietnamese military received technologically advanced weapons. Air strikes, con- ducted with television-guided and laser-guided bombs, destroyed the villages. Napalm, agent orange, and other chemical defoliants destroyed the land. As a result of American operations, the rural population was killed, relocated in "strategic hamlets," or forced into the cities. The destruction of families and villages produced feelings of rootlessness. Dependent on American technological superiority, urban Vietnamese felt hopeless, resigned, and fatalistic. Inert and politically powerless, they failed actively to support either the Saigon government or the NLF. When in August 1973 the U.S. Congress suspended American assistance and banned further U.S. military operations in Vietnam, defenders of the Saigon government felt demoralized, betrayed, and abandoned. Morale to pursue the war plummeted.

The North Vietnamese government practiced greater national self- reliance. True, President Ho Chi Minh worked for the Comintern during the 1920s; he also tried to maintain good relations with the People's Republic of China. Despite the Soviet and Chinese assistance to the war, these two foreign powers gave less assistance to the DRV than the U.S. government provided the Saigon armed forces. No Soviet troops fought beside Vietnamese soldiers. No Russian pilots conducted air strikes against the south. Compared with the PRC, the Soviet Union granted more military assistance to North Vietnam. Yet these weapons consti- tuted mainly light and medium tanks, some 130-millimeter, long-range artillery, mortars, machine guns, and AK-47 automatic rifles—less techni- cally advanced equipment than the weapons available to the South Vietnamese army.[16] In sum, neither superior firepower nor economic assistance provided by the U.S.S.R. explains the Communists' victory in the south. Rather, they overwhelmed the Saigon military bureaucracy by creating a more powerful organizational network, strengthening the traditional spirit of national independence, and reinterpreting precolonial values to meet modern structural conditions.

## Political Changes in the Socialist Republic of Vietnam

After gaining control of southern Vietnam in 1975, the Communist party leaders continued their mobilization activities. Although the war against the South Vietnamese armed forces had ended, another military struggle began against the Chinese army and the Cambodian guerrilla forces of the Khmer Rouge—two Communist powers. Militarily, the Vietnamese people mobilized for war. Economically, they mobilized for the construction of a socialist society. In this new struggle against foreign enemies and domestic "counterrevolutionaries," Vietnamese communism became militarized. The elitist mobilization system assumed more bureaucratic forms. Let us explore these trends by examining the changes that the Vietnamese Communist party (VCP) has tried to secure in the political culture, the power of the state, and the content of public policies.

*Reshaping the Political Culture*

With a stress on pragmatism, technology, material incentives, and the expansion of economic production, the current political beliefs articulated by the top Communist party leaders convey bureaucratic overtones. Like the precolonial mandarins, Vietnamese Marxists emphasize the need for both virtue and talent (*tai duc*). According to them, the new socialist person should serve as a moral example to others by embodying such values as purity, discipline, selflessness, austerity, honesty, courage, tenacity, and dedication to the socialist cause. Besides securing greater moral legitimacy for the new Communist regime, VCP leaders base the party's legitimacy on fulfilling certain material objectives. In the Socialist Republic of Vietnam (SRV), the scientific/technological revolution takes precedence over the cultural/ideological revolution. To achieve the major task of expanding economic production, party elites stress the need for hard work, pragmatic techniques, technical skills, professionalism, expertise, and mastery over the material environment—all achievement-oriented values. Material incentives—economic rewards for higher labor output—are used to stimulate greater economic production. Adaptable, flexible means, rather than abstract ideological ends, constitute the core of the new political belief system.

VCP elites uphold collectivist values rather than the pursuit of individual interests. Linking individualism to the consumerist mentality of the U.S.-dominated Thieu regime, they urge Vietnamese to embody such collective virtues as workers' solidarity, proletarian internationalism, patriotism, people's "collective mastery," respect for the public welfare, and support for the rules of collective life. Loyalty to the party, commitment to the state, and defense of the "socialist homeland" assume priority over reverence for individual self-expression and freedom.

Political elitism triumphs over civil liberties. The VCP asserts its role as the vanguard force that unites, organizes, and leads the Vietnamese people. According to article 4 of the SRV constitution:

> The Communist Party of Vietnam, the vanguard and general staff of the Vietnamese working class, armed with Marxism-Leninism, is the only force leading the state and society, and the main factor determining all successes of the Vietnamese revolution.[17]

Through the mass associations, the party educates, motivates, and mobilizes the masses. The party coordinates and directs the state agencies, which then implement party directives. Unlike military-technocratic bureaucrats in non-Communist dictatorships, however, the Vietnamese Communists blend political elitism with a focus on socioeconomic equality, especially on assistance to the needy, sick, and uneducated. By expanding health care and educational opportunities for women, montagnard ethnic minorities, and poor peasants, the party and state elites aim to build a more egalitarian socialist society.[18]

### Restructuring Political Organizations

After the Vietnamese Communists won the war against the South Vietnamese army, they established a stronger state than had functioned during either the precolonial period or the French colonial era. The Vietnamese state became more coercive, centralized, and coordinated. Although social pluralism weakened, the scope of power exercised by the state grew stronger.

Especially in the south, coercive power prevails over consensus formation; the army and military police play crucial political roles. Three agencies of state coercion—the People's Army of Vietnam, the military police, and the People's Security Forces—control dissident behavior. By handling arrests, trials, imprisonments, and executions, they apply extensive physical coercion. From 1975 through 1982, the regime executed more than 60,000 persons, mainly high-ranking military officers within the ARVN. Around 200,000 detainees have spent time in "reeducation" camps, where they suffered from malnutrition, malaria, tuberculosis, and other diseases. State expropriations of many private firms have strengthened economic coercion. Upper-class professionals associated with the Thieu regime have faced difficulties finding a job. Noncompliance with party-state directives can cause dismissal from a job or expulsion to a new economic zone, where dismal economic conditions prevail. The People's Army of Vietnam runs the state farms, supervises life in the new economic zones, and directs forced labor campaigns. Under this program, rebellious youth and ex-ARVN officers build roads, dig irrigation canals, or plant sweet potatoes. Vietnamese who disobey the party-state elite also risk losing their ration cards, thereby hindering their access to food and scarce consumer goods. Besides physical and economic coercion, normative (ideological) coercion pervades the society. At reeducation camps, former employees of the Thieu regime—and even individuals who opposed it—receive political indoctrination, confess their political sins, and seek forgiveness from the party elite. Spies and informers monitor "deviant" behavior of such out-groups as speculators, smugglers, "pilferers of socialist property," "puppet soldiers and administrators" (personnel employed by the Thieu regime), "comprador exploiters" (mainly Chinese small traders and shopkeepers), "landowning robber barons," and supporters of the "neocolonialist" American forces. Normative violations of the secular political religion as interpreted by the party elite thus incur severe punishment.

Why has the party-state elite applied such a heavy dosage of physical, economic, and ideological coercion in southern Vietnam? The main reason revolves around the lack of widespread support that the Communist victors found in the southern cities. Even during the precolonial period, the southern Vietnamese held less Spartan values than did the northerners. Unlike their northern colleagues, the southerners were more spontaneous, informal, leisurely, self-assertive, and distrustful of authority. Under colonial rule, the French gained the greatest influence over the southern region. Here French individualist values became more accepted than in the north. Village cohesion remained weaker. Wealthier than the two northern areas, the southern economy provided greater opportunities for individual labor mobility. After the French withdrew from Vietnam in 1954, the Americans took their place in the south. As American air strikes and forced draft urbanization programs depopulated the rural areas, the villagers fled to the cities. Whereas in 1960 around one-third of the South Vietnamese population lived in urban areas with populations greater than 500,000, by 1975 nearly 45 percent inhabited the cities. Influenced by American individualist, consumer-oriented values, the urban residents became dependent on the U.S. government's military presence, financial assistance, and support for the Thieu regime. A large proportion of the people living in Saigon opposed a Communist victory, even if they displayed little enthusiasm for the Thieu government.

The Communist military victory in 1975 brought not only greater political coercion but also a more centralized state. Village leaders no longer enjoyed the autonomy they had exercised under the Vietnamese monarchy or even under French colonialism. Political power now became concentrated in Hanoi. The southern-based organizations linked to the NLF either dissolved or merged with agencies controlled by the Vietnamese Communist party. For instance, during 1976 the National Liberation Front merged with the Fatherland Front. The People's Liberation Armed Forces joined the People's Army of Vietnam. The People's Revolutionary Party cadres became members of the Vietnamese Communist party. The Provisional Revolutionary Government, formerly dominated by the PRP, disappeared, replaced by the Socialist Republic of Vietnam.

As in the typical elitist mobilization system, the dominant party coordinates government activities. Although some non-Communist delegates serve in the National Assembly, most representatives are members of the Vietnamese Communist party. Comprising about 3 percent of the Vietnamese population, the VCP directs such central government agencies as the Council of Ministers, the Supreme People's Court, the Supreme People's Organ of Control, and the National Defense Council. At all levels of the military hierarchy, party officials control military personnel. The Central Military Party Committee, along with the Ministry of Defense Party Committee, formulate key defense policies. Within provincial, district, and village governments, the party sets the general line for actions taken by local people's and administrative committees. Although the party claims to supervise and guide government organizations, party agencies often try administering public policies. As a result of this organizational overlap between party and government, the policy process becomes stalemated. Evasion of responsibility and local resistance to central party directives plague the regime.

The Vietnamese Communist party also moved swiftly to weaken the vestiges of pluralism remaining under the overthrown Thieu regime. Party and state gained control over primordial, religious, and economic groups. Pledged to a unitary state that administers one people, the VCP pursued an assimilationist policy toward ethnic minorities such as the mountain people who live in the central highlands and along the borders with China. After 1975, the state abolished the autonomous regions for ethnic minorities and limited their political autonomy. From 1978 through early 1980, the government expelled thousands of urban Chinese who dominated trade in rice, fertilizers, and medicines; in 1981, however, state authorities began to allow Chinese merchants greater economic freedom. Although during the 1960–1975 period women gained more opportunities to participate in local party and government organizations, after the war ended their political influence declined. In the mid-1980s women comprised fewer than 20 percent of party members and around 10 percent of local VCP people's committees. The VCP directed the Vietnam Women's Union, which concentrated on constructing socialism, defending the socialist homeland, raising women's political consciousness, and educating them about child care and family planning.

Catholic priests and Buddhist monks have lost their religious and political freedoms. To control the Catholic population, the VCP established the Committee for Solidarity of Patriotic Vietnamese Catholics. Although Catholics can attend church services, the government monitors priests' sermons and limits the number of newly ordained priests. The state closed or requisitioned some Catholic churches. Priests cannot easily establish new churches. Especially in the new economic zones, several parishes have no priests. Regarded as second-class citizens, Catholics face difficulties securing employment in schools and hospitals. Buddhist monks have also endured restrictions, especially when they oppose government policies. In 1981 the state instituted the Unified Buddhist Church to cement loyalty toward the regime. The Vietnamese Communist party arrogates for itself the creation of the new socialist person, the new proletarian culture, and a new socialist society. Directed by the state, party, and revolutionary youth organizations such as the Ho Chi Minh Communist Youth Union, VCP cadres educate young people. Political education takes precedence over religious training.

After the Communist victory in 1975, the party-state elite tried to restrict the power of the urban private business sector. Especially in Ho Chi Minh City and Haiphong, the Chinese controlled small-scale trade and industry. Vietnamese small industrialists manufactured laundry powder, cigarettes, candy bars, and salad oil. Other small businessmen traded goods, often on the black market. In 1978 the state attempted to supplant the private economic sector. State stores and state trading companies replaced privately owned shops. Many small-scale industrialists had to join handicraft cooperatives. Former managers of private firms became the managers of state-owned industries or joint state-private enterprises. To consolidate its control over the economic sector, the party established a network of mass associations, such as the Vietnam Confederation of Trade Unions, that directed the activities of factory workers and employees of state firms.

After the reunification of the nation in 1975, the state assumed more responsibilities over the economic, educational, and health sectors. Banks, foreign trade establishments, large industrial plants, and transportation facilities became nationalized. The government seized control of schools, universities, and hospitals that the Catholic church had formerly managed. Under this expansion of state power, the Communist party elite became actively engaged in formulating and implementing a broad range of public policies, including economic, educational, and health care decisions.[19]

### Making and Implementing New Public Policies

After winning the civil war in 1975, the Vietnamese Communist party instituted a state socialist economic policy in the southern region. Perceiving Vietnam in the early stage of the transition from small-scale production to larger-scale socialist production, the party-state elite interpreted socialism to mean expanded public ownership. The government converted the largest businesses into state-owned industries, which produced machine tools, steel, chemicals, coal, tires, textiles, and porcelains. Some privately owned firms became joint state-private enterprises. Although many small traders and shopkeepers had to join cooperatives, such as handicraft and marketing cooperatives, other private businessmen managed to retain some autonomy over their enterprises. Particularly in the southern cities, small-scale traders and manufacturers supplied Vietnamese with consumer goods such as food, soap, glasses, buckets, kerosene lamps, plastic baskets, sandals, embroidered silk, and cigarettes. Tailors, barbers, hairdressers, and restaurant owners operated private firms. Throughout the rural areas the collectivization of agriculture took place, with state farms, agricultural cooperatives, and production collectives the dominant agrarian institutions. Unlike other Asian state socialist societies, such as North Korea and Mongolia, where 40 percent of the labor force works in agriculture, Vietnam remains an agrarian economy; in 1980 about two-thirds of the employed population worked on the farms. Compared with North Korean government administrators, Vietnamese state officials have gained less control over the farm population, especially in the southern region. Protesting pre-1979 government policies that set low prices for rice and interfered with the market exchange of food and consumer goods, peasants refused to harvest rice on cooperative land, expended their energy on small family plots, fed their rice to pigs, and failed to deliver grain to state agencies. Because of these protest activities, in 1979 the government introduced some decentralized market features that spurred agricultural production.

Although remaining committed to state socialist economic policies, during the early 1980s the party-state elite instituted market incentives, particularly in the agrarian sector. Government officials wield only limited control over the market. Private firms, which usually employ fewer than twenty personnel, control the wholesale and retail trade of food, fish, and forest products. (In 1983 about 70 percent of all retail trade occurred through private exchange networks.) Even though cooperative farms feature public ownership of crop land, machinery, and irrigation facilities, the nuclear family has regained the dominant role. Family members transplant rice, breed fish, make handicrafts, and raise pigs, chickens, vegetables, and fruit. According to the contract system, farmers deliver a certain quota of their grain output to the state in exchange for fertilizers, insecticides, equipment, and veterinarian services. After meeting their quota, farmers can sell the remaining produce on the free market. Under the subcontracting arrangements, a nuclear family leases land owned by the cooperative and agrees to render a certain share of rice or other food to the cooperative. The nuclear family also controls food production on private plots, which comprise 5 percent of total cooperative land. Low taxes on land and higher prices for food produced above a state quota represent other material incentives to stimulate agricultural output.

Under the bureaucratic aspects of state socialism, government agencies set prices, distribute goods, and plan the economic development process. Expansion of agricultural production and light industries, including those making consumer goods, has become the primary objective. To increase production the party elite encourages material rewards to the technical expert, who assumes the major responsibility for applying the latest technological, scientific, and mechanical methods to the economy. The expansion of economic production also requires foreign economic assistance, which the SRV government has obtained mainly from the Soviet Union and the East European Communist states. By joining COMECON (the Council for Mutual Economic Assistance, composed of East European states, Mongolia, and Cuba), Vietnam has secured credits, technical assistance, industrial supplies, and food.

What effects did these economic policies exert on economic growth? Particularly between 1976 and 1980, the Socialist Republic of Vietnam realized a low growth rate, especially in food and consumer goods. Both objective conditions—bad weather, war damage—and policy performance explain the economic stagnation. Drought, floods, and typhoons struck the nation during 1977 and 1978, causing shortages of rice, other grains, peanuts, beans, sugar, tea, and coffee. The lengthy war with the United States destroyed land, cities, villages, power stations, ports, roads, and transportation facilities. After 1975 trained Vietnamese fled their country, which thus lost vital human capital. Many remaining urban southerners resented the imposition of party discipline and felt no incentive to expand economic output. As a result of the U.S. embargo, Vietnam lost credits and spare parts not only from the United States but also from West European nations, Japan, the Asian Development Bank, and the International Monetary Fund. The war against the Khmer Rouge increased the military budget but reduced government expenditures for domestic economic production. Because the export of such goods as rubber, tea, coffee, pineapples, bananas, and handicrafts failed to expand, a trade deficit ensued, thereby causing a shortage of foreign exchange. Battles with China on the northern borders brought an end to Chinese economic assistance and led skilled Chinese—entrepreneurs in the south as well as dockworkers and coal miners in the north—to emigrate from Vietnam. The wars with the United States and China meant that the Vietnamese government became too dependent on the Soviet Union for trade, loans, technical assistance, and such resources as oil, steel, machinery, fertilizer, and coal. Since Vietnam lacked the money to pay for all these goods, shortages of coal, gasoline, kerosene, and diesel oil impeded the drive for rapid industrialization. Industrial production failed to match expectations because the state lacked investment capital as well as technically trained managers and skilled factory workers. Bureaucratism, centralization, corruption, and incompetence diminished managerial efficiency. In short, several related factors—a high foreign debt, primitive technology, inefficient management, wartime devastation, lack of foreign exchange, and shortages of coal, machinery, electric power, and chemical fertilizers—contributed to the low growth rate during the late 1970s. With the institution of more flexible decentralized market mechanisms based on material incentives, agricultural and small handicrafts production increased from 1980 through 1985. Yet large-scale industrial production continued to lag; many factories operated under one-half their potential capacity.

The same factors that caused low economic growth also accounted for severe inflationary pressures that plagued Vietnam during the late 1970s and early 1980s, when prices rose between 50 and 80 percent a year. Both supply and demand variables produced the steep price increases. The excess aggregate demand stimulated by the wars with the Khmer Rouge and China inflated the economy. Supply restrictions also created severe inflation. Typhoons, floods, and droughts led to food shortages, as did the wars against the Chinese and their allies, the Khmer Rouge. Seeking higher prices for their produce, some farmers refused to sell their food to the state but instead sold it on the free market. Hoarding and speculation carried out mainly by Chinese entrepreneurs caused additional shortages. The worldwide increase in oil prices exacerbated Vietnam's inflationary problems, since gasoline, diesel oil, and kerosene bore high costs on the world market. Devaluation of the currency raised import prices. Finally, inefficient planning by state and party officials aggravated the inflation. Without competent personnel, state agencies faced especially severe difficulties in channeling food from rural areas to the cities and in allocating agricultural equipment from the industrial centers to the farmers. Most farmers lacked tractors, harvesters, and water pumps needed to expand agricultural output.

Besides severe inflation, high unemployment has plagued the southern region of Vietnam. During the early 1980s, around 20 percent of the work force was jobless. The major reason for the high unemployment stems from the withdrawal of the American armed forces prior to 1975. Under the Thieu regime, the Saigon economy was geared to serving the consumer needs of U.S. troops and to maintaining the Vietnamese military in power. When the United States ended its military involvement in 1973, the jobless rate escalated, especially for those employed as translators, secretaries, maids, hotel managers, importers of luxury goods, drug dealers, "bar girls," and prostitutes. After the Vietnamese Communists defeated the Saigon army, bureaucrats, military personnel, and police associated with the Thieu administration became unemployed. The withdrawal of American, French, and Taiwanese investors after 1975 also left some industrial employees jobless, since the Vietnamese state lacked the capital equipment, raw materials, and trained personnel needed to run these industries. Another cause of unemployment derives from urban overpopulation. During the war, air strikes and guerrilla attacks impelled the villagers to flee the rural areas for the cities. By creating new economic zones in the central plateau, the Mekong Delta, and the coastal regions, the Vietnamese government hopes to lower urban unemployment as well as increase agricultural production. Despite these policy objectives, contemporary Vietnam remains far less industrialized than North Korea, another state socialist regime, and hence lacks the industrial base to provide jobs for school graduates.

Although the expansion of economic production has proved difficult, the party elite has attained greater success in its struggle for greater equality. By levying cheap rents, supplying inexpensive rationed goods (such as rice, oil, and clothing), and allocating land to poor farmers in the agricultural cooperatives, economic policies have led to a more egalitarian distribution of wealth. Nevertheless, the regime has hardly instituted full economic equality. Factory workers' wages now derive from their productivity, efficiency, and product quality. This reliance on material incentives and the opposition to wage equality have brought less egalitarian incomes. Farmers in the Mekong Delta are now more prosperous than most urban residents, especially workers in the state factories and even government civil servants. Traders on the free market earn higher incomes than do most state employees. Although the political elite—government ministers, managers, directors, party cadres—may not receive high incomes, they do gain greater access than the masses to educational institutions, health-care facilities, and special state stores where they can buy food and consumer goods.[20]

Despite some elitist aspects of the educational system, the socialist government has expanded popular access to schooling. During the late 1970s the government established a new educational system that provided schooling for nearly all the population. Infants under six years old attend nursery schools. The general education program includes primary, junior secondary, and senior secondary schools. At the higher education level, students can take a vocational program, attend a middle-level professional school for engineering training, or enroll in colleges and universities, which stress science, economics, and technology—subjects needed for future technicians, managers, specialists, and administrators. Workers in the agricultural cooperatives, factories, and government offices have access to various adult education programs, such as evening classes, work-and-study courses, and on-the-job classes. Here they learn literacy skills and technical knowledge. Despite shortages of teachers and such facilities as classrooms, textbooks, paper, chalk, and blackboards, by 1983 nearly 80 percent of the Vietnamese adult population over fifteen years old had acquired literacy skills. Few other low-income countries in Asia or Africa have such a high literacy rate.

The content of the new school curriculum stresses not only basic literacy but also the need for children to learn political values, role behaviors, and certain cognitive skills. Focusing on the ideas of Ho Chi Minh and Marxist-Leninist beliefs, the normative model promotes political reeducation. Consistent with the precolonial heritage, political education has become moral education. Charged with creating a "new socialist person," teachers emphasize the moral values proclaimed by President Ho: love for the homeland, hard work, unity, discipline, cleanliness, modesty, courage, and honesty. For the party-state elite, socialism means industrialization of the Vietnamese nation; thus, the need for economic achievement occupies a high place on the value of hierarchy. In school young children learn about national heroes of the past, such as poor peasant Nguyen Hien, who, during the thirteenth century, studied hard and became the first doctor of the nation. Taking Nguyen Hien as a model, contemporary Vietnamese teachers urge their students to work hard, show self-reliance, and achieve for the national good. They hope that these values will become incorporated into their students' political and economic behavior. Politically, the new socialist person exemplifies the ideal role for future citizens. Economically, the socialist division of labor includes the following important occupational roles: skilled factory workers, farmers on agricultural cooperatives, office employees in state agencies, technicians, engineers, scientists, and managers. Besides preparing students for these politico-economic roles, the schools also give some attention to cognitive development. Although Marxist-Leninist dogma hinders the learning of new cognitive skills, the Vietnamese curriculum also stresses science and mathematics — subjects that require an empirical orientation, receptiveness to new abstract ideas, and a critical stance toward orthodox teachings.[21]

Advances in health care have lagged behind the educational accomplishments. In both the northern and the southern regions, the war with the United States and the Thieu administration left deep scars. American pilots dropped chemical defoliants over all the Vietnamese territory. Unexploded shells and land mines still dot the countryside. Air strikes destroyed some hospitals. The wars with the Khmer Rouge and the Chinese army have brought shortages of foods, drugs, and medicines. The U.S. government dissuaded the European Economic Community from continuing shipments of food to Vietnamese children's hospitals. Party-state control of the public health system and the abolition of private health care caused many physicians to leave the country. Faced with these problems, the regime has still tried to expand access to health programs. Most villages now have a health-care station that provides first aid, social hygiene programs, and maternity care. Doctors, auxiliary doctors, midwives, nurses, and pharmacists provide general medical practice in these village health centers. More specialized treatment takes place in district and provincial hospitals. Particularly at the village level, Vietnamese health policies try to synthesize traditional with modern medicines. Besides using advanced Western medical techniques, Vietnamese doctors rely on such traditional methods as acupuncture and antibacterial medicines from local plants. To implement this health program, the party-state elite mobilizes professional health specialists as well as the Vietnamese Communist party and the mass associations that it directs, including the Ho Chi Minh Communist Youth Union, the Women's Union, the Elders' Association, and the Traditional Medicine Association. Despite the obstacles to securing a healthy population, these policy efforts that blended the professional approach with populist strategies produced health conditions comparing favorably with infant mortality and life expectancy rates in all òther low-income societies except China and Sri Lanka. In 1984, around fifty children for every thousand live births died before age one; life expectancy at birth reached sixty-five years.[22]

In conclusion, the Vietnamese modes for handling the basic issues in the policy process exemplify the typical elitist mobilization system. Over the last fifty years, the Communist leaders have blended a will to attain fundamental socioeconomic changes with a sensitivity to the objective conditions blocking the voluntarist orientation. Motivated by a powerful need for achievement, the party-state elite instituted policies that helped reduce illiteracy, increase economic equality, and raise life expectancy. All these policy objectives were attained despite hostile objective conditions: poverty, Chinese military intrusions, war with the Khmer Rouge, continued U.S. government hostility, and some southern resistance. Policy efforts to expand production, reduce inflation, and decrease southern unemployment proved less successful.

Like other elitist mobilizers, the Vietnamese Communists have historically asserted the dominance of political organization over social-group spontaneity as the primary way to transform society. Although the pervasive organizational network enabled the Vietnamese Communists to defeat the Saigon army, it also led to the bureaucratization of the mobilization system after the civil war ended. Even top party leaders themselves have criticized tendencies toward bureaucratic arrogance, elitism, mandarinism, incompetence, and corruption. Especially in the south, the Vietnamese Communist party organization remains weak. The party and its mass associations, especially the youth groups and unions, seem unable to attract large memberships. Many party cadres show incompetent, corrupt behavior: They gain special privileges for themselves, including benefits such as access to canned milk, bikes, cars, transistor radios, and houses. Some local party activists accept bribes and practice extortion. Faced with party malfeasance, particularly in the southern areas, the top VCP leaders have tried to purify the party and state administration. They have purged corrupt cadres from the party. In 1986 the three highest-ranking VCP officials—Truong Chinh, Pham Van Dong, and Le Duc Tho—voluntarily resigned from the Political Bureau and Central Committee. As a result, younger members gained the opportunity to wield greater influence over party decision-making.[23]

Policymaking in the Socialist Republic of Vietnam combines ideological consensus with conflict toward out-groups opposed to socialist transformation. Through ideological reeducation programs, the Communist party attempts to organize a consensus behind the new regime. Yet because the party never developed as broad a popular support base in the south as it did in the north, the armed forces and police wield extensive coercive power throughout the southern region. They mobilize conflict against domestic out-groups such as the bourgeoisie, the Catholic church, the Buddhist sects (Hoa Hao, Cao Dai), and the urban supporters of the Thieu regime, as well as against such foreign adversaries as the Khmer Rouge and the Chinese army. In these pervasive struggles, political life becomes militarized. Militaristic images bombard the economic policy process as the "battle for production" takes place. Despite the stress on ideological unity, the difficulties in stimulating rapid economic growth have produced intense policy conflicts among the party-state elite. As in most Marxist-Leninist regimes, the ideological purists ("Reds") struggle against the pragmatists ("experts"). Committed to ideological orthodoxy, the Reds favor centralized state planning by party leaders, the promotion of heavy industry, government price controls, moral incentives for workers, and the collectivization of agriculture and industry. In their view, the party must establish socialism quickly. By contrast, the more pragmatic experts assume that the transition to socialism will take a longer time. They prefer a policy emphasis on decentralized management by specialists, the promotion of light industry and agriculture, flexible market prices, material incentives (wage differentials) for workers, and the retention of a small-scale private sector. Within the top organs of the party and state, but not in the mass public arena, the elite debate these policy options and try to reach a consensus.[24]

Finally, although dedicated to the socialist transformation of society, Communist party leaders in the SRV have always stressed the need to modernize tradition, learn from national history, and retain a continuity with the past order that provides significance to social change. The Vietnamese national identity extends nearly four thousand years back into history; wars against Chinese imperialism strengthened their attachment to the Vietnamese nation. From the Confucian ethos and precolonial village traditions, the Communist party elite have taken such notions as pragmatism, collectivism, communal cohesion, cooperation in mutual assistance clubs, reverence for education, and rule by an educated bureaucratic elite. The injunction to defend the homeland elevates family values from the local village to the entire nation. During the early 1980s, as during the precolonial era, powerful families dominated the central government. For example, after the civil war ended in 1975, the relatives of Le Duan and Le Duc Tho gained control over party agencies, civilian government organs, the security apparatus, and the military. As under the Vietnamese monarchies, some power over political and economic policymaking has been decentralized to provinces and especially villages. With the contract system, the nuclear family has regained its control over economic production of farm produce and handicrafts.

Yet the party-state elite has introduced new practices taken from Marxist-Leninist ideology that stresses social equality and fundamental sociopolitical change. Although Vietnamese have inherited a military tradition based on their historical struggles with China, the Khmer Empire, and the Champa Empire, no imperial army ever gained the power or status currently shown by the People's Army of Vietnam. Marxism-Leninism also upholds the need for a powerful political party that organizes the revolution; certainly, no such dominant party ever ruled the more pluralistic precolonial Vietnam. Like classical Leninists, the Vietnamese Communist party leaders interpret socialism to mean state control and ownership of the economy. Whereas the imperial Vietnamese court ruled a decentralized agrarian bureaucracy that provided some poor relief to citizens, today in Vietnam a stronger central government performs more extensive activities.[25] Wielding power through three centralized organizations—party, state, and army—the Communists have constructed an elitist mobilization system that has tried to realize more far-reaching changes than Vietnam ever experienced before the twentieth century.

# Notes

1 For analyses of political life in precolonial Vietnam, see Tran Nhu Trang, *The Transformation of the Peasantry in North Viet Nam* (Ph.D. dissertation, Department of Political Science, University of Pittsburgh, 1972), 30–103; John T. McAlister, Jr., and Paul Mus, *The Vietnamese and Their Revolution* (New York: Harper Torchbooks, 1970), 31–57, 78–92; Frances FitzGerald, *Fire in the Lake: The Vietnamese and the Americans in Vietnam* (Boston: Little, Brown, 1972), 3–47, 142–145; Samuel L. Popkin, *The Rational Peasant: The Political Economy of Rural Society in Vietnam* (Berkeley: University of California Press, 1979), 83–132; Alexander B. Woodside, *Community and Revolution in Vietnam* (Boston: Houghton Mifflin, 1976), 109–118; John K. Whitmore, "Communism and History in Vietnam," in *Vietnamese Communism in Comparative Perspective*, ed. William S. Turley (Boulder, Colo.: Westview Press, 1980), 11–44; John K. Whitmore, "Social Organization and Confucian Thought in Vietnam," *Journal of Southeast Asian Studies* 15 (September 1984): 296–306; David W. Haines, "Reflections on Kinship and Society under Vietnam's Lê Dynasty," *Journal of Southeast Asian Studies* 15 (September 1984): 307–314; Alexander B. Woodside, "Medieval Vietnam and Cambodia: A Comparative Comment," *Journal of Southeast Asian Studies* 15 (September 1984): 315–319.
2 McAlister and Mus, *The Vietnamese and Their Revolution*, 78.
3 *Émile Durkheim: Selected Writings*, ed. and trans. Anthony Giddens (London: Cambridge University Press, 1972), 144–146.
4 McAlister and Mus, *The Vietnamese and Their Revolution*, 78.
5 For analyses of the effects of colonial rule, see Virginia Thompson, *French Indo-China* (New York: Macmillan, 1937), esp. 58–98, 249–264; Nguyên Thê Anh, "The Vietnamese Monarchy under French Colonial Rule, 1884–1945," *Modern Asian Studies* 19 (February 1985): 147–162; Woodside, *Community and Revolution in Vietnam*, 14–28; FitzGerald, *Fire in the Lake*, 53–64, 151; Trang,

*Transformation of the Peasantry*, 103–134; John T. McAlister, Jr., *Vietnam: The Origins of Revolution* (Garden City, N.Y.: Doubleday Anchor, 1971), 37–97; Popkin, *The Rational Peasant*, 133–183; Samuel L. Popkin, "Corporatism and Colonialism: The Political Economy of Rural Change in Vietnam," *Comparative Politics* 8 (April 1976): 431–464; Milton Osborne, "Continuity and Motivation in the Vietnamese Revolution: New Light from the 1930's," *Pacific Affairs* 47 (Spring 1974): 37–55; Martin J. Murray, *The Development of Capitalism in Colonial Indochina (1870–1940)* (Berkeley: University of California Press, 1980).

6 McAlister, *Vietnam*, 106.

7 Huynh Kim Khanh, "The Vietnamese August Revolution Reinterpreted," *Journal of Asian Studies* 30 (August 1971): 761–782; McAlister, *Vietnam*, 126–127, 171–337; Trang, *Transformation of the Peasantry*, 160–164, 181, 191, 205–218; Woodside, *Community and Revolution in Vietnam*, 118–148, 160–234; Popkin, *The Rational Peasant*, 184–242; Vu Ngu Chieu, "The Other Side of the 1945 Vietnamese Revolution: The Empire of Viet-Nam (March–August 1945)," *Journal of Asian Studies* 45 (February 1986): 293–328.

8 See *The New York Times*, September 4, 1969, p. 17; Woodside, *Community and Revolution in Vietnam*, 160–200; Milton Osborne, "Makers of the 20th Century: Ho Chi Minh," *History Today* 30 (November 1980): 40–46; William J. Duiker, *The Communist Road to Power in Vietnam* (Boulder, Colo.: Westview Press, 1981), 7–43.

9 See *The Viet-Nam Reader*, rev. ed., ed. Marcus G. Raskin and Bernard B. Fall (New York: Vintage Books, 1967), 97.

10 For analyses of the political beliefs of Lao Dong leaders, NLF cadres, and Saigon military officers, see McAlister and Mus, *The Vietnamese and Their Revolution*, 11–139; FitzGerald, *Fire in the Lake*, 72–137, 212–227, 236–263; Nguyen Khac Vien, *Tradition and Revolution in Vietnam*, trans. Linda Yarr, Jayne Werner, and Tran Tuong Nhu (Berkeley, Calif.: Indochina Resource Center, 1974), 15–52; William Darryl Henderson, *Why the Vietcong Fought* (Westport, Conn.: Greenwood Press, 1979), 48–60, 77–86; Douglas Pike, *History of Vietnamese Communism, 1925–1976* (Stanford, Calif.: Hoover Institution Press, 1978), 55–71; Woodside, *Community and Revolution in Vietnam*, 201–300; Alexander Woodside, "Ideology and Integration in Post-Colonial Vietnamese Nationalism," *Pacific Affairs* 44 (Winter 1971/1972): 487–510; Paul Berman, *Revolutionary Organization: Institution-Building within the People's Liberation Armed Forces* (Lexington, Mass.: D. C. Heath/Lexington Books, 1974), 35–88.

11 Jeffery M. Paige, *Agrarian Revolution: Social Movements and Export Agriculture in the Underdeveloped World* (New York: The Free Press, 1975), 278–333, 369–376, esp. 331–333; Jeffery M. Paige, "Social Theory and Peasant Revolution in Vietnam and Guatemala," *Theory and Society* 12 (November 1983): 699–737; Robert Scigliano, *South Vietnam: Nation under Stress* (Boston: Houghton Mifflin, 1964), 101–129, 130–159; FitzGerald, *Fire in the Lake*, 72–137, 236–263, 349–359; Anthony J. Russo, Jr., "Economic and Social Correlates of Government Control in South Vietnam," in *Anger, Violence, and Politics: Theories and Research*, ed. Ivo K. Feierabend, Rosalind L. Feierabend, and Ted Robert Gurr (Englewood Cliffs, N.J.: Prentice-Hall, 1972), 314–324.

12 Pike, *History of Vietnamese Communism*, 94, 115–130; Douglas Pike, *Viet Cong: The Organization and Techniques of the National Liberation Front of South Vietnam* (Cambridge, Mass.: MIT Press, 1966), 166–209; Jon M. Van Dyke, *North*

*Vietnam's Strategy for Survival* (Palo Alto, Calif.: Pacific Books, 1972), 92–107;
Edwin E. Moise, "Land Reform and Land Reform Errors in North Vietnam,"
*Pacific Affairs* 49 (Spring 1976): 70–92; R. B. St. John, "Marxist-Leninist Theory
and Organization in South Vietnam," *Asian Survey* 20 (August 1980): 812–828;
Trang, *Transformation of the Peasantry*, 218–219, 268–269, 290–296; Truong Nhu
Tang, with David Chanoff and Doan Van Toai, *A Vietcong Memoir* (New York:
Harcourt Brace Jovanovich, 1985), 130–144; Stephen J. Morris, "Human Rights
in Vietnam under Two Regimes," in *Freedom in the World: Political Rights and
Civil Liberties 1982*, ed. Raymond D. Gastil (Westport, Conn.: Greenwood
Press, 1982), 219–253.

13 Henderson, *Why the Vietcong Fought*, 40–47, 64–121; John C. Donnell, "South
Vietnam in 1975: The Year of Communist Victory," *Asian Survey* 16 (January
1976): 1–13; Tang, *A Vietcong Memoir*, 156–175, 186–199; Berman, *Revolutionary
Organization*, 89–190.

14 Nancy Wiegersma, "Agrarian Differentiation in Southern Vietnam: A Com-
ment," *Journal of Contemporary Asia* 15, no. 4 (1985): 474–481; Berman, *Revolu-
tionary Organization*, 66–77; William S. Turley, "Women in the Communist
Revolution in Vietnam," *Asian Survey* 12 (September 1972): 793–805; Van Dyke,
*North Vietnam's Strategy for Survival*, 100–109; FitzGerald, *Fire in the Lake*,
165–211, 160–424; Richard Shultz, "The Limits of Terrorism in Insurgency
Warfare: The Case of the Viet Cong," *Polity* 11 (Fall 1978): 67–91; Jeffrey Record,
"Viet Cong: Image and Flesh," *Trans-action* 8 (January 1971): 46–52; Huynh
Kim Khanh, "Year One of Postcolonial Vietnam," *Southeast Asia Affairs 1977*,
vol. 4 (Singapore: Institute of Southeast Asian Studies, FEP International,
1977), 294–295; Gareth Porter, "Vietnam's Long Road to Socialism," *Current
History* 71 (December 1976): 209–210; William Broyles, Jr., "The Road to Hill
10," *Atlantic Monthly* 255 (April 1985): 91–118; Tang, *A Vietcong Memoir*, 167.

15 Pike, *History of Vietnamese Communism*, 92–133; Pike, *Viet Cong*, 109–231;
William S. Turley, "Civil-Military Relations in North Vietnam," *Asian Survey* 9
(December 1969): 879–899.

16 Donnell, "South Vietnam in 1975," 1–13; Edmund Stillman, "Smart Bombs and
Dumb Strategy," *Saturday Review of the Society* 55 (July 29, 1972): 27–32; Stephen
T. Hosmer, Konrad Kellen, and Brian M. Jenkins, "The Fall of South Vietnam,"
*Conflict* 2, no. 1 (1980): 1–8.

17 William J. Duiker, *Vietnam since the Fall of Saigon*, rev. ed. (Athens: Ohio
University Center for International Studies, 1985), 181.

18 *Vietnam Courier* 16, no. 3 (1980): 4, 5, 7; Paul Isoart, "Les Institutions politiques
des deux Vietnams," *Revue juridique et politique: Indépendance et coopération* 24
(September 1970): 368–372; Claude Lange, "Le Catholicisme face au pouvoir
socialiste depuis la réunification du Viet-nam," *Mondes Asiatiques*, nos. 9–10
(Spring/Summer 1977): 77–93; Stephen B. Young, "Vietnamese Marxism:
Transition in Elite Ideology," *Asian Survey* 19 (August 1979): 770–779; David W.
P. Elliott, "North Vietnam since Ho," *Problems of Communism* 24 (July/August
1975): 35–52; Porter, "Vietnam's Long Road to Socialism," 227; William S.
Turley, "Vietnam since Reunification," *Problems of Communism* 26 (March/April
1977): 36–54; David W. P. Elliott, "Institutionalizing the Revolution: Vietnam's
Search for a Model of Development," in Turley, ed., *Vietnamese Communism in
Comparative Perspective*, 200; Phan Hien, "The Penal Code of the Socialist
Republic of Vietnam," *Vietnam Courier* 21, no. 9 (1985): 4–6.

19 For analyses of state power in contemporary Vietnam, see Alexander

Woodside, "Problems of Education in the Chinese and Vietnamese Revolutions," *Pacific Affairs* 49 (Winter 1976/1977): 664–665; Alexander Woodside, "Nationalism and Poverty in the Breakdown of Sino-Vietnamese Relations," *Pacific Affairs* 52 (Fall 1979): 381–409; Carlyle A. Thayer, "Dilemmas of Development in Vietnam," *Current History* 75 (December 1978): 221–225; Carlyle A. Thayer, "Development Strategies in Vietnam: The Fourth National Congress of the Vietnam Communist Party," *Asian Profile* 7 (June 1979): 275–286; Tai Sung An, "The All-Vietnam National Assembly: Significant Developments," *Asian Survey* 17 (May 1977): 432–439; Claude Lange, "Controverses sur la 'Liberté Religieuse' au Vietnam," *Mondes Asiatiques*, no. 12 (Winter 1977/1978): 329–342; Lange, "Le Catholicisme face au pouvoir socialiste," 77–93; William S. Turley, "Urban Transformation in South Vietnam," *Pacific Affairs* 49 (Winter 1976/1977): 607–624; Khanh, "Year One of Postcolonial Vietnam," 287–305; Pike, *History of Vietnamese Communism*, 134–152; Douglas Pike, "Inside Vietnam: The Recycling of a Society," *Strategic Review* 6 (Summer 1978): 48–55; Milton Osborne, "The Indochinese Refugees: Cause and Effects," *International Affairs* 56 (January 1980): 37–53; *The Boat People: An 'Age' Investigation with Bruce Grant* (New York: Penguin Books, 1979), 82–109; U.S. Congress, House Committee on International Relations, *Human Rights in Vietnam: Hearings before the Subcommittee on International Organizations*, 95th Cong., 1st sess., 1977, pp. 76–99; Elliott, "Institutionalizing the Revolution," 199–223; Jacqueline Desbarats and Karl D. Jackson, "Vietnam 1975–1982: The Cruel Peace," *Washington Quarterly* 8 (Fall 1985): 169–182; Peter Eng, "Vietnam's Re-education Camps Punish Thousands of Ex-Civil War Foes," *Los Angeles Times*, November 22, 1984, part I-B, p. 3; *Amnesty International Report 1984* (London: Amnesty International Publications, 1984), 267–270; Nguyen van Canh with Earle Cooper, *Vietnam under Communism, 1975–1982* (Stanford, Calif.: Hoover Institution Press, 1983), 100–119; Nguyen Long with Harry H. Kendall, *After Saigon Fell: Daily Life under the Vietnamese Communists* (Berkeley: Institute of East Asian Studies, University of California, 1981), 14–32; Doan van Toai and David Chanoff, *The Vietnamese Gulag*, trans. Sylvie Romanowski and Françoise Simon-Miller (New York: Simon and Schuster, 1986), 185–331; Douglas Pike, *PAVN: People's Army of Vietnam* (Novato, Calif.: Presidio Press, 1986), 145–161; Nguyên duc Nhuân, "Do the Urban and Regional Management Policies of Socialist Vietnam Reflect the Patterns of the Ancient Mandarin Bureaucracy?" *International Journal of Urban and Regional Research* 8 (March 1984): 84; Broyles, "The Road to Hill 10," 91–118; Carlyle A. Thayer, "Vietnam's Two Strategic Tasks: Building Socialism and Defending the Fatherland," in *Southeast Asian Affairs 1983*, ed. Pushpa Thambipillai (Aldershot, Hampshire, England: Gower Publishing Company, 1983), 299–324; Ng Shui Meng, "Vietnam in 1983: Keeping a Delicate Balance," in *Southeast Asian Affairs 1984*, ed. Pushpa Thambipillai (Singapore: Institute of Southeast Asian Studies, 1984), 346; Nguyên duc Nhuân and Vo Nhan Tri, eds., "Le Vietnam dix ans après: Bilan et perspectives," *Problèmes politiques et sociaux*, no. 531 (March 7, 1986): 20; Robert Shaplen, "A Reporter at Large: Return to Vietnam—II," *New Yorker* 61 (April 29, 1985): 106–107, 118; Jayne Werner, "Women, Socialism, and the Economy of Wartime North Vietnam, 1960–1975," *Studies in Comparative Communism* 14 (Summer/Autumn 1981): 165–190; Nguyen Thi Dinh, "Vietnamese Women and the Revolution," *Vietnam Courier* 22 (March 1986): 13–18; World Bank, *World Development Report, 1979* (New York: Oxford University

Press, 1979), 164; Walker Connor, *The National Question in Marxist-Leninist Theory and Strategy* (Princeton, N.J.: Princeton University Press, 1984), 101–120, 342–345, 454–456; Irene Norlund, "The Role of Industry in Vietnam's Development Strategy," *Journal of Contemporary Asia* 14, no. 1 (1984): 94–107; William J. Duiker, "Vietnam in 1984: Between Ideology and Pragmatism," *Asian Survey* 25 (January 1985): 100; Lewis M. Stern, "The Overseas Chinese in the Socialist Republic of Vietnam, 1979–82," *Asian Survey* 25 (May 1985): 521–536; William J. Duiker, "Vietnam in 1985: Searching for Solutions," *Asian Survey* 26 (January 1986): 109–110.

20 For analyses of economic policies and performance of the Vietnamese government, see Xavier Guillaume, "Tendances et difficultés de l'économie vietnamienne," *Mondes Asiatiques*, no. 11 (Autumn 1977): 197–217; *Vietnam Courier* 15, no. 2 (1979): 23; Thayer, "Dilemmas of Development in Vietnam," 223–225; Thayer, "Development Strategies in Vietnam," 281–286; Claude Lange, "Révolution socialiste au Vietnam du Sud," *Mondes Asiatiques*, no. 7 (Autumn 1976): 321–324; Porter, "Vietnam's Long Road to Socialism," 209–212, 226–228; Woodside, "Nationalism and Poverty in the Breakdown of Sino-Vietnamese Relations," 393–409; Philippe Devillers, "Vietnam in Battle," *Current History* 77 (December 1979): 214–218, 225–226; A. D. Cao, "Development Planning in Vietnam: A Problem of Postwar Transition," *Asia Quarterly*, no. 4 (1978): 263–276; A. D. Cao, "Investment and Trade Opportunities in the New Vietnam," *Asia Quarterly*, no. 2 (1979): 115–127; Louis Peronne, "La Politique intérieure du Vietnam," *Politique étrangère* 44 (December 1979): 235–249; Ton That Thien, "Vietnam's New Economic Policy: Notes and Comments," *Pacific Affairs* 56 (Winter 1983–1984): 691–712; Christine Pelzer White, "Everyday Resistance, Socialist Revolution and Rural Development: The Vietnamese Case," *Journal of Peasant Studies* 13 (January 1986): 49–63; Christine White, "Agricultural Planning, Pricing Policy and Co-operatives in Vietnam," *World Development* 13 (January 1985): 97–114; Jayne Werner, "Socialist Development: The Political Economy of Agrarian Reform in Vietnam," *Bulletin of Concerned Asian Scholars* 16, no. 2 (1984): 48–55; Ngo Vinh Long, "Agrarian Differentiation in the Southern Region of Vietnam," *Journal of Contemporary Asia* 14, no. 3 (1984): 283–305; Nguyen van Canh, *Vietnam under Communism*, 100–102; Melanie Beresford, "Household and Collective in Vietnamese Agriculture," *Journal of Contemporary Asia* 15, no. 1 (1985): 5–36; Melanie Beresford, "Vietnam's Economic Challenge," *AfricAsia*, no. 18 (June 1985): 30–31; Tran Van Ha, "The Family Economy of the Vietnamese Peasants," *Vietnam Courier* 22 (February 1986): 14–16; Doan Vu, "An Economic Reform with a Revolutionary Character," *Vietnam Courier* 21, no. 10 (1985): 10–12; Vo Van Kiet, "The Vietnamese Economy at the Threshold of the New Five-Year Plan," *Vietnam Courier* 22 (February 1986): 6–8; Nguyen Ngoc Triu, "Problems, Achievements, and Prospects of Vietnamese Agriculture," *Vietnam Courier* 22 (February 1986): 9–13; Charles Fourniau, "Vietnam: La Construction du socialisme à l'heure de vérité," *Recherches internationales*, no. 20 (April/May/June 1986): 7–28; Nguyên duc Nhuân and Vo Nhan Tri, eds., "Le Vietnam dix ans après," 21–36; Tetsusaburo Kimura, "Vietnam: Ten Years of Economic Struggle," *Asian Survey* 26 (October 1986): 1039–1055; John H. Esterline, "Vietnam in 1986: An Uncertain Tiger," *Asian Survey* 27 (January 1987): 92–103; Robert Shaplen, "A Reporter at Large: Return to Vietnam—I," *New Yorker* 61 (April 22, 1985), 104–125; Ng Shui Meng, "Vietnam in 1983," 343–357; R. D. Hill and Cheung

Man Biu, "Vietnamese Agriculture: Rhetoric and Reality," *Contemporary Southeast Asia* 7 (March 1986): 292–305; Derek Martin da Cunha, "Aspects of Soviet-Vietnamese Economic Relations," *Contemporary Southeast Asia* 7 (March 1986): 306–319; World Bank, *World Development Report 1986* (New York: Oxford University Press, 1986), 238–239.

21 See Viet Chung, "General Education in the Socialist Republic of Vietnam," *Vietnam Courier* 21, no. 10 (1985): 15–16; Hoang Xuan Tuy, "Higher Education and Secondary Vocational Education," *Vietnam Courier* 21, no. 10 (1985): 16–17; *Vietnam Courier* 15, no. 10 (1979): 609; *Vietnam Courier* 15, no. 11 (1979): 10; *Vietnam*, no. 235 (1978): 18–19; *Vietnam*, no. 231 (1978): 18–19; Devillers, "Vietnam in Battle," 225; Lange, "Révolution socialiste au Vietnam du Sud," 316–321; Alexander Woodside, "The Triumphs and Failures of Mass Education in Vietnam," *Pacific Affairs* 56 (Fall 1983): 401–427; Thai Quang-Nam, "Éducation et travail productif au Vietnam," *Canadian and International Education* 8, no. 2 (1979): 92–99; Nguyen van Canh, *Vietnam under Communism*, 145–163; Ruth Leger Sivard, *World Military and Social Expenditures 1986*, 11th ed. (Washington, D.C.: World Priorities, 1986), 38.

22 Alexander Casella, "Dateline Vietnam: Managing the Peace," *Foreign Policy*, no. 30 (Spring 1978): 180; Hoang Bao Chau, "Combining Traditional and Modern Medicines in Vietnam," *Vietnamese Studies*, no. 50 (1979): 7–28; Khanh, "Year One of Postcolonial Vietnam," 292; François Rémy, "Viet Nam: Guaranteed for Life," *World Health* (May 1978): 12–15; Arthur W. Galston and Ethan Signer, "Education and Science in North Vietnam," *Science* 174 (October 22, 1971): 379–385; Herbert A. Schreier, "Medicine versus Health: A Comparison of Two Systems," *Pharos* 38 (July 1975): 125–129; World Bank, *World Development Report 1986*, 180, 232; Dang Hoi Xuan, "Achievements in Health Work since the Triumph of the August 1945 Revolution," *Vietnam Courier* 21, no. 8 (1985): 26–27; Nguyen Long, *After Saigon Fell*, 92–101; Don Luce, "Making Vietnam 'Feel Pain,'" *Nation* 234 (March 27, 1982): 363–364.

23 See Douglas Pike, "Vietnam in 1980: The Gathering Storm?" *Asian Survey* 21 (January 1981): 84–92; Thayer, "Vietnam: Beleaguered Outpost of Socialism," 165–176; Elliott, "Institutionalizing the Revolution," 199–223; William S. Turley, "Political Participation and the Vietnamese Communist Party," in Turley, ed., *Vietnamese Communism in Comparative Perspective*, 171–197; Thayer, "Vietnam's Two Strategic Tasks," 299–324; Michael Williams, "The Shakeup in Vietnam," *World Today* 43 (February 1987): 19–20.

24 William S. Turley, "Hanoi's Domestic Dilemmas," *Problems of Communism* 29 (July/August 1980): 42–61; Carlyle A. Thayer, "Vietnam's New Pragmatism," *Current History* 82 (April 1983): 158–161, 183–185.

25 Thomas Hodgkin, "Scholars and the Revolutionary Tradition: Vietnam and West Africa," *Oxford Review of Education* 2, no. 2 (1976): 111–120; Young, "Vietnamese Marxism," 770–779; Truong Nhu Tang, "The Myth of a Liberation," *New York Review of Books* 29 (October 21, 1982): 31–36; Nguyên duc Nhuân, "Do the Urban and Regional Management Policies of Socialist Vietnam Reflect the Patterns of the Ancient Mandarin Bureaucracy?" 73–89.

# 5

## POLITICAL CHANGE IN CUBA

Condemn me. It does not matter.
History will absolve me.
—Fidel Castro (1953)

All the people should be organized, because for people in the midst of a revolution the most important task is organizing their forces. No matter how great its enthusiasm, no matter how great its morale and fighting spirit, an unorganized populace is ineffective because it disperses its forces.
— Fidel Castro (1961)

The revolution is now an institution.

— Fidel Castro (1984)

As an elitist mobilization system, Cuba under Fidel Castro shares many similarities with Vietnam. Both systems have tried to mobilize the masses for the construction of a socialist society. Gaining political power through armed struggle, the Vietnamese Communists and Fidel Castro based their mobilization campaigns on a military model. As the struggle mounted against internal resistance and hostility from foreign powers, political life became militarized. The Spartan military virtues of austerity, discipline, selflessness, and dedication to the national cause took priority over popular consumption, leisure, and individualism. Even economic decision-making assumed militaristic images, as shown by the stress on the battle for production. Like the Vietnamese, the Cubans have achieved greater success in redistributing income, expanding educational opportunities, and providing health care than in stimulating economic production. Both nations have depended on the Soviet Union to supply them with weapons, oil, economic credits, technical assistance, and industrial equipment. In exchange for this economic and military aid, Cuba and Vietnam have generally followed the Soviet foreign policy line; as a result, Chinese leaders have ridiculed Vietnam as the Cuba of Asia. Both the Vietnamese and Cubans live in the shadow of a more powerful neighboring state. While Vietnam has sought to overcome the dominance of China, Cuba has resisted the structural control wielded by the U.S. government, which militarily occupied Cuba from 1899 to 1902, 1906 to 1910, and 1917 to 1923. Although historically fighting against Chinese domination, the Vietnamese modified Confucian values to suit national conditions. Similarly, since winning independence in 1902, Cubans have been influenced by values expressed in the American mass media: individualism, consumerism, and entrepreneurial freedom. Fidel Castro represents the first major Cuban leader who has attempted to shift these values toward those of a more collectivist socialist culture.

Despite these similarities, striking differences also separate Vietnam from Cuba. Compared with Fidel Castro, the Vietnamese Communists have shown a greater reliance on Leninist techniques for exercising political power. Ho Chi Minh was one of the founding members of the French Communist party and also worked for the Communist International (the Comintern) in Asia. In 1930 he organized the Vietnamese Communist party; under its direction, Vietnam won independence from France. Between 1954 and 1975 the Lao Dong (Workers) party in the Democratic Republic of Vietnam (DRV) guided the People's Army of Vietnam toward eventual triumph in the south. Although President Ho Chi Minh served as the preeminent figure in the DRV, he never renounced the importance of collective leadership. When he died in 1969, a peaceful succession to power took place; the pattern of political decision-making remained the same. Today Vietnamese Communist party leaders use Marxist-Leninist phraseology in their speeches, which uphold the need for political organization, the vanguard party, the dictatorship of the proletariat, and collective leadership.

By contrast, the Cuban leadership, especially Fidel Castro, remains less indebted to the Leninist organizational framework. In Cuba personal leadership takes precedence over organizational rule. All institutions depend on the will of Fidel Castro. Whether we regard him as a "socialist caudillo" or a "revolutionary Robin Hood,"[1] Castro has dominated the Cuban policy process since 1959. Yet unlike Ho Chi Minh, he has never maintained such lengthy ties with the international Communist movement. Indeed, not until late 1961—three years after overthrowing the regime of Fulgencio Batista—did Castro declare himself a Marxist-Leninist. His Rebel Army, not a Communist party, engineered Batista's downfall. Before 1958 the Popular Socialist party (PSP), which maintained close ties with the Soviet Union, actually supported the Batista government rather than Castro's insurgent movement. Immediately after gaining government power in early 1959, Castro ruled through the army, not a dominant party. Only in 1965 did he finally organize the ruling Communist Party of Cuba to govern the nation. Today most top party leaders consist of the comrades who fought with Castro in the Sierra Maestra to defeat Batista; former PSP activists play a less significant role in party politics.

Although Castro's charismatic leadership did lead to Batista's downfall, the highly personal style of political decision-making has hindered the operation of Cuba's state socialist economy. A modern complex economy requires a strong institutional base associated with clear procedures, delegation of authority, shared agreements on governmental responsibilities, and adaptable organizations that can efficiently process information. Rule by a single person, however, impedes policy formulation and implementation, especially in a regime where the state exercises a comprehensive scope of power. During the 1970s, under Soviet pressure, Castro moved to "institutionalize" the revolution. Political decision-making became more bureaucratized. Nevertheless, even though institutional forms gained more importance, the method of policymaking remained about the same. As leader of the revolution, Castro has continued to dominate all key institutions, including the government, armed forces, and party.

The following sections explore two general questions related to systems change in Cuba. First, why did the Batista regime collapse so easily? That is, what factors explain the transition from a bureaucratic-authoritarian to an elitist mobilization system? Second, why did the Castro regime become more bureaucratized during the 1970s?

## The Revolutionary Seizure of Power

Although the Cuban revolutionaries struggled for a much briefer time than did the Vietnamese revolutionaries to gain governmental control, similar reasons explain the downfall of the old regime. As we have seen, the Vietnamese Communists pursued a fifty-year campaign to reunify the nation; in Cuba, however, Castro and his guerrilla followers fought less than three years before emerging victorious. As in Vietnam, the revolutionaries succeeded because they maintained a stronger group cohesion, operated a more powerful organizational apparatus, and expressed a stronger commitment to an ideological cause than did incumbent government officials. The policy failures of the Batista government and the withdrawal of U.S. support during 1958 also weakened the regime's power.

### Political Cohesion of Social Groups

From the time that Batista staged a coup in 1952 until his overthrow in late 1958, he never developed a cohesive base of group support to consolidate his rule. At the end, nearly all groups—religious, ethnic, and especially economic—withdrew their support from the Batista government. The Catholic church never played a powerful role in Cuban political life. During the 1950s, 80 percent of priests were Spanish, not Cuban. Rather than strongly supporting the Batista government, church officials remained politically quiescent, encouraging their mainly urban parishioners to seek spiritual salvation, not changes in the political world. Yet some reformist Catholic groups, such as the Catholic Action, the Young Christian Workers, and the Student Christian movement, did oppose Batista and cast their lot with the Castro opposition. Non-Catholic groups also offered no strong support to the Batista government. Protestant churches identified more with the United States than with the Cuban government. Seeking a theocratic order where Jesus Christ rules as king, the Jehovah's Witnesses opposed all secular governments.[2]

The main ethnic cleavages in Cuba have divided blacks (about 27 percent of the population) from whites; Batista retained the wholehearted support of neither group. Batista's politics took an ambivalent stand toward race relations. On the one hand, he did uphold the efforts of the Cuban Confederation of Labor to end economic discrimination against blacks. As a result, both white and black skilled factory workers earned about the same income. On the other hand, under the Batista regime social discrimination still remained; blacks could not gain entrance to certain resorts, hotels, beaches, parks, and social clubs. Economically, blacks also suffered. Generally, they occupied positions at the bottom of the economic stratification system. Compared with whites, blacks earned lower wages, gained less schooling, worked fewer months a year, experienced higher unemployment rates, and held fewer professional jobs, particularly in U.S.-owned industries, the Cuban foreign service, and the armed forces. For these reasons, blacks gave somewhat stronger support to Castro's revolution. Whites also expressed disenchantment with the Batista government policy toward race relations; some felt that as a mulatto, Batista showed excessive enthusiasm about equalizing racial opportunities.[3]

During the 1950s, economic cleavages, not ethnic divisions, led to the collapse of the Batista regime. The major economic cleavage split Havana from the rest of the nation, especially the rural areas. Compared with other Latin American nations, Cuba had attained a relatively high level of socioeconomic development. In 1958 it ranked fifth in gross national product per capita, fourth in urbanization, and fifth in literacy. Yet outside Havana dismal economic conditions prevailed. More than 20 percent of the rural people were illiterate. They suffered from bad housing and inadequate health care. Particularly in Oriente province, Castro's birthplace and the area from which had come his earliest support, most peasants did not own land. Early in the twentieth century, small farmers had lost land to the United Fruit Company and to other corporations, such as the Cuban-American Sugar Company. Between 1899 and 1902, the U.S. military commanders created a Rural Guard that allied with the landowners to protect their estates from rural bandits. Through the 1950s landowners and the Rural Guard continued evicting the numerous squatters who seized land. Workers could gain employment for only half the year in the Oriente sugar mills. To the rural squatters and under-employed sugar workers, Castro appeared as the champion of the rural people against the Havana economic elite. He acted like a revolutionary Robin Hood, a social bandit who robbed from the rich and gave to the poor.

Although Castro came to power by appealing to the rural poor, he also initially won the support of urban economic groups that had grown disillusioned with Batista. Not only the poorer urban residents but also some wealthy groups rallied to the Castro insurgent movement. During 1958, unemployment grew from 7 percent in March to 18 percent in December; at the end of that year, even the urban factory workers, who had formerly supported Batista, abandoned him because of their deteriorating economic conditions. Along with its bad economic performance, the political repression of the Batista administration alienated wealthier groups that had once defended his rule. Some bankers, industrialists, sugar-mill owners, and professionals, such as doctors and lawyers, supplied money to the Rebel Army. The younger "bourgeois radicals" joined Castro to fight against the Batista army. At the end of 1958, the only major groups that continued to ally with Batista were American investors and Cuban businessmen connected to U.S. industrial firms. These industrialists, who controlled electric power production, telecommunications, transportation, shipping, luxury hotels, banks, tourism, gambling, and prostitution, feared that a guerrilla triumph would end their control over vital sectors of the Cuban economy.[4]

In sum, Fidel Castro and his Rebel Army emerged victorious because he attracted a broad coalition of social groups. Catholic reformists wanted a more humane society. Blacks desired greater racial equality and improved employment opportunities. Squatters in the Oriente province sought access to land. The unemployed and underemployed perceived that Castro, rather than Batista, would implement government policies to lower the jobless rates. Some wealthy groups thought that Batista's overthrow would bring more political order and economic growth. Professionals looked for an end to government corruption and repression. Among the middle-class opponents of Batista, the radical bourgeoisie joined the guerrilla movement to reshape the political culture toward socialist values, institute a more egalitarian economic order, and lessen the cleavages separating the urban sector from the underdeveloped rural areas.

## The Power of Political Organizations

Another reason for Castro's victory revolves around his success in developing a more powerful organization base than did Batista. Under the bureaucratic Batista regime, the mechanisms of coercive control and consensus formation disintegrated. Political consensus rested on the government's ability to supply economic payoffs to organized groups, such as the sugar growers, sugar-mill owners, bankers, and trade unionists. When the economy declined in 1958, the political consensus evaporated. Not only during his last year in office but from the beginning of his rule, Batista had always placed greater reliance on coercive power than on consensus to maintain himself in power. Perceiving that he would not win the 1952 presidential election, he staged a coup d'état three months before the election took place. From then until his overthrow, he suspended the civil liberties that Cubans had previously known, such as the freedoms guaranteed to the press, voluntary associations, and political parties. Yet particularly during 1958, his coercive power also began to deteriorate. Repression waxed and waned. When opposition emerged, he suppressed the dissidents. Then, after Cubans and Americans protested the curtailment of civil liberties, the government lessened its harsh treatment. This inconsistent use of coercive power angered Batista's opponents but lessened their fear of attacking his rule. Hence, the bureaucratic system destabilized.

Although Batista governed a bureaucratic-authoritarian system, the government, army, and political parties exercised only weak power. Controlled by personal factions, the political parties had few activities to perform in the repressive system. Among the government agencies, neither the parliament nor the courts played a significant role. Instead, the executive dominated the policy process. Backed by the military and police, Batista ruled through executive decree. Even the bureaucracy, however, failed to wield strong influence. Corrupt and faction-ridden, it often came under the control of powerful interest groups attached to the government bureaus. For example, although the government supposedly regulated the sugar industry, actually sugar-mill owners and sugar growers determined the decisions taken by the Sugar Stabilization Institute. Faced with weak government agencies and political parties, Batista relied on the military to maintain his power. Yet the armed forces also proved an unstable base of support. Rather than base advancement on professional criteria, he promoted military officers according to political criteria—that is, personal loyalty to him. As a result, military morale declined. Battles with the guerrilla forces, who had popular support in the Sierra Maestra, further demoralized the armed forces. Although the police remained loyal to Batista, a large segment of the army troops withdrew their support from the government in 1958. Some stopped fighting. Others joined the Rebel Army. Encouraged by the State Department, which opposed Batista, the U.S. government suspended arms shipments to Cuba in March 1958. Because of Batista's declining coercive capabilities, the guerrilla forces led by Castro toppled the Batista regime at the end of the year.

Confronted by the disintegrating bureaucratic system, Castro organized a mobilization movement that overthrew Batista. Unlike the Vietnamese situation, however, in Cuba the Rebel Army, not the Communist party, led the revolutionary campaign. Whereas the Vietnamese Communist party leaders created the People's Liberation Armed Forces and the People's Army of Vietnam, the Cuban Rebel Army arose before the organization of the Cuban Communist party. Castro and his followers perceived the Rebel Army, not the party, as the vanguard of the revolution. Yet as in Vietnam, the revolutionaries in Cuba triumphed not because of their superior weapons or troop strength but because the incumbent government ruled through a disintegrating institutional base. Although Batista's army included over 30,000 men, in mid-1958 the Rebel Army comprised less than 500 troops. Whereas Batista had access to advanced weapons from the United States, Castro obtained no military assistance from the Soviet Union until after he came to government power; instead, his army captured weapons from government forces. Castro overcame these obstacles by better organizing the more limited resources at his disposal. Faced by the corrupt government bureaucracy, the ineffective political parties, and the demoralized army, the Rebel Army operated as the dominant organization spearheading the revolution. Between late 1956 and 1958, it established a dual government in Oriente province. Besides directing the military struggle, the Rebel Army performed several tasks associated with a civilian government. For instance, it supervised educational programs, created hospitals, administered business enterprises (arms repair, shoemaking, small industries), enacted land redistribution programs, levied taxes, and implemented a legal system. By educating the rural residents, providing them health care, improving their economic status, and protecting them from the arbitrary attacks of Batista's Rural Guard, Castro and his followers gained increased legitimacy from the populace and thereby further weakened the Batista government.[5]

## The Strength of Ideological Commitment

When the political and economic situation deteriorated during the late 1950s, Batista's legitimacy waned. As in the typical industrial bureaucratic-authoritarian system, he justified his right to rule on the achievement of political order and economic payoffs. Government policies, however, failed to attain these goals. Partly because of police brutality, arbitrary arrests, and the inconsistent use of repression, violence and disorder increased. By 1958 not only the rural areas but also the cities experienced growing disorder. Guerrillas won victories in the Sierra Maestra. Sabotage and general strikes plagued the cities. During 1958 economic performance also declined. Real wages as a percentage of domestic national income declined. Particularly in the rural areas, unemployment, bad housing, and unhealthy living conditions prevailed. For most citizens, corruption seemed the most effective way to improve their economic status. Yet the wealthy, rather than the unorganized poor, seemed to benefit from the corrupt practices. Operating a bureaucratic-authoritarian system that provided few concrete benefits, Batista also failed to develop a strong commitment to a moral cause that would rally the population behind his administration. Thus neither material nor moral legitimacy enabled him to overcome the challenge posed by Fidel Castro.

Unlike the Vietnamese Communists, who adapted Marxism-Leninism to their national conditions, Castro never articulated such a comprehensive, systematic ideology to gain power. Instead, national populism, not Marxism-Leninism, helped mobilize his following. As a charismatic figure, a revolutionary Robin Hood, he promised to deliver the Cuban masses from the evils of the Batista regime—graft, corruption, economic inequality, gambling, prostitution, and the general urban decadence associated with the Havana elite. Rather than stressing the need for socialist economic policies and politico-economic independence from the United States, Castro appealed for support on a populist program that echoed the same themes voiced by nineteenth-century poet and journalist José Martí. These moral values included racial equality, honest government, and social justice for the poor. Stressing a more equal distribution of goods and services, Castro secured material legitimacy when he pledged land to the squatters, health care to the sick, educational opportunities to the illiterate, and decent housing for the homeless. This populist platform enabled Castro and his Rebel Army to gain a multiclass backing, which brought about the downfall of the Batista regime.[6] As in Vietnam, a revolutionary mobilization system supplanted the discredited bureaucratic-authoritarian system.

## The Revolutionaries in Power

The elitist mobilization system installed on January 1, 1959, instituted several changes in Cuban society. Changes occurred in the dominant beliefs, social stratification patterns, political organization, and public policies that had prevailed under Batista. Over the twenty-year period between 1960 and 1980, the style of decision-making also altered, as the mobilization system became more bureaucratized during the 1970s. From the cultural perspective, this change toward an "institutionalized," bureaucratic order involved a shift from egalitarian values and moral incentives toward a stress on more elitist values and material incentives. Structurally, the charismatic authority of Castro declined, while institutional authority became more prominent. During the 1970s the Cuban Communist party, the professionalized army (the Revolutionary Armed Forces), government agencies, and unions strengthened their power. Whereas in the late 1960s the army and mass associations like the Committees for the Defense of the Revolution performed general tasks, the 1970s saw greater specialization of functions; the army, government civil service, and party each performed a different function. Consistent with these trends in beliefs and structures, changes in the public policy process focused on the need to stimulate economic production. Placing less emphasis on an equal distribution of goods, policymakers urged greater attention to economic efficiency and increased production. Highly educated professionals—managers, supervisors, technicians, experts, specialists—gained greater control over political and economic decision-making. Faced with continuing U.S. government hostility, the Castro regime in the 1970s became more dependent on the Soviet Union to supply economic credits, technical assistance, machinery, industrial supplies, oil, and consumer goods.[7]

## Changes in Political Beliefs

For the last thirty years, Castro has worked to transform Cubans' political beliefs from those associated with the individualist, consumer-oriented culture of the United States to those of a collectivist, socialist value system. Equating individualism with capitalist selfishness, he wants the "new socialist person" to express collective virtues: altruism, cooperation, austerity, sacrifice, discipline, loyalty to the national regime, and a strong commitment to "socialist internationalism." Both freedom and equality assume collectivist interpretations. For Castro, Cuba's national freedom from U.S. domination and the right of workers and peasants to free themselves from class exploitation take precedence over individual civil liberties. According to him, the Cuban media must serve the Revolution, not air the views of dissidents. Giving voters a free choice in elections becomes less important than establishing "organs of people's power" that provide the masses opportunity to participate in political life. Although upholding greater socioeconomic equality, especially for rural people, workers, and women, Castro shows less sympathy for political equality. He assumes that the Cuban Communist party and its leadership will exercise dominant power over the political process. Even though Castro repudiates popular checks on political decision-making by either competitive elections or independent mass media, he still maintains that the Cuban revolution acts for the people, if not by them. According to his interpretation, democracy means that the people feel a part of state power.

Castro's socialist ideology has blended moral values with material benefits. Influenced by Ernesto "Che" Guevara, Castro during the 1960s placed greater emphasis on moral incentives as a way to stimulate production. Those citizens who worked hard, showed high rates of labor productivity, cooperated to increase community output, and behaved altruistically received approval from the government. By emulating the socialist example of Fidel Castro, they earned special praise—for example, the title of Hero of Labor, Hero of Moncada, or Heroic Guerrilla. During this period, nearly all workers, regardless of their output, received equal wages; only narrow income differences separated the workers. However great the idealistic intentions of this campaign to create a new socialist person, the economic consequences of stressing moral incentives disappointed Castro. Between 1967 and 1970, the gross domestic product declined each year. High rates of absenteeism, combined with low labor productivity, partly accounted for decreasing growth rates. Thus during the early 1970s Castro began placing greater reliance on material incentives as a way to stimulate increased growth. Although workers still received verbal approval, titles, and medals for increasing labor output,

128

workers who fulfilled their quotas on time, expanded their productivity, and improved the quality of their goods received tangible, concrete payoffs: higher wages, better housing, television sets, refrigerators, sewing machines, and vacations at a beach resort. Specialists and technicians also earned higher incomes than did unskilled workers. Against the charge that these material incentives meant the reintroduction of capitalism into Cuba, Castro claimed that his socialist economic policies encouraged Cubans to work for the good of the whole community, not for their private gain as under capitalism.[8]

To what extent have Cuban workers actually internalized the values associated with the "new socialist person"? Empirical studies suggest that not all Cubans have accepted *socialismo*. On the contrary, some have fallen prey to *sociolismo*—the pursuit of self-interest on the job. Neither moral nor material incentives have succeeded in eradicating such behavioral traits as absenteeism, pilfering, corruption, bribery, and negligence. Inefficiency and lack of labor discipline still plague the workplace. Whatever their job performance, most workers interpret socialism in reformist terms. They seek healthier working conditions, higher wages for hazardous work, freedom to transfer from one job to another, nutritious food in the dining hall, more day-care centers, and greater educational opportunities.[9] For the typical Cuban worker, socialism thus entails more equal opportunities and access to concrete benefits, rather than collective ownership of productive resources. A more equal distribution of social benefits takes priority over increased economic production.

### Changes in the Social Stratification System

Although Castro has opposed complete wage equality, his policies have produced a more egalitarian social stratification system than existed under Batista. In particular, blacks, women, and lower-income groups have gained concrete benefits since the revolutionaries came to power. The Castro government has given blacks greater educational opportunities, increased access to schooling, more employment opportunities, higher-status jobs, and the right to visit vacation resorts, beaches, and recreational centers formerly closed to them. Even though blacks are still underrepresented in the top ranks of the army and government, in 1986 they held two seats on the Cuban Communist party Political Bureau and 28 percent of the posts in the party's Central Committee—a proportion equal to their share of the population.

Like blacks, women have secured greater socioeconomic and political power. During the 1970s women moved into more varied occupations, such as office work, administration, education, health care, geology, light industry, and day-care centers. By 1985 women made up 37 percent of the labor force. They also obtained more educational opportunities; during the early 1980s nearly one-half the postsecondary student population included women. A Family Code passed in 1974 asserted that both men and women must equally share responsibility for rearing children and handling household chores, even though Castro himself admits that most Cuban men still hold patriarchal attitudes toward a woman's role at home. Women have also gained more access to political power. In 1985 they comprised more than two-fifths the *militantes* of the Union of Communist Youth, about half the base leaders of the Committees for the Defense of the Revolution, and around one-fifth the total membership of the party, the Central Committee, and the National Assembly. Despite these advances, women still occupy few top leadership roles in government ministries and the Cuban Communist party, especially the Political Bureau and Secretariat.[10]

The public policies of the revolutionary government have also extended equality to economic groups. Between 1959 and 1978 the economic stratification system became more equal than under the Batista regime. Whereas in 1953 the poorest 20 percent of the population received about 2 percent of the national income, twenty-five years later that figure rose to 11 percent. In 1953 the wealthiest fifth of Cubans obtained 60 percent of the Cuban income; however, by 1978 their share of the national income had fallen to 36 percent. Wage equality increased. Public policies authorized free social services (education, health, pensions), low rents, inexpensive housing, and subsidized meals at schools and workplaces. All these benefits raised poor people's incomes.[11]

Although the revolutionary government destroyed the Cuban capitalist class, a new bureaucratic class has gained power. Operating the state socialist economy, government bureaucrats, party cadres, technicians, supervisors, and managers now control access to the means of production. Although still committed to income equality, they instituted during the early 1970s a more elitist stratification system than had prevailed in the late 1960s. Whereas during the late 1960s neither the quality nor the quantity of labor output determined a person's wages, the next decade saw a greater reliance on material incentives to stimulate economic productivity. Individuals who produced the most goods, performed high-quality workmanship, contributed overtime labor, fulfilled the greatest responsibilities, attended adult education classes, and engaged in voluntary work earned the highest wages. The party-state elite secured several fringe benefits: housing, an automobile, travel/vacation opportunities, consumer goods unavailable through the ration system, and special hospital care. Few farmers or factory workers held positions in the National Assembly or top party organs. Instead, the technical-professional elite —

state administrators, technocrats, party leaders, and military officers—dominated these political structures and wielded decisive power over the policy process.

## Changes in Political Organization

The institution of a revolutionary government meant that the armed forces, civil service, and dominant party exercised greater power than under the Batista regime. After Fidel Castro captured government control in early 1959, he began reinforcing the power of the Revolutionary Armed Forces (FAR). Military expenditures in 1958 comprised about 2.3 percent of the gross national product; troops in the regular armed forces, as well as army and naval reserves, included nearly 50,000 men. By 1962 military expenses had risen to 8 percent of the gross national product; around 300,000 troops served in the Revolutionary Armed Forces. FAR officers dominated party organizations and government ministries. For example, in 1965 military officers constituted nearly 60 percent of the members on the Central Committee of the Cuban Communist party—a higher percentage than in the Soviet Union, Vietnam, or China. They headed government ministries, such as Industry, Transportation, Education, and Interior. Besides carrying out professional military duties, the FAR performed other diffuse tasks. They operated various schools, including ones for junior and senior high school students, technical workers, cadets, and high-ranking officers. In the economic sector, the FAR helped harvest the sugarcane, build roads, and construct hydroelectric plants. As an internal security agency, the FAR maintained social control.

During the 1960s both the government bureaucracy and the political party remained weaker than the armed forces. A charismatic political leader, Castro rejected bureaucratic rule. Instead, he and his comrades from the Sierra Maestra guerrilla struggle exercised informal personalized rule. Neither the government civil service nor the party bureaucracy gained extensive power. Whereas Raúl Castro organized the Revolutionary Armed Forces as a successor to the Rebel Army in late 1959, the Cuban Communist party did not form until 1965. Two earlier political organizations—the Integrated Revolutionary Organizations and the United Party of the Socialist Revolution—collapsed before they had the opportunity to consolidate their political functions. Between 1965 and the early 1970s, even the Cuban Communist party played only a limited role in the power structure. Since its membership comprised less than 1 percent of the Cuban population, it could hardly develop close links with the masses; instead, the Committees for the Defense of the Revolution, organized in 1960, assumed the greatest responsibilities for mobilizing the masses.

From 1970 through 1986, a greater balance of political power emerged among the three dominant organizations: the government, the army, and the party. Although the army remained a focal institution, it became more professionalized. In line with growing bureaucratic dominance, its functions were more differentiated from activities performed by the party, government, and other military agencies. Organized by the Ministry of the Armed Forces, the Army of Working Youth mainly helped cut sugarcane. Rather than fight a conventional war, it waged the battle for sugar production. The Territorial Troops Militia served as a citizens' force that mobilized the population for national defense against foreign invaders. Performing largely specialized tasks, the FAR concentrated on fighting overseas wars, such as in Angola and Ethiopia. Signaling a reduced political role for the armed forces, several army officers relinquished their formal military roles and took positions in the government or party. In 1986 around 20 percent of members of the party's Central Committee came from military ranks. Over 90 percent of the military officers belonged to the Cuban Communist party or to its auxiliary organization, the Union of Communist Youth. During the 1970s, the party assumed greater responsibilities. Within the armed forces, it politically educated the troops. It coordinated some government activities. The party directed the mobilizing process carried out by the mass organizations. Including around 5 percent of the population, it became more active in the fields, factories, and schools, mobilizing the masses behind Fidel's latest campaign. The government bureaucracy also strengthened its role in political decision-making. Professionals, administrators, technocrats, and specialists within the civil service retained greater autonomy to implement public policies and manage state enterprises.[12]

The revolutionary takeover in 1959 marked the emergence of a stronger state. As in a typical elitist mobilization system, the central government under Castro's leadership operates in a coercive, centralized, and coordinated fashion. Social groups exert little autonomy from the government or dominant party. Compared with the Batista regime, the Castro government has extended the scope of government power more deeply into economic, educational, and health activities.

Although Fidel Castro has tried to win broader consensual support by making charismatic appeals, extending educational opportunities, improving the health care system, and equalizing income, his rule still rests on a coercive base. From 1960 through 1985, U.S. specialists on Latin America rated the twenty largest Latin American states on their degree of civil liberties: free speech, competitive elections, independent judiciary, civilian supremacy over the military, and freedom to organize political parties. According to these criteria, Cuba ranked sixteenth most repressive in 1960, nineteenth in 1965 and 1970, fourteenth in 1975, twelfth in 1980, and sixteenth in 1985.[13] Throughout this period the government used physical, economic, and ideological (normative) coercion against opponents. Physical coercion included indefinite detention, imprisonment, and execution of political dissidents—those individuals who expressed opposition to the Cuban socialist system, government policies, or Castro's personal rule. Economic coercion also prevailed. Some people who voiced "deviant" political views were fired from a job in a state enterprise. Loyalty to the political regime, rather than economic performance, often determined job promotion. The government sent to a work camp those who engaged in "antisocial" behavior or refused military service, which was compulsory for men between fifteen and twenty-seven years old. As in a typical mobilization system, ideological coercion deterred antiregime actions. People labeled as ideological outcasts included those who refused to work, wanted to leave Cuba for the United States, attacked the socialist state, endangered social order, defamed government leaders, or opposed the revolution. Castro urged manual and intellectual workers, small farmers, students, and soldiers to report the oppositional activities carried out by ideological out-groups— for example, the "lumpen," "scum," *gusanos* (worms), loafers, and parasites. Stationed in each neighborhood, the Committees for the Defense of the Revolution, which included more than four-fifths of the adult Cuban population, played the major role in overseeing everyone's behavior. Dissidents who persisted in their "counterrevolutionary" actions were often sent to a camp for socialist reeducation.

Government decision-making in contemporary Cuba remains highly centralized. Within the top party-state agencies—the Political Bureau and the Secretariat of the Cuban Communist Party, the executive committee of the Council of Ministers, and the Council of State (executive committee of the National Assembly—Fidel Castro, Raúl Castro, and their supporters make the crucial public policies. Through these central organs, they set public goals, allocate national resources, plan the economy, and oversee policy performance. Yet this highly centralized system has created bottlenecks at the local level. Responding to these local pressures, which seek greater resources to resolve problems, Castro has decentralized middle-level and lower-level management. Local managers in state enterprises, along with administrators who work for provincial and municipal government agencies, have gained the power to initiate local projects involving health, education, public transportation, and housing. These administrators can also allocate local resources to projects that they initiate.

As a way to stimulate greater local participation in the policy process, the 1976 Cuban Constitution established "organs of people's power," specifically assemblies at the municipal, provincial, and national government levels. Yet citizens have the right to elect directly only delegates to the municipal assembly, not to the provincial or national legislatures. The municipal assembly operates as an agency of political communication between citizens and their legislators. Citizens complain to municipal delegates about policy implementation—for example, about low-quality bread, shortages of building materials, bad bus service, inconsiderate treatment at health clinics, and inefficient garbage collection, water supplies, and sanitation. All these concrete policy demands revolve around ways to make the existing system work better. In turn, the elected delegates report these complaints to either local government administrators or higher government officials. Finally, the municipal delegates report the decision or nondecision taken by the government bureaucracy to their constituents. Despite this trend toward greater decentralized management, the centralized Cuban Communist party (Partido Comunista de Cuba—PCC) retains supervisory control over operation of the organs of local power. Ultimately responsible to Fidel Castro, the local PCC executive committee oversees the performance of the municipal and provincial governments.[14]

Besides operating a coercive, centralized government, Fidel Castro administers a highly coordinated government. Yet in contrast to Vietnam, where the Communist party under collective leadership coordinates government decision-making, in Cuba coordination reflects more personalized rule. Today, Fidel Castro, Raúl Castro, educated professionals, and members of the July 26 guerrilla movement (the group led by Fidel that attacked the Moncada army barracks on July 26, 1953) dominate the top party-state central organizations. For example, Fidel Castro is first secretary of the Central Committee of the Communist Party of Cuba, President of the Council of Ministers, President of the Council of State, and Commander-in-Chief of the Revolutionary Armed Forces. He also oversees such government ministries as armed forces, interior (police, internal security), public health, and culture. Raúl is second secretary of the PCC, vice president of the Council of Ministers, vice president of the Council of State, General of the Army, and minister of the Revolutionary Armed Forces. Young professionals—managers, supervisors, technicians—along with the Castro brothers' guerrilla comrades, direct the remaining government and party organs. As the supreme coordinator of government activities, Fidel Castro controls the Cuban Communist party and the central ministries. The party supervises the mass associations and government bureaucracy. Yet the personal power wielded by Castro seems greater than the control exerted by the impersonal party organization. The *comandante en jefe* and leader of the revolution, Castro arbitrates disputes among competing elite factions and tries to steer the society toward socialism.[15]

As in the typical elitist mobilization system, Castro's revolutionary government allows few social groups to function independently from the state. In line with the revolutionary socialist ideology, the class struggle takes precedence over the racial struggle. Government officials discourage Afro-Cuban writers from expressing their ideas about race relations in Cuba. Black solidarity organizations have no freedom to press their demands. Religious groups enjoy few civil liberties. True, all churches, except the Jehovah's Witnesses, can freely conduct worship services. Catholic and Protestant seminaries still continue their religious education. Ministers within the Cuban Ecumenical Council—mainly Reformed Presbyterians, Methodists, and Free Baptists—have the freedom to travel overseas. Yet viewing religion as a private concern, government officials deny churches the freedom to publish their own print media, to proselytize new members, and to criticize the state, the Communist party, and the Revolution. No practicing Christian may hold membership in the Cuban Communist party or the Union of Communist Youth. Economic groups also lack the autonomous power to express their civil liberties.

Rather than encourage spontaneous voluntary political participation, the Cuban revolutionary government mobilizes all social groups toward objectives determined by the elite. Political mobilization takes several forms. At mass rallies, demonstrations, and "people's marches," Cubans shout slogans, express their support for the Castro government, and listen to him deliver lengthy orations. Socialist emulation campaigns strive to induce Cuban students and workers to follow the example set by Fidel and Che Guevara. Since 1959 the government has staged quasi-military campaigns to defend the fatherland, promote economic development, and improve social services. In 1961 the government mobilized the Cuban masses against the Bay of Pigs military invasion conducted by Cuban exiles and the U.S. government. During 1960 and 1961 a mass education drive reduced the illiteracy rate from 20 percent to only 4 percent. In 1970 Castro tried but failed to mobilize the whole Cuban population to produce a ten-million-ton sugar harvest.

Mass associations controlled by Cuban Communist party leaders play a crucial mobilizational role in leading these campaigns. The Federation of Cuban Women, headed by Vilma Espín, the wife of Raúl Castro, organizes women's participation. The National Association of Small Farmers (ANAP), the Confederation of Cuban Workers (CTC), and the National Union of Cuban Writers and Artists (UNEAC) mobilize diverse economic groups. ANAP promotes expanded food production. Even

135

though CTC unions have some power within a factory to participate in economic planning, restrain the arbitary decisions of state enterprise managers, and persuade party leaders to dismiss a manager, unions remain subordinate to party and state leadership. They concentrate on increasing production and on educating workers about ways to raise labor output. State officials hire and fire all managers. Party *militantes* offer general guidance about factory operations. The UNEAC keeps watch over writers and artists to ensure that they "serve the revolution." The largest mass associations, the Committees for the Defense of the Revolution, operate at the local neighborhood level; they perform comprehensive activities such as crime reduction, political surveillance, education, health care, housing construction, and harvesting of the sugar cane.[16]

Pursuing a state socialist policy, the Cuban government today wields a more comprehensive scope of power than under Batista's rule. Around 90 percent of the labor force now works for state enterprises. The government operates all educational institutions except religious seminaries. Public health services have spread to the rural areas. Except in Havana, few doctors maintain a private practice.[17]

### Changes in Public Policies
The major economic policy changes introduced by the Castro government have strengthened state control over the economy and increased economic dependence on the U.S.S.R. Today the state owns most manufacturing and entrepreneurial firms. In the urban areas a small private sector does operate, especially in such services as dentistry, medicine, hairdressing, tailoring, carpentry, plumbing, gardening, auto mechanics, appliance repairs, taxi driving, shoeshining, and ice cream sales. Over half the Cuban people own homes; under 1985 housing law, renters gained the opportunity to purchase their residences. Agriculture includes three sectors. State farms manage around 80 percent of the land, with small private farms (8 percent of land) and agricultural cooperatives (12 percent) forming the remaining fifth. Farmers on individual plots, cooperatives, and state farms receive services such as free health care and subsidized housing, but the state farmers and members of production cooperatives secure more social services and greater access to tractors, combines, irrigation facilities, pesticides, seeds, fertilizers, and low-interest loans. Although in 1980 farmers on private land and cooperatives gained the right to sell a portion of their produce to consumers at free markets, in 1986 Fidel Castro abolished these markets, claiming that they promoted commercialism, speculation, and economic inequalities.[18]

The implementation of state socialist economic policies has led to greater economic dependence on the Soviet Union, especially during the

1970s. Yet this dependence differs somewhat from the type of dependence that Cuba maintained with the United States before 1959. Under Bastista, American corporations owned extensive private property in Cuba; they dominated banks and the electric-power, telephone, railroad, nickel-production, and petroleum-refining industries. These American private investors aimed to maximize their profits, which were remitted to the United States, rather than reinvested in Cuba. By contrast, the U.S.S.R. owns no private means of production in Cuba; state officials, not private investors, bargain with one another. Instead of striving to maximize profits, the Soviet government has sought strategic goals—to maintain an independent Cuban state allied to the Soviet Union. To retain its influence in Cuba, Soviet officials have extended interest-free loans, supplied cheap oil imports, offered a guaranteed market for Cuban sugar, and since 1973 purchased its sugar at prices above the world market price. Despite these favorable economic tradeoffs for Cuba, reliance on the Soviet Union has made Cuba vulnerable to Soviet economic coercion. If Fidel Castro fails to accept Soviet policies, then he risks having the U.S.S.R. government delay oil shipments, refuse to import sugar, or reduce technical credits.[19]

What impacts have state control and reliance on the Soviet Union exerted on such economic variables as growth, inflation, unemployment, and income distribution? The Cuban government has faced the greatest difficulties realizing consistently high economic growth between 1961 and 1985. During the latter 1960s, economic growth sharply declined from its 1961–1965 performance. Although rapid growth occurred in the early 1970s, it fell during the second half of that decade. From 1981 through 1985, the growth rate once again accelerated. Several factors explain the failure of the growth rate to match Cuban leaders' expectations. The continued U.S. embargo on trade with Cuba lessened the availability of hard currency, raw materials, spare parts, and technical innovations. Declining credits from Western Europe impeded the purchase of industrial and agricultural inputs from Western suppliers. Often the industrial technology imported from the Soviet Union proved inefficient. Most important, falling world market prices for sugar from 1976 to 1979 lowered the growth rate. Organizational problems, such as low worker productivity, absenteeism, and managerial bureaucratism impeded efficient economic performance. The diversion of resources from domestic capital goods to military expenditures, which ranged between 7.8 percent and 9.8 percent of the gross domestic product from 1977 through 1984, also hindered the expansion of economic output.

Between 1960 and 1980 Cuban inflation rates showed an inverse relationship with growth rates. When growth declined during the late

1960s, prices rose. In the 1970s, especially 1971 to 1975, Cubans experienced the highest growth and lowest inflation. Price controls and rationing represented the primary policies for restraining price increases. Cubans received free health care; they did not have to pay directly for rising medical costs. Price controls on rents, foods, and communications/ transportation facilities weakened inflationary pressures on consumer necessities. During the late 1970s consumers purchased more than two-thirds of the total supply of foods such as rice, beef, milk, sugar, bread, and beans through the rationing system. State ministries also set the prices of goods purchased in "parallel markets," where a product cost less than a similar item sold on the black market but more than inexpensive rationed goods. Despite these government efforts to curb price increases, high aggregate demand combined with low supplies produced surging inflation during the late 1960s. The same supply problems that caused low growth aggravated inflationary pressures. By standardizing wages, implementing full employment, and providing some free services (health care, education, public phones), the government expanded consumers' incomes. However, the production of consumer goods occurred at a slower rate than the rise in potential aggregate demand. The embargo placed by the United States on trade with Cuba meant that Cuban firms could no longer obtain the spare parts and advanced technology needed to operate an efficient economy. Often machinery imported from the U.S.S.R. was inappropriate or obsolete; thus production of consumer goods lagged. Faced with rising prices, the Castro government in the early 1970s took actions to expand supply and reduce aggregate demand. By importing consumer goods from Japan, securing technical credits from the Soviet bloc, and gearing wages to labor productivity, Cuban policymakers tried to increase production. Although price controls remained on medicines, clothing, and some foods, the state lifted controls from other consumer goods, such as cigarettes, tobacco, restaurant meals, television sets, radios, cameras, and refrigerators. The abolition of some price controls lowered aggregate demand but raised the prices of decontrolled products. Like other Third World governments, the Cuban administration could not easily devise appropriate economic policies that would maintain low inflation rates; during the 1980s inflation became a more severe problem.

As a revolutionary Robin Hood, Fidel Castro scored his greatest victories in lowering unemployment and creating a more egalitarian society. During the Batista regime unemployment ranged between 7 percent and 20 percent of the labor force; however, under Castro the jobless rate fell to around 1 percent in 1970. It ranged between 3 percent and 5 percent from 1972 through 1981. Although workers lacked the full freedom to choose the job they desired, the state did guarantee employment opportunities to all who sought work. In particular, people in the sugar industry who once worked only six months a year gained yearlong jobs on state farms. From 1965 to 1984 the industrial growth rate averaged around 6 percent a year. Whereas in 1960 22 percent of the labor force worked in industry, by 1981 that proportion had increased to 31 percent—a higher share than in any other Latin American country except Uruguay, Argentina, and Trinidad-Tobago. The expansion of steel, machinery, electrical equipment, electronics, metal products, and tire manufacturing industries created jobs for skilled factory workers. Government agencies providing social services (education, health care, housing, social security) employed large staffs. Teachers, construction workers, technicians, and medical personnel served in Cuba's overseas programs in Nicaragua, Angola, Mozambique, Ethiopia, Somalia, Tanzania, Guinea, South Yemen, Libya, and Vietnam. The private service sector provided employment to those entrepreneurial Cubans unwilling to work in the state enterprises, government bureaucracies, or overseas programs.

Several government policies took wealth from the rich and distributed it to the poor. The ban on U.S. private investment prevented American corporate executives from remitting profits on their Cuban enterprises back to the United States. By eliminating the gambling and prostitution industries in Havana, the government uprooted the economic power of organized crime. Cuban real estate speculators who made huge profits from land sales no longer enjoy this opportunity to gain wealth. Along with higher wage increases for agricultural workers, the greater employment opportunities, schooling, and housing allocated to the rural population brought more equality between the cities and the countryside.[20]

Like economic policies, the education policies pursued by the Cuban government express a commitment to securing mass equality through mobilizing the population. Various types of schools provide a mass education. The government expanded the number of primary schools, especially those in the rural areas. Junior high and senior high youths attended *escuelas en el campo* (schools in the countryside). At these boarding schools, students combined formal classroom learning with work experience on farms, spending one-half the day in school and the remaining time at farm work. The growth of educational enrollments at technical secondary institutes and universities gave low-income youths greater opportunities to secure a higher education. Older men and women benefited from the adult education programs. Several mobilizing agencies, especially the Committees for the Defense of the Revolution, have organized mass educational campaigns. Assisted by the Federation of Cuban Women, the CDRs led the drive in 1961 to reduce illiteracy.

Going to the rural areas, "people's teachers," *brigadistas* (student volunteers organized in micro-brigades), workers in the Patria o Muerte Brigade, and trained educators spearheaded the drive to upgrade the literacy rate. After the anti-illiteracy campaign ended in 1962, the CDRs continued to promote school attendance in their neighborhoods. Within the schools, youth organizations—the José Martí Pioneer Organization for primary school students, the Federation of Students of Intermediate Education, the Federation of University Students, and the Union of Communist Youth—teach new socialist values and mobilize young people behind the campaigns sponsored by the revolutionary government. The Confederation of Cuban Workers takes charge of politically educating adult workers. In short, these mobilization policies have made education widely available to all segments of the Cuban population.

The Cuban government gives the highest priority to teaching moral values and training students for new occupational roles. According to Fidel Castro, teachers should serve as moral exemplars of the socialist revolution:

> Our teachers must be an example of socialist morality; they must resolutely oppose any deviation from the new set of values created by the Revolution. The teacher must be a permanent student of Marxism-Leninism. He or she must be well informed on national and international events; and must be in the forefront of today's ideological struggle.[21]

In line with this directive, Castro urges teachers to uphold socialist morality, educational excellence, and the revolutionary politics of the Cuban Communist party. As a vanguard group, schoolteachers must impart such values as punctuality, discipline, love of work, selflessness, modesty, and collective responsibility. Through participation in flag salutes, cults of national heroes, socialist emulation campaigns, and revolutionary sociodramas, children are supposed to learn these normative beliefs. As each schoolday opens, youths salute the Cuban flag and sing such songs as "Los niños socialistas marchamos a la paz." Taking Che Guevara as their moral exemplar, they pledge: "We shall be like Che." Young Pioneers engage in "socialist emulation" campaigns in which they compete with one another to demonstrate such virtues as punctuality, good study habits, care for school property, productive labor, and hygienic behavior. Each year, on July 26, some Young Pioneers take part in a revolutionary sociodrama in which they reenact the assault on the Moncada army barracks, an event in 1953 that marked the beginning of the armed struggle to overthrow the Batista regime.

The Cuban schools not only teach revolutionary values but also prepare youth for future occupational roles. The worker—one who has united mental with physical labor—represents the ideal role. The secondary school curriculum concentrates on mathematics, physics, chemistry, and biology. At polytechnical institutes, universities, and such elite pre-university schools as the Lenin school in Havana, courses stress training for technical/professional workers: scientists, technicians, managers, engineers, doctors, teachers, economists, and accountants.

Compared with the normative and role-allocation tasks of the schools, the cognitive development function assumes less importance. The heavy political content of the curriculum—the emphasis on loyalty to the revolution, obedience to the socialist cause, and commitment to Fidel's campaigns—hinders free inquiry in the Cuban schools. Rote learning, high scores on written examinations, and the attainment of superior course grades take precedence over abstract thinking, creative problem-solving, and critical examination of political issues.[22]

Public health programs blend the professional approach with a populist orientation that mobilizes the local community behind more egalitarian goals. Health equality signifies expanded access to medical facilities as well as the recruitment of health personnel from a broader segment of the population. Since the revolutionaries assumed power in 1959, the government has focused on recruiting more doctors who are women, blacks (Afro-Cubans), and persons from working-class and rural backgrounds. The promotion of equal access to health care has involved expanding medical facilities in the rural areas. Doctors who recently graduated from medical school have the obligation to practice at least two or three years in rural health centers. Sanitary brigades of nurses help physicians and mass associations improve rural hygiene. Although health planning takes place at the central government level in the Ministry of Public Health, the actual administration of health policies is decentralized. Physicians working in community health centers—the polyclinics—retain considerable autonomy. At each polyclinic, specialists in pediatrics, obstetrics-gynecology, internal medicine, and dentistry treat patients. Besides these polyclinics, other health facilities—child health clinics, maternity hospitals, nutritional rehabilitation centers—enable doctors to make medical care more accessible to the Cuban population. In 1985 the government instituted the family physician program, which serves people in their neighborhoods, workplaces, and schools. Under this program, the polyclinics provide technical training, laboratory assistance, and consultation with medical specialists. At the local level, public health commissioners coordinate the activities of physicians as well as the members of the mass associations involved in health-care programs.

Nearly every mass organization becomes mobilized behind a public health campaign. The Committees for the Defense of the Revolution administer polio vaccinations, organize blood donations, and encourage mothers and their children to make regular visits to their neighborhood polyclinic. Sanitary brigades of the Federation of Cuban Women provide cancer smears, fumigate against mosquitoes, promote family nutrition, and conduct health discussions. The Confederation of Cuban Workers organizes first-aid stations in factories. The National Association of Small Farmers helps treat animal diseases. Youth groups such as the Pioneer Organization and the Union of Communist Youth lead public hygiene campaigns.

Partly as a result of these mass mobilization activities, life expectancy has risen and infant mortality has fallen, especially since the early 1970s. Because housing, sanitation, water, and nutrition have improved, the incidence of malaria, tuberculosis, polio, typhoid fever, dysentery, and venereal diseases has fallen. Nearly all babies are born in a hospital; mothers receive extensive prenatal and postnatal medical care. The government grants them a six-week leave from work before the child's birth and a twelve-week leave after its birth. For these reasons, Cuba has achieved the lowest infant mortality and highest life expectancy rates in Latin America. In 1985, for every 1000 live births, 15 infants died before age one. Average life expectancy at birth reached 74 years.[23]

In conclusion, the way that Castro and his comrades have handled the basic issues in the policy process reflects the change toward a more institutionalized elitist mobilization system during the 1970s and 1980s. Castro fuses voluntarism with determinism. At mass rallies, he closes each speech with this moral imperative: "Patria o Muerte. Venceremos." ("Fatherland or Death. We shall overcome".) According to this view, revolution means that personal will guides political action in all efforts to overcome obstacles. Yet during the early 1970s, Castro toned down this idealist, subjectivist orientation, claiming that the revolutionary leadership must also become more sensitized to the objective politico-economic conditions limiting rapid economic development—conditions such as the shifting world market prices for sugar, a lack of advanced technology, and dependence on the Soviet Union for economic assistance and military hardware. Faced with continuing opposition of the U.S. government to state socialist policies, Cuba in the 1970s came under greater Soviet influence. As the revolution became more institutionalized, Castro placed greater stress on political organization, rather than personal will, as the major way to attain a socialist society. When economic conditions deteriorated during the mid-1980s because of reduced Soviet subsidies, lower foreign exchange earnings, and supply shortages, Castro reasserted a more voluntarist policy position. Rather than decentralize the economy and institute more market mechanisms, as did the Vietnamese

Communists, he proclaimed the need for political education, ideological renewal, rectification of errors, and revolutionary will as ways to overcome Cuba's objective problems. Moral values—altruism, courage, hard work, thrift, austerity, honesty—assumed priority over material incentives, commercialism, private trade, and the profit motive. According to Castro, the Cuban Communist party, which he regarded as the vanguard force, the "soul of the Cuban Revolution," had to take the initiative in mobilizing the population behind the battle against economic adversity.[24]

Beginning in the 1970s the dominant organizations came to perform differentiated activities superseding the more spontaneous, ad hoc style of decision-making that had pervaded the previous decade. Today the Cuban Communist party formulates general policies, which government agencies staffed by educated professionals then implement. CTC unions have gained more financial resources, greater autonomy from state enterprise managers, and expanded opportunities to participate in a factory's economic planning.

Both a conflict orientation and a focus on consensus pervade the policy process. Conflict with certain out-groups or enemies—the U.S. imperialists, the *gusanos*, the counterrevolutionaries, the lumpen bourgeoisie, and the parasites—becomes a way to mobilize solidarity among the workers, small farmers, students, and compañeros.[25] Consensus rests less on a faith in a systematic, comprehensive Marxist-Leninist ideology than on a personal commitment to emulate the examples of Fidel Castro, Che Guevara, Camilo Cienfuegos, and Celia Sánchez. Personal loyalty to Fidel, not ideological mystique, supplies solidarity to the Cuban policy process.

Finally, Fidel Castro has focused on change, not continuity, as the central feature of the revolutionary experience. Through mass mobilization and extensive party-state control, his policies have sought to end Cuban dependence on the United States, eliminate the capitalist sector, industrialize the economy, diversify Cuban exports, and create a more egalitarian social stratification system. He had attained all these goals except export diversification.

Despite this revolutionary orientation, the Cuban policy process does retain some continuity with traditional ways. Like prerevolutionary regimes, the Castro administration remains economically dependent on a foreign power—not the United States but the Soviet Union. As before the revolutionary takeover, the sale of sugar on the world market still supplies the main foreign earnings. Most important, under the Castro regime, as in previous administrations, personal leadership still dominates the policy process. Despite the greater institutional power of the party, government, mass associations, and armed forces, a socialist

143

*caudillo*, Fidel Castro, commands the key party, state, and military organizations. Edward Gonzales points out:

> Fidel is the supreme orator in a country that has traditionally been noted for its addiction to talking and that has always valued the art of rhetoric. . . . He is the dominating *caudillo*, the commanding personality, the national *patrón* in a society that has seen the likes of Machado and Batista and whose social fabric traditionally was held together by strong personal attachments and by patron-client relationships. Cuba has thus not entirely escaped her past in the *fidelista* quest for radical change.[26]

Amid the socioeconomic changes that the elitist mobilization system has brought to Cuba, the personal style of political decision-making hence retains a link with the prerevolutionary traditions.

## Notes

1 In *Cuba under Castro: The Limits of Charisma* (Boston: Houghton Mifflin, 1974), 168–189, Edward Gonzalez calls Castro a "socialist caudillo." David E. Apter, *The Politics of Modernization* (Chicago: University of Chicago Press, 1965), 324–325, refers to Castro as a "Robin Hood" figure.
2 Margaret E. Crahan, "Salvation through Christ or Marx: Religion in Revolutionary Cuba," *Journal of Interamerican Studies and World Affairs* 21 (February 1979): 156–184; Margaret E. Crahan, "Cuba: Religion and Revolutionary Institutionalization," *Journal of Latin American Studies* 17 (November 1985): 319–324; John M. Kirk, "From Counterrevolution to *Modus Vivendi*: The Church in Cuba, 1959–84," in *Cuba: Twenty-Five Years of Revolution, 1959–1984*, ed. Sandor Halebsky and John M. Kirk (New York: Praeger, 1985), 94–96.
3 Johnetta B Cole, "Race toward Equality: The Impact of the Cuban Revolution on Racism," *Black Scholar* 11 (November/December 1980): 2–24; Jorge I. Domínguez, "Racial and Ethnic Relations in the Cuban Armed Forces," *Armed Forces and Society* 2 (February 1976): 273–280; Geoffrey E. Fox, "Race and Class in Contemporary Cuba," in *Cuban Communism*, 3d ed., ed. Irving Louis Horowitz (New Brunswick, N.J.: Transaction Books, 1977), 421–442; Maurice Zeitlin, *Revolutionary Politics and the Cuban Working Class* (Princeton, N.J.: Princeton University Press, 1967), 66–88.
4 Jorge I. Domínguez, *Cuba: Order and Revolution* (Cambridge, Mass.: Harvard University Press, 1978), 54–133, 431–437; George I. Blanksten, "Fidel Castro and Latin America," in *The Revolution in World Politics*, ed. Morton A. Kaplan (New York: Wiley, 1962), 113–136; Maurice Zeitlin, "Cuba: Revolution without a Blueprint," in *Cuban Communism*, 199–210; Zeitlin, *Revolutionary Politics and the Cuban Working Class*, 288; Nelson Amaro Victoria, "Mass and Class in the Origins of the Cuban Revolution," in *Cuban Communism*, 155–185; Bert Useem, "Peasant Involvement in the Cuban Revolution," *Journal of Peasant Studies* 5 (October 1977): 99–111; Louis A. Perez, Jr., "The Pursuit of Pacification: Banditry and the United States' Occupation of Cuba, 1898–1902," *Journal of Latin American Studies* 18 (November 1986): 313–332.

5  See Morris H. Morley, "The U.S. Imperial State in Cuba, 1952–1958: Policy-making and Capitalist Interests," *Journal of Latin American Studies* 14 (May 1982): 143–170; D. E. H. Russell, *Rebellion, Revolution, and Armed Force* (New York: Academic Press, 1974), 16–28, 115–120; Domínguez, *Cuba*, 64–133, esp. 125; Nelson P. Valdés, "Revolution and Institutionalization in Cuba," *Cuban Studies* 6 (January 1976): 1–4; Louis A. Perez, Jr., "Army Politics in Socialist Cuba," *Journal of Latin American Studies* 8 (November 1976): 252–258.

6  Domínguez, *Cuba*, 118–131, 199; Antoni M. Kapcia, "The Cuban Enigma," *Problems of Communism* 29 (January/February 1980): 85; Gonzalez, *Cuba under Castro*, 89–95; Tad Szulc, *Fidel: A Critical Portrait* (New York: William Morrow, 1986), 21–22, 92–94.

7  Valdés, "Revolution and Institutionalization in Cuba," 1–37; Sergio Roca, "Cuban Economic Policy in the 1970s: The Trodden Paths," *Studies in Comparative International Development* 12 (Spring 1977): 86–114; Carmelo Mesa-Lago, "Building Socialism in Cuba: Romantic versus Realistic Approach," *Latin American Perspectives* 3 (Fall 1976): 117–121; Carmelo Mesa-Lago, *Cuba in the 1970s: Pragmatism and Institutionalization*, rev. ed. (Albuquerque: University of New Mexico Press, 1978), 30–61, 112–115.

8  Richard R. Fagen, *The Transformation of Political Culture in Cuba* (Stanford, Calif.: Stanford University Press, 1969), 13, 139–140, 180–222; *Fidel Castro Speaks*, ed. Martin Kenner and James Petras (New York: Grove Press, 1969), 80, 85–87, 308–309; Fidel Castro, *Education in Revolution* (Havana, Cuba: Instituto Cubano del Libro, 1975), 144–147, 175–177; Barbara Walters, "An Interview with Fidel Castro," *Foreign Policy*, no. 28 (Fall 1977): 22–51; *MacNeil/Lehrer News Hour*, "Conversation with Castro: Part II, Touching Old Wounds," Transcript 2447, February 12, 1985, p. 4; Frank T. Fitzgerald, "A Critique of the 'Soviet-ization of Cuba' Thesis," *Science and Society* 42 (Spring 1978): 1–32; Mesa-Lago, *Cuba in the 1970s*, 46–47, 57; Carmelo Mesa-Lago, *The Economy of Socialist Cuba: A Two-Decade Appraisal* (Albuquerque: University of New Mexico Press, 1981), 34; Joel C. Edelstein, "Economic Policy and Development Models," in *Cuba: Twenty-Five Years*, 181–189; Roca, "Cuban Economic Policy in the 1970s," 86–90; Robert M. Bernardo, "Moral Stimulation and Labor Allocation in Cuba," in *Cuban Communism*, 338–371; Jorge F. Pérez-López, "Real Economic Growth in Cuba, 1965–1982," *Journal of Developing Areas* 20 (January 1986): 162.

9  John Womack, Jr., "The Revolution Tightens Its Belt," *New Republic* 182 (May 31, 1980): 19–23; Marifeli Pérez-Stable, "Institutionalization and Workers' Response," *Cuban Studies* 6 (July 1976): 31–54.

10  Domínguez, *Cuba*, 224–227, 494–504; Fox, "Race and Class in Contemporary Cuba," 421–442; *Granma Weekly Review*, March 16, 1980, p. 3; Carollee Bengelsdorf and Alice Hageman, "Emerging from Underdevelopment: Women and Work in Cuba," *Race and Class* 19 (Spring 1978): 361–378; Carollee Bengelsdorf, "On the Problem of Studying Women in Cuba," *Race and Class* 27 (Autumn 1985): 35–50; Nelson Valdés, "The Changing Face of Cuba's Communist Party," *Cuba Update* 7 (Winter/Spring 1986): 1, 4, 7, 16; Brian Latell, "Cuba after the Third Party Congress," *Current History* 85 (December 1986): 426; Isabel Larguía and John Dumoulin, "La mujer en el dessarollo: Estrategia y experiencias de la Revolución Cubana," *Casa de las Américas* 25 (March/April 1985): 37–53; Alfred Padula and Lois Smith, "Women in Socialist Cuba, 1959–84," in *Cuba: Twenty-Five Years*, 79–90; Marvin Leiner, "Cuba's Schools: 25 Years Later," in *Cuba: Twenty-Five Years*, 31.

11 Claes Brundenius, "Cuba: Redistribution and Growth with Equity," in *Cuba: Twenty-Five Years*, 202; Mesa-Lago, *The Economy of Socialist Cuba*, 141–174; Juan M. del Aguila, *Cuba: Dilemmas of a Revolution* (Boulder, Colo.: Westview Press, 1984), 144–145; Nelson P. Valdés, "The Cuban Revolution: Economic Organization and Bureaucracy," *Latin American Perspectives* 6 (Winter 1979): 13–37; David Lehmann, "The Cuban Economy in 1978," *Cambridge Journal of Economics* 3 (September 1979): 319–326; Mesa-Lago, "Building Socialism in Cuba," 117–121; Irving Louis Horowitz, "Authenticity and Autonomy in the Cuban Experience: Toward an Operational Definition of Revolution," *Cuban Studies* 6 (January 1976): 67–74; Victoria, "Mass and Class in the Origins of the Cuban Revolution," 155–156.

12 Perez, "Army Politics in Socialist Cuba," 251–271; Jorge I. Domínguez, "Institutionalization and Civil-Military Relations in Cuba," *Cuban Studies* 6 (January 1976): 39–65; Domínguez, *Cuba*, 341–378, esp. 347; Jorge I. Domínguez, "Revolutionary Politics: The New Demands for Orderliness," in *Cuba: Internal and International Affairs*, ed. Jorge I. Domínguez (Beverly Hills, Calif.: Sage Publications, 1982), 22–25, 53–59; Mesa-Lago, *Cuba in the 1970s*, 67–68; William M. LeoGrande, "The Communist Party of Cuba since the First Congress," *Journal of Latin American Studies* 12, no. 2 (1980): 397–419, esp. 414; William M. LeoGrande, "Continuity and Change in the Cuban Political Elite," *Cuban Studies* 8 (July 1978): 1–31; William M. LeoGrande, "Civil-Military Relations in Cuba: Party Control and Political Socialization," *Studies in Comparative Communism* 11 (Autumn 1978): 278–291; William M. LeoGrande, "Party Development in Revolutionary Cuba," *Journal of Interamerican Studies and World Affairs* 21 (November 1979): 457–480; Edward Gonzalez, "Political Succession in Cuba," *Studies in Comparative Communism* 9 (Spring/Summer 1976): 80–107; Stockholm International Peace Research Institute, *World Armaments and Disarmament: SIPRI Yearbook 1985* (London: Taylor and Francis, 1985), 284; Juan del Aguila, "Political Developments in Cuba," *Current History* 85 (January 1986): 14; Valdés, "The Changing Face of Cuba's Communist Party," 16.

13 *Statistical Abstract of Latin America*, vol. 25, ed. James W. Wilkie and David Lorey (Los Angeles: University of California at Los Angeles Latin American Center Publications, 1987), 179; *Amnesty International Report 1986* (London: Amnesty International Publications, 1986), 143–146; Aryeh Neier, "Castro's Victims," *New York Review of Books* 33 (July 17, 1986): 28–31.

14 Archibald R. M. Ritter, "The Organs of People's Power and the Communist Party: The Nature of Cuban Democracy," in *Cuba: Twenty-Five Years*, 270–290; Rhoda Pearl Rabkin, *Cuban Socialism: A Case Study of Marxist Theory in Practice* (Ph.D. dissertation, Department of Government, Harvard University, 1982), 162–163; Edward Gonzalez, "The Party Congress and *Poder Popular*: Orthodoxy, Democratization, and the Leader's Dominance," *Cuban Studies* 6 (July 1976): 1–14; William M. LeoGrande, "The Theory and Practice of Socialist Democracy in Cuba: Mechanisms of Elite Accountability," *Studies in Comparative Communism* 12 (Spring 1979): 39–62; Max Azicri, "The Institutionalization of the Cuban State: A Political Perspective," *Journal of Interamerican Studies and World Affairs* 22 (August 1980): 315–344; Ernesto E. Rodríguez, "Public Opinion and the Press in Cuba," *Cuban Studies* 8 (July 1978): 51–65.

15 Azicri, "The Institutionalization of the Cuban State," 315–321, 326–341; Leo Grande, "Continuity and Change in the Cuban Political Elite," 1–31; Mesa-Lago, *Cuba in the 1970s*, 79–80; *Latin America Weekly Report*, January 18, 1980,

146

p. 2; Edward Gonzalez, "Complexities of Cuban Foreign Policy," *Problems of Communism* 26 (November/December 1977): 7; Domínguez, "Revolutionary Politics," 19–66; Frank Thomas Fitzgerald, *Politics and Social Structure in Revolutionary Cuba: From the Demise of the Old Middle Class to the Rise of the New Professionals* (Ph.D. dissertation, Department of Sociology, State University of New York at Binghamton, 1985); W. Raymond Duncan, "Castro and Gorbachëv: Politics of Accommodation," *Problems of Communism* 35 (March/April) 1986): 52.

16 Rhoda Peal Rabkin, "Cuban Political Structure: Vanguard Party and the Masses," in *Cuba: Twenty-Five Years*, 251–267; Marifeli Pérez-Stable, "Class, Organization, and *Conciencia*: The Cuban Working Class after 1970," in *Cuba: Twenty-Five Years*, 291–303; Pérez-Stable, "Institutionalization and Workers' Response," 31–54; Linda Fuller, "Changes in the Relationship among the Unions, Administration, and the Party at the Cuban Workplace, 1959–1982," *Latin American Perspectives* 13 (Spring 1986): 6–32; Domínguez, *Cuba*, 225, 260–305, 410–413; Domínguez, "Revolutionary Politics," 50–52; LeoGrande, "Theory and Practice of Socialist Democracy in Cuba," 39–62; Kapcia, "The Cuban Enigma," 80–86; James M. Wall, "Worshipping God in a Communist State," *Christian Century* 97 (April 29, 1981): 467–469; Crahan, "Cuba: Religion and Revolutionary Institutionalization," 332–340; Caleb Rosado, *Sect and Party: Religion under Revolution in Cuba* (Ph.D. dissertation, Department of Sociology, Northwestern University, 1985), esp. 255–336; Kirk, "From Counterrevolution to *Modus Vivendi*," 93–111; *Granma Weekly Review*, May 11, 1980, p. 3; del Aguila, *Cuba*, 154–159.

17 Domínguez, *Cuba*, 136–139; Mesa-Lago, *Cuba in the 1970s*, 94.

18 Nancy Forster, "Cuban Agricultural Productivity: A Comparison of State and Private Farm Sectors," *Cuban Studies* 11 (July 1981–January 1982): 105–125; David Lehmann, "Smallholding Agriculture in Revolutionary Cuba: A Case of Under-Exploitation?" *Development and Change* 16 (April 1985): 251–270; Lehmann, "The Cuban Economy in 1978," 319–326; Carmelo Mesa-Lago, "Farm Payment Systems in Socialist Cuba," *Studies in Comparative Communism* 9 (Autumn 1976): 275–284; *Cuba Update* 1 (September 1980): 1–2; *Latin America Weekly Report*, July 18, 1980, p. 7; Medea Benjamin, Joseph Collins, and Michael Scott, *No Free Lunch: Food and Revolution in Cuba Today*, rev. ed. (New York: Grove Press, 1986), 168–187.

19 Susan Eckstein, "Capitalist Constraints on Cuban Socialist Development," *Comparative Politics* 12 (April 1980): 253–274; William M. LeoGrande, "Cuban Dependency: A Comparison of Pre-Revolutionary and Post-Revolutionary International Economic Relations," *Cuban Studies* 9 (July 1979): 1–28; Kosmas Tsokhas, "The Political Economy of Cuban Dependence on the Soviet Union," *Theory and Society* 9 (March 1980): 319–362; Richard Turits, "Trade, Debt, and the Cuban Economy," *World Development* 15 (January 1987): 163–180.

20 Brundenius, "Cuba: Redistribution and Growth with Equity," 193–210; Claes Brundenius, "Growth with Equity: The Cuban Experience (1959–1980)," *World Development* 9 (November/December 1981): 1083–1096; Claes Brundenius, "Some Notes on the Development of the Cuban Labor Force, 1970–80," *Cuban Studies* 13 (Summer 1983): 65–77; Mesa-Lago, *The Economy of Socialist Cuba*, 7–53, 109–198; Carmelo Mesa-Lago, "The Economy: Caution, Frugality, and Resilient Ideology," in *Cuba: Internal and International Affairs*, 113–161; Carmelo Mesa-Lago and Jorge Pérez-López, *A Study of Cuba's Material Product System, Its*

*Conversion to the System of National Accounts, and Estimation of Gross Domestic Product per Capita and Growth Rates,* World Bank Staff Working Papers 770 (Washington, D.C.: World Bank, 1985), 46–73; Jorge Péréz-López, "Cuban Economy in the 1980's," *Problems of Communism* 35 (September/October 1986): 16–34; Pérez-López, "Real Economic Growth in Cuba," 151–172; Andrew Zimbalist, "Editor's Introduction: Cuba's Socialist Economy toward the 1990s," *World Development* 15 (January 1987): 1–4; Andrew Zimbalist and Susan Eckstein, "Patterns of Cuban Development: The First Twenty-Five Years," *World Development* 15 (January 1987): 5–22; Andrew Zimbalist, "Cuban Industrial Growth, 1965–84," *World Development* 15 (January 1987): 91; Gordon White, "Cuban Planning in the Mid-1980s: Centralization, Decentralization, and Participation," *World Development* 15 (January 1987): 153–161; Andrew Zimbalist, "Cuban Economic Planning: Organization and Performance," in *Cuba: Twenty-Five Years,* 213–227; Edelstein, "Economic Policy and Development Models," 177–192; Domínguez, *Cuba,* 173–184, 227–229; Tsokhas, "The Political Economy of Cuban Dependence on the Soviet Union," 319–362; Lehmann, "The Cuban Economy in 1978," 319–326; Michael S. Lewis-Beck, "Some Economic Effects of Revolution: Models, Measurement, and the Cuban Evidence," *American Journal of Sociology* 84 (March 1979): 1127–1149; Joseph A. Kahl, "Cuban Paradox: Stratified Equality," in *Cuban Communism,* 241–264; Susan Eckstein, "The Debourgeoisement of Cuban Cities," in *Cuban Communism,* 443–474; Susan Eckstein, "The Impact of Revolution on Social Welfare in Latin America," *Theory and Society* 11 (January 1982): 43–94; Susan Eckstein, "Structural and Ideological Bases of Cuba's Overseas Programs," *Politics and Society* 11, no. 1 (1982): 95–121; Susan Eckstein, "The Impact of the Cuban Revolution: A Comparative Perspective," *Comparative Studies in Society and History* 28 (July 1986): 502–534; World Bank, *World Development Report 1984* (New York: Oxford University Press, 1984), 259; World Bank, *World Development Report 1985* (New York: Oxford University Press, 1985), 215; World Bank, *World Development Report 1986* (New York: Oxford University Press, 1986), 239; *World Armaments and Disarmament: SIPRI Yearbook 1986* (New York: Oxford University Press, 1986), 246.

21 *Granma Weekly Review,* July 19, 1981, p. 2.

22 Fidel Castro, "Discurso pronunciado por el comandante en jefe Fidel Castro Ruz, an el acto de graduación de 10 mil 658 egresados del destacamento pedagogico universitario 'Manuel Ascunce Domenech,' el Día 7 de julio de 1981," *Educación: Revista trimestral del Ministerio de Educación* 11 (July–September 1981): 3–16; Marvin Leiner, "Two Decades of Educational Change in Cuba," *Journal of Reading* 25 (November 1981): 202–214; Leiner, "Cuba's Schools," 27–42; Manuel Pastor, "Cuba," *Integrated Education* 20 (November 1983): 9–10; William Messmer, "Cuban Agriculture and Personnel Recruitment Policy," *Studies in Comparative International Development* 19 (Spring 1984): 3–28; Domínguez, *Cuba,* 165–173; Karen Wald, *Children of Che: Childcare and Education in Cuba* (Palo Alto, Calif.: Ramparts Press, 1978), esp. 63–64, 125, 148–159, 185–193, 214, 255, 324, 344–345, 361; Chris Rawlence, "Jo at School in Havana," *New Society* 51 (January 3, 1980): 10–12; Paul Harrison, "Cuba: Qualifying for Tomorrow," *People* 7, no. 2 (1980): 12–13; Jonathan Kozol, "A New Look at the Literacy Campaign in Cuba," *Harvard Educational Review* 48 (August 1978): 341–377; Castro, *Education in Revolution,* 146–147, 171–172; Abel Prieto Morales, "The Literacy Campaign in Cuba," *Harvard Educational Review* 51 (February 1981): 31–39; *Granma Weekly Review,* July 5, 1981, pp. 3–4.

23 Josef Gugler, "'A Minimum of Urbanism and a Maximum of Ruralism': The Cuban Experience," *Studies in Comparative International Development* 15 (Summer 1980): 27–44; Douglas Campos-Outcalt and Edward Janoff, "Health Care in Modern Cuba," *Western Journal of Medicine* 132 (March 1980): 265–271; Richard Garfield, "Nursing, Health Care and Professionalism in Cuba," *Social Science and Medicine* 15A (January 1981): 63–74; Ross Danielson, *Cuban Medicine* (New Brunswick, N.J.: Transaction Books, 1979), 127–211; Ross Danielson, "Medicine in the Community: The Ideology and Substance of Community Medicine in Socialist Cuba," *Social Science and Medicine* 15C (December 1981): 239–247; Ross Danielson, "The Cuban Health Area and Polyclinic: Organizational Focus in an Emerging System," *Inquiry* 12 (June 1975 Supplement): 86–102; Howard Waitzkin, "Health Policy and Social Change: A Comparative History of Chile and Cuba," *Social Problems* 31 (December 1983): 235–248; Sergio Roca, "Cuba Confronts the 1980's," *Current History* 82 (February 1983): 76; Sally Guttmacher and Ross Danielson, "Changes in Cuban Health Care: An Argument against Technological Pessimism," *International Journal of Health Services* 7, no. 3 (1977): 383–400; Philip M. Boffey, "Health Care as a Human Right: A Cuban Perspective," *Science* 200 (June 16, 1978): 1246–1250; Milton I. Roemer, "Health Development and Political Policy: The Lesson of Cuba," *Journal of Health Politics, Policy and Law* 4 (Winter 1980): 570–580; Paul Harrison, "Cuba: Health—Star of the Revolution," *People* 7, no. 2 (1980): 10–11; Eilif Liisberg, Iraj Takibzadeh, and Albert Ezban, "Revolution in Health," *World Health* (April 1975): 14–19; Domínguez, *Cuba*, 184–185, 221–224; Harry Nelson, "Cuba's Health Care Reaches Its People," *Los Angeles Times*, June 16, 1980, pp. 1, 3, 20, 21, 22; *Granma Weekly Review*, June 22, 1980, p. 1; *Statistical Abstract of Latin America*, vol. 20, ed. James W. Wilkie (Los Angeles: University of California at Los Angeles Latin American Center Publications, 1980), 82, 90–91; "Comparative Figures from the Reports of Second and Third Congresses," *Cuba Update* 7 (Winter/Spring 1986): 7; United Nations Children's Fund, *The State of the World's Children 1987* (New York: Oxford University Press, 1987), 128–129; Sarah M. Santana, "The Cuban Health Care System: Responsiveness to Changing Population Needs and Demands," *World Development* 15 (January 1987): 113–125; Jorge Aldereguia Valdes-Brito and Jorge Aldereguia Henriquez, "Health Status of the Cuban Population," *International Journal of Health Services* 13, no. 3 (1983): 479–485; José Gutierrez Muniz, José Camaros Fabian, and José Cobas Manriquez, "The Recent Worldwide Economic Crisis and the Welfare of Children: The Case of Cuba," *World Development* 12 (March 1984): 254. From 1955 through 1958, Cuba had the lowest infant mortality rate and the highest life expectancy in all Latin America, even though data supplied by the Batista government probably underestimated the rural infant mortality rates. During the 1960s the infant mortality rate rose; only by 1971 had the childhood death rate fallen below the 1958 figure. Not until the early 1970s did the Castro government succeed in training enough health specialists and in mobilizing the sufficient community participation needed to raise the level of health care.
24 *Latin American Weekly Report*, January 15, 1987, pp. 10–11; *Granma Weekly Review*, February 1, 1987, pp. 2–4; Szulc, *Fidel*, 19–27, 75–76, 649–653; Tad Szulc, "Cuba: A Run-Down Revolution," *Los Angeles Times*, January 11,

1987, part V, p. 1; David Slater, "Socialism, Democracy and the Territorial Imperative: Elements for a Comparison of the Cuban and Nicaraguan Experiences," *Antipode* 18 (September 1986): 170.

25  Fagen, *The Transformation of Political Culture in Cuba*, 219–220.
26  Gonzalez, *Cuba under Castro*, 11.

# 6

## POLITICAL CHANGE IN CHILE

Chile today is faced with the necessity of finding a new way to build a socialist society — our revolutionary path is the pluralist path, anticipated by the classic theorists of Marxism but which has never before become a concrete fact. . . . We shall have the energy and the capacity to carry our effort forward, to the first socialist society built according to the principles of democracy, plurality, and liberty.

— Salvador Allende

The existence and propagation of Leninist-Marxism in the world today represents the destruction of the basic foundations from which the Western and Christian civilizations derive. . . . Society is under the obligation of drastic self-defense, thus giving birth to new restrictive measures in the exercise of personal liberty or lawful rights, in order to reconcile these with the imperative of security which every community justly demands.

— Augusto Pinochet

As a Latin American nation that attempted revolutionary changes during the mid-twentieth century, Chile shares several similarities with Cuba. Compared with other countries in South America, both nations have attained high rates of social modernization. Like Cuba, Chile is fairly urbanized. More than 90 percent of the people are literate. Individualism, achievement, and social equality have influenced the popular culture. No large Indian groups retain an identification with traditional values.

Despite this relatively high modernity, severe economic inequalities and stagnant economic growth plagued both nations on the eve of the revolutionary effort to transform their social structures. In particular, a deep chasm split the urban from the rural areas. Compared with city residents, those in the countryside experienced greater poverty, more severe economic repression, lower literacy, poorer health, and less adequate housing conditions. Both countries also suffered from slow growth rates. Stagnating production combined with unequal distribution of wealth to exacerbate political tensions.[1]

Determined to overcome these economic crises, leftist political parties and unions played a more important role in both nations than in most other Latin American societies. The Communist parties enjoyed support among the urban working class. Although in Cuba the Popular Socialist party won only 7 percent of the votes to the Cuban legislature in 1948, it formed the best organized party. The Chilean Communist party secured greater electoral support; its popular vote for congressional candidates rose from 10 percent in 1945 to 16 percent in 1969.[2] Outside the legislature, the Communist parties in both countries exercised greater strength, since they dominated key labor unions. To the left of the Communist parties stood political movements that advocated more revolutionary strategies for gaining political power. As we have seen, in Cuba the followers of Fidel Castro and the July 26th movement staged an armed struggle to overthrow the Batista regime. Until Castro's victory seemed imminent in late 1958, the Popular Socialist party leaders denounced Castro for his adventurism. In Chile the leftist wing of the Socialist party, along with the youthful members of the Movement of the Revolutionary Left (Movimiento de Izquierda Revolucionaria—MIR), expressed more enthusiasm for violence and spontaneity as ways to gain political power than did the Chilean Communist party, which placed greater faith in the electoral process and trade-union organizing activities. After Castro took over government control in early 1959, the PSP and the July 26th movement operated in an uneasy coalition. By 1962 the guerrilla followers of Fidel had emerged triumphant. In Chile the leftist Unidad Popular attained executive power when its candidate Salvador Allende won the presidential election in 1970. As in Cuba, however, the two wings on the left governed in a fragile alliance. Unlike Castro, Allende never gained a dominant position over the left or the government establishment, especially the military, which opposed his policies.

The most striking difference between Cuba and Chile is that the Cuban revolutionaries vanquished their political opponents, but the Chilean revolutionaries lost government power after only three years in office. In 1973 a military coup dedicated to extirpating the Marxist influence in Chile overthrew the Allende government. The different outcomes partly stem from the diverse background conditions separating the two countries. Opponents of the socialist revolution retained greater power in Chile than in Cuba. Under the Batista government, the Cuban capitalists, especially the sugar-mill owners, exerted economic influence primarily through ties with American corporations and the U.S. government. Lacking national legitimacy, the Cuban industrialists relied on the armed forces to retain their dominance. In 1958 the Cuban military began to disintegrate as troops and even officers refused to fight the Rebel Army, defected to Castro's guerrilla forces, and even collaborated with the July 26th movement in attempts to overthrow Batista. When the U.S. government, encouraged by State Department opposition to Batista, placed an embargo on arms shipments to Cuba in the spring of 1958, that action signaled a withdrawal of U.S. support for Batista.

In Chile, however, the capitalist class and armed forces posed a much stronger opposition to the socialist revolutionaries. Chilean industrialists wielded greater control over the domestic economy. Although U.S. corporations during the late 1960s dominated such vital industries as nitrates, copper, iron, and the telephone utility, private Chilean oligopolies controlled major manufacturing industries. Unlike the Cuban military under Batista, the Chilean armed forces showed greater professionalism, that is, corporate autonomy, expertise, morale, and cohesion. Attempting to deter opposition to his policies, Allende increased military expenditures, granted salary raises to the armed forces, continued military assistance from the United States, and appointed officers to high positions in his government. Rather than appease the military, these actions reinforced its power. Given the weaker role played by the U.S. government and American multinational corporations in Chilean domestic affairs, the socialist revolutionaries experienced greater difficulties fusing the anticapitalist class struggle with the anti-imperialist nationalist struggle.[3]

Compared with the Chileans, Cubans have lived through a more autocratic history. Founded by Spain around 1500, Cuba did not gain political independence until 1902. As a military base for Spanish incursions into Latin America, Cuba thus experienced a four-hundred-year heritage of military dictatorship. After political independence, autocratic rule continued. The best known military dictators who gained power through coups d'état were General Gerardo Machado (1925–1933) and Fulgencio Batista, whose first term of office lasted from 1933 through 1944 and whose second term began in 1952 and ended in 1958. Only for brief periods between these military dictators did Cubans enjoy such civil liberties as free speech, free press, and competitive elections.

By contrast, Chileans had longer experience with reconciliation systems. At least until the brutal military coup that occurred in 1973, they prided themselves on the comparative strength of their democratic traditions. Founded by Spain in the early sixteenth century, Chile won her political independence in 1818, nearly a century before Cuba's split from Spanish colonial rule. Although Chilean historians have labeled the period from 1830 through 1890 as the "autocratic republic," actually a competitive oligarchy governed after 1860. True, the president dominated the government process. Yet he shared power with a faction-riven legislative elite that included copper-mine owners, nitrate-mine owners, manufacturers, bankers, railroad executives, shippers, merchants, landowners, and grain-mill operators. Although only a small proportion of the population voted, elections among competing political parties did take place. Peasants and working-class individuals enjoyed few economic rights; however, the elite did support such civil liberties as a free press, free speech, and competitive elections. From 1891 through 1920, Chileans managed a parliamentary system under which the congress, not the president, wielded dominant power. Between 1932 and 1973 a more democratic reconciliation system began to emerge as more and more groups gained the right to participate in political life. A balance of power developed between the congress and the presidency; the president needed to cooperate with the legislature for effective policymaking to take place. Throughout its history, the Chilean military has rarely intervened directly into civilian political matters. From 1851 through 1973 armed forces officials served as president only during two periods: 1891–1896 and 1924–1932. After 1932 until 1973, a few military plots to stage a coup did occur in 1939, 1946, 1948, 1951, 1955, and 1969; however, all these conspiracies failed. Thus, on most indicators of formal democracy—free speech, competitive elections, freedom for party organizations, independent judiciary, and civilian supremacy over the government—scholars in the post–World War II period (1945–1973) consistently ranked Chile among the three most democratic nations in Latin America. Cuba, however, usually scored in the bottom half, especially after 1952.[4]

Influenced by this democratic, pluralistic heritage, Salvador Allende had neither the will nor the power to take the autocratic road toward socialism. Although a self-styled Marxist, he was not a Leninist or a Stalinist. A vanguard political party seemed antithetical to the competitive party system. Because the professionalized military forces retained considerable power and legitimacy, the organization of a guerrilla force to wage an armed struggle appeared not only futile but also contradictory to democratic norms. Thus the reconciliation heritage hindered the effective wielding of coercive power through either a vanguard political party or a rebel army. President Allende believed that a consensual strategy represented the best way to institute socialism in Chile. Pluralists, however, need sufficient time to develop a consensus, negotiate compromises, and form effective coalitions. Yet the lengthy process needed for consensus formation also gives opponents opportunity to mobilize against the reconciliation system. Unfortunately for President Allende, time ran out before he could organize coalitions with groups on both his ideological left and right. Unable to wield effective coercive or consensual power, the Allende government succumbed to a military coup on September 11, 1973.

## The Reconciliation System of the Unidad Popular

The Unidad Popular (Popular Unity) government, which held executive power from late 1970 through September 1973, exemplified a reconciliation political system. President Salvador Allende supported civil liberties. Structurally, both the social stratification system and the government institutions functioned in a pluralist manner. Most social groups enjoyed autonomy from the government. Rather than polarized, they revealed internal conflicts of interests. Policymaking power was divided among different political parties and diverse government institutions.

### Political Beliefs
A longtime member of the legislature, Salvador Allende participated in Chile's pluralist institutions for over thirty years. First elected to the lower house of parliament in 1937, Allende briefly served as a minister of health in the Popular Front government during 1939. Between 1945 and 1970 he held a seat in the Senate, from which he conducted four campaigns for president in 1952, 1958, 1964, and 1970. After three unsuccessful attempts, he finally was elected president in 1970. As head of the Unidad Popular coalition, an alliance of mainly Radicals, Communists, and Socialists, he won 36 percent of the popular vote, compared with 35 percent obtained by Jorge Alessandri, the conservative National party candidate, and 28 percent secured by Radomiro Tomic, who represented the Christian Democrats. Since Allende gained a plurality of votes, the congress elected him to the presidency.[5]

Throughout his brief tenure in office, President Allende upheld political freedom. In his view, Chilean socialists must respect legality, show tolerance for opposition views, and institute a peaceful transition to socialism. Rejecting the Soviet, Chinese, and Cuban models, Allende wanted to base Chilean socialism on a pluralist foundation.[6]

Compared with the West European social democrats, Allende gave less priority to protecting the economic freedoms of the capitalists. As a Marxist humanist, he wanted to implement state ownership of capital goods and financial institutions. His concept of socialism not only involved greater state ownership but also expanded freedom for workers to control the government and industrial plants. According to him, the policies pursued by the Unidad Popular government should enlarge workers' freedom to gain greater upward mobility in the social stratification system.

Allende's interpretation of equality placed him between social democratic and Leninist beliefs. Even though he sought to empower the workers, he also expressed some leanings toward political elitism. Opposed to the vanguard party and the dictatorship of the proletariat, he nevertheless wanted the workers and small farmers to grant him the discretion to make independent decisions. Certainly, he opposed populist mobilizations, such as factory takeovers and land seizures, carried out independently from government direction.[7] Although taking an ambivalent view toward political equality, Allende consistently expressed strong support for economic and cultural equality. For him, socialism meant the abolition of class divisions through income redistribution programs that narrowed wage differences. According to him, the government must also expand the equal opportunities to receive an education, gain access to health care, and find a job. Culturally, Allende wanted his followers to treat others as compañeros, as human beings who deserve equal respect.[8]

As in a typical reconciliation system, the concepts of legitimacy voiced by President Allende stressed the separation of moral and material legitimacy, with material ends taking priority. Rather than advocating a secular political religion, a cult of Marxist-Leninist ideology, for example, he stressed the need for a secular, pragmatic orientation. Opposed to dogmatic theorizing, Allende had no desire to sacrifice individuals on the altar of abstract Marxist doctrines. He acknowledged: "I am no theorist of Marxism. . . . If by chance we were to mar the virginity of orthodox theoreticians and yet accomplish something, I would be content with the latter."[9] He wanted Chileans to judge his government according to its effectiveness in bringing concrete material benefits to the workers—more income equality, greater educational opportunities, and expanded popular access to health care. From his perspective, moral legitimacy stemmed mainly from a commitment to uphold the law, the constitution, and the electoral process.

The major ideological dilemma that Allende never reconciled centered on the contradiction between revolutionary ends and reformist means, between the goal of a mobilization system and reconciliation tactics to realize that system. Anxious to bring fundamental changes to Chilean society, Allende wanted to institute more radical transformations than the Popular Front government (a shaky alliance of Radicals, Socialists, Communists, and other smaller parties) had achieved between 1938 and 1941. He also worked to transcend the reformist policies that he identified with the Christian Democratic Eduardo Frei administration (1964–1970). For Allende and his supporters, the Unidad Popular government had the duty to lead the nation toward socialism, which they interpreted to mean a mobilized society: workers' control of the state, increased government ownership of capital, greater workers' participation in management, expanded consumption for workers and small farmers, and a more egalitarian distribution of wealth. Allende sought to achieve these socialist ends through the nonviolent, democratic means associated with a pluralist reconciliation system. By gaining control of the presidency, he hoped to implement redistributionist policies that would strengthen his popular base among the factory workers, draw to him more small farmer support, and attract some clerks, technicians, and professionals. Through these tactics, Allende believed that the Unidad Popular would gradually win control over other government institutions, including the congress and the courts. This reconciliation strategy failed because the articulation of revolutionary socialist objectives impeded the accommodation of group differences in the Chilean reconciliation context.[10]

### Political Parties and Social Groups

Since the nineteenth century, a competitive party system thrived in Chile until the 1973 coup. During the Allende administration, several different political parties competed at elections and shared government power. As in the typical pluralist reconciliation system, the parties drew support from diverse groups.

Neither religious nor especially ethnic cleavages formed the basis for partisan differences. Compared with some other Latin American countries, Chile is more ethnically homogeneous. The ancestors of most contemporary Chileans originally emigrated from Spain. During the nineteenth century, Germans and Italians migrated to Chile, yet they comprised a smaller share of the population than in Brazil or Argentina. From the Middle East came Syrians and Palestinians who went into textile manufacturing. The native Indians constitute less than 3 percent of the Chilean population. Conquered first by the Spanish army and later by the Chilean military, they live mainly as subsistence farmers in the southern regions. Deprived of land, they supported the efforts of MIR to stage land seizures.[11]

A homogeneous nation of Catholics, Chile has never experienced the bitter religious conflicts that have divided fervent Catholics from secular anti-Catholics in France, Italy, Spain, and Mexico. Unlike the Roman Catholic church in Colombia, which has maintained tight conservative control over the state, Chilean Catholic church leaders have followed a reformist path; in the twentieth century, they have upheld the separation of the state from the church. Rather than favoring only the conservative parties, Catholics have offered their support to all parties: left, center, and right. True, during the early 1970s, the conservative National party attracted greater support from practicing Catholics than from voters who remained indifferent to the Catholic religion. Like the National party, the Christian Democrats drew their strongest appeal from the most devoted Catholics, that is, voters who regularly attended church services. In contrast, Chileans who rejected any identification with the Catholic faith voted for the leftist Unidad Popular. Despite these ties between religion and partisan voting, more practicing Catholics shifted toward the left-wing parties after the 1970 presidential election. Some devoted Catholics even joined leftist movements that worked for a radical transformation of society. These groups included the Movement of United Popular Action (MAPU, composed of ex-Christian Democrats), the Christian Left, and Christians for Socialism. Activist leaders within MIR included a few Catholic priests. Articulating a liberation theology, these left-wing Catholics wanted to revolutionize both the church and society. For them, a socialist economic policy represented the best means to liberate oppressed workers and peasants from their misery.[12]

Economic divisions, not religious cleavages, better explain electoral support for different political parties. Even though each party appealed to distinctive economic groups, no class polarization split the parties into two opposing camps. Economically, Chile functioned under a complex, differentiated stratification system, rather than a simple, polarized class structure. Political conflicts within each class seemed more pervasive than the conflict between opposed classes, such as the struggle between the bourgeoisie and the proletariat. Each class faction articulated diverse interests; overall class solidarity remained weak, especially among lower-income groups. Given this low class cohesion, most parties managed to attract votes from diverse economic groups. Let us explore first the partisan voting behavior of economic groups in the urban areas and then analyze the partisan basis of the rural class structure.

At the top of the urban social stratification system stood the industrialists, bankers, manufacturers, top-ranking managers, technicians, and professionals. As the economic group that dominated the Chilean society and state before the 1960s, the upper class allied most strongly with the National party. This group rejected the Unidad Popular program to expand state ownership of industry and to enlarge the share of national income received by workers.[13]

Of all the economic groups, the middle-class service sector showed the strongest tendency to split its vote among different political parties. Composed of diverse groups—state civil servants, private white-collar salaried employees, self-employed businesspeople (retail merchants, truck drivers), and professionals such as teachers, doctors, and lawyers— the middle class supported leftist, centrist, and rightist parties. Opposed to high inflation, price controls, high wage increases for workers, and state ownership of industries, self-employed businesspeople leaned toward the National party, although some supported the Christian Democrats. Salaried employees such as office and sales workers backed the National and Christian Democratic parties. Reformist professionals who favored government efforts to equalize opportunities preferred the Christian Democratic party. More left-wing professionals, especially civil servants, teachers, students, artists, journalists, and even a few doctors, voted for the Unidad Popular candidate in the 1970 election.[14]

Among industrial factory workers, the Unidad Popular drew only fragmented support. During the 1970 presidential election, Salvador Allende received between 40 and 50 percent of the working-class vote. He especially attracted voters who belonged to leftist unions, worked in large factories (mines, manufacturing plants, textile industries, food-processing establishments), and remained indifferent to religion. About 25 percent of industrial workers preferred the Christian Democratic candidate; another quarter voted for Alessandri, the National party candidate for president. The Nationalists and Christian Democrats managed to attract blue-collar workers who worked in small firms, belonged to no unions, and regularly attended Catholic church services.[15]

Similarly, in the rural areas, the Unidad Popular failed to win over all the farmers. Naturally, the landed elite—the *latifundistas* who owned more than 80 basic irrigated hectares (BIH) (about 200 acres)—favored the National party, since they had lost their land under the agrarian reform policies implemented by both the Frei Christian Democratic government and the Allende Unidad Popular administration. Landowners who held medium-sized commercialized farms between 40 and 80 BIH (100 to 200 acres of high-quality land) supported the National party. Like the *latifundistas*, they rejected the UP program for state ownership and land redistribution. Although the Unidad Popular never expected to attract any support from these wealthy landowners, its appeals to less prosperous farmers also met resistance. Farmers who had benefited from the Frei administration's agrarian reform policies favored the Christian

Democratic party. These included primarily the *asentados*, members of the *asentamientos* (cooperative settlements) who gained extensive concrete benefits: a monthly wage, fertilizers, seeds, economic credits, use of farm equipment, a private garden plot, and the right to cultivate some of the cooperative land for the farmer's own private benefit. Having won economic and political power from the *asentamiento* structure instituted by the Frei government, the *asentados* opposed UP efforts to establish new farm structures that would restrict their rights. Thus, they continued to back the Christian Democrats. Poorer farmers who had not gained benefits from the Christian Democratic agrarian reform policies offered the greatest electoral support to the UP candidates. Most notably, the *afuerinos* (landless migrant farm workers who received a wage for two or three months labor) and some *minifundistas* (subsistence farmers who owned less than 12 acres) backed the Socialists, MAPU, and MIR. Anxious to gain more land, the *afuerinos* and *minifundistas*, especially the Mapuche Indians, showed the greatest enthusiasm for staging land seizures—actions discouraged but not repressed by the Allende government.[16]

In sum, like the urban class structure, the rural stratification system during the Allende presidency showed a differentiated, complex pattern. No cohesive peasant or proletarian class ever emerged to back the Unidad Popular government. Instead, conflicts of interests among the urban middle class, the working class, and the farm sector weakened the Allende government's control over Chilean society.

The fragmented nature of the party system impeded the ability of the Unidad Popular to manage government activities. The Unidad Popular constituted a coalition of divergent parties. Allende's first cabinet consisted of four Socialists, three Communists, three Radicals, two Social Democrats, two Independents, and one MAPU leader. The smaller parties—Radicals, Social Democrats, Independents—did not adhere to a Marxist program; instead, they drew their support from the small business sector. Communists and left-wing Socialists disagreed on both tactics and economic policies. This attitudinal disunity on the left constituted a major reason for the downfall of the Allende regime. Of the several factions within the Socialist party, the left wing exercised the dominant power. Sympathetic to the MIR position, it wanted Salvador Allende to accelerate the revolutionary program for making the transition to socialism. Although a longtime Socialist party leader, Allende tended to side with the Communist view toward tactics and policies. Tactically, President Allende, the right Socialists, and the Communists wanted to expand the governing coalition to include more diverse groups, including "progressive" middle-class segments, reformist Christian Democrats, and sympathetic military officers. The left-wing Socialists, however, placed less faith in these alliance tactics. They repudiated compromises with Christian Democratic leaders in the congress. Instead of allying with Christian Democratic (PDC) elites, the Socialists sought to win over PDC supporters.

Besides these tactical differences, economic policy stands also split the Socialists from the Communists. The Socialists generally urged Allende to pursue a more "revolutionary" strategy. From 1972 on, they wanted to extend state ownership of firms. They also supported increased worker participation in factories, seizures of factories and farms, and greater authority to "organs of popular power" such as farm workers' committees, factory committees, neighborhood commands, industrial district workers' councils, and price control and supply committees. By contrast, the Communist party urged Allende to continue more conciliatory economic policies, such as respect for the private property rights of the small business sector. Opposed to factory and farm takeovers, the Communists after 1971 also rejected further nationalization of private business enterprises. In the Communist view, the government must concentrate on improving the efficiency of the firms already brought under state ownership. At this stage of the transition toward socialism, expanded production hence took priority over further egalitarian redistribution and workers' control.[17]

The control of congress by two opposition parties—the Christian Democrats and the Nationalists—further weakened the Unidad Popular's power to make government policies. Historically, Chileans have lived under a multiparty system. As Table 6.1 indicates, since World War II usually four or more major parties have competed for seats in the Chilean legislature. No single party has ever won a majority of popular votes in elections to the Chamber of Deputies or the Senate. No Chilean president ever commanded a majority of legislators from his own party. Thus, if the president wanted to obtain congressional approval of his program, he had to strike bargains with leaders of the opposition parties. When Salvador Allende assumed the presidential office in late 1970, slightly over 60 percent of members of both the Senate and the Chamber of Deputies belonged to opposition parties, mainly the National and Christian Democratic. During the first year of his term, the divisions between these two parties, combined with the reformist views of some leftist Christian Democrats, enabled Allende to begin implementing some policies proposed by the Unidad Popular electoral platform.

By 1972 the power of the PDC reformist wing declined, and the National and Christian Democratic parties became more unified in their opposition to the Unidad Popular government.[18] They resented not only

161

## TABLE 6.1
### POLITICAL PARTIES IN CHILE

#### I. POPULAR VOTES FOR MAJOR PARTIES IN CONGRESSIONAL ELECTIONS, 1945–1973 (PERCENTAGES OF TOTAL VOTES)

| Parties | 1945 | 1949 | 1953 | 1957 | 1961 | 1965 | 1969 | 1973 |
|---|---|---|---|---|---|---|---|---|
| Socialist | 13% | 9% | 14% | 11% | 11% | 10% | 12% | 19% |
| Communist[a] | 10 | — | — | — | 11 | 12 | 16 | 16 |
| Radical[b] | 20 | 28 | 16 | 22 | 21 | 13 | 13 | 4 |
| Christian Democrat[c] | 3 | 4 | 3 | 9 | 15 | 42 | 30 | 29 |
| Liberal | 20 | 19 | 11 | 15 | 16 | 7 | — | — |
| Conservative | 24 | 23 | 14 | 18 | 14 | 5 | — | — |
| National[d] | | | | | | | 20 | 21 |
| Others[e] | 10 | 17 | 42 | 25 | 12 | 11 | 9 | 11 |

#### II. NUMBER OF SEATS HELD BY POLITICAL PARTIES IN THE CHILEAN LEGISLATURE BEFORE AND AFTER MARCH 1973 ELECTION

| PARTIES | CHAMBER OF DEPUTIES (N =150 SEATS) | | SENATE (N = 50 SEATS) | |
|---|---|---|---|---|
| | pre-election | post-election | pre-March | post-March |
| Unidad Popular | 57 | 63 | 18 | 20 |
| Socialists | 14 | 27 | 4 | 7 |
| Communists | 22 | 26 | 6 | 9 |
| Radicals | 12 | 5 | 4 | 2 |
| Others[f] | 9 | 5 | 4 | 2 |
| Opposition to UP | 93 | 87 | 32 | 30 |
| Christian Democrats | 47 | 50 | 20 | 19 |
| Nationalists | 33 | 34 | 5 | 8 |
| Others[g] | 13 | 3 | 7 | 3 |

Sources: Arturo Valenzuela, *The Breakdown of Democratic Regimes: Chile* (Baltimore: The Johns Hopkins University Press, 1978), 35, 85; *Latin America* 7 (March 9, 1973): 73.

[a] Between 1948 and 1958 the Communist party was banned from participating in elections.

[b] In the 1973 election the old Radical party fragmented into three different parties. One segment, the Radical party, supported the Unidad Popular. The two other radical parties, the Democratic Radicals and the Left Radicals, allied with the opposition to the Unidad Popular.

[c] The Christian Democratic party formed in 1957; before then it was called the Falange Nacional.

[d] After the 1965 election, the Liberals and Conservatives allied to become the National party.

[e] In the 1973 elections, 5 percent of the "Others" category voted for minor parties supporting the Unidad Popular. These small parties included MAPU (Movement of United Popular Action, 2.5 percent), the Christian Left (1 percent), API (Independent Populist Action, 1 percent), and the Popular Socialist Union (0.5 percent). Around 6 percent of the "Others" category voted for minor parties opposed to the Unidad Popular; these parties included the Left Radicals (2 percent) and the Democratic Radicals (2 percent).

[f] The smaller parties allied with the Unidad Popular held the following number of seats in the two houses of Congress after the March 1973 elections: MAPU (2 seats), Christian Left (2 seats), API (2 seats), and the Popular Socialist Union (1 seat).

[g] The smaller parties allied with the Christian Democratic–Nationalist opposition to the Unidad Popular held the following number of seats in the two houses of Congress after the March 1973 elections: Left Radicals (4 seats) and the Democratic Radicals (2 seats).

the state ownership policies implemented by Allende but also his tendency to avoid congressional approval for these policies. By reinterpreting some laws passed during the twelve-day "Socialist Republic" of 1932, the Allende government justified state takeovers of private industries, including major banks, financial institutions, steel plants, textile industries, mines, the ITT telephone company, and General Tire's Chilean subsidiary. Opposed to these executive actions, Christian Democratic and Nationalist legislators impeached cabinet ministers and tried to veto presidential initiatives. By gaining two-thirds of the congressional seats in the March 1973 elections, they also hoped to impeach President Allende himself. That tactic, however, failed. Instead, the parties allied to the Unidad Popular increased their share of the popular vote to around 44 percent; they gained 42 percent of the seats in the Chamber of Deputies and 40 percent of the Senate seats. The opposition thus still lacked the two-thirds vote needed either to override a presidential veto or to impeach Allende. Compromise between the UP parties and the opposition became increasingly difficult to achieve. Within the Unidad Popular, the left-wing Socialists rejected any coalition with reformist PDC legislators. Within the Christian Democratic party, the rightist faction had grown dominant and supported an alliance with the National party, not the Unidad Popular. As the centrist position weakened, the two partisan extremes strengthened their power. Unable to reconcile conflicts within the Unidad Popular or to negotiate a compromise with the reformist wing of Christian Democrats, President Allende faced a political deadlock.[19] As party heads spent more and more time trying to reconcile their conflicts, government decision-making became increasingly stalemated.

### Government Institutions and Social Groups

During his brief presidency, Salvador Allende governed a weaker state than operates in either a mobilization or a bureaucratic-authoritarian system. As head of a reconciliation system, he faced several structural contradictions. Although formal government institutions in Santiago wielded centralized power, the high degree of interest-group pluralism weakened central government control. The populist mobilization system at the local level came into conflict with the reconciliation bargaining strategy preferred by national government elites. Groups opposing President Allende retained extensive power to block his policies. While the Unidad Popular platform advocated an expanded scope of government power, no organization or political leader had the power to coordinate government decision-making. Unable to overcome these structural contradictions, Allende's government eventually lost power to the military.

Throughout his tenure President Allende never used state coercion against his opponents on the right or the left. The Catholic church and mass media had the freedom to oppose government policies. The Catholic church conducted worship services, administered pastoral programs, and operated their schools free from state interference. Channel 13, the television station owned by the Catholic University of Chile, broadcast programs critical of leftist organizations and Unidad Popular policies. About three-fourths of the radio stations throughout Chile voiced opposition to the Unidad Popular. Newspapers and magazines that took an anti-Allende stand outsold those media backing his administration. The *El Mercurio* chain, which had ties with the National party, dominated the newspaper business. Christian Democratic sympathizers controlled other mass media.[20]

Although from a legalistic standpoint the national government officials in Santiago wielded centralized power over formal government agencies, actually local government institutions, especially municipal councils, handled important responsibilities. City councils formulated policies that dealt with community health, housing, recreation, education, culture (libraries, museums), and mass transportation. Because the central government controlled the raising of most revenues for local government projects, the mayor and the municipal councilors had to bargain with national legislators and civil servants in Santiago to secure public funds for sewage systems, water projects, electric streetlights, paved streets, schools, gymnasiums, hospitals, and flood-control projects. In Santiago local government officials also tried to obtain personal favors for their constituents, including higher pensions, larger retirement benefits, jobs, and judicial pardons. The competitive nature of the municipal party system meant that low-income citizens gained some concrete benefits. Voters elected their municipal councilors; all Chilean political parties actively competed for seats on the city councils. During the 1971 city elections, parties supporting the Unidad Popular gained about half the total votes, slightly more than the Christian Democratic and National parties.[21]

No person or government agency coordinated the policy process in the Allende administration; an extensive dispersal of power prevailed. True, of all the government institutions, the presidency probably exercised the greatest influence. The president assumed the major responsibility for planning economic development, directing the social security system, and organizing the administration. Besides initiating some economic legislation, he could use legal decrees over such policies as taxation, expenditures, and government employment. Yet other institutions, especially Congress, placed important checks on presidential power. Congress levied taxes. It authorized the specific areas in which the president could legislate by decree. Within the legislative standing committees, members of opposition parties bargained with government officials about the contents of bills submitted by the president. Usually, committee members modified the president's proposals. Thus if the president wanted to translate his policy preferences into laws, he needed to cooperate with the congress.

Government civil servants retained considerable independence from direct presidential control. Responsible for implementing policies, the bureaucracy was fragmented into competing political parties and interest groups. Along with civil servants and technicians, interest-group representatives (business-people, union leaders, landowners) served on many government agencies. State bureaucrats themselves held membership in different political parties, including the Socialist, Communist, Radical, and Christian Democratic. Christian Democratic officials in particular showed weak enthusiasm for administering the Unidad Popular programs. Since several different ministries and public agencies handled a similar policy, the overlapping jurisdictions among these various bureaucracies further hindered effective presidential coordination. President Allende, party leaders, and heads of such government institutions as the Ministries of Finance and the Economy, the central bank, and the Corporation for Promotion of Production (CORFO), which managed state enterprises, failed to unify the policy process.

Despite the weak coordination that President Allende achieved over government decision-making, the Unidad Popular regime still expanded the scope of state power. It enlarged the state-owned sector, increased state planning, and more actively regulated private firms. The government assumed greater responsibility for securing equal access to health care and educational opportunities.[22] All these economic, educational, and health policies increased central government activities.

### Public Policies

By raising aggregate demand and expanding state control over the economy, the public policies pursued by the Allende government tried to overcome Chile's grave economic problems. Since World War II, Chileans had faced high inflation, high jobless rates, stagnant economic growth, and severe income inequalities. The Unidad Popular policymakers stimulated total demand by raising government expenditures, incurring fiscal deficits, and expanding the money supply. Fiscal and monetary policies increased aggregate demand. Government expenditures rose especially for social services, such as education, public health, housing, social security, family allowances, day-care centers, school lunches, and recreational facilities. Yet as expenditures rose, taxes declined. The congress failed to raise progressive taxes on property or income; only sales taxes on cigarettes, beer, and gasoline increased during the Allende years. As a result, fiscal deficits escalated from 2.9 percent of the gross domestic product in 1970 to 24.6 percent in 1973. Monetary policies also followed an expansionary line. The state-owned banks made generous loans to firms in both the public and private sectors. The money supply increased about 100 percent in both 1971 and 1972, soaring to over 260 percent in 1973; all these figures reflect higher yearly rises in the money supply than occurred during the last years of the Frei government.

Under the Unidad Popular regime, large sectors of the economy came under government ownership or control. The Unidad Popular program envisioned three economic sectors: the *area of social property* dominated by state ownership, a *mixed* sector where state ownership included between 50 percent and 80 percent of enterprises, and a *private* sector. By August 1973 the state had acquired major control over banks, mines, and enterprises that manufactured products such as oil, rubber, basic metals, chemicals, and textiles. Nearly one-third of the industrial labor force worked for enterprises included under the area of social property. In the countryside the Allende government destroyed the old *latifundo* system by expropriating nearly all the landed estates of more than 80 BIH (200 acres). Most of the expropriated estates transformed into either *asentamientos* or *comités campesinos de la reforma agraria*, farm structures that gave male heads of households (in an *asentamiento*) and permanent farmers (in a *comité campesino*) the dominant politico-economic influence. The government converted about 10 percent of the expropriated farms into *centros de reforma agraria* and *centros de producción*. *Centros de reforma agraria* were large farms that gave all farm workers—permanent residents and part-time migrant laborers, both young and old—rights to participate in economic decisions. *Centros de producción* were large state farms that produced timber and livestock. By 1973 around one-fifth of farm laborers worked in the agrarian reformed sector, which comprised 40 percent of the highest-quality land. Despite the extension of the agrarian reformed sector during the Allende administration, medium-sized commercial farmers still owned 40 percent of the best land, with subsistence farmers controlling the remainder.

To what extent did the Unidad Popular succeed in realizing its goals of lowering unemployment, expanding income equality, curtailing inflation, and stimulating higher economic growth? From early 1971 through August 1972, industrial output rose each successive month. During this period consumer prices showed only moderate increases. For example, whereas the 1970 inflation rate stood at 33 percent, it declined to 19 percent in 1971—a lower rate than during any year of the Frei administration. During 1971 the Allende government's policies for expanding aggregate demand lowered unemployment and raised plant capacity to nearly full use; thus, the real growth rate rose 9 percent without creating severe inflationary pressures. After mid-1972, however, industrial output nosedived; each month from September 1972 until September 1973 the economy experienced a negative growth rate. In 1972 the real gross domestic product declined 1.2 percent; the next year it fell 5.6 percent.

Several factors explain the changing pattern of industrial output. Facing price controls, low profits, and possible nationalizations, most private enterprisers, both Chileans and foreigners, refused to make additional investments. Although public investment increased under the Allende regime, the government concentrated on expanding the output of basic consumer goods such as food, beverages, clothes, textiles, and furniture. Compared with the two previous administrations, the Allende regime gave lower priority to investments in capital goods (machinery, electrical equipment, and construction equipment) needed to expand industrial output. Since the rises in public investment failed to counterbalance the falling private investment, the growth rate declined after mid-1972.

The actions of the U.S. government, private multinational corporations, and international lending agencies also contributed to lagging economic growth. During all three years of the Allende presidency, Chile faced a negative balance of payments; that is, imports exceeded exports. The declining price of copper on the world market meant a fall in the income received from exports. The need to import expensive food and about 80 percent of capital goods from Western nations further depleted foreign exchange reserves. Under pressure from the Nixon administration, U.S. and international financial institutions reduced loans to the Chilean government. Unable to obtain short-term credits or spare parts from Western, particularly U.S., sources, Chilean economic production collapsed.

Along with the failure to obtain capital equipment, spare parts, and loans, the declining labor productivity also exacerbated the growth problems. Especially in firms placed under the area of social property, strikes, absenteeism, and the failure to maintain the machinery led to a falling output per hour. This declining productivity occurred less often in enterprises where workers played the greatest role managing the plant. When workers participated in decisions about employment, dismissal, transfers, labor relations, job safety, investments, and wage levels, labor productivity either increased or remained the same relative to levels under private ownership. Unlike industries where workers' representatives held little influence over management decisions, industries with high worker participation showed less absenteeism, fewer strikes, fewer thefts, more job security, more job training courses, greater innovations, more investment, and greater cooperation among workers, including the exchange of technical information needed to expand labor productivity. Yet since professional managers dominated the decision-making processes in most state-controlled firms, expanded worker participation in only a few enterprises failed to raise the overall labor output.

Agricultural production resembled the industrial growth pattern. Although food production increased a bit in 1971, it fell during 1972 and 1973. Fearing either expropriation or land seizure, many private landowners ceased producing agricultural crops. In the publicly owned reformed sector, *asentamientos* and *comités campesinos de la reforma agraria* contributed to declining agricultural productivity. Many of these cooperative farms lacked the machinery (tractors, harvesters) needed to cultivate land. Several reform units had little access to trained agricultural experts who would help the farmers raise agricultural output. Since general consumer prices rose faster than the prices for food bought by the state purchasing agency, farmers in the reformed sector felt little economic incentive to expand production. Often they sold food produced on communal lands or on their private garden plots for higher prices on the black market, which accelerated the inflationary pressures.

During 1972 and 1973 Chileans suffered not only from declining production but also from skyrocketing inflation. Prices increased 77 percent in 1972 and then soared to 353 percent in 1973—the highest world inflation rate. The astronomical price rises stemmed from both demand-pull and cost-push variables. Although aggregate demand increased, supplies decreased. Because the Chilean congress refused to raise income or property taxes to finance increased government expenditures, the fiscal deficits increased. Unable to obtain tax increases or foreign loans, the Allende administration ordered the central bank to print more money. By raising total demand far above increased production, the fiscal deficits and growth in the money supply stimulated higher inflation. Reduced supplies also exacerbated inflationary problems. Supply shortages resulted from falling production, domestic hoarding, panic buying, sabotage, and lockouts. Strikes by private truck drivers in October 1972 and again in July 1973 curtailed the distribution of needed supplies, both food and capital goods.

Labor unions, private industries, and government pushed up costs, which further contributed to the skyrocketing inflation. Wage increases generally outstripped gains in labor productivity, especially in privately owned plants. Workers in the publicly controlled area of social property received lower wage hikes than employees working for private enterprises. Fearing nationalization and growing trade union influence, private business executives felt pressured to grant high raises. They also increased prices for their goods at a faster rate than did managers operating the state-controlled industries. Despite the extensive nationalizations, private entrepreneurs still owned vital sectors of the economy, such as food, wood, furniture, paper, and some capital goods. Since concentrated industries (oligopolies) dominated the private economic sector, they felt few competitive pressures to minimize costs. Public policies toward foreign exchange relationships and the nationalized firms also pushed up costs. The devaluation of the Chilean currency vis-à-vis Western currencies meant that Chileans had to pay higher prices for imported capital equipment, oil, steel, and chemicals; thus, the costs of vital industrial inputs escalated. Most nationalized industries placed under the area of social property faced high deficits, especially the chemical, steel, and energy plants. Unable to reduce costs by decreasing wages or making high price increases, these state-controlled firms relied on government loans for operating funds. Because the congress refused to raise sufficient taxes, the Allende administration financed these deficits by expanding the money supply. High inflation followed.

Although during 1972 and 1973 the Allende policymakers failed to halt rising prices, they did lower unemployment and secure more income equality. During the 1960s the unemployment rate in greater Santiago hovered between 4 percent and 7 percent of the labor force. When the Unidad Popular governed the country, the jobless rate averaged 4.1 percent in 1970, 4.2 percent in 1971, 3 percent in 1972, and 4.8 percent in 1973. Unemployment was low mainly because the Allende administration enacted economic policies that raised aggregate demand. Its investment policies concentrated on labor-intensive, rather than capital-intensive, programs. Unskilled workers in particular benefited from the increased employment opportunities made available in the state enterprises.

To a large extent, the Unidad Popular policies also led to greater income equality. True, not all programs produced egalitarian results for every worker. For instance, even though in 1971 the real income of industrial workers rose (that is, wage increases exceeded rises in general consumer prices), by 1973 the soaring inflation rates brought a decline in real income; that year, prices rose faster than the wage hikes. As in the Frei administration, the land redistribution policies pursued by the Allende regime gave greater income to the *asentados*—the permanent farm residents—than to the *minifundia* subsistence farmers or to the landless migrant farm laborers. Within the expropriated farms, the permanent residents employed mainly their family relatives and expelled the landless agricultural laborers, who migrated to the city in search of work. Nevertheless, most Unidad Popular policies lessened income

169

inequalities. The agrarian reform program destroyed landed estates, thereby ending the *latifundo* system. Not only the rural poor but also the urban low-income citizens gained access to education, health care, and inexpensive housing. In the urban areas, the falling unemployment rates meant rising incomes for blue-collar workers, especially the unskilled laborers who gained jobs in state factories. During the first year of the Allende presidency, wages increased more rapidly than prices; hence, the real income of workers rose. Finally, during 1972 and 1973—times of hoarding, black markets, and food shortages—the price control and supply committees distributed inexpensive food (sugar, flour, rice) to poor people. All these programs implemented by the Unidad Popular hence raised the share of the national income going to poor people and factory workers.[23]

The education policies pursued by the Allende government also showed a commitment to greater social equality. Although all parties within the Unidad Popular coalition wanted to expand equality, divisions arose between those committed to democratizing the educational system and others who placed the highest priority on "proletarian socialism." Salvador Allende, right-wing Socialists, Communists, and Radicals believed in using the state to make the educational system more democratic. They sought comprehensive schools that would increase educational opportunities for the lower-income population. Under their educational arrangements, teachers, parents, and students would gain greater influence in helping the professional educators operate the schools. By contrast, the left Socialists, MAPU, and MIR wanted to mobilize the working class to transform the educational system toward a "proletarian socialist" model. According to their normative view, the schools must give students the ideological and technical education that would prepare them to conquer political power for the working class.

Divided by these two normative orientations, the Unidad Popular experienced difficulties following an ideologically consistent educational policy. The programs actually enacted pursued a pragmatic course. Particularly in the rural areas, the Allende government mounted a campaign against illiteracy. Adult education programs expanded, as did educational opportunities for workers. From 1971 through 1973 enrollments in kindergarten, primary, secondary, and postsecondary schools increased. Even though children of professionals, managers, clerks, and salespeople continued to have greater access to secondary and university education than did farmers' children, students from all social classes gained expanded educational opportunities. Children of urban industrial workers probably secured the greatest educational benefits, compared with their previous opportunities. A slight enrollment shift from private

170

to public schools also conformed to UP objectives. Whereas in 1970 about 23 percent of students attended private primary and secondary schools, in 1973 this figure fell to 20 percent. At the postsecondary level, educators expanded scientific, technical, and professional training programs.

The more controversial program to establish proletarian socialist schools failed. Even within the Unidad Popular, President Allende, the right-wing Socialists, the Communists, and the Radicals opposed this educational strategy. The considerable power of the Christian Democrats in both the public and private schools also blocked the proletarian socialist programs. Christian Democrats led the Federation of Secondary School Students of Santiago. In most Chilean universities students elected Christian Democrats to the rectorship and gave them majority control on university councils. At the pre-university level, PDC supporters also dominated parents' associations, mothers' centers, and neighborhood committees. Because of this educational influence exerted by the Christian Democratic party, the Allende government generally continued the reformist educational policies that had begun during the Frei administration. Attempting to attract greater support from the left wing of the PDC, the UP policymakers retained the same level of state subsidies to pre-university private schools as under President Frei. Indeed, government grants to Catholic universities increased during the Allende presidency.[24] Given the power of the private educational sector and the influence of Christian Democrats over school administration, the Unidad Popular government pursued a pragmatic, reformist path. Although educational opportunities became more equal, the need to reconcile differences among Unidad Popular factions and with the Christian Democrats muted the leftwing socialist drive to use the schools as an instrument for constructing proletarian socialism.

Like its educational policies, the health policies implemented by the Allende government gave priority to expanding equal access to social services and to democratizing the administration of these services. Pregnant mothers and children under sixteen years old received a half liter of free milk each day. The government encouraged more doctors to begin their practices in rural and low-income urban areas. It built additional hospitals, maternity clinics, and especially neighborhood health centers that remained open longer hours to serve the poor. Improved sanitation and housing facilities for low-income neighborhoods also equalized health care benefits. As a partial result of these populist, egalitarian programs, the infant mortality rate fell from 86 deaths of infants under one year old for every 1000 live births to 70 in 1973. To democratize the administration of health policies, the Unidad Popular leaders established hospital councils and local health councils in neighborhood health centers. Intended to expand popular participation in health decision-making, these councils gave community workers, health service employees, local government officials, and central government civil servants the right to review budgetary decisions. Naturally, the health professionals such as physicians and hospital administrators resented their lessened influence.

Although the Allende government did expand health-care access to the poor, it achieved less success in securing fundamental transformations of the health system. Popular participation in local health decision-making increased, yet professional physicians retained the dominant influence over major policies. The failure to widen popular control stemmed from the powerful position held by the Chilean Medical Association (CMA), which rejected the Unidad Popular health policies. Only about 30 percent of physicians, primarily those in the public health movement and the schools of public health, supported the UP health programs. The remaining 70 percent, especially those dominating the Chilean Medical Association, opposed policies that expanded equal access to health care, gave workers and consumers greater control over health professionals, and increased the number of paraprofessionals. These populist proposals threatened the economic interests of physicians identifying with the CMA. Aligning themselves with the organized opposition to the Unidad Popular government, they went on strike during October 1972 along with the private truck drivers. As the analysis of educational policies suggested, the pluralist nature of Chilean society limited the power of the Allende government to mobilize support behind efforts to secure fundamental transformations in the policy process.[25]

In summary, the ineffectiveness shown in the policy process during the brief Allende presidency partly derives from the conflicting styles of political decision-making that struggled for dominance. Reconciliation, mobilizational, and bureaucratic-authoritarian modes contended with one another. Until the military coup of September 1973, no single style ever emerged dominant. Despite their "revolutionary" rhetoric, Salvador Allende, the right-wing Socialists, the Communists, and the leftist Christian Democrats chose a reconciliation style. Striving to reach a consensus, they saw the need to compromise their differences with the opposition. For the reconcilers, the congress had an important role to play in the policy process along with the presidency. Although the attempt proved unsuccessful, this group sought an alliance within the congress between UP supporters and left-wing Christian Democrats—an alliance that would have improved the prospects for congressional approval of the UP programs.

The left-wing Socialists, MAPU, and the Movement of the Revolutionary

172

Left rejected this reconciliation strategy, favoring instead a populist mobilization style. For them, class struggle, not class accommodation, energized the policy process. Opposed to the power exerted by the "bourgeois" parliament, they backed strong presidential initiatives supported by local revolutionary organizations. Rather than attain socialism from above through electoral politics and representative democracy, the populist mobilizers wanted to institute socialism from below via participatory democracy and the politics of direct action. In the sense that no powerful party-state elite directed the mass activities, they illustrate a populist type of mobilization. For example, in the cities the *pobladores*— squatters and slum dwellers—organized *campamentos* (squatter settlements) that pressured the Allende government to build houses, construct new schools, and provide jobs. Neighborhood associations such as councils, fronts, blocks, and an elected executive mobilized the squatters and provided arenas for popular participation. Urban radicals sponsored numerous organizations that assumed crucial decision-making powers when the truckowners, bus drivers, retail merchants, factory owners, doctors, and dentists staged a strike during October and November 1972. After factory owners called a lockout, *cordones industriales* (industrial district workers' councils) organized workers to maintain production and alleviate shortages. Leaders of these *cordones* repudiated any attempts by a "paternalistic" government bureaucracy to interfere with workers' autonomy. *Comandos comunales* (neighborhood commands) coordinated the activities of groups such as neighborhood councils, mothers' centers, and student groups. When the food distribution network broke down and food became scarce, *juntas de abastecimiento y precios* (committees of price control and supply) tried to enforce the fixed price schedules and to secure an adequate supply of rationed food. In the rural areas, *consejos comunales campesinos* (farm workers' committees) encouraged farmers to continue supplying food to the cities. Even after the strike ended in early November 1972, all these populist organizations remained in operation, urging the Allende government to take a more revolutionary stance. Some on the Left, especially the left-wing Socialists and the MIRistas, viewed nongovernmental agencies like industrial belts, neighborhood commands, committees of price control and supply, and farm workers' committees as part of a "dual power" system that would accelerate the drive toward a fully socialist society à la 1917 Russian soviets.

However fervent their revolutionary rhetoric, the leftist mobilizers lacked the organizational power wielded by the elites, who advocated a bureaucratic-authoritarian style of decision-making. These elites dominated key power centers in Chile: the concentrated industries, the state civil service, the professionalized military, the National party, and

173

the right wing of the Christian Democratic party. For the authoritarian bureaucrats, order arose through elite imposition of policy priorities, not through peaceful accommodation of group differences. Horrified by the social conflict, political disorder, and policy wrangling that they saw destroying the Chilean body politic, the armed forces leaders staged a *golpe de estado* to cleanse the political system of both the mobilization and reconciliation styles.[26]

## The Golpe of the Generals

Despite the long democratic history of Chile, the September 1973 military coup occurred mainly because the Unidad Popular government proved unable to reconcile the severe political conflicts, mobilize the populace behind administration policies, and crush the bureaucratic opposition. Fragmentation of group support, weak institutional backing, declining legitimacy, and ineffective policy performance all contributed to the *golpe de estado*.

### Fragmentation of Group Support

During the Unidad Popular regime, the cohesion of economic groups supporting the government remained weak. As a Marxist socialist, President Allende sought to base his support on the "working class," which he broadly defined to include industrial laborers, small farmers, and certain segments of the middle class: professionals, white-collar employees, and technicians. Yet neither the structural unity nor the attitudinal cohesion of these groups ever reached a level high enough to consolidate Allende's rule.

Structurally, not all industrial workers belonged to a single union organization backing the Unidad Popular administration. Around one-half the industrial wage earners worked in firms with only ten or fewer employees. These privately owned enterprises were rarely unionized. The percentage of workers who belonged to unions constituted no more than 40 percent of the total blue-collar and white-collar labor force. This proportion included most public employees, workers in mines, large manufacturing plants, and construction firms, but only about a quarter of persons employed by private businesses. The major union confederation, the Central Única de Trabajadores, which gave strong backing to the Allende government, organized only around 65 percent of the total unionized labor force. Split into factions supporting the Socialist, Communist, and Christian Democratic parties, the national CUT wielded little control over the autonomous local unions.

174

The industrial working class also demonstrated attitudinal disunity. Some workers, especially those in small firms, perceived no conflicting interests between them and their employers. Another group looked for a charismatic leader to bring downtrodden people out of their misery. Others who identified with the Christian Democrats preferred a Christian socialist policy that humanized relations between workers and managers. Only a fraction of blue-collar workers—probably no more than a fourth or a fifth—adopted a Marxist position. Among these workers, the majority favored a peaceful road to socialism; only a small segment perceived the need for an armed struggle to attain a socialist revolution.

The two other segments of the Unidad Popular group coalition, small farmers and segments of the middle class, showed even greater disunity than factory workers. During the early 1970s, only about a quarter of the Chilean population lived in the countryside; farmers proved more difficult to organize into unions than did industrial laborers. Probably less than a fifth of the agrarian population, mainly farmers earning a wage, joined a peasant union. The rural unions split their support among the Christian Democrats, the Christian Left, MAPU, Socialists, and Communists. Similarly, large segments of the urban middle classes were disunified. Although some professionals supported the Unidad Popular, the majority sided with the Christian Democratic–National opposition. Most self-employed urban businesspeople—artisans, repair workers, retail shopkeepers, and truck drivers—rejected the Allende government's collectivist ideology, its programs for state ownership, and the soaring inflation that plagued Chile during 1972–1973. The lower-middle class generally backed either the National party or the Christian Democrats. Most private-sector white-collar office employees allied with the PDC rather than the Unidad Popular.

Compared with groups supporting the Unidad Popular, the groups opposed to the Allende administration demonstrated greater political cohesion. In particular, the urban and rural upper class maintained high solidarity. Concentrated industries headed by elite families dominated the urban private economy; they formed alliances with the landed aristocracy. These industrialists, corporate executives, well-paid technicians, upper-income professionals, and large landowners maintained close ties through intermarriage, membership in social clubs, and participation in powerful organizations. Their *gremios* (trade and professional associations)—such as the National Industrial Society, the National Society of Agriculture, the Confederation of Rural Employers, the National Front of the Private Sector, and the Confederation of Professional Associations—rallied the opposition against government policies to extend state ownership and to secure greater income equality. All these organizations reinforced the structural solidarity of groups rejecting UP economic policies. Public opinion surveys taken in 1972 indicate that upper-income and middle-income Santiago residents showed stronger opinion solidarity than did poorer citizens. The higher the income level, the more negative became the evaluation of the Allende government's performance. Compared with the wealthy, lower-income people were more divided in their assessments. Whereas nearly three-fourths of the upper-income residents viewed the government's performance as bad, only one-quarter of the poorer Santiago population voiced a favorable evaluation; one-third gave the administration a bad rating, and the remainder perceived it as fair.[27]

In sum, from both an attitudinal and structural perspective, the Allende government did not fall because of class polarization; rather, political polarization brought about its downfall. No class struggle pitted the bourgeoisie against the proletariat. Instead, intraclass conflicts, especially within both the industrial working class and the small farming sector, overwhelmed the interclass divisions. Even though some segments of the middle and upper classes supported the Unidad Popular, the opposition of these economic groups to the Allende administration showed stronger cohesion than did the government's support among the industrial workers and small farmers. Thus by 1973 the Chilean political system had polarized between the government and its opposition. President Allende succumbed to a military coup because his opponents controlled more powerful political institutions than did his defenders.

### The Fragility of Institutional Support

The Allende regime fell because it lacked strong institutional support from the legislature, courts, and armed forces. The Supreme Court and another independent judicial agency, the Contraloría (Office of the Controller General) ruled that the executive had acted illegally when it nationalized some private enterprises. The Contraloría also declared that the president needed approval from a majority in the congress to implement his executive decrees regulating economic activities. These two judicial institutions hence sided with the Christian Democratic–National party opposition in the legislature. Agrarian tribunals established under the 1967 land reform law usually favored the landowners who opposed the UP land redistribution policies. As challenges to the legitimacy of government policymaking grew more severe, violence increased. Unable to coordinate the policy process effectively, President Allende in the fall of 1972 gave military officials greater power to manage the government.

From November 1972 to March 1973, the armed forces gained increasing responsibilities for coordinating government decision-making. A larger number (ten) of military officers served as cabinet members in the Allende administration than in the two previous administrations of Eduardo Frei (one officer) and Jorge Alessandri (none). For example, military officers directed the Interior ministry, the Public Works and Transportation ministry, and the Ministry of Mines. Both active and retired armed forces leaders assumed key responsibilities in the state bureaucracy. They held high positions in the Chilean Development Corporation, the nationalized mines formerly owned by Anaconda and Kennecott, and state enterprises such as telecommunications, shipping, and steel. Military officers also achieved dominant control in "emergency zones," that is, those geographic areas subject to a high degree of violence. Particularly in the southern region, where farm seizures by the Mapuche Indians threatened the landed elite, military commanders managed local government activities. As turbulence escalated during late 1972 and 1973, military officers hence came to play a relatively independent government role. Mainly educated in Catholic schools, they had close ties with the provincial middle and upper classes, such as business executives, professionals, and southern landowners. In particular, the navy and air force officers maintained friendly contacts with National party leaders. Although some military personnel sympathized with the Unidad Popular program, a large segment took an anti-Marxist stand. When the economic crisis became more severe in 1973 and the Allende government seemed unable to cope with public disorder, some officers began planning a military coup. Their experience working in state enterprises, the cabinet, and the emergency zones reinforced their belief that they could operate the government better than President Allende or the Marxist parties. By summer 1973 most high-ranking military personnel no longer viewed the UP government as legitimate.[28]

*The Decline of Political Legitimacy*

Compared with the opposition, the Unidad Popular government never developed as strong an ideological commitment to its socialist cause—a commitment that would have strengthened its political legitimacy. Neither the UP elites nor their mass supporters reached agreement about the precise meaning of "socialism." Within the Socialist party, ideological eclecticism prevailed. Some activists sympathized with the ideas of Marshal Tito, Mao Zedong, or Fidel Castro; others articulated a uniquely Chilean view of socialism. President Allende favored a nondogmatic Marxist-humanism interpretation. Communist party leaders adhered to the Soviet version of Marxism-Leninism. MAPU tried to blend Christian socialism with Marxism. The Radicals and Social Democrats, who occupied five posts in Allende's first cabinet, did not even espouse Marxist beliefs.

Few groups backing the Unidad Popular expressed a strong commitment to Marxism or Leninism. Farmers and industrial workers generally interpreted "socialism" to mean government provision of more concrete benefits, that is, a more egalitarian distribution of employment opportunities, education, health care, housing, and inexpensive consumer goods. Most factory workers wanted the government to implement "progressive reforms" through a nonviolent, electoral approach. Fewer workers advocated nationalization of all industries than favored either a private enterprise economy or state ownership of heavy industry and transportation. Similarly, in the countryside, MIRista attempts to mobilize the poor farmers behind the socialist cause proved difficult. Farmers desired more land, agricultural credits, farm equipment, fertilizers, seeds, better housing, improved health care, and greater educational opportunities. After mobilizing to seize a farm, the peasants quickly demobilized and returned to their private concerns: improved life conditions for themselves and their families. One organization formed by the MIR, the Front of Revolutionary Women, showed greater interest in learning about first-aid techniques than in becoming politically educated about the revolutionary role for women in a new socialist Chile. Another group organized by the MIRistas, a Young People's Center, preferred to play soccer rather than to participate in "consciousness-raising" sessions. In short, support for the Unidad Popular depended on its ability to supply concrete benefits to its supporters. In 1973 governmental legitimacy waned when inflation soared, the "real" disposable income of workers declined, and the food distribution system deteriorated.

Unable to mobilize its supporters around an ideological cause, the Allende government also lost its procedural legitimacy during 1973. To ensure the maintenance of a reconciliation system, leaders need to develop a procedural consensus, a widely accepted agreement on the rules that regulate group conflicts. In Chile, this consensus on the rules for bargaining, negotiating, and compromising disintegrated during the Unidad Popular regime. Threatened groups refused to accept Allende's policymaking procedures as legitimate. Within the government institutions, the Supreme Court, the Contraloría, and the congressional opposition viewed Allende's actions as illegal; they blocked his attempts to resolve the economic difficulties. The National party leaders, the Supreme Court justices, and the Controller General favored a military coup. Christian Democratic legislators hoped that a short-lived military intervention would restore political order, constitutional government, and rule by civilians. Outside the formal government structures, mobilizers from both left and right derided the procedural consensus needed in a reconciliation system. On the right, Patria y Libertad (Fatherland and

Freedom) and other paramilitary organizations assassinated government officials, police, army officers, and civilians. They blew up buses, railroad tracks, bridges, electricity plants, oil lines, and gas lines. By these actions, they intended to discredit the Allende government, foment political disorder, and thus encourage the military to stage a coup. On the left, the MIRistas expressed contempt for the "bourgeois democracy" they associated with electioneering, parliamentary rule, constitutional government, and incremental reformist policies. As the Unidad Popular's procedural legitimacy declined, President Allende found it increasingly difficult to reconcile conflicting groups and to implement policies that would help resolve the grave economic crises.[29]

### The Ineffectiveness of Policy Performance

The ineffective policy performance by the Allende government contributed to its declining power and legitimacy. Operating under a pluralistic style of political decision-making, the Unidad Popular administration could not easily act on the information the policymakers received from diverse sources. Faced with a fragmented power system, President Allende had no powerful organization through which to realize fundamental changes. Although the UP policies did lower unemployment and secure more equal income distribution, the Allende administration's inability to curtail price rises and to increase economic growth rates contributed to its declining support.

Besides the Unidad Popular regime's own failures to effectively manage the economy, the actions taken by the Nixon administration worsened a deteriorating economic situation. Although external pressures from the U.S. government did not create the coup, its assistance to conservative elites who opposed Allende facilitated his removal from office. Both Richard Nixon and Henry Kissinger worked to overthrow Allende. In their view, Allende represented a threat to the national security interests of the United States. According to Kissinger, President Allende was not a Social Democrat but a totalitarian Marxist-Leninist dictator who would establish a second Communist-dominated state in Latin America. To avert this possibility, President Nixon ordered U.S. government officials to institute economic sanctions against Chile. From 1971 to 1973, credits from the Agency for International Development and the U.S. Export-Import Bank declined, as did multilateral loans from the World Bank and the Inter-American Development Bank. Credits from U.S. private banks ceased. The Nixon policymakers also placed an embargo on spare parts headed for Chile and demanded the immediate payment of its foreign debt. All these actions caused higher inflation and falling production. During this period, however, aid to the anti-Allende opposition increased. Military sales and economic assistance to the Chilean armed forces grew larger. The U.S. government helped finance strikes by truckowners, mineworkers, taxi drivers, bus owners, and airline pilots; by bringing a halt to production and distribution, these strikes worsened the inflationary situation. U.S. government subsidies to the Christian Democratic party, the National party, Patria y Libertad, the *gremios*, and the mass media (especially *El Mercurio*), reinforced the opposition's power to attack the Allende government for its ineffective policy performance.

Although the U.S. government financed opposition activities, the Soviet Union failed to provide similar economic support to the Allende regime. Soviet officials viewed Latin America as part of the United States' sphere of influence. They worked to weaken U.S. power in Chile but felt little inclination to subsidize a second Communist state in the Western Hemisphere along with Cuba. According to their rationale, the anti-UP opposition posed a powerful barrier to creating a state socialist economy. For this reason, Soviet policymakers granted the Allende government little economic assistance or military equipment.[30]

However great the impact of these external influences, a more important reason for the *golpe de estado* stemmed from the Unidad Popular's inability to reconcile the ways of handling the four policy issues: voluntarism versus determinism, spontaneity versus organization, conflict versus consensus, and change versus continuity. Rather than blend these diverse modes, the UP policymakers acted with excessive voluntarism, spontaneity, and conflict. President Allende took a voluntarist position about moving Chile toward a socialist society. Dedicated to realizing a fundamental transformation of the socioeconomic situation, he underestimated the difficulties that impeded the transition to socialism. These objective conditions included the cultural attitudes of groups opposed to a socialist society, the extensive economic power held by urban private entrepreneurs, the opposition of the U.S. government and multinational corporations, and the political power wielded by such institutions as the armed forces, the national police, the congress, and the courts.

In the Unidad Popular regime, no powerful political organization coordinated the policy process; instead, spontaneity from below impeded central coordination. Allied with the Allende government but striving to accelerate the revolutionary movement, the left-wing Socialists, MIRistas, and MAPUchistas staged land seizures, factory takeovers, and occupations of government buildings. This *espontaneísmo* stimulated countermobilizations by right-wing movements. Horrified by the strikes, factory takeovers, land seizures, high inflation, and state nationalizations of private enterprises, the rightists mobilized to topple the Allende regime.

Fearing state seizures of their enterprises, *gremio* leaders organized strikes and lockouts. Middle-class women marched in the streets, banging their empty pots to protest against rationing, black markets, food shortages, and inflation. This polarization between leftist and rightist mobilizers led to growing political disorder, which weakened the central government's power.[31]

A reconciliation system needs consensus for effective decision-making; however, when the politico-economic crises grew more severe, President Allende faced greater difficulties reaching a consensus, not only within the Unidad Popular but also between the UP and the left wing of the Christian Democrats. Rising polarization pitted the government against the opposition, leftist movements against right-wing organizations. Particularly after the March 1973 elections, when both the right-wing Nationalists and the leftist Socialists increased their electoral strength, the rhetoric became more violent, as evidenced by MIRista and left-wing Socialist calls for arming the workers. Despite the revolutionary rhetoric, most UP supporters remained unarmed. As Karl Marx had warned in *The Eighteenth Brumaire of Louis Bonaparte*, a gap between stated intentions and the means to attain these goals leads to defeat by more powerfully organized professional armed forces:

> If the Montagne [a radical-democratic party in the Second French Republic, 1848–1851] wanted a parliamentary victory, it ought not to have given the call to arms. If it gave the call to arms in parliament, it ought not to have behaved in a parliamentary fashion in the streets. If the peaceful demonstration was meant seriously, it was foolish not to foresee that it would be received in a warlike manner. If a real struggle was intended, it was very odd to lay down the weapons with which it would have to be fought.[32]

Like the unsuccessful French revolutionaries in the mid-nineteenth century, the Unidad Popular policymakers failed to reconcile means and ends. They sought to create a revolutionary mobilization system in a pluralist reconciliation context. Whereas the establishment of a mobilization system requires a high degree of ideological conflict and armed struggle, a reconciliation system depends on procedural consensus and the ability to form alliances. Lacking both procedural consensus and a powerfully organized political party or rebel army, the Unidad Popular found itself attacked "in a warlike manner."

Finally, the UP administration never reconciled the tensions between change and continuity. President Allende wanted to achieve radical socioeconomic changes but still retain the constitutional government, respect for legality, and electoral traditions that Chileans had experienced during most of the twentieth century. Yet his strategy for securing change

181

differed from the path followed by the Swedish Social Democrats. They extended social services to the whole citizenry, expanded income equality, and gave the factory working class greater economic power in the plants. However, they retained the monarchy, the established Lutheran church, and private ownership of industry. As a Marxist socialist, President Allende seemed reluctant to pursue this reformist strategy. To the powerful military officers and conservative elites, Allende's policies for expanding state ownership and equalizing income distribution represented excessive change. Frightened by the revolutionary Marxist rhetoric and deprived of some material benefits, the upper classes allied with the professional military officers to overthrow the Unidad Popular administration. In its place, they established a new regime that marked a more drastic change from the past order than President Allende ever achieved.

## The Military Bureaucratic-Authoritarian System

The transformation of the Unidad Popular reconciliation system into an industrial bureaucratic-authoritarian system represented a more fundamental political change than carried out by either the Vietnamese Communists or Fidel Castro. In Vietnam and Cuba after World War II, mobilization systems replaced bureaucratic regimes. Despite changes in policy priorities, policy contents, and policy impacts, the revolutionary governments that emerged from the civil wars still ruled in a centralized, coercive manner, as did their predecessors. By contrast, in Chile the military government that seized power on September 11, 1973 brought about sweeping changes in nearly all parts of the political system. Whereas President Allende had articulated a democratic socialist ideology, with a high value placed on both civil liberties and socioeconomic equality, Augusto Pinochet, the army general who became president, rejected civil liberties, pluralism, and equality. The military officers established a stronger state—a more coercive, centralized, coordinated, and monistic state; yet the scope of government power, especially over economic activities, declined. In contrast, Allende had expanded the scope of state power; however, government operations remained more consensual, decentralized, uncoordinated, and pluralistic. Through their economic, health, and educational policies, Unidad Popular officials sought to create a more egalitarian social stratification system that gave poor farmers and factory workers more opportunities for upward mobility. Committed to restoring the political power of the upper classes, the military officers who dominated the new bureaucratic order created a more rigid, elitist social stratification system. For them, increasing the economic growth rate took precedence over equalizing income distribution. Policies to curtail inflation became more important than government actions that would lower the unemployment rate.

In short, the military government transformed political structures, stratification, policy priorities, and the content of government decisions — all aspects of the political system. From this perspective, the *golpe de estado* secured a sharper break with previous administrations than did the Unidad Popular presidential victory in 1970. That election marked the transition from one democratic reconciliation system to a more radical reconciliation regime. The coup, however, brought to power authoritarian bureaucrats who sought to extirpate pluralism from the Chilean body politic.

## The New Political Ideology

The political values guiding Chile's bureaucratic elite blend the *monistic conservatism* of Hispanic colonial traditions with the *free-market* principles linked to monetarist economic policies. Like the Unidad Popular reconciliation system, the Pinochet administration confronts a tension between ends and means. The authoritarian means of a military-police state contradict the goal of a pluralistic free-market economy. President Pinochet articulates a monistic interpretation of conservatism that rejects ideological pluralism. Equating civil liberties with disorder, anarchy, license, chaos, class conflict, and polarization, he stresses the need for national security, order, authority, discipline, and obedience. In his view, political freedom for the individual or group would give Chile's internal "enemies" (Marxists, Communists) and their external allies (the U.S.S.R. and Cuba) the right to threaten Chilean national security. To avert this danger, President Pinochet has worked to eliminate the pluralism, intellectual criticism, parliamentary freedom, and competitive electoral politics that have thrived in Chile during the twentieth century. According to his concept of "authoritarian democracy," the Chilean state must strengthen presidential authority and protect society from Marxist parties. For him, the main political liberty worth preserving is the freedom of the nation to remain independent from internal Marxist tyranny and from foreign domination, whether by the U.S.S.R. or by the United States.

In the military's value hierarchy, economic freedom for private entrepreneurs assumes highest importance. Perceiving Chile as a "nation of entrepreneurs and owners," not a nation of workers, Pinochet upholds freedom for Chilean private enterprisers to own property, to accumulate capital, and to trade with other nations. Freedom for multinational corporations to invest in Chile and to sell their imports on the Chilean market also receives his approval. However, he accords factory workers less economic freedom, especially the rights to strike, engage in nationwide collective bargaining, and participate in managing a plant.

Besides rejecting civil liberties in the new bureaucratic state, Pinochet expresses a similar contempt for equality. Like the Hispanic monistic conservatives, he believes in political hierarchy, not political equality. For him, the superior elites must dominate the inferior masses. Rule by the meritorious should replace rule by the mediocre. He repudiates the attempts of the Allende government to secure greater income equality among the Chilean citizenry. Instead, Pinochet supports equality of opportunity. He assumes that equal opportunities to achieve unequal economic rewards will give talented, ambitious, industrious people the incentive to maximize production. Those born with superior abilities and those who demonstrate their meritorious achievements will thus rise to higher positions. Consistent with his attitude toward politico-economic equality, Pinochet's view of cultural equality voices the same disdain for egalitarian social interaction. Whereas Salvador Allende wanted people to address him as *compañero*, President Pinochet has assumed the title "His Excellency," a form of address signifying the need for the masses to defer to their "superiors." Under the military regime, the poor must defer to the rich, the young to the old, and subjects to their masters. Not only status equality but also spiritual equality receives low priority. According to Pinochet, Chileans are locked in a bitter war with the domestic Marxists and the Soviet imperialists. The nationalists, Christians, and private property holders are the favored people. Disfavored groups include the international communists, the atheists, and the poor.

Attempting to legitimate the new military bureaucratic state, Pinochet has blended moral values with material benefits; however, the moral and material concepts of legitimacy diverge from President Allende's beliefs. Whereas Allende stressed a more equal distribution of concrete goods, Pinochet stresses the need to attain rapid economic growth and curtail inflation. Expanding material production takes precedence over equalizing income distribution. Allende wanted Chileans to internalize the moral values of Marxist humanism. By contrast, Pinochet regards Chile not as a Marxist society but as a Christian nation where love of God, Catholic spiritual values, and the traditional moral teachings of the Church maintain national solidarity.

Collectivist values, rather than individualism, pervade Pinochet's concept of political legitimacy. He warns that in the new "authoritarian democracy," no individual has the right to assert his interests against the state. National security supersedes individual freedom. Pinochet asserts that under the military regime, the state will exercise full sovereignty;

individuals will no longer possess the authority to endanger the nation's common good. In the new bureaucratic state, he expects Chileans to live in organic harmony, undisturbed by class conflicts, political polarization, and social disorder.

Although the free-market technocrats who advocate monetarist economic policies agree with Pinochet that Chile needs an authoritarian state committed to freedom for the private entrepreneur, they reject his emphasis on collectivism and traditional Catholic values. For the "Chicago boys"—the Chileans who studied under Milton Friedman and Arnold Harberger at the University of Chicago—the type of democracy under Presidents Frei and Allende threatened the free market. Irrational voters lacked the information and judgment to make sound electoral choices. Hence, a rational, enlightened technocratic elite must rule an authoritarian state, strengthen the private market system, and educate individuals about the virtues of free–market policies, including the need for free trade, foreign investment, privatization, state deregulation, and expanded marketplace competition. From this technocratic perspective, individual self-interest takes priority over social solidarity. Rather than stress cooperative efforts and the provision of social services (health, education, income maintenance), the free-market ideology upholds individual economic success, atomization, and the consumption of luxury goods by the wealthy. Christian moral values based on altruism and self-sacrifice seem less important than the pursuit of material goods by private enterprisers. In short, unlike the Allende administration policymakers, who supported democratic socialism, Christian socialism, Marxism, or Leninism, the Chicago boys reject this ideological eclecticism. They see the need for a dictatorial state to guide Chileans toward a free-market system in which irrational socialist policies and a paternalistic government no longer wield dominant influence.[33]

### The New Bureaucratic State

The bureaucratic regime established by the army, navy, air force, and national police rules a stronger state than Chileans ever experienced during the twentieth century. Compared with the Unidad Popular reconciliation system, it exercises more coercive, centralized, coordinated, and monistic power. Although in these respects the state has grown stronger, its scope of power has become more limited, since the state plays a less active role supplying economic benefits, educational opportunities, and health services to Chilean citizens, especially the poor.

The severe political coercion wielded by the military regime represents the most striking departure from previous administrations. During 1985 Latin American scholars in the United States ranked Chile as the nineteenth most coercive state in Latin America; among the twenty largest nations, only Haiti secured lower civil liberties scores. By contrast, from 1945 through 1970 American scholars evaluated Chile as the second or third most democratic country in Latin America.[34]

Unlike the Unidad Popular government, the military bureaucratic state has applied a high degree of physical, economic, and normative coercion. Police raids, arbitrary arrests, indefinite detention, torture (beatings, electric shocks, sleep deprivation, forcing of live snakes into detainees' throats), and executions coerce the regime's opponents. Abusive treatment has occurred in prisons, concentration camps, and detention centers. Kidnappings, assassinations, internal exile, and expulsion from Chile illustrate other forms of physical coercion. The state security police agencies—first the Dirección de Inteligencia Nacional (DINA) and after mid-1977 the Central Nacional de Informaciones (CNI)—the Intelligence Service of Carabineros, the Chilean Anti-Communist Action Squad, and the Intelligence Service of Agriculture have kidnapped and tortured opposition leaders, mainly leftists who supported the Unidad Popular regime. The Chilean secret police have even ordered the executions of Chilean exiles living overseas. For example, General Carlos Prats (former minister of the interior, minister of defense, and commander of the army under the Allende government) was assassinated in Argentina. An auto explosion killed Orlando Letelier, former Chilean ambassador to the United States, in Washington, D.C. An attempt to assassinate Christian Democratic leader Bernardo Leighton in Rome failed.

Economic coercion deprives Allende followers of their livelihood. Government civil servants, intellectuals, professors, teachers, doctors, factory workers, and farmers who supported the Unidad Popular have lost their jobs. Blacklists have prevented them from securing employment. Although opposed to state ownership of private property, the military government has seized the property held by the Unidad Popular parties.

Book burnings, censorship, closing of plays, and bans on Marxist literature represent the main forms of normative coercion. Censors even ban literature about cubism, the art movement, for its supposed sympathy with the Cuban revolution. Through these repressive techniques, the military state has tried to eliminate "the cancer of Marxism" from the Chilean body politic.

In accord with its coercive orientation, the new bureaucratic regime moved to suppress the extensive social pluralism that prevailed during previous administrations. Formerly autonomous ethnic and religious groups have lost their political independence. In the south of Chile, the large landowners, army, and national police (*carabineros*) quashed the

Mapuche Indians by abolishing their communal land, killing resisters, ending their political autonomy, and centralizing state control over them. Although the Roman Catholic church now acts as the primary agency of national reconciliation and as the main institutional opposition to the military regime, it, too, exercises less political freedom than before the coup. Claiming to govern a "Christian nation," the military officers can hardly completely repress church activities. In early 1976 Cardinal Raúl Silva Henríquez organized the Vicariate of Solidarity, which supplies health care, food, employment information, and legal services to the poor and oppressed. Through organizations such as the Vicariate, church personnel assist political prisoners and provide data on missing persons. Naturally, the military rulers look askance at these church activities. Attempting to deter church opposition, the army and police have raided church buildings, arrested priests and nuns, tortured them, and even desecrated the graves of Cardinal Silva's parents. In response to this harassment, Cardinal Silva told an interviewer in 1975: "The Church had more freedom under Allende than it does now. . . . Marxists respected the power of the Church, much more than did the old liberals. . . . The government of Allende, despite all its problems, was a government with which poor people identified, but in no way do they identify with this government."[35]

Whereas Presidents Frei and Allende incorporated nearly all economic groups in government decision-making, under the military regime diverse economic associations no longer constrain state power; instead, state officials, allied with large landowners, corporate executives, and especially financiers, bankers, and technocrats, repress factory workers and small farmers. Immediately after seizing power, the military bureaucrats outlawed peasant associations and the major union organization, the Central Única de Trabajadores. The rights to strike and engage in collective bargaining were curtailed. Today the government restricts union activities to the plant or enterprise level. Often several different unions operate in the same company; fragmented into dispersed organizations, the union movements possess neither the right to bargain collectively above the company level nor the authority to negotiate any matter except wage settlements. Although the state now allows workers the legal right to strike, no strike can last longer than sixty days. Because of the high unemployment and state repression of labor union federations, even this right gives workers little bargaining power against management. Nevertheless, strikes have occurred at copper mines, textile plants, and steel factories. Government-supported candidates have lost union elections to Christian Democratic, Socialist, and Communist activists. They have protested government policies that have frozen wages, reduced salaries, and increased joblessness. All these protests represent signs of continuing labor opposition to the bureaucratic-authoritarian state.

Controls over the private mass media have also tightened. Whereas the Allende government granted television channels, radio stations, newspapers, and magazines the freedom to criticize Unidad Popular policies, the military regime allows the media few such opportunities. Although most media are privately owned, the state regulates their content to ensure that opposition to the military government remains mute. Only a few magazines with low circulations among intellectuals express even mild opposition to government policies. State bureaucrats respond to this moderate criticism by harassing the journals' editors. The *El Mercurio* newspaper chain, which enthusiastically welcomed the military coup, dominates the national press. Still attacking the menace of domestic Marxism and international communism, it offers mainly apologies for government policies. After the *El Mercurio* publishing company incurred severe financial losses in 1983, the state-owned Banco del Estado supplied loans to the company and thereby gained control over a majority of its shares. As a result, the chain came under tighter state supervision by executives (general editor, company lawyers, economic advisers) even more loyal to the Pinochet regime than before. Whereas in the Allende period radio and television stations presented lively political debate, under the military bureaucratic state most have become depoliticized.

The bureaucratic-authoritarian state dominating Chile does allow more pluralism than do such elitist mobilization systems as North Korea, Vietnam, and Cuba; yet this limited pluralism remains vulnerable to state repression. Immediately after the coup, the military officers outlawed leftist trade unions and religious organizations such as the Christians for Socialism. The major opposition groups that retain some autonomy from state control are attached to the Catholic Church. The Vicariate of Solidarity assists the unemployed, feeds the poor, provides health services, and publicizes government violations of human rights. The Workers' Pastorate helps urban union members. Through basic Christian communities, low-income housewives and students seek redress of local grievances. Private church-related institutes that conduct research include the Center of Research and Development in Education, the Latin American Institute of Doctrine and Social Studies, and the Academy of Christian Humanism. At the Latin American Faculty of Social Sciences (FLACSO) and the Center of Economic Research and Planning, scholars also have the power to carry out research projects. Sports clubs, cultural centers, mutual aid societies, professional associations, and trade unions try to organize women, merchants, doctors, lawyers, teachers, students, truck drivers, factory workers, and slum dwellers against the Pinochet administration's policies.

Compared with leftist organizations, right-wing associations have retained greater freedom to pursue their activities. Groups such as the *gremios*, the National Agricultural Society (SNA), the National Industrial Society (SOFOA), the National Association of Advertisers, the Chilean Association of Advertising Agencies, and the Society for the Defense of Tradition, Family, and Property advise government officials.

In short, under the conditions of limited pluralism now prevailing in Chile, the military bureaucrats deny most groups, except right-wing organizations, the right to participate in political decision-making. Yet so long as the Catholic church concentrates on spiritual functions (faith and morals), trade unions negotiate wage settlements at the local plant, sports clubs organize soccer matches, and private research institutes restrict their activities to studying, not changing, society, these organizations retain some autonomy. According to this policy, opposition associations must perform apolitical, specialized tasks if they want their operations unhindered by state repression.

The antiparty state established by the military bureaucrats demobilized all political parties. Whereas under previous administrations political life revolved around active party competition, the military officers associated party competition with *politiquería*, "dirty politics," which the armed forces linked to parliamentary wrangles, opportunistic compromises, and secret deals. Immediately after seizing political power, the military first banned the Marxist parties—the Socialists, Communists, MAPU, Christian Left—and later outlawed all other parties, including the Christian Democratic and the National parties. Only in 1987 did the military junta legalize political parties that repudiated Marxism, championed government doctrines, and pledged to defend national security. Because President Pinochet has shown little enthusiasm for restoring civilian rule, most Christian Democratic leaders have grown increasingly disenchanted with the military government. Even some former National party activists long for a restoration of the parliamentary system. Although the state has outlawed the Communist party, it operates today in various front organizations, such as sports clubs and pop groups. It also has tried to strengthen its influence among students, urban slum dwellers, and the unemployed. Compared with the Communists, the Socialist party has suffered greater losses from military repression, mainly because it had a weaker organization during the Allende administration.

Despite government efforts to weaken parties, their leaders have formed three broad coalitions that correspond with the party formations under the Allende regime. On the Left the Popular Democratic Movement

189

rallies the Communists, left-wing Socialists, and supporters of MIR. Convinced that the repressive Pinochet government will never permit a peaceful road to leftist power, this movement since 1980 has supported not only nonviolent activities (rallies, demonstrations, strikes, negotiations with armed forces officers) but also armed struggle and sabotage as ways to topple the military regime. Allied with the Communist party, the Manuel Rodríguez Patriotic Front has bombed U.S. banks, destroyed electric power stations, and assassinated military officials. In the center, the Democratic Alliance tries to organize Christian Democratic activitists along with leaders of smaller parties: centrist and "humanist" Socialists, Social Democrats, Radicals, and MAPUistas (the Obrero y Campesino wing). Rejecting an alliance with the Communists and left-wing Socialists, the Democratic Alliance has pledged itself to more peaceful tactics, including attempts to secure a dialogue with Pinochet administration officials about the possibilities of greater civilian participation within the regime. On the Right stand the former political party leaders, such as the Nationalists, who most enthusiastically welcomed the military coup. Whereas some right-wingers urge support for Pinochet, others oppose his rule and seek a more democratic alternative. Although these three coalitions retain some freedom to discuss ways of dislodging the Pinochet government from power, each lacks the structural solidarity and attitudinal consensus needed for waging an effective campaign. Divided by ideological conflicts, policy differences, personality clashes, and tactical disputes, members within each fragmented coalition cannot develop sufficient unity against the cohesive army and police that maintain Pinochet's power.[36]

Besides repressing social pluralism and competitive political parties, the bureaucratic-authoritarian state centralized government power. By dissolving the more than 250 municipal councils through which elected local politicians delivered concrete benefits to their constituents, the Pinochet government became even more centralized than the pre-1974 formal institutional structure. Military officials fired, tortured, imprisoned, or killed those mayors who supported the Unidad Popular. In the Allende administration, the municipal councilors elected the mayor, except in Santiago, Valparaíso, and Viña del Mar, where the president selected the mayor. Under the military regime, however, President Pinochet appoints all mayors. Most of his appointments have been former National party supporters, a few Christian Democrats, and military officers. Although the mayor has become the dominant executive official, he remains subordinate to the central government junta. Military commanders now dominate provincial and departmental posts. They are directly accountable to the president. Cities have fewer funds than before the coup.[37]

Government power in the bureaucratic-authoritarian state has become more coordinated around the president. Formerly, the president shared policymaking powers with the congress, courts, and a fairly autonomous civil service. Now the coordinating power over government decisions centers on Pinochet, who rules as president, commander in chief of the armed forces, and head of the army. After leading the coup in 1973, he quickly eliminated his rivals within the navy and air force and gained dominant control over the state bureaucracy, the national police, the secret police, intelligence services, and the armed forces. Pinochet's power over military appointments, promotions, and retirements consolidates his domination. Partly because he has retained support from financiers, industrialists, and the united, professionalized army, he has held office longer than any other president in Chilean history. In his roles as President, Captain General, and Supreme Chief of the Nation, Pinochet coordinates government policies made by military officers and civilian technocrats. Whereas military officials direct such agencies as defense, communications, and the State Development Corporation, civilian technocrats take main responsibility for economic decision-making.

As in other bureaucratic-authoritarian states, in Chile several factions struggle to influence the top ruler. Factional conflicts pit the *duros* (hard-liners) against the *aperturistas*, who prefer reduced military control. The *duros* support the continuation of military rule; for them, national security assumes the dominant policy priority. Less committed to free-market principles, they favor some government-provided social services to the poor and advocate a government party that will mobilize support for the military regime among the general populace. By contrast, the *aperturistas* envision a greater political role for civilians, particularly those economic classes supporting monetarist policies. Opposed to the *duros'* backing for protectionism and stronger state control over the private economy, they prefer free trade, minimal social services to the poor, and privatization of state industries. From their perspective, apolitical technocrats, not military-sponsored party politicians, should govern Chile. Arbitrating these factional disputes, Pinochet usually sides with the *duros* in their support for military dictatorship but with the *aperturistas* in their economic policy preferences.[38]

Although the military-dominated state has become more coercive, monistic, centralized, and coordinated, its scope of political power has lessened, especially over economic and health policies. More precisely, the military regime combines political autocracy with free-market economic policies. Under Pinochet's rule, the state has strengthened its repressive controls over factory workers, subsistence farmers, agricultural wage earners, leftist intellectuals, and opposition leaders. In the economic, health, and educational sectors, however, private enterprises have gained greater power. The government has sold several public enterprises brought under state control during the Frei and Allende administrations. The state no longer supplies so many services and concrete benefits to poor people, who now must depend on Catholic charity and private business beneficence. Private medical centers and private pension fund associations administer health programs that cater to the urban wealthy. Since the government provides fewer scholarships and low-cost educational opportunities for the poor than during the Allende regime, the post-primary educational system now operates mainly for the children of the middle and especially upper classes. Hence, the reduced scope of government power has brought major policy benefits to the economic elite.

### Public Policy Transformations and
### Political Restratification

The public policies pursued by the military regime have restored the upper classes to their former dominant position. Presidents Allende and Frei sought to open the social stratification system by creating more opportunities for small farmers, factory workers, and white-collar personnel. By contrast, the military bureaucracy has reestablished the rigid social stratification system that existed before the 1960s. Under the military regime, the main groups benefiting from government policies have included top-ranking military officers, Chilean bankers, heads of insurance firms, Chilean industrialists allied with foreign corporations, overseas investors, and large-scale landowners who raise food for export. In both urban and rural areas, the class structure has become less differentiated. As more and more small business firms go bankrupt, the economy has come under the domination of economic "clans," or families, that control the private financial sector (banking, insurance), large-scale industries, the mass media, agriculture, and fishing. In the rural areas as well, a simplified class structure has emerged. The agro-industrialists and medium-sized commercial farmers who grow crops for export have reaped the greatest gains from the military government's economic policies. The subsistence farmers (*minifundistas*), many of whom work as temporary wage laborers, have borne the costs. During the post-Allende period, the proportion of the agrarian population employed as subsistence farmers and wage laborers rose; the wealthy agro-industrial exporters also became more numerous. Through its economic policies, the bureaucratic-authoritarian state has restratified Chilean society.[39]

The fiscal policies implemented by the Pinochet government have brought more benefits to the politico-economic elite than to the poor.

Whereas during the Allende administration military expenditures as a share of the gross domestic product remained under 3 percent, from 1974 through 1984 they ranged between 6.1 percent and 9.5 percent, the highest in Latin America except for Cuba. These defense expenditures gave military officials higher salaries, larger pensions, more luxurious residences, free health care, and more technologically advanced weapons. During the latter 1970s government spending on public works and on such social services as education, health care, housing, family allowances, old-age pensions, and public transportation declined as a proportion of total government expenditures. At the same time, Chileans paid increased fees for education, public housing, public transportation, and medical services. According to the social security program implemented during the early 1980s, the government and employers terminated their payments to the old-age pension fund. Now the employer contributes only to the work injury insurance program; the government finances family allowances and unemployment insurance. Employees pay the contributions for pensions, disability insurance, and health insurance. These contributions—nearly a fifth of a worker's monthly salary—are invested by privately owned pension-fund conglom-erates that maintain close ties with the leading banks. Under this social security plan, enterprises gain investment funds and inexpensive credit. Although the government has guaranteed that each retired employee will receive a minimum pension, the retirement benefits under the new system amount to less than half the monthly pension that the worker would have gained from the old program. The new tax policies also exert a regressive effect. The government levied a new value-added tax, which hurt low-income consumers. It decreased corporate income taxes and abolished taxes on profits, bank interest, and capital gains; these tax reductions obviously benefited the wealthy.

Monetary policies have lessened total demand, thereby deflating the economy. During the 1970s the yearly increases in the money supply peaked in 1974 and began to decline thereafter. Whereas in 1974 the quantity of money grew about 315 percent, by 1984 the monetary rise totaled less than 20 percent. As the money supply declined, real domestic interest rates rose; loans became more difficult to secure. Although the Chilean oligopolies could secure loans at lower interest rates from such foreign institutions as the International Monetary Fund, the World Bank, the Inter-American Development Bank, Man-ufacturers Hanover Trust, Chase Manhattan, the National Bank of Paris, Citibank, and Bankers Trust, the small-business sector had no such access to cheap foreign credit. Instead, Chilean bankers and financiers imposed high interest rates on small-scale manufacturers, traders, and farmers. Unable to secure inexpensive credit, many faced bankruptcy.

The government's regulatory policies have exerted a deleterious impact on blue-collar workers, small businesspeople, subsistence farmers, and the poor. Whereas President Allende's incomes policy controlled prices and increased wages, the military bureaucratic state has pursued the opposite tack; it abolished price controls on most goods but regulated wage hikes so that wages increased at a slower rate than consumer prices. According to the government labor code, the minimum wage no longer covers agricultural laborers, young apprentices from fourteen to twenty-one years old, and adults over sixty-five. As a result of these labor policies—longer working hours, reduced wage increases, limitations on personnel covered by the minimum wage—the real wages of workers have drastically declined; in 1982 workers had less purchasing power than in 1971. Foreign trade policies also brought few benefits to low-income citizens. Committed to monetarist policies formulated at the University of Chicago, the economic technocrats sought to expand free trade with the United States, Japan, and West European nations. The government reduced tariffs and customs duties. Currency devaluations from late 1973 through 1979 helped expand the export trade, particularly of fishmeal, fresh fruit (grapes, apples, peaches), wine, and pine wood (logs, sawn timber)—all products grown by the wealthy agro-industrialists. Since the coup the production of cereals, potatoes, soybeans, lamb, and eggs—foods grown by small farmers and consumed especially by low-income people—has decreased. The reduced tariffs on imported goods have promoted greater price competition but at the expense of small farmers and small businesspeople. Without access to low interest rates, they must operate at high production costs; hence, they cannot match the lower prices of imported goods. As a result, small-scale Chilean farms and firms have gone bankrupt, their land and enterprises sold to wealthy Chileans or to executives managing overseas multinational corporations.

Government programs for denationalizing state enterprises brought few benefits to the small-scale Chilean business sector; instead, the Chilean oligopolists and foreign private investors reaped the greatest gains. Dedicated to a private enterprise market economy, the military government removed from state ownership most of the firms that had been nationalized as far back as 1939. Even the General Cemetery of Santiago, operated by the government for over a hundred years, fell under private ownership. State enterprises were sold at a low price (about half their market value) either to Chilean corporations or to foreign multinationals such as Exxon, Firestone, General Tire, and Dow

Chemical. Although most copper industries remained in the public sector, private contractors now operate in the state-owned copper mines and pay lower wages than the state managers. By the mid-1980s the state owned around twenty non-financial public enterprises, mainly electric, telephone, transportation, oil, mining, steel, and coal industries.

Despite this trend toward deregulation and privatization of the economy, the state still controls vital sectors. During late 1982 the economic depression and speculative lending practices caused several large private banks and financial institutions to go bankrupt because of unpaid loans. The state central bank underwrote the payment of these debts. Government managers took charge of lending practices, allocation of any profits, and dividend payments, so that by early 1985 the state owned or controlled 70 percent of banks. Businesspeople and upper-class individuals became dependent on state loans to repay their debts. Nationalization of private liabilities hence accompanied denationalization of state assets.

In the rural areas, public policies that encourage private landowner-ship rewarded large landowners and agro-industrialists. The government returned nearly one-third of the land that comprised the agrarian reform sector to its former owners; around 10 percent was sold at auctions to the urban wealthy, including businesspeople and government officials. The ex-*asentados* gained individual ownership rights to 40 percent of this land. (The government retained the rest as state-owned forest lands or as cooperatives intended for subdivision.) Small farmers secured few benefits from the restoration of privately owned land. When the government reduced price supports for food, small farmers earned lower incomes. The sale of state-owned facilities such as marketing agencies to private enterprises benefited the bankers. The government ended most technical assistance to small farmers, who can no longer obtain inexpensive tractors, harvesters, irrigation facilities, seed, fertilizers, pesticides, and credits. Instead, private enterprises and banks supply these agricultural inputs at higher prices than the government used to charge. Unable to repay their debts, small-scale farmers sold their land to large landowners and agro-industrialists who manage farms over one hundred irrigated acres. At the beginning of the 1980s, no more than one-fifth of former *asentados* retained the land that they had gained under the agrarian reform programs of Presidents Frei and Allende.

Unlike the Unidad Popular regime, the military government of President Pinochet has scored its greatest success in expanding pro-duction and curtailing inflation, rather than lowering unemployment and reducing income inequality. (See Table 6.2.) Particularly after 1976 consumer price rises began to decline to double-digit figures, compared with the triple-digit inflation rates that plagued Chile from 1973 through 1976. Except for 1975, when the real gross domestic product decreased by nearly 13 percent, the GDP rose each year between 1974 and 1981. During 1982–1983, however, Chile suffered from negative growth rates. The bureaucratic-authoritarian state's record on employment and income distribution also diverge from the Allende administration's performance. Whereas the UP government lowered unemployment and expanded income equality, the military regime increased the jobless rolls; between 1975 and 1985 official unemployment figures for greater Santiago ranged between 9 percent and 20 percent of the work force, compared with less than 5 percent during the early 1970s. Youths twenty-five years old or younger faced especially high jobless rates. Under the military bureaucracy, income distribution became less equal. Whereas the wealthiest fifth of the population increased their share of the total national income, the poorest 60 percent secured a lower proportion. Wealthy people who derived their incomes from profits, dividends, and rent made the

TABLE 6.2
UNEMPLOYMENT, INFLATION, AND ECONOMIC GROWTH RATES IN CHILE

| YEAR | PERCENTAGE OF WORK FORCE UNEMPLOYED IN GREATER SANTIAGO | YEARLY CONSUMER PRICE INCREASES | YEARLY CHANGES IN REAL GROSS DOMESTIC PRODUCT |
|------|---------------------------------------------------------|---------------------------------|-----------------------------------------------|
| 1970 | 4.1% | 33% | 1.4% |
| 1971 | 4.2 | 19 | 9.0 |
| 1972 | 3.3 | 77 | −1.2 |
| 1973 | 4.8 | 354 | −5.6 |
| 1974 | 8.3 | 505 | 1.0 |
| 1975 | 15.0 | 375 | −12.9 |
| 1976 | 17.1 | 212 | 3.5 |
| 1977 | 13.9 | 92 | 9.9 |
| 1978 | 13.7 | 40 | 8.2 |
| 1979 | 13.4 | 33 | 8.3 |
| 1980 | 12.0 | 35 | 7.8 |
| 1981 | 9.0 | 20 | 5.5 |
| 1982 | 20.0 | 10 | −14.1 |
| 1983 | 17.1 | 27 | −0.7 |
| 1984 | 18.5 | 20 | 6.3 |
| 1985 | 15.3 | 31 | 2.4 |

Sources: *International Financial Statistics Yearbook 1986* (Washington, D.C.: International Monetary Fund, 1986), 113, 155; *Year Book of Labour Statistics 1980, 1986*, vols. 40, 46 (Geneva: International Labour Office, 1980, 1986), 281, 524.

greatest gains from the economic policies implemented by the free-market technocrats.

The economic growth rates from 1976 to 1981 derived mainly from the rises in the export trade, domestic commerce, and financial services, rather than from higher capital investment and industrialization. The 1975–1979 currency devaluations led to expanding export sales from 1976 through 1980, the years of highest economic growth. During the late 1970s copper attracted a high price on the world market, thus stimulating Chilean enterprises to increase production for sales overseas. The greater mechanization of agriculture expanded the production of food exports such as table grapes, wine, peaches, apples, nectarines, plums, and asparagus. The economic growth rates did not stem from vast increases in capital investment. New investment in capital goods stood at a lower percentage of the gross domestic product in the late 1970s than in 1970 or 1971. Despite the government's efforts to encourage foreign private investment, few overseas corporations during the late 1970s expanded their investments in Chile, except in financial institutions and mines. Because of the deflationary economic policies, Chilean investors had little incentive to add new machinery, equipment, and plants. Since unemployment rates remained high and consumers' purchasing power had declined, the majority of Chileans had less money to spend. Thus plant capacity usage stayed at low levels. Although the Chilean military government and private firms received extensive credits from the World Bank, the Inter-American Development Bank, and overseas private banks, Chileans used these loans to lend money at high interest rates and to pay the soaring foreign debts, rather than to invest in capital equipment.

The drop in inflation rates after 1974 primarily stemmed from government policies to curtail demand and restrain wage costs. Committed to deflationary economic policies, the bureaucratic-authoritarian state raised taxes and cut government expenditures, especially for low-income citizens. As a consequence, the budgetary deficit fell to under 2.5 percent of the gross domestic product during the 1975–1978 period; from 1979 to 1982 the government realized a fiscal surplus. Lower increases in the money supply, combined with higher domestic interest rates, further deflated the economy. These fiscal and monetary policies decreased aggregate spending by government, business, and households; hence, inflation rates declined. Economic policies also lowered the costs incurred by workers, business managers, and government officials. The state restricted labor unions, especially their right to strike and engage in collective bargaining. It made sure that wage increases fell behind rises in the consumer price index. The minimum wage covered a lower percentage of workers than during the Allende period. As a result, labor costs decreased. The encouragement of free trade by overseas firms placed pressures on domestically-owned Chilean businesses to lower their costs and thus their prices. The sale of most state enterprises to private entrepreneurs reduced governmental costs, since the state no longer had to increase the money supply to finance the deficits incurred by public enterprises.

Although the military government's deflationary policies partly contributed to a lower inflation rate, especially after 1976, they also brought about dramatic rises in the jobless rates. When policymakers decreased government expenditures, increased regressive taxes, raised the interest rates, and lowered the increases in the money supply, total demand by government, consumers, and small businesses naturally fell. With the sale of most state enterprises, unskilled workers could no longer secure well-paid government employment; instead, they or their spouses had to work at low wages as servants for the Chilean upper classes. Entrepreneurs who managed the mines, as well as the domestically owned concentrated industries, operated capital-intensive enterprises; hence, unskilled laborers faced greater difficulties finding work. The bankruptcies of the labor-intensive small business firms further added to the jobless rolls. The mechanization of agriculture, which benefited mainly the agro-industrialists who grew crops for export, signaled declining employment opportunities in the rural areas, especially for subsistence farmers and seasonal wage laborers, many of whom fled the countryside to seek jobs in the urban areas. There they joined the ranks of the unemployed living in squalid shantytowns.

Besides increasing joblessness, the deflationary economic policies caused greater income inequality. Wage reductions, decreased government expenditures for social services (pensions, health care, housing, education), and policies that promoted the growth of concentrated industries, especially financial conglomerates, all led to a greater gap between the rich and poor. The growth in the low-paid urban service sector (artisans, shopkeepers, street vendors, mechanics, shoemakers, watch repairers), combined with a declining percentage of the labor force employed in high-wage manufacturing jobs, meant greater income disparities. Although factory workers earned lower real wages, managers, professionals, and technocrats employed in the concentrated industries increased their incomes. In short, the fiscal, monetary, regulatory, and ownership policies of the bureaucratic-authoritarian state brought higher income inequalities. By so doing, they helped restore the politico-economic dominance of the Chilean elites.[40]

Like the economic policies pursued by the military government, its education policies combine economic elitism with political coercion. The bureaucratic state reduced educational opportunities for women, blue-collar workers, and the poor. It gained coercive control over all schools, both public and private. Committed to a normative model that seeks a "moral resurrection" from the evils of Marxism, military officials who control teachers, education administrators, and the curriculum attempt to scrub students' minds clean and teach the values of national unity, patriotism, order, stability, obedience, discipline, hierarchy, political elitism, free markets, and private property. According to the bureaucratic elite, schoolteachers should train their students to be politically passive subjects but economically active entrepreneurs.

The educational program implemented by the military government reflects this commitment to political authoritarianism and economic elitism. Immediately after the coup, military officers, primarily retired ones, seized control over elementary schools, secondary schools, and universities, which relinquished the political autonomy they had enjoyed under the Allende administration. Not only in public institutions but in private schools too, students, teachers, and administrators who had sympathized with the Unidad Popular government lost their positions. The military rectors who gained control over public and Catholic universities fired about one-third of the professors and expelled nearly one-fifth of the students. Many teachers, especially those supporting the UP, were imprisoned or exiled. Even though in the 1980s municipal governments gained authority to manage public primary and secondary schools, President Pinochet appointed the mayors who controlled the schools. The central government's Ministry of Education financed their expenditures and determined their curricula.

Government officials impose an ideologically monistic curriculum on students. Administrators censor the content of courses and encourage teachers to practice "self-censorship." Courses taught in primary and secondary schools stress moral values, Chilean spiritual traditions, national glory, military history, love for the fatherland, and opposition to Marxism. Rather than encourage voluntary political participation based on conflict over public issues, the courses strike an apolitical note. The government has banned any courses that stress group conflict as the main basis of historical analysis. Identifying "politics" with ideological controversies, conflicts of interest, class conflicts, and anarchy, the curriculum developers urge a passive respect for established authorities. Economic values taught in the primary and secondary schools focus on the need to work hard and respect private property. Universities train students for professional, technocratic jobs in private enterprises. The military rectors heading the universities have downgraded the humanities and social sciences (especially political science and sociology), emphasizing instead coursework in business, engineering, architecture, medicine, the natural sciences, and national security. Of all the social sciences, only economics receives special attention. In accordance with the military regime's ideological orientation, faculty who profess the free-market doctrines of Milton Friedman, Friedrich Hayek, James Buchanan, or Gordon Tullock gain the right to teach economics courses. Despite these efforts to impose Hispanic conservative and free-market values on students, elections to the Federation of University Students indicate that the indoctrination attempt has failed. In 1986 the left-wing Popular Democratic Movement and the centrist Christian Democratic slates each secured about 40 percent of the Federation vote, with right-wing candidates obtaining less than 20 percent.

The military regime not only curtailed educational pluralism but also ended the Unidad Popular program for widening access to the schools. Since 1974 enrollments in postsecondary institutions have declined; children from lower-income families no longer can gain the financial assistance available during the Allende period. The bureaucratic state has reduced funds to Catholic schools, which now offer fewer scholarships to poor students. Government policymakers have also curtailed funds to public schools. Whereas in the past the government financed most educational expenses in the state universities, under the military government students themselves must pay higher tuition to attend a university. Deprived of their scholarships and forced to rely on their own resources for financing a university education, low-income students have mainly withdrawn from higher education programs. To a greater extent than before the coup, working-class children now finish their formal education in primary school. Declaring education beyond primary school to be a "privilege," not a right, the military elites have encouraged the expansion of private secondary schools and universities, which serve mainly students from wealthy families.[41]

The health policies made by the military bureaucratic state blend an elitist market model with political autocracy. Through their control over state coercion, the military officials fired about one-third of those Chilean doctors who had supported President Allende's egalitarian health policies. Some judged "irredeemable" by the junta were imprisoned, tortured, and executed. Other UP-supporters among physicians and health-care workers were expelled from the Chilean nation. Opposed to the system of hospital councils and neighborhood health centers established under the Allende administration, the military bureaucrats abolished the local health councils and hospital councils. Devastated by the dismissal of ten thousand health personnel, the National Health

Service had to curtail its programs for low-income citizens. The government decreased expenditures for nutritional programs that benefited children over five years old. Medical care offered by private physicians superseded the former emphasis on government-provided health services. Terminating most free medical programs, state officials encouraged greater competition among private medical groups for patients. Despite this movement toward private medical care, physicians no longer possessed the extensive authority they had held under the Allende administration. The Chilean Medical Association became a purely voluntary association, rather than a professional organization enrolling all physicians and advising government administrators about health policies. Since 1973 nonphysicians have usually directed the Ministry of Health. Bureaucrats who head the local health agencies control both private and public health organizations. Their authority derives from personal loyalty to President Pinochet, not from their professional competence as physicians.

Under the new health-care system instituted during the late 1970s and early 1980s, Chileans secure less egalitarian access to health services than they enjoyed during the Unidad Popular regime. Wealthy urban residents, who rely on private medical centers, can most easily visit a trained physician and use advanced medical facilities. Other high-income individuals participate in private prepaid insurance schemes offered by provisional health institutes. Most Chileans gain health benefits through the National Health Service System (SNSS) or the National Health Fund. Many salaried employees and wage earners contract for health-care benefits with private agencies, which are funded by payroll deductions. Yet the expensive fees charged by these private health institutions deter poor workers from joining them. Low-income persons must use the SNSS public health clinics, which suffer from physician shortages, long waits, overflowing toilets, and a lack of bandages.

Despite the curtailment of health care for the poor, the infant mortality rate declined from around 78 deaths under a year old for every 1000 live births in 1972 to 22 in 1985, a lower rate than in any other large Latin American country except Cuba and Costa Rica. Even though children over five years old received fewer government-financed lunches after 1974, infants under six years continued to secure food at public health centers, where nurses checked the children for childhood diseases. Mothers and infants obtained prenatal and postnatal care from nurses and medical assistants. Under nutritional programs for the poor, pregnant mothers received supplemental milk at emergency malnutrition recuperation centers. All these public programs that gave priority to pregnant mothers and children under six years old helped reduce the infant mortality rate.[42]

In conclusion, the ways that the military regime handles basic policy issues reflect the shift from a reconciliation system to an industrial bureaucratic-authoritarian system. Voluntarism blends with determinism. As head of the bureaucratic state, President Pinochet asserts his will to extirpate the Marxist cancer from the Chilean body politic. Although pledged to reassert Chile's national glory, Pinochet and his advisers still recognize the objective conditions limiting the attainment of their economic goals. For example, Chilean economic growth rates partly depend on the sale of exports. Although far weaker than under the Frei or the Allende administrations, the trade unions still have the power to stage strikes and work slowdowns, actions that affect productivity as well as inflation rates. Sensitive to these objective conditions, the military bureaucrats thus urge the Chilean populace to lower its economic expectations about governmental policy impacts.

Opposed to the severe internal conflicts that beset the Allende regime, the military officials imposed a forced consensus on Chilean society. They suppressed the party conflicts, institutional disputes, and class cleavages that brought about the downfall of the Unidad Popular. Rather than formulating policies through bargains, negotiations, and compromises with diverse participants, the military state rules through decree. Factional policy disputes between the *aperturistas* and the *duros* take place behind the scenes, not in open assemblies. Appeals for national unity constitute the major way that the military government has attempted to strengthen its consensual foundation. Since procedural consensus still remains weak, the policy process shows a rigid style; the military officers, civilian technocrats, and oligopolists who make economic policies face difficulties adapting to new information.

Consistent with the bureaucratic-authoritarian model, state organization takes precedence over social-group spontaneity. Military officers, policemen, civil servants, and technocrats dominate the policy process. Although dedicated to a "free-market" economy, they remain horrified by the social spontaneity that erupted during both the Frei and Allende administrations. According to the bureaucratic view, such populist mobilization activities as strikes, factory takeovers, land seizures, rallies, and demonstrations pulled Chile into anarchy, disorder, and chaos. One primary reason for the *golpe de estado* was to repress this *espontaneísmo* and restore order to Chile. Despite state attempts to crush the populist mobilization, spontaneous movements still maintain vitality. Populist mobilizers in the shantytowns of Santiago organize cooperative purchase associations, soup kitchens, housing committees, health centers, employment workshops, cultural clubs, women's groups, and basic Christian communities. The Roman Catholic church offers support to all these groups, but poor people themselves lead the populist mobilization drive. They stage street demonstrations, utility bill payment strikes, land seizures of vacant housing, and raids on supermarkets, warehouses, and trucks. Most political decisions occur in general assemblies and involve extensive popular participation by the shantytown dwellers, especially youths and women. Committed to "Popular Power" and "shantytown mobilization," the United Slumdwellers Committee coordinates the *pobladores'* activities. Even though the military and police have forcibly relocated the *pobladores* and mounted night raids against the poor, these populist mobilization activities continue functioning. Thus the Chilean state rules through extensive coercion. Yet its control over social groups remains more limited than in an elitist mobilization regime such as Cuba.[43]

Rather than maintain continuity with the pluralist decision-making procedures of the Frei and Allende administrations, the military officers who staged the 1973 coup brought drastic changes to Chile. Although they wanted to establish a technologically advanced capitalist economy, their political style marked a return to the eighteenth century, when the Spanish army ruled Chile as a political autocracy.[44] Unlike the political situation two hundred years ago, today the military elite has allied with civilian "free-market" technocrats. From their perspective, the "true" revolutions of the modern era are not the Soviet or Cuban revolutions but the technological advancements secured through electronics developments. Claiming to know the interests of the bourgeoisie better than private business executives themselves, the technocrats rely on the army to guide Chile toward a more modernized capitalist society based on science and technology. By operating a rigid bureaucratic-authoritarian system, the military elite has hindered opportunities for peaceful sociopolitical change.

# Notes

1 See Robert L. Ayres, "Economic Stagnation and the Emergence of the Political Ideology of Chilean Underdevelopment," *World Politics* 25 (October 1972): 34–61; Michael S. Lewis-Beck, "Some Economic Effects of Revolution: Models, Measurement, and the Cuban Evidence," *American Journal of Sociology* 84 (March 1979): 1127–1149.

2 Jorge I. Domínguez, *Cuba: Order and Revolution* (Cambridge, Mass.: Harvard University Press, 1978), 108; Arturo Valenzuela, *The Breakdown of Democratic Regimes: Chile* (Baltimore, Md.: The Johns Hopkins University Press, 1978), 35.

3 Maurice Zeitlin, "Cuba: Revolution without a Blueprint," in *Cuban Communism*, 3d ed., ed. Irving Louis Horowitz (New Brunswick, N.J.: Transaction Books, 1977), 199–210; Maurice Zeitlin and Richard E. Ratcliff, "The Concentration of National and Foreign Capital in Chile," in *Chile: Politics and Society*, ed.

Arturo Valenzuela and J. Samuel Valenzuela (New Brunswick, N.J.: Transaction Books, 1976), 297–337; Liisa North, "The Military in Chilean Politics," *Studies in Comparative International Development* 11 (Summer 1976): 73–106, esp. 85, 90–93.

4 See *Statistical Abstract of Latin America*, vol. 20, ed. James W. Wilkie (Los Angeles: University of California at Los Angeles Latin American Center Publications, 1980), 543; Jorge Tapia-Videla, "The Chilean Presidency in a Developmental Perspective," *Journal of Interamerican Studies and World Affairs* 19 (November 1977): 451–481; Maurice Zeitlin, *The Civil Wars in Chile* (Princeton, N.J.: Princeton University Press, 1984); Brian Loveman, *Chile: The Legacy of Hispanic Capitalism* (New York: Oxford University Press, 1979), 176–182; North, "The Military in Chilean Politics," 79–80; George I. Blanksten, "Fidel Castro and Latin America," in *The Revolution in World Politics*, ed. Morton A. Kaplan (New York: Wiley, 1962), 115–121. As Loveman, 177, 180–181, points out, even between 1840 and 1890, during the period of the "autocratic republic," the Chilean congress strengthened its power over the executive, gaining veto power over taxes, the budget, and the size of the armed forces.

5 Robert J. Alexander, *The Tragedy of Chile* (Westport, Conn.: Greenwood Press, 1978), 118–128.

6 Salvador Allende, *Chile's Road to Socialism*, trans. J. Darling (Baltimore, Md.: Penguin Books, 1973), 52–68, 140.

7 Laurence Birns, ed., *The End of Chilean Democracy: An IDOC Dossier on the Coup and Its Aftermath* (New York: Seabury Press, 1974), 31; Allende, *Chile's Road to Socialism*, 71–74.

8 Allende, *Chile's Road to Socialism*, 63, 143–145.

9 Ibid., 171–172. See also 94–97, 111, 161.

10 See Paul W. Drake, *Socialism and Populism in Chile, 1932–52* (Urbana: University of Illinois Press, 1978), 318–341; Thomas John Bossert, *Political Argument and Policy Issues in Allende's Chile* (Ph.D. dissertation, Department of Political Science, University of Wisconsin—Madison, 1976), 273; Radomiro Tomic, "Christian Democracy and the Government of the Unidad Popular," in *Chile at the Turning Point: Lessons of the Socialist Years, 1970–1973*, ed. Federico G. Gill, Ricardo Lagos E., and Henry A. Landsberger (Philadelphia: Institute for the Study of Human Issues, 1979), 209–239. Sergio Bitar, *Chile: Experiment in Democracy*, trans. Sam Sherman (Philadelphia: Institute for the Study of Human Issues, 1986), 227–228.

11 Laurence Whitehead, "The Socialist Experiment in Chile," *Parliamentary Affairs* 25 (Summer 1972): 235–236; George I. Blanksten, "The Politics of Latin America," in *The Politics of the Developing Areas*, ed. Gabriel A. Almond and James S. Coleman (Princeton, N.J.: Princeton University Press, 1960), 461.

12 Brian H. Smith, *The Church and Politics in Chile: Challenges to Modern Catholicism* (Princeton University Press, 1982), 130–133, 216–220; Brian H. Smith and José Luis Rodríguez, "Comparative Working-Class Political Behavior: Chile, France, and Italy," *American Behavioral Scientist* 18 (September 1974): 59–96; Michael Dodson, "The Christian Left in Latin American Politics," *Journal of Interamerican Studies and World Affairs* 21 (February 1979): 45–68.

13 See César Caviedes, *The Politics of Chile: A Sociogeographical Assessment* (Boulder, Colo.: Westview Press, 1979), 91–107; Barbara Stallings, *Class Conflict and Economic Development in Chile, 1958–1973* (Stanford, Calif.: Stanford University Press, 1978), 34–37, 42–46, 54–55; James D. Cockcroft, "Impact of Trans-

national Corporations on Chile's Social Structure," *Summation* 5 (Summer/Fall 1975): 7–32; Maurice Zeitlin, Lynda Ann Ewen, and Richard Earl Ratcliff, "'New Princes' for Old? The Large Corporation and the Capitalist Class in Chile," *American Journal of Sociology* 80 (July 1974): 87–123; Zeitlin and Ratcliff, "The Concentration of National and Foreign Capital in Chile," 297–337.

14 Caviedes, *The Politics of Chile*, 107–122; Stallings, *Class Conflict and Economic Development in Chile*, 55, 244–245; Robert Ayres, "Unidad Popular and the Chilean Electoral Process," in *Chile: Politics and Society*, 30–66; Smith and Rodríguez, "Comparative Working-Class Political Behavior," 67; Ian Roxborough, Philip O'Brien, and Jackie Roddick, *Chile: The State and Revolution* (New York: Holmes and Meier, 1977), 246.

15 Smith and Rodríguez, "Comparative Working-Class Political Behavior," 64–71; Smith, *The Church and Politics in Chile*, 153; Caviedes, *The Politics of Chile*, 123–135; Stallings, *Class Conflict and Economic Development in Chile*, 55–57, 217–220, 245.

16 For analyses of the agrarian class structure, see Peter Winn and Cristóbal Kay, "Agrarian Reform and Rural Revolution in Allende's Chile," *Journal of Latin American Studies* 6 (May 1974): 135–159; Cristóbal Kay, "Agrarian Reform and the Transition to Socialism in Chile, 1970–1973," *Journal of Peasant Studies* 2 (July 1975): 418–445; Cristóbal Kay, "Agrarian Reform and the Class Struggle in Chile," *Latin American Perspectives* 5 (Summer 1978): 117–140; Ian Roxborough, *The Political Mobilization of Farm Workers during the Chilean Agrarian Reform, 1971–1973: A Case Study* (Ph.D. dissertation, Department of Sociology, University of Wisconsin—Madison, 1977), 272–291; Roxborough, O'Brien, and Roddick, *Chile*, 135–143; Daniel Hellinger, "Electoral Change in the Chilean Countryside: The Presidential Elections of 1958 and 1970," *Western Political Quarterly* 31 (June 1978): 253–273.

17 See Bossert, *Political Argument and Policy Issues in Allende's Chile*, 216–258; Drake, *Socialism and Populism in Chile*, 309–332; Benny Pollack, "The Chilean Socialist Party: Prolegomena to Its Ideology and Organization," *Journal of Latin American Studies* 10 (May 1978): 117–152; Carlos Altamirano, "Critical Reflections on the Chilean Revolutionary Process," *Socialist Thought and Practice* 16 (September 1974): 79–103; Eusebio M. Mujal-Léon, "The Communist Party of Chile, 1969–1973: The Limits of Pluralism," *World Affairs* 136 (Fall 1973): 132–151; Andrew Zimbalist, "The Dynamic of Worker Participation: An Interpretive Essay on the Chilean and Other Experiences," *Administration and Society* 7 (May 1975): 43–54; Juan G. Espinosa and Andrew S. Zimbalist, *Economic Democracy: Workers' Participation in Chilean Industry, 1970–1973* (New York: Academic Press, 1978), 105–107; Andy Zimbalist and Barbara Stallings, "Showdown in Chile," *Monthly Review* 25 (October 1973): 1–24; Alexander, *The Tragedy of Chile*, 256–257.

18 David Lehmann, "The Political Economy of Armageddon: Chile, 1970–1973," *Journal of Development Economics* 5 (June 1978): 107–114; Zimbalist and Stallings, "Showdown in Chile," 5–22; James Petras, *Politics and Social Forces in Chilean Development* (Berkeley: University of California Press, 1969), 197–219; Roxborough, *Political Mobilization of Farm Workers*, 150–157; Jack Spence, "Class Mobilization and Conflict in Allende's Chile: A Review Essay," *Politics and Society* 8, no. 2 (1978): 134; Michael Fleet, *The Rise and Fall of Chilean Christian Democracy* (Princeton, N.J.: Princeton University Press, 1985), 128–175; Radomiro Tomic, "The PDC during the Allende Years and Some Comments

on the Origin of the Christian Democratic Left Wing," in *Chile at the Turning Point*, 328–340.

19 Luis Quirós-Varela, *Agrarian Policies in Chile: Stagnation, Reform and Counter-Reform in the Countryside* (Ph.D. dissertation, Department of Political Science, University of North Carolina at Chapel Hill, 1979), 125; Roxborough, O'Brien, and Roddick, *Chile*, 69, 82, 96; Laurence Whitehead, *The Lesson of Chile*, Fabian Research Series 317 (London: Fabian Society, 1974), 38–39; *Latin America 7* (March 9, 1973): 73; Peter A. Goldberg, "The Politics of the Allende Overthrow in Chile," *Political Science Quarterly* 90 (Spring 1975): 93–116; Tapia-Videla, "The Chilean Presidency in a Developmental Perspective," 451–481; Valenzuela, *The Breakdown of Democratic Regimes: Chile*, 35, 85; J. Biehl del Río and Gonzalo Fernandez R., "The Political Pre-requisites for a Chilean Way," *Government and Opposition* 7 (Summer 1972): 314–317.

20 Smith, *The Church and Politics in Chile*, 189–190, 196–208, 225; Alexander, *The Tragedy of Chile*, 247; Patricia Fagen, "The Media in Allende's Chile," *Journal of Communication* 24 (Winter 1974): 59–70; Lehmann, "The Political Economy of Armageddon," 112; Jorge Nef, "The Politics of Repression: The Social Pathology of the Chilean Military," *Latin American Perspectives* 1 (Summer 1974): 60–61.

21 Federico G. Gil, *The Political System of Chile* (Boston: Houghton Mifflin, 1966), 129–131; Valenzuela, *The Breakdown of Democratic Regimes: Chile*, 53–54; Arturo Valenzuela, *Political Brokers in Chile: Local Government in a Centralized Polity* (Durham, N.C.: Duke University Press, 1977).

22 For analyses of the structural incoherence in the Allende administration's processing of policy issues, see Bitar, *Chile*, 219–221, 234–235; Valenzuela, *Breakdown of Democratic Regimes: Chile*, 13–19; Arturo Valenzuela, "Political Constraints to the Establishment of Socialism in Chile," in *Chile: Politics and Society*, 3–9, 14–25; Tapia-Videla, "The Chilean Presidency," 466–472; H. Zemelman and Patricia Leon, "Political Opposition to the Government of Allende," *Government and Opposition* 7 (Summer 1972): 328–330; Roxborough, O'Brien, and Roddick, *Chile*, 88–93, 111–112; Bossert, *Political Argument and Policy Issues in Allende's Chile*, 113–115; Quirós-Varela, *Agrarian Policies in Chile*, 125, 189.

23 For analyses of economic policies and impacts during the Allende regime, see the following studies: Stallings, *Class Conflict and Economic Development in Chile*, 49–50, 125–226, 252, 260–262; Espinosa and Zimbalist, *Economic Democracy*, 46–50, 141–185; Alejandro Foxley, Eduardo Aninat, and José P. Arellano, "Chile: The Role of Asset Redistribution in Poverty-Focused Development Strategies," *World Development* 5 (January/February 1977): 69–88; John Strasma, "Campesinos, Land, and Employment under Unidad Popular," in *Chile at the Turning Point*, 195–204; Pío García, "The Social Property Sector: Its Political Impact," in *Chile at the Turning Point*, 160–182; Thomas G. Sanders, "Counter-reform in the Chilean Campo," *American Universities Field Staff Reports*, no. 32 (June 1980): 4; Kay, "Agrarian Reform and the Transition to Socialism in Chile," 418–445; Kay, "Agrarian Reform and the Class Struggle in Chile," 117–140; Roxborough, *Political Mobilization of Farm Workers*, 275–293; Quirós-Varela, *Agrarian Policies in Chile*, 140–149, 183–206; Brian Loveman, *Struggle in the Countryside: Politics and Rural Labor in Chile, 1919–1973* (Bloomington: Indiana University Press, 1976), 279–334: Loveman, *Chile*, 265–267, 335–340; Valenzuela, *The Breakdown of Democratic Regimes: Chile*, 50–59, 64–65; Zeitlin

and Ratcliff, "The Concentration of National and Foreign Capital in Chile," 297–327; Markos J. Mamalakis, compiler, *Historical Statistics of Chile: National Accounts* (Westport, Conn.: Greenwood Press, 1978), 164–165; *International Financial Statistics Yearbook 1984* (Washington, D.C.: International Monetary Fund, 1984), 79, 103, 123; Sebastian Edwards, "Stabilization with Liberalization: An Evaluation of Ten Years of Chile's Experiment with Free-Market Policies, 1973–1983," *Economic Development and Cultural Change* 33 (January 1985): 227; Andres Drobny, "The Influence of Minimum Wage Rates on the Level and Distribution of Real Wages in Chile, 1960–1972," *Bulletin of Latin American Research* 2 (May 1983): 17–38; *Year Book of Labour Statistics 1980* (Geneva: International Labour Office, 1980), 281; Paul E. Sigmund, *The Overthrow of Allende and the Politics of Chile, 1964–1976* (Pittsburgh, Penn.: University of Pittsburgh Press, 1977), 279–283.

24 See Pedro Castro, *La educación en Chile de Frei a Pinochet* (Salamanca, Spain: Ediciones Sígueme, Tierra dos Tercios, 1977), 123–197; Smith; *The Church and Politics in Chile*, 189–199; Ernesto Schiefelbein and Joseph P. Farrell, "Selectivity and Survival in the Schools of Chile," *Comparative Education Review* 22 (June 1978): 326–341; Sigmund, *The Overthrow of Allende*, 163–170, 189–190, 202–206; Arthur Liebman and James F. Petras, "Class and Student Politics in Chile," *Politics and Society* 3 (Spring 1973): 329–345; Kathleen B. Fischer, *Political Ideology and Educational Reform in Chile, 1964–1976* (Los Angeles: University of California at Los Angeles Latin American Center Publications, 1979), 59–117.

25 Vicente Navarro, *Medicine under Capitalism* (London: Croom Helm, 1976), 33–57; Hilary Modell and Howard Waitzkin, "Health Care and Socialism in Chile," *Monthly Review* 27 (May 1975): 29–40; Hilary Modell and Howard Waitzkin, "Medicine and Socialism in Chile," *Berkeley Journal of Sociology* 19 (1974–1975): 1–20; Diana Chanfreau, "Professional Ideology and the Health Care System in Chile," *International Journal of Health Services* 9, no. 1 (1979): 87–105; *Statistical Abstract of Latin America*, vol. 20, p. 90.

26 For analyses of populist mobilization during the Allende presidency, see Peter Winn, *Weavers of Revolution: The Yarur Workers and Chile's Road to Socialism* (New York: Oxford University Press, 1986), esp. 120–245; Tapia-Videla, "The Chilean Presidency," 465–476; Smith, *The Church and Politics in Chile*, 136–141, 237; Dennis Burnett, "Grass Root and Political Struggle—the *Pobladores* Movement in Chile 1968–1973," *Vierteljahresberichete*, no. 78 (1979): 375–383; Paul W. Drake, "Corporatism and Functionalism in Modern Chilean Politics," *Journal of Latin American Studies* 10 (May 1978): 83–116, esp. 110–115; Drake, *Socialism and Populism in Chile*, 325–333; Stallings, *Class Conflict and Economic Development in Chile*, 39–40, 57–59, 141–144; Robert R. Kaufman, *Transitions to Stable Authoritarian Corporate Regimes: The Chilean Case?* Sage Professional Papers in Comparative Politics, vol. 5, series no. 01–060 (Beverley Hills, Calif.: Sage Publications, 1976); Brian Loveman, "Allende's Chile: Political Economy of the Peaceful Road to Disaster," *New Scholar* 5, no. 2 (1978): 313; Spence, "Class Mobilization and Conflict in Allende's Chile," 131–164; Henry A. Landsberger and Tim McDaniel, "Hyper-Mobilization in Chile, 1970–1973," *World Politics* 28 (July 1976): 502–541; Harvey Waterman, "Political Mobilization and the Case of Chile," *Studies in Comparative International Development* 13 (Spring 1978): 60–70; María de los Angeles Crummett, "El Poder Feminino: The Mobilization of Women against Socialism in Chile," *Latin American Perspectives* 4 (Fall 1977): 103–113; Lehmann, "The Political Economy of Armageddon," 119–123;

Alexander, *The Tragedy of Chile*, 273–283, 301–305. "Populist mobilization" does not mean that the poor people organized themselves. Most often, students, intellectuals, left-wing professionals, and young, well-educated workers from leftist families led the mobilization activities. Nevertheless, the mobilization sprang from below, not from above in the form of a powerful state and centralized party. In this sense, the mobilization was populist.

27 Whitehead, *The Lesson of Chile*, 30–35; Alain Wallon, "Perspectives actuelles du mouvement ouvrier au Chili," *Les Temps modernes*, no. 323 (June 1973): 1989–1990; Julio Samuel Valenzuela, "The Chilean Labor Movement: The Institutionalization of Conflict," in *Chile: Politics and Society*, 135–164; Landsberger and McDaniel, "Hyper-mobilization in Chile," 502–541; Waterman, "Political Mobilization and the Case of Chile," 65–66; Stallings, *Class Conflict and Economic Development in Chile*, 40–41; Peter Winn, "Loosing the Chains: Labor and the Chilean Revolutionary Process, 1970–1973," *Latin American Perspectives* 3 (Winter 1976): 71–72; Kay, "Agrarian Reform and the Class Struggle in Chile," 117–140; Alejandro Foxley and Oscar Muñoz, "Income Redistribution, Economic Growth, and Social Structure: The Case of Chile," *Oxford Bulletin of Economics and Statistics* 36 (February 1974): 21–44; Richard E. Ratcliff, "Capitalists in Crisis: The Chilean Upper Class and the September 11 Coup," *Latin American Perspectives* 1 (Summer 1974): 78–90; Zeitlin and Ratcliff, "The Concentration of National and Foreign Capital in Chile," 117–120; James W. Prothro and Patricio E. Chaparro, "Public Opinion and the Movement of Chilean Government to the Left, 1952–72," *Journal of Politics* 36 (February 1974): 37–40; Bitar, *Chile*, 196–235.

28 Drake, *Socialism and Populism in Chile*, 325–334; Bossert, *Political Argument and Policy Issues in Allende's Chile*, 230–249; Roxborough, O'Brien, and Roddick, *Chile*, 108–112, 266; Cristóbal Kay, "Chile: The Making of a Coup d'État," *Science and Society* 39 (Spring 1975): 3–25; Cristóbal Kay, "Chile since 1920," *Latin American Research Review*, 14, no. 3 (1979): 264–279; James F. Petras, "Chile: Crime, Class Consciousness and the Bourgeoisie," *Crime and Social Justice*, no. 7 (Spring/Summer 1977): 14–22; North, "The Military in Chilean Politics," 73–106; Frederick M. Nunn, "New Thoughts on Military Intervention in Latin American Politics: The Chilean Case, 1973," *Journal of Latin American Studies* 7 (November 1975): 271–304; Stallings, *Class Conflict and Economic Development in Chile*, 46–50, 61; Antonio Moreno Rivas, "Sobre la democracia y los militares: El caso chileno," *Revista Mexicana de Sociología* 37 (July-September 1975): 737–765.

29 Pollack, "The Chilean Socialist Party," 151–152; Christian Lalive d'Epinay and Jacques Zylberberg, "Une Variable oubliée de la problématique agraire: Le prolétariat urbain," *Civilisations* 23/24, nos. 1/2 (1973/1974): 51–64; Landsberger and McDaniel, "Hyper-mobilization in Chile," 510–514, 517–521; Goldberg, "The Politics of the Allende Overthrow in Chile," 115; Roxborough, *Political Mobilization of Farm Workers*, 533–577; Smith, *The Church and Politics in Chile*, 210–228, 287–288; Valenzuela, *The Breakdown of Democratic Regimes: Chile*, 59, 69–70, 101; Tomic, "Christian Democracy and the Government of the Unidad Popular," 234–235.

30 Francisco Zapata, "Strikes and Political Systems in Latin America," *Die Dritte Welt* 7, no. 1 (1979): 93–97, 105; Morris Morley and Steven Smith, "Imperial 'Reach': U.S. Policy and the CIA in Chile," *Journal of Political and Military Sociology* 5 (Fall 1977): 203–216; James Petras and Morris Morley, "Chilean Destabilization and Its Aftermath: An Analysis and a Critique," *Politics* 11 (November

1976): 140–148; James Petras and Morris Morley, "On the U.S. and the Overthrow of Allende: A Reply to Professor Sigmund's Criticism," *Latin American Research Review* 13, no. 1 (1978): 205–221; William J. Barclay, "State and Capital: The Case of 'Chilean' Copper," *Summation* 5 (Summer/Fall 1975): 32–44; William Shawcross, "Nixon's Way with Allende," *New Statesman* 86 (September 21, 1973): 371–372; Elizabeth Farnsworth, "Chile: What Was the U.S. Role? (1) More than Admitted," *Foreign Policy*, no. 16 (Fall 1974): 127–141; Elizabeth Farnsworth, Richard Feinberg, and Eric Leenson, "The Invisible Blockade: The United States Reacts," in *Chile: Politics and Society*, 338–373; Henry Kissinger, *White House Years* (Boston: Little, Brown, 1979), 653–683; U.S. Congress, Senate, *Covert Action in Chile: 1963–1973*, Staff Report of the Select Committee to Study Government Operations with Respect to Intelligence Activities, 94th Cong., 1st sess., December 18, 1975; U.S. Congress, Senate, *Alleged Assassination Plots Involving Foreign Leaders*, An Interim Report of the Select Committee to Study Governmental Operations with Respect to Intelligence Activities, S. Rept. 94–465, 94th Cong., 1st sess., November 20, 1975, pp. 225–254, 262; Valenzuela, *The Breakdown of Democratic Regimes: Chile*, 56–57; Stallings, *Class Conflict and Economic Development in Chile*, 238; Clodomiro Almeyda Medina, "The Foreign Policy of the Unidad Popular Government," in *Chile at the Turning Point*, 76–103, esp. 97–100; Joseph L. Nogee and John W. Sloan, "Allende's Chile and the Soviet Union: A Policy Lesson for Latin American Nations Seeking Autonomy," *Journal of Interamerican Studies and World Affairs* 21 (August 1979): 339–368.

31 Jorge Tapia-Videla, "The Difficult Road to Socialism: The Chilean Case from a Historical Perspective," in *Chile at the Turning Point*, 41–43.

32 Karl Marx, *Surveys from Exile: Political Writings*, vol. 2, ed. David Fernbach (New York: Vintage Books, 1974), 178–179. Three months before the coup, Miguel Enriques, MIRista leader who was later killed by the military government, declared: "The working class is today a structured army, bent on fighting for its interests and resisting the onslaught of the reactionaries. The working class and the people . . . have given notice to their political leadership that the struggle has left the corridors of parliament and that they will not permit setbacks or concessions." Quoted in Valenzuela, *The Breakdown of Democratic Regimes: Chile*, 101.

33 See "Speech by Augusto Pinochet Ugarte," in *The Politics of Antipolitics: The Military in Latin America*, ed. Brian Loveman and Thomas M. Davies, Jr. (Lincoln: University of Nebraska Press, 1978), 200–207; "Pinochet's Campaign Platform: A Review of His Latest Literary Effort," *Latin America Regional Reports Southern Cone*, March 7, 1986, p. 4; P. Bule, "Elements for A Critical Analysis of the Present Cultural System," in *Chile at the Turning Point*, 359–367; Smith, *The Church and Politics in Chile*, 294–295, 304; Gabriel Marcella, "The Chilean Military Government and the Prospects for Transition to Democracy," *Interamerican Economic Affairs* 33 (Autumn 1979): 3–19; Hernán Vidal, "The Politics of the Body: The Chilean Junta and the Anti–Fascist Struggle," *Social Text* 1 (Summer 1979): 104–111; Michael Moffitt, "Chicago Economics in Chile," *Challenge* 20 (September/October 1977): 35; *The Chile Monitor*, no. 5 (April 1974): 11; Alejandro Foxley, *Latin American Experiments in Neoconservative Economics* (Berkeley: University of California Press, 1983), 101–102; Sergio Bitar, "Monetarism and Ultraliberalism, 1973–80," *International Journal of Politics* 12 (Winter, 1982/1983): 10–47; Karen L. Remmer, "Public Policy and

Regime Consolidation: The First Five Years of the Chilean Junta," *Journal of Developing Areas* 13 (July 1979); 441–461.

34 *Statistical Abstract of Latin America*, vol. 25, ed. James W. Wilkie and David Lorey (Los Angeles: University of California at Los Angeles Latin American Center Publications, 1987), 179. See also the following sources for details of the coercive power wielded by the military government: "Terror in Chile," *New York Review of Books* 21 (May 30, 1974): 38–44; "UN and Human Rights in Chile," *Human Rights Review* 1 (Autumn 1976): 145–156; Karen L. Remmer, "Political Demobilization in Chile, 1973–1978," *Comparative Politics* 12 (April 1980): 282–283; Alexander, *The Tragedy of Chile*, 357, 390–394; Mark A. Uhlig, "Pinochet's Tyranny," *New York Review of Books* 32 (June 27, 1985): 35–40; Hugo Fruhling, "Stages of Repression and Legal Strategy for the Defense of Human Rights in Chile: 1973–1980," *Human Rights Quarterly* 5 (November 1983): 510–533; Rodolpho Borquez, "La Répression culturelle sous la dictature," *Socialisme* 30 (September/October 1983): 435–449; Jim Guy, "The Case of the Mapuche and Chile's 'Bad' Law 2568," *International Perspectives* (September/October 1981): 14–16; *Amnesty International Report 1986* (London: Amnesty International Publications, 1986), 132–137; *Latin American Regional Reports Southern Cone*, February 5, 1987, p. 2.

35 Smith, *The Church and Politics in Chile*, 208, as well as 317–322. See also Thomas G. Sanders, "Popular Religion, Pastoral Renewal, and National Reconciliation in Chilean Catholicism," *American Universities Field Staff Reports*, no. 16 (March 1981): 1–11.

36 Drake, *Socialism and Populism in Chile*, 340–341; Drake, "Corporatism and Functionalism in Modern Chilean Politics," 83–88, 114–116; Nef, "The Politics of Repression," 71–76; Bob High, "Chile: Five Years Later," *NACLA Report on the Americas* 12 (September/October 1978): 34–41; Thomas G. Sanders, "Military Rule in Chile," *Common Ground* 2 (April 1976): 21–32; Raquel Salinas Bascur, "Chilean Communications under the Military Regime: 1973–1979," *Current Research on Peace and Violence* 2, no. 2 (1979): 80–95; Quirós-Varela, *Agrarian Policies in Chile*, 289–293; Alexander, *The Tragedy of Chile*, 426–443; David Stephen, "Legitimising a Reign of Terror," *New Statesman* 99 (January 25, 1980): 120–122; Crummet, "El poder feminino," 103–113; Sanders, "Popular Religion, Pastoral Renewal, and National Reconciliation in Chilean Catholicism," 4–11; Thomas G. Sanders, "Education and Authoritarianism in the Southern Cone," *American Universities Field Staff Reports*, no. 12 (January 1981): 13–14; James Petras, "The Chicago Boys Flunk Out in Chile," *Nation* 236 (February 19, 1983): 193, 210–211; Nigel Haworth and Jackie Roddick, "Labour and Monetarism in Chile 1975–80," *Bulletin of Latin American Research* 1 (October 1981): 49–62; Lois Oppenheim, "Democracy and Social Transformation in Chile: The Debate within the Left," *Latin American Perspectives* 12 (Summer 1985): 59–76; Uhlig, "Pinochet's Tyranny," 35–40; Claudio Duran, "Return to Chile," *Canadian Forum* 64 (April 1984): 6–9; Arturo Valenzuela, "Prospects for the Pinochet Regime in Chile," *Current History* 84 (February 1985): 77–80, 89–90; Alan Angell, "Pinochet's Chile: The Beginning of the End?" *World Today* 41 (February 1985): 27–30; Carmelo Furci, "The Chilean Communist Party (PCCh) and Its Third Underground Period, 1973–1980," *Bulletin of Latin American Research* 2 (October 1982): 81–95; Fleet, *The Rise and Fall of Chilean Christian Democracy*, 199–207; Jorge Edwards, "Books in Chile," *Index on Censorship* 13 (April 1984): 20–22; Michael Moneteón, "Chile under the Dictator," *Socialist*

*Review* 16 (May-August 1986): 99–118; Ariel Dorfman, "The Challenge in Chile," *New York Times Magazine*, June 29, 1986, pp. 22–29; Francisco Zapata, "Crisis económica y movilización social en Chile (1981–1984)," *Foro Internacional* 26 (October-December 1985): 221–225; Arturo Valenzuela and J. Samuel Valenzuela, "Party Oppositions under the Chilean Authoritarian Regime," in *Military Rule in Chile: Dictatorship and Oppositions*, ed. J. Samuel Valenzuela and Arturo Valenzuela (Baltimore: The Johns Hopkins University Press, 1986), 184–229; Brian Loveman, "Military Dictatorship and Political Opposition in Chile, 1973–1986," *Journal of Interamerican Studies and World Affairs* 28 (Winter 1986–1987): 1–38; Guy Bajoit, "Mouvements sociaux et politiques au Chili," *Problèmes d'Amérique Latine*, no. 79 (1986): 5–27; Manuel Barrera and J. Samuel Valenzuela, "The Development of Labor Movement Opposition to the Regime," in *Military Rule in Chile*, 230–269; Alan Angell, "Why Is the Transition to Democracy Proving so Difficult in Chile?" *Bulletin of Latin American Research* 5, no. 1 (1986): 25–40; Pamela Constable, "Pinochet's Grip on Chile," *Current History* 86 (January 1987): 17–20, 38–40; Martin Andersen, "Staying the Course in Chile," *SAIS Review* 7 (Winter/Spring 1987): 169–183; Alfred Stepan, "State Power and the Strength of Civil Society in the Southern Cone of Latin America," in *Bringing the State Back In*, ed. Peter B. Evans, Dietrich Rueschemeyer, and Theda Skocpol (New York: Cambridge University Press, 1985), 317–343; *Latin American Weekly Report*: January 27, 1984, p. 5, May 4, 1984, p. 3, June 22, 1984, p. 5, January 22, 1987, p. 9, February 26, 1987, p. 9; *Latin American Regional Reports Southern Cone*: March 9, 1984, p. 9, May 25, 1984, p. 7, April 19, 1985, pp. 6–7, June 28, 1985, p. 3.

37  Camilo Taufic, *Chile en la hoguera: Crónica de la represión militar* (Buenos Aires: Ediciones Corregidor, 1974), 264; *Latin America* 8 (May 17, 1974): 148–149; Valenzuela, *Political Brokers in Chile*, xi–xii, 221–231.

38  Quirós-Varela, *Agrarian Policies in Chile*, 253–256; *Latin America Weekly Report*, July 18, 1980, p. 5; *Latin America Regional Reports*, August 1, 1980, p. 3; Harold Blakemore, "Back to the Barracks: The Chilean Case," *Third World Quarterly* 7 (January 1985): 44–62; Arturo Valenzuela, "Eight Years of Military Rule in Chile," *Current History* 81 (February 1982): 64–68, 88; Arturo Valenzuela, "Chile's Political Instability," *Current History* 83 (February 1984): 68–72, 88–89; Alan Angell, "Pinochet's Chile: Back to the Nineteenth Century?" *World Today* 38 (January 1982): 18–25; Genaro Arriagada Herrera, "The Legal and Institutional Framework of the Armed Forces in Chile," in *Military Rule in Chile*, 117–143.

39  Quirós-Varela, *Agrarian Policies in Chile*, 328–332, 340–351; *Latin America Weekly Report*, January 11, 1980, pp. 8–9; Cristóbal Kay, "The Monetarist Experiment in the Chilean Countryside," *Third World Quarterly* 7 (April 1985): 301–322; Leonardo Castillo and David Lehmann, "Chile's Three Agrarian Reforms: The Inheritors," *Bulletin of Latin American Research* 1 (May 1982): 21–43; Lovell S. Jarvis, *Chilean Agriculture under Military Rule: From Reform to Reaction, 1973–1980* (Berkeley: Institute of International Studies, University of California, Berkeley, 1985).

40  For information about the economic policies and impacts of the Pinochet government, see the following sources: *International Financial Statistics Yearbook 1986*, vol. 39 (Washington, D.C.: International Monetary Fund, 1986), 89, 113, 155; *International Financial Statistics Supplement on Exchange Rates*, no. 9 (Washington, D.C.: International Monetary Fund, 1985), 15–21; *Government*

*Finance Statistics Yearbook,* vol. 10 (Washington, D.C. International Monetary Fund, 1986), 254; *Year Book of Labour Statistics 1986,* vol. 46 (Geneva: International Labour Office, 1986), 524; Stockholm International Peace Research Institute, *World Armaments and Disarmament: SIPRI Yearbook 1979* (London: Taylor and Francis, 1979), 54–57; *World Armaments and Disarmament: SIPRI Yearbook 1986* (New York: Oxford University Press, 1986), 246–247; Morgan Guaranty Trust Company of New York, *World Financial Markets,* May 1985, pp. 1–11; Foxley, *Latin American Experiments in Neoconservative Economics,* 40–90, 124; Edwards, "Stabilization with Liberalization," 223–254; Roberto Zahler, "Recent Southern Cone Liberalization Reforms and Stabilization Policies: The Chilean Case, 1974–1982," *Journal of Interamerican Studies and World Affairs* 25 (November 1983): 509–562; Ricardo Lagos and Victor E. Tokman, "Monetarism, Employment and Social Stratification," *World Development* 12 (January 1984): 43–65; Carlos Fortin, "The Failure of Repressive Monetarism: Chile, 1973–1983," *Third World Quarterly* 6 (April 1984): 310–326; Philip O'Brien, "Authoritarianism and Monetarism in Chile, 1973–1983," *Socialist Review* 14 (September/October 1984): 44–79; Ricardo Lagos, "The Emergent Bourgeoisie," *International Journal of Politics* 12 (Winter 1982/1983): 48–68; Bitar, "Monetarism and Ultraliberalism," 10–47; Angell, "Pinochet's Chile: The Beginning of the End?" 27–30; Angell, "Pinochet's Chile: Back to the Nineteenth Century?" 18–25; Arthur J. Mann and Carlos E. Sanchez, "Labor Market Responses to Southern Cone Stabilization Policies: The Cases of Argentina, Chile, Uruguay," *Inter-American Economic Affairs* 38 (Spring 1985): 19–39; Barbara E. Kritzer, "Chile Changes Social Security," *Social Security Bulletin* 44 (May 1981): 33–37; Oscar Altimir, "Poverty, Income Distribution and Child Welfare in Latin America: A Comparison of Pre- and Post-recession Data," *World Development* 12 (March 1984): 261–282; Remmer, "Public Policy and Regime Consolidation," 441–461; Petras, "The Chicago Boys Flunk Out in Chile," 193, 210–211; Ricardo Ffrench-Davis, "Exports and Industrialization in an Orthodox Model: Chile, 1973–78," *Vierteljahresberichte,* no. 75 (1979): 15–34; Paul E. Sigmund, "The Rise and Fall of the Chicago Boys in Chile," *SAIS Review* 3 (Fall 1983): 41–58; Antonio Schneider, "Supply-Side Economics in a Small Economy: The Chilean Case," in *Free Market Conservatism: A Critique of Theory and Practice,* ed. Edward J. Nell (London: George Allen and Unwin, 1984), 209–228; Jarvis, *Chilean Agriculture under Military Rule;* Kay, "The Monetarist Experiment in the Chilean Countryside," 301–322; Castillo and Lehmann, "Chile's Three Agrarian Reforms," 21–43; Sebastian Edwards, "Monetarism in Chile, 1973–1983: Some Economic Puzzles," *Economic Development and Cultural Change* 34 (April 1986): 535–559; Thomas Scheetz, "Gastos militares en Chile, Peru y la Argentina," *Desarrollo económico* 25 (October/December 1985): 315–327; José-Pablo Arellano, "Social Policies in Chile: An Historical Review," *Journal of Latin American Studies* 17 (November 1985): 397–418, esp. 405; Carlos Ominami, "Un Nouveau Type de financement extérieur pour un nouveau modèle de croissance, un example: Le Chile (1974–1979)," *Problèmes d'Amérique Latine,* nos. 4599–4600 (December 31, 1980): 102–127; *Latin American Regional Reports Southern Cone:* October 11, 1985, p. 6, February 5, 1987, p. 3; Javier Martínez and Eugenio Tironi, "La Estratificación social en Chile," *Pensamiento iberoamericano,* no. 6 (July-December 1984): 93–116; Julio Galvez and James Tybout, "Microeconomic Adjustments in Chile during 1977–81: The Importance of Being a *Grupo,*" *World Development* 13 (August 1985): 969–994; Angell,

"Why Is the Transition to Democracy Proving so Difficult in Chile?" 27–29; R. N. Gwynne, "The Deindustrialization of Chile, 1974–1984," *Bulletin of Latin American Research* 5, no. 1 (1986): 1–23; Joseph Ramos, *Neoconservative Economics in the Southern Cone of Latin America, 1973–1983* (Baltimore: The Johns Hopkins University Press, 1986), esp. 12–23, 64–66, 174–183; Alfredo Rodríguez, "Santiago, viejos y nuevos problemas," *Pensamiento iberoamericano*, no. 7 (January–June 1985): 117–138.

41  Bule, "Elements for a Critical Analysis of the Present Cultural System," 367–398; Smith, *The Church and Politics in Chile*, 320–322; Alexander, *The Tragedy of Chile*, 387–390; Castro, *La educación en Chile de Frei a Pinochet*, 199–234; *Life in Chile under the Military Regime*, Report 2 (London: Chile Committee for Human Rights, 1974), 28–40; *Report on Chilean University Life*, no. 1 (Winter 1979): 4–6; *Latin America Regional Reports*, March 7, 1980, p. 5; Sanders, "Education and Authoritarianism in the Southern Cone," 10–15; Fischer, *Political Ideology and Educational Reform in Chile*, 121–148; Alvaro García H. and John Wells, "Chile: A Laboratory for Failed Experiments in Capitalist Political Economy," *Cambridge Journal of Economics* 7 (September–December 1983): 287–304; Rafael Echeverría, "Política educacional y transformación del sistema de educación en Chile a partir de 1973," *Revista Mexicana de Sociología* 44 (April–June 1982): 529–557; John Walsh, "New University Law Decreed in Chile," *Science* 211 (March 27, 1981): 1403, 1406; Daniel C. Levy, *Higher Education and the State in Latin America: Private Challenges to Public Dominance* (Chicago: University of Chicago Press, 1986), 66–113; Alejandro Foxley and Dagmar Raczynski, "Vulnerable Groups in Recessionary Situations: The Case of Children and the Young in Chile," *World Development* 12 (March 1984): 223–246; Noel McGinn and Susan Street, "Educational Decentralization: Weak State or Strong State?" *Comparative Education Review* 30 (November 1986): 471–490; Daniel C. Levy, "Chilean Universities under the Junta: Regime and Policy," *Latin American Research Review* 21, no. 3 (1986): 95–128; *Latin American Weekly Report*, November 13, 1986, p. 5; Tim Frasca, "Chilean Frustration Builds over Pinochet's Brand of Education," *Christian Science Monitor*, March 9, 1987, p. 17.

42  Chanfreau, "Professional Ideology and the Health Care System in Chile," 99–103; Modell and Waitzkin, "Health Care and Socialism in Chile," 35–40; Modell and Waitzkin, "Medicine and Socialism in Chile," 20–22; Navarro, *Medicine under Capitalism*, 57–60; *Life in Chile under the Military Regime*, 23–27; Foxley and Raczynski, "Vulnerable Groups in Recessionary Situations," 227–239; Clara S. Haignere, "The Application of the Free-Market Economic Model in Chile and the Effects on the Population's Health Status," *International Journal of Health Services* 13, no. 3 (1983): 389–405; Joseph L. Scarpaci, "Restructuring Health Care Financing in Chile," *Social Science and Medicine* 21, no. 4 (1985): 415–431; Anamaria Viveros-Long, "Changes in Health Financing: The Chilean Experience," *Social Science and Medicine* 22, no. 3 (1986): 379–385; Dorfman, "The Challenge in Chile," 26; Vergara, "Changes in the Economic Functions of the Chilean State under the Military Regime," 101; United Nations Children's Fund, *The State of the World's Children 1987* (New York: Oxford University Press, 1987), 129; World Bank, *World Tables*, vol. 2, 3d ed. (Baltimore, Md.: The Johns Hopkins University Press, 1983), 20.

43  Fernando Ignacio Leiva and James Petras, "Chile: New Urban Movements and the Transition to Democracy," *Monthly Review* 39 (July–August 1987): 109–124; Fernando Ignacio Leiva and James Petras, "Chile's Poor in the Struggle for

Democracy," *Latin American Perspectives* 13 (Fall 1986): 5–25; Mariana Schkolnik, "La Société civile recomposée," *Autogestions*, no. 17 (October 1984): 61–71; Francisco Zapata, "Mouvements sociaux et alliances politiques," *Autogestions*, no. 17 (October 1984): 93–101; Lois Hecht Oppenheim, "State Repression and the Organization of Urban Grass-Roots in Chile" (Paper delivered at the 1987 annual meeting of the Western Political Science Association, Anaheim, California, March 27, 1987).

44 Loveman, *Chile*, 135–138, 148–149, 349–356; Sigmund, *The Overthrow of Allende*, 262–273.

# 7

## POLITICAL CHANGE IN NIGERIA

It is now fashionable in Nigeria to pretend that a military regime is an aberration and that the return to a civil government means a return to democracy. That is false. We have never had democracy in Nigeria. . . . Democracy remains an illusion in our country so long as politicians are not ready to accept all the duties associated with it.
— General Theophilus Danjuma

In our present situation, the need to reconcile our partisan political interests with our constitutional responsibilities to our people who elected us cannot be over-emphasized. . . . The successful operation of the new constitution calls for co-operation rather than confrontation, accommodation instead of intolerance and fairness to all instead of discrimination on the basis of one's political, ethnic or religious views.
— President Shehu Shagari

In *Things Fall Apart* the Nigerian novelist Chinua Achebe portrayed the social changes that the British colonialists brought to Igboland during the late nineteenth century. Politically, under the imposition of colonial rule, Igbo elders lost their power to British soldiers, police, and especially the district commissioner, who presided over native courts at the local level. Assisted by educated Nigerian court messengers, clerks, and interpreters, the district commissioner acted as local lord who made the crucial decisions about village life. The British also introduced churches, trading stores, new schools, and hospitals supplanting the authority that Igbo leaders had previously wielded. British military officers, merchants, missionaries, and district commissioners came to play the dominant roles; they helped undermine Igbo religious values, family ties, and the traditional system of justice. Achebe's novel describes the fate of one man, Okonkwo, in the Igbo village of Umuofia. His eldest son joined a Christian church, became literate, trained as a teacher in a new college, and no longer worshipped the Igbo god Chukwu, the earth goddess Ala, and the ancestral spirits. Chagrined at the changes occurring in his family and village, Okonkwo met with other men in the village market to protest the British intrusion into their lives. When court messengers appeared at the meeting and tried to disband the meeting, Okonkwo used a machete to decapitate one messenger and shortly thereafter hanged himself. Okonkwo's world had fallen apart. Faced with these violent protests against colonial rule, the British district commissioner made plans to write a book entitled *The Pacification of the Primitive Tribes of the Lower Niger*.[1]

For Nigerians, things fell apart not only with the imposition of colonial rule but also when they gained political independence in 1960. From 1960 through 1985 Nigerians faced several political changes: a coup by Igbo officers who overthrew the elected civilian government in January 1966, a Northern-led coup in July 1966, the ouster of one set of military officers by another set in July 1975, an abortive coup in February 1976 that led to the top general's assassination, the restoration of civilian government in October 1979, the return to power by the armed forces in December 1983, and another military coup in August 1985. Like many Latin American nations, Nigeria since independence has alternated between military bureaucratic-authoritarian regimes and reconciliation systems.

Unlike Chile, which underwent a sharp break with past democratic practices when the military staged the 1973 coup, Nigeria has experienced less fundamental sociopolitical changes under diverse regimes. Bureaucratic-authoritarian governments have featured reconciling tendencies; bureaucracies have ruled the competitive oligarchies. From 1970 to 1983 both military and elected civilian governments administered similar public policies, which brought no dramatic transformation of society. Amid the periodic changes in government personnel and formal institutions, two features — oligarchical political rule and mercantile capitalism — have remained constant. From the beginnings of colonial rule until today, a bureaucratic oligarchy has controlled the country; the masses have become marginally involved in political life. Merchant capitalists, both Nigerian and foreign, have dominated the economy. Even though elected civilian governments have allowed greater political competition and encouraged more groups to share in economic decision-making, the state bureaucrats, professionals (lawyers, physicians, educators), and merchant capitalists have continued to wield decisive power. By examining

216

the interactions among government bureaucrats, professionals, Nigerian traders, and foreign capitalists, we can better understand the marginal sociopolitical changes occurring during the twentieth century.

## The Colonial Bureaucratic System

From 1900 through 1960 the British colonialists ruled Nigeria through less repressive, more pluralist tactics than did the French in Vietnam or the Spanish in Cuba. Along with the British civil servants, social groups, especially merchants and missionaries, dominated the policymaking process. Before 1900 a British trading firm, the Royal Niger Company, ruled part of present-day Northern Nigeria. The British Foreign Office controlled the eastern region as the Niger Coast Protectorate. The British Colonial Office dominated Lagos, the capital city, and most of Western Nigeria. On January 1, 1900, the Royal Niger Company and the British Foreign Office yielded control of their regions to the Colonial Office, which established a united Nigerian territory. Yet even after this amalgamation, the country remained politically decentralized. North and south retained separate administrations and judicial systems. Governed by a British governor and Fulani aristocrats, northerners lived under more autocratic rule than did the southerners, who had the opportunity to elect Africans to a legislative council in Lagos. Throughout Nigeria social groups, especially trading firms and churches, retained autonomous power. Muslim clergy in the north controlled education, family life, and some courts. In the southern region Christian missionaries supplied educational and health-care services to the Nigerians. Given this social pluralism and mild repression, the Nigerian independence movement after World War II never faced the obstacles that the French colonialists mounted against the Vietnamese nationalists.[2]

### The Power of Social Groups

The native authority system established by the British gave heads of ethnic groups, especially in the north, some power over the policy process. The Hausa-Fulani ethnic group dominated the north. Ruling fairly centralized kingdoms, the emirs and chiefs maintained autocratic authority over their people under the British indirect rule system. In the south more democratic institutions originally governed the western Yoruba and eastern Igbo. Yoruba obas, alafins, and councils of chiefs relied on consultative mechanisms that provided constitutional checks and balances against autocratic personal rule. The Igbos, who inhabited the southeast region, governed themselves through decentralized village structures that gave village councils, elders, age grades, and occupational groups the right to participate in political decision-making. The British imposed more bureaucratic structures on the southern ethnic groups than on the northern Hausa-Fulani. In the south, the colonial governor, resident, and district commissioner made the crucial policies. They either operated through traditional southern leaders or created new warrant chiefs, as in Igboland. Whatever the case, British bureaucrats, not Nigerians, dominated political life. Educated Nigerians mainly served as clerks, messengers, and interpreters for British colonial officials.

Under colonial rule the British promoted religious diversity, especially in the southern region. There the Methodist, Church Missionary Society (Anglican), Baptist, and Catholic clergy evangelized the population, introduced Western education, and trained Nigerians to become clerks, interpreters, teachers, and missionaries. As a result of their exposure to Western education, southerners held the most skilled occupational positions as lower-ranking civil servants, postal employees, bank clerks, technicians, and traders. In the north, British officials prevented Christian missionaries from establishing schools among the Hausa-Fulani Moslem emirs, who were encouraged to establish their own Islamic-based educational institutions. Until World War.II few northerners gained a British education or mastered the English language; those who knew Arabic and Hausa worked mainly for the native authority system.

Economic groups maintained extensive freedom during the colonial period. Unlike Vietnam, where the French colonialists allocated land to French settlers and established a few manufacturing industries (rubber, zinc, coal, tin), in Nigeria the British maintained the traditional land tenure system, never created settler plantations, and invested few resources on manufacturing. Instead, they concentrated on trade. At the top of the economic stratification system stood the British merchant capitalists, especially managers from such trading firms as the Royal Niger Company (later the United Africa Company) and the John Holt Company. They controlled the export trade, including banks, shipping, and air transport. British investors also dominated insurance, communications, and mining. Below them Lebanese, Greek, and Syrian merchants conducted smaller-scale commerce with Nigerians. Most Africans worked as farmers or traders. A few served as commercial agents of British firms. Particularly in the southern region, a market system operated during the colonial period; even though the British capitalists wielded the greatest political power over government policy, Nigerian traders had some freedom to pursue their economic interests. Between the two world wars Nigerian trade unions began organizing civil servants, railway workers, and teachers.

*The Colonial Government Structure*

Although the British colonialists administered a bureaucratic-authoritarian system in Nigeria, they encouraged more reconciliation procedures than did the French in Vietnam. Soldiers and police wielded coercive rule; yet, especially after World War II, the British relied on consensual power. Whereas before the war the legislative council included only representatives from Lagos and the southern province, after 1945 Nigerians from throughout the territory became legislative council members. During the 1950s political parties spread to the northern region and became more active in the south. Party leaders negotiated the terms of political independence with the British.

British colonial rule combined centralized policy formation with extensive regional decentralization. At the end of the nineteenth century the British instituted centralized rule over diverse African political structures: the Sokoto kingdom in the north, the centralized chiefdoms of Yoruba and Benin in the west, such village republics as the Igbo and the Tiv in the east, and the institutions of two hundred other ethnic groups. The British governor general acted as the top policy formulator over all Nigeria. Yet because of the ethnic diversity within Nigeria, British civil servants decentralized policy implementation to the regions. From 1900 until 1946 the northern and southern regions maintained separate administrations. In 1939 the southern region split into eastern and western provinces. The 1946 constitution established a central legislative council for all Nigeria and three regional legislatures; within each region, the governor and lieutenant governor wielded decisive power. According to the 1954 federal constitution, the regional government run by civil servants from each region became the crucial policymaking agency. On the eve of political independence, the central government lacked significant authority, including control over revenues.

The colonial state carried out more economic activities than had been performed by Nigeria's precolonial political institutions. British civil servants, who coordinated different government agencies, established a legal order, instituted a cash-based tax system, created a common currency, built an economic infrastructure (ports, roads, railroads, some electric power facilities), operated a few factories (cotton gins, stone quarries, sawmills, furniture plants), and promoted the export trade, particularly such crops as palm oil, cotton, cocoa, and peanuts. Raising revenues through commodity marketing boards, civil servants rewarded private businesses seeking loans, contracts, and licenses from the government. By paying Nigerian farmers a lower price for their crops than they could earn on the world market, these marketing boards gained surplus funds that initially benefited British merchants and, after 1954, Nigerian businesspeople.

Committed to creating a legal order and economic infrastructure, British colonial officials devoted far less attention to supplying educational and health-care services to the Nigerians. Religious authorities, such as Christian missionaries in the south and Muslim malaams in the north, operated most educational institutions. The colonial government built a few hospitals, except those in some urban areas that served British armed forces, British civil servants, and the educated Nigerian elite who worked for the colonial government. Either Christian churches or the native authority system operated most urban hospitals and rural dispensaries; these health-care institutions lacked the trained staff and expenditures needed to provide adequate health care to the Nigerian masses, especially those living in the rural areas.

### The Attainment of Political Independence

Because colonial rule in Nigeria rested on a pluralistic, decentralized, and largely consensual base, the attainment of political independence in 1960 occurred through gradualist, nonviolent tactics. No mass mobilization movement ever formed to unite all Nigerians in a struggle for national independence. The country's ethnic diversity and decentralized regional governments impeded the formation of a political party with roots in all geographic areas. Instead, the process of securing political independence from Britain featured elite negotiations, not mass involvement by farmers, artisans, and factory workers. Educated Nigerians— mainly lawyers, teachers, clerks, and small businesspeople—resented the paternalistic behavior shown by the British ruling elite: senior civil servants, army officers, and managers of foreign-based firms such as the United Africa Company. For the nationalistic middle sectors, independence meant the expansion of opportunities that the British had denied them. With the achievement of national independence and the establishment of the first republic, these educated, middle-class Nigerians gained dominant political power. Yet despite the new reconciliation system, the bureaucratic-authoritarian mode of decision-making inherited from the British continued to shape the policy process. The Nigerian elite ruled a competitive oligarchy rather than a pluralist democracy with mass political participation.[3]

## The First Nigerian Republic

Nigerians secured their political independence from Britain in 1960, established a republican government in 1963, and experienced the first military coup in early 1966; during this six-year period a competitive oligarchical system governed Nigeria. Both beliefs and structures reflected an accommodationist orientation, with a stress on the need for government and private business elites to reconcile their differences. Yet no powerful procedural consensus ever developed. Subnational loyalties took precedence over national ties. The fragmented power structure immobilized the policy process and facilitated a military takeover.

### Political Beliefs

The political beliefs of the three dominant leaders in the first republic — Prime Minister Abubakar Tafawa Balewa, President Nnamdi Azikiwe, and key opposition figure Obafemi Awolowo — expressed a commitment to social pluralism, dispersed government power, and toleration. The need for making frequent compromises with diverse influential groups exerted a strong pragmatic influence on these politicians' beliefs. The Nigerian federal system encouraged a legalist outlook — that is, a a greater concern with procedures than with substantive goals. The objectives focused on maintaining diversity, checking concentrated power, and securing national unity. Reflecting a reconciliation orientation, these Nigerians hoped to realize a national community sentiment from pluralist diversity. Prime Minister Balewa assumed the role of the national reconciler, the evoker of toleration and consensus. According to him, a common loyalty, agreement on legal procedures, and a spirit of reconciliation had to transcend the group struggle, so that political elites could peacefully settle their differences.[4]

### Political Structures

Despite their commitment to reconciliation beliefs, Nigerian leaders in the first republic faced difficulties operating political structures that accommodated regional differences. As in a typical competitive oligarchy, government institutions exercised weak power. Government coercion was limited. The federal government had neither the power nor the will to coerce dissidents. Although regional governments tried to repress the opposition, especially in the north, the police could not control the protests that western cocoa farmers launched against regional political authorities.

The decentralized government institutions established during the 1950s under British colonial rule continued into the first republic. Regional governments, not the federal government, wielded decisive power. At the time of independence in 1960, three regions — the north, west, and east — competed for resources. In 1963 a fourth, midwestern, region reduced the western region by one-third in population and area. Each regional government controlled the most important activities, including pre-university education, socioeconomic development projects, banking, and the regulation of commerce. Although northern leaders, who inhabited the most populous region, dominated the central government, the wealthier, better-educated western and eastern regions held the greatest resources.

At both the central and the regional levels, the coordination of government activities proved difficult. The dispersion of powers in a federal system fragmented the policy process. Within the national government the president and prime minister competed for dominance. Cabinet ministers, legislators, and civil servants retained autonomous power. Bureaucrats—permanent secretaries, deputy permanent secretaries, senior assistant secretaries—provided whatever coordination that did emerge from this pluralist network.

Consistent with the model of a reconciliation system, social groups maintained their independence from government control. As in the colonial period, ethnic groups exerted considerable political power, particularly over the regional governments. The Hausa-Fulani controlled the north, the Yoruba the west, and the Igbo the east. The Bini, Igbo, and Urhobo formed the three largest ethnic groups in the smaller midwestern region. These regional governments recruited civil servants according to their ethnic affiliations. Bureaucrats implemented policies based on ethnic loyalties; for example, businesspeople from the dominant ethnic group received the greatest subsidies, contracts, licenses, and loans. Even within the federal government, ethnic considerations shaped personnel decisions. The quota system for allocating military officials to the general staff, defense headquarters, and field command ensured that the north would secure 50 percent, the east 25 percent, and before 1964 the west 25 percent; after 1963 the West received 21 percent of appointments and the midwest 4 percent. Thus, ethnic representation permeated both the central and regional governments.

Religious groups maintained the political independence they had secured during the colonial period. In the north, Muslim leaders controlled the educational and judicial systems and reinforced the power of the Hausa-Fulani aristocracy. In the south, churches played a less important political role. Even though Muslims and Christians competed for conversions among the Yoruba people, their ancestral city (family birthplace), not their religious affiliation, shaped political allegiances. Most Igbo joined Christian churches, which provided the educational opportunities needed for upward social mobility into the governmental and private business sectors.

Occupational pluralism also characterized the first Nigerian republic. Dominant economic groups included the Fulani business elites, Hausa merchants, and Igbo and Yoruba executives. Below them in the economic stratification system came some lower-ranking professionals (doctors, lawyers, teachers), small-scale traders, and clerks. A few Nigerians worked in coal mines, textile factories, construction firms, ports, and railroad networks. Around 80 percent of the labor force farmed the land, raising food either for their subsistence needs or for the export market. Even though all these economic groups had the freedom to articulate their policy preferences, the business elites possessed the greatest organizational ability to press their claims on government officials.

In this pluralist system several political parties competed for influence over the policy process, yet no party ever gained the power to mobilize the masses throughout all Nigeria. Business executives and ethnic group leaders controlled the major parties—the Northern People's Congress (NPC), the Action Group (AG), and the National Convention of Nigerian Citizens (NCNC). One party dominated each region and attracted its major electoral support from a single ethnic group: The NPC represented the Northern Hausa-Fulani, the AG served Yoruba interests, and the NCNC gained the greatest influence among the Igbo in the east and midwest. Despite this ethnic-regional strength, the internal organizational power of the parties remained weak. Faction-ridden and split by divergent policy preferences, the parties operated as elite parties with a limited mass base. Patron-client ties united the party leaders with their electoral supporters. In exchange for votes, the party officials promised their followers concrete benefits: jobs, educational opportunities, and health-care programs for the masses and government contracts, import licenses, and subsidies for the business elites. Political party activists thus made ethnic appeals to voters and rewarded businesspeople who supported the party with control over marketing boards, development projects, and state corporations.

During the first republic, government agencies wielded a greater scope of power than they had under colonial rule. Regional governments performed especially important activities. Although the federal government lacked the financial resources to pursue ambitious socioeconomic development projects, regional governments controlled the commodity marketing boards that regulated the prices received by farmers for their export produce. Because the marketing boards paid the farmer a lower price than his or her food could earn on the world market, they gained the funds used by regional government development boards to establish banks, insurance companies, housing corporations, and hotels. Loans went to private businesses that produced textiles, shoes, and soft drinks. Regional governments also controlled primary and secondary schools.

Neither the federal government nor the regional governments devoted any attention to establishing a comprehensive public health program. Although senior civil servants gained free health care, few rural people ever secured access to physicians, nurses, or medicine. As in the colonial period, the health program brought the greatest benefits to the urban wealthy.

## Overthrow of the First Republic

The major reason for the January 1966 coup, which overthrew the first Nigerian republic, stemmed from the elite polarization that immobilized the policy process. Subnational group cohesion overwhelmed national solidarity. As ethnic regionalism became stronger, both westerners and easterners opposed northern domination of the central government. Political leaders faced difficulties wielding either coercive or consensual power. Civilian politicians lacked effective control over the military and police. Coalition formation also proved difficult. Regional governments controlled educational institutions and courts, which could not organize the populace behind civil values and rule by a national civilian administration. The federal government alliance linking the NPC with the NCNC dissolved in 1963. Because the two major southern parties, the NCNC and the AG, attracted main support from their own groups, the Igbo and the Yoruba, they could not easily form an alliance that transcended ethnic appeals. Ineffective policy performance further weakened the civilian governments, both federal and regional. As the regional elites strove for greater concrete benefits—contracts, subsidies, loans—the federal government became immobilized by a growing imbalance between sectional demands and scarce financial resources needed to fulfill them. Combined with rigged elections, weak procedural consensus, and general corruption, this policy ineffectiveness undermined the military's belief in civilian government legitimacy. Electoral irregularities and violence, which plagued both the 1964 federal elections and the 1965 western regional elections, created doubts among the armed forces about civilian leaders' right to govern Nigeria. Unwilling to differentiate between the public good and the private interest, civil servants and politicians made decisions according to ethnic loyalties and kin ties rather than according to achievement-based criteria. This corruption strengthened the military's determination to stage a coup d'état that would cleanse the political system, end group polarization, and create a stronger national unity.[5]

## Rule by the Federal Military Government

From 1966 through 1979 several military governments ruled Nigeria. Igbo officers staged the first coup in January 1966. Attempts to institute a unitary state led to another coup in July by northern soldiers, who placed General Yakubu Gowon in power as top leader. In July 1975 the armed forces overthrew Gowon and installed General Murtala Mohammed as the dominant political figure. An abortive coup in February 1976 caused Mohammed's assassination and the rise to power of Lieutenant General Olusegun Obasanjo, who remained in office until October 1979, when an elected civilian government took control of government institutions throughout the nation.[6] These military governments brought important sociopolitical changes to Nigeria, particularly during the 1970s. Elite political beliefs became more nationalistic, stressing the need for discipline, duty, and responsibility, not conflict. The central government wielded an expanded scope of power over economic and educational activities. Although the military established a bureaucratic-authoritarian system, a competitive oligarchy continued to make the crucial policies. The Nigerian masses neither participated in the coups nor shaped basic government decisions. As under colonial rule and the first republic, government officials, professionals, and private business executives still dominated the policy process.

### The Political Culture of
### the Armed Forces

Guiding a bureaucratic-authoritarian regime, the military officers placed a low value on individual freedom and political equality. From their perspective, the pursuit of individual freedom and civil liberties brought too much chaos and disorder to the first republic. Rather than stressing political equality, they focused on the need for discipline, loyalty, and duty to the military establishment.

Like the civilian politicians who governed the first republic, the military elites perceived nationalism and rapid economic development as the most appropriate values for legitimating their regime. According to them, economic growth should benefit the whole nation. Pledged to combat tribalism, ethnic divisiveness, regionalism, and other sectional interests, armed forces officers expected that nationalism would become the dominant collective value. They tried to expand Nigeria's influence throughout Africa. Attacks on South Africa's apartheid policy and support for the MPLA government in Angola represented the Nigerian govern ment's efforts to articulate a more nationalistic orientation that lessened dependence on Britain and the United States.[7]

225

## Institutional Changes

In the federal military government, the key structures of government coercion, the armed forces and the police, gained the dominant power; yet they never established such a professional, hierarchical organization as the repressive one that governed Chile after the 1973 coup. The Nigerian civil war between 1967 and 1970 reinforced the power of the national armed forces; compared with the pre-civil war recruitment practices, appointments and promotions to senior military positions depended less on regional or ethnic ties. In 1972 the military regime created a national police force that replaced the former regional police. Controlled by the inspector general in Lagos and by state commissioners, the police repressed demonstrations by students and unions, banned political meetings on university campuses, and dissolved political rallies that became "too disorderly." The military government also banned political party activity until 1978 and tried to dissolve ethnic associations. Yet particularly after the civil war ended in early 1970, government coercion lessened. The regime showed leniency toward the secessionist Igbos and released most political prisoners from jail.

The military government instituted a more centralized government structure than had operated under the first republic. As the regime created more states—twelve in 1967 and nineteen in 1976—the federal government strengthened its power over the state governments. At the federal level the Supreme Military Council and the Federal Executive Council formulated policies for economic development, education, health, housing, and transportation. The federal government allocated funds for implementing these programs to the states, which lacked their own resources to finance the development projects. At the state government level, military governors, aided by expanded state bureaucracies, administered the policies decreed by central authorities.

Under this centralized federalism, military officers and civilian bureaucrats coordinated government activities at all levels. The Supreme Military Council, composed almost exclusively of armed forces and police personnel, made the crucial decisions. The Federal Executive Council, comprising military and civilian commissioners, supervised policy implementation. Within the state governments the military governors and their permanent secretaries coordinated the policy process. In the national, state, and local council institutions, civil servants played a key policy role. The most powerful bureaucrat in Nigeria, the secretary to the military government and the head of the civil service, unified the whole administrative structure. At both the national and state levels, permanent secretaries wielded the dominant power. The local government secretary, a civil servant, ran the town councils. All these bureaucrats performed a wide range of activities.

Even though the federal military government curtailed the extensive social pluralism that prevailed in the first republic, it never quashed group autonomy. The regime banned ethnic associations, but they organized farmer protests against high taxes. The creation of nineteen states also strengthened the power of minority ethnic groups. Under the first republic the three major ethnic groups, which formed around two-thirds of the Nigerian population, controlled the three largest regions. The Hausa-Fulani dominated the north, the Hausa the west, and the Igbo the east. In 1976 the establishment of nineteen states meant that these three ethnic groups held a demographic majority in twelve states. The Hausa-Fulani dominated Bauchi, Kano, Kaduna, Niger, and Sokoto. Yoruba controlled Lagos, Ogun, Oyo, Ondo, and Kwara. The Igbo comprised the majority in Anambra and Imo. Ethnic minorities—for example, Ede, Ibibio, Ijaw, Tiv, Kanuri—gained greater representation in the other seven states.

Economic interest groups, especially business and professional associations, played a key policy role. Organized into the Nigerian Medical Association and the National Association of Resident Doctors, physicians maintained extensive influence over the decisions made by the Ministry of Health. The Lagos Chamber of Commerce and Industry, the Nigerian Association of Chambers of Commerce, Industry, Mines, and Agriculture, the Manufacturers' Association of Nigeria, and the Nigeria Employers' Consultative Association helped shape economic policies. Although from 1969 to 1976 the military regime declared strikes illegal, mandated state arbitration, and banned electoral political activity by unions, labor union activity grew increasingly important after the civil war ended. Particularly among civil servants and teachers, union membership rose. By the end of the 1970s, the largest unions within the National Labour Congress, the dominant labor organization, comprised teachers, junior civil servants, traders, public utilities workers, and agricultural laborers. Because of Nigeria's underdeveloped manufacturing sector, industrial workers wielded less influence over union activities. Harassed by the government, union members still mounted demonstrations and strikes, particularly during the 1974–1977 period. Thus, military efforts to repress organizational pluralism failed to curb group demands for greater material benefits: higher pay, expanded housing, lower taxes, more generous contracts, and cheaper credit.

Under the military regime, the central government expanded its scope of power, undertaking projects intended to promote national integration and economic development. In 1977 federal and state governments took control over all radio and television stations. Nigerian civil servants and private business executives secured the opportunity to purchase shares in foreign-owned enterprises. Government regulation over prices and wages increased. Government loans went to capital-intensive industries and agribusinesses. Under the 1978 land use decree, the state governor gained the authority to allocate urban land. Local land allocation committees, composed of traditional chiefs, civil servants, lawyers, and land surveyors, regulated the transfer of rural land. Federal government policies expanded primary education and university enrollments. All these activities increased the national government's power and brought the main rewards to the wealthy urban elite, mainly businesspeople and professionals.[8]

## Policy Changes

The Federal Military Government introduced policy changes that expanded state control over the economy and increased the power of Nigerian capitalists vis-à-vis multinational corporations, especially those from Britain. During the 1970s several decrees broadened state ownership, instituted joint ventures with foreign-owned firms, and encouraged private Nigerian business firms to consolidate their holdings. By 1979 the government sector included ownership over mining, manufacturing (steel plants), the economic infrastructure (ports, airports, airlines, shipping lines, railways, electric power, irrigation facilities, radio, television, telecommunications), banking, and insurance. Under the "indigenization" program implemented during the 1970s, Nigerian governments and private business executives purchased shares—from 40 percent to 60 percent—in foreign-owned enterprises, such as banks, insurance firms, oil corporations, iron and steel companies, engineering plants, and construction firms. Both the federal government and the state governments bought shares in the multinational corporations. By supplying loans for the purchase of these shares by Nigerians, government banks enriched senior civil servants, military officials, urban business executives (traders, bankers), and educated professionals (lawyers, physicians). Even though Nigerian capitalists and government officials purchased shares and sat on boards of multinationals, Nigerians still did not make these enterprises' key decisions. Whereas Nigerians handled public relations, legal matters, and recruitment of personnel, foreign managers, usually British, controlled finances, production, and technology.

Under the military regime, federal government expenditures and revenues rose to higher percentages of the national income than during the first republic. When world market prices for oil soared during the 1970s, the high surtaxes on multinational oil corporations supplied the federal government with increased revenues. Whereas in 1965 oil revenues accounted for only 8 percent of total federal government revenues, by 1973 that percentage grew to 67 percent; from 1974 through 1979 it increased to around 80 percent. Between 1965 and 1978 federal government revenues doubled from 10 percent of the gross domestic product to 22 percent. Government expenditures expanded rapidly for the military. In the first republic defense spending never exceeded 1 percent of the gross national product; however, after the military coup in January 1966, this proportion ranged between 3 percent and 7 percent. Around 90 percent of these defense expenditures went to pay military officers' salaries. After 1970 federal government expenditures for education also increased; however, the health sector remained an under-financed sector, with military health facilities receiving the greatest resources.

What impact did these economic policies exert on growth, inflation, unemployment, and income equality? First, the growth rate depended mainly on the prices earned by oil exports on the world market, not on increased agricultural productivity. From 1960 through 1965, the annual rise in the real gross domestic product averaged around 5 percent. During the post–civil war years, when oil prices skyrocketed (1970–1979), the real gross domestic product increased around 8 percent a year. Yet over the latter period, agriculture showed a negative yearly growth rate. Whereas in 1965 farm products constituted more than 60 percent of domestic exports, by 1975 they had fallen to less than 5 percent; oil comprised 93 percent of total export earnings. Despite government efforts to promote capital-intensive agricultural corporations that would grow export crops, these policies failed to expand food output for either the export trade or domestic consumption. Although large-scale farmers and agribusiness executives received major bank loans to purchase agrarian inputs such as tractors, combines, seed, and fertilizers, most small farmers lacked credit to buy these inputs. The government paid low prices for domestically-produced food. The overvalued Nigerian currency meant low prices for food imports. Because of these policy disincentives, agricultural productivity declined; the government imported food, especially wheat and rice.

Second, inflation posed a more severe problem under the military government than during the first republic. Whereas consumer prices rose around 3 percent a year from 1960 to 1965, they increased more than 12 percent between 1966 and 1979. The rapid rise in world oil prices partially contributed to the escalating inflation by expanding the money supply. Food shortages, combined with greater urban spending on food, also accounted for the higher general price rises.

Third, the underdeveloped manufacturing sector hindered the expansion of employment opportunities. Increased oil production created relatively few jobs. Except for construction and the economic infrastructure, industrial growth occurred at a slow pace. Whereas in 1965 10 percent of the labor force worked in the industrial sector, by 1980 that share had risen to only 12 percent. When government policies failed to pay high prices for food and resources (loans, agrarian inputs) went mainly to agribusinesses, many small farmers lost their land and migrated to the cities, where some found jobs in construction or trade.

Fourth, during the late 1970s income inequalities based on region and class grew more severe. Economic disparities split the northern region from the southern. With fewer industries, national resources, and educated personnel, the north was much less wealthy than the southern states, which had more industries, greater oil supplies, easier access to the coast, and a better-educated labor force, especially in the west, the two Igbo provinces (Anambra, Imo), Bendel, and Lagos, the capital. The cleavage between the urban and rural areas also became more pronounced under the military regime. Compared with city dwellers, most rural residents had less favorable educational opportunities, health-care facilities, and employment prospects. Government policies that benefited agribusinesspeople and large-scale landowners worsened the small farmers' lot and plunged them into greater poverty. Senior government officials, businesspeople, and skilled professionals (lawyers, managers, accountants) became wealthier, while small farmers, unskilled workers, unemployed school leavers, and the urban underemployed (traders, artisans) in the informal sector failed to share the benefits of rapid economic growth. Composed of high-ranking military officers and senior civil servants, the government elite secured lucrative rewards from armed-forces rule. Besides earning high salaries, they received generous fringe benefits: housing subsidies, rental allowances, car allowances, low-interest auto loans, free electricity and water, free health care, and overseas training. With income gained from high salaries, foreign bank loans, and kickbacks for granting government contracts to foreign firms, the bureaucratic elite purchased urban real estate, productive farmland, and shares in foreign enterprises. Private businesspeople, especially contractors, merchants, and realtors, reaped economic rewards from government contracts, licenses, and loans. In this merchant capitalist economy, commercial enterprises made higher profits than did industrialists, who remained subordinate to British-owned corporations.[9]

Like economic policies, the education policies during the military regime reflected increased state involvement, a more nationalistic orientation, and greater inequalities. In 1976 the federal government began implementing a Universal Primary Education (UPE) program that nearly doubled primary school enrollments. Financed initially by the federal government with supplemental expenditures by the state governments, the UPE program originated as a way to symbolize national prestige and to win greater support for the armed forces, especially among southerners, who highly value a formal western education. Policymakers stressed the normative purposes of the primary schools. Students sang a national anthem, saluted the national flag, pledged allegiance to "Nigeria my country," and promised to "defend her unity and to uphold her honour." Cognitively, the curriculum focused on the need for primary pupils to become literate in either English or Hausa. Instructors taught both political and economic role behaviors. They encouraged students to respect authority and act as obedient citizens. Rather than emphasizing vocational or agricultural training, the secondary school courses transmitted skills relevant to clerical and managerial occupations.

During the late 1970s the military government failed to equalize educational opportunities. Inequalities divided north and south, urban and rural areas. Rural schools lacked qualified staff, adequate funds, and sufficient resources (books, equipment). In the wealthier south, rural residents and women benefited from the UPE program. Northerners resisted a non-Islamic western education for girls. Particularly in the rural north, most states had low secondary school enrollments. State governments lacked the revenues to finance these schools, and families lacked the income to pay secondary school fees.

Educational institutions produced neither obedient citizens nor an employed work force. Facing dim prospects for employment, secondary and university students staged strikes and demonstrations against the military government. Primary school leavers gained neither jobs nor the opportunity to pursue a secondary education. Preferring employment as clerks or skilled workers, Nigerian students learned after graduation that the demand for such high-paying jobs outstripped the supply.[10]

Even though health expenditures expanded during military rule, the health system brought the major benefits to the urban elite. At the federal and state government level, professionals in the Ministry of Health formulated basic policies. Then the state Health Services Management Board implemented these policies, provided health services, purchased drugs and medical equipment, and administered hospitals, health centers, and health clinics. Located mainly in the cities, specialist hospitals contained amenity wards for the elite and general wards for rank-and-file citizens. Health centers, health clinics, and local government dispensaries supplied medical services to rural residents. These public health-care institutions served no more than one-third of the population. Physicians operated private clinics regulated by the government, but these clinics lacked adequate equipment or staff. Both regional and economic inequalities marked the performance of the health-care system. Rural areas faced several shortages: personnel, drugs, hypodermic needles, and ambulances. The system provided the greatest care to the urban wealthy and to the government elite, including senior civil servants, military governors, permanent secretaries, and professionals within the Ministry of Health and the state Health Services Management Board. They received prompter treatment, special drugs, and the opportunity for overseas health care—benefits unavailable to the general population. As a result of these inegalitarian health policies, Nigerians faced low life expectancy and high infant mortality rates. In 1978 over 150 children for every 1000 live births died before age one; life expectancy at birth reached only forty-eight years—unfavorable rates for even the sub-Saharan African region.[11]

## Relinquishment of Control
## to the Civilians

For the following three reasons, top military officers decided after 1974 to give civilian politicians formal control over government institutions. First, ineffective policy performance plagued the Gowon administration, which ruled from July 1966 until July 1975. Rapid price increases, growing inequalities, and corruption by military governors marred the military government's record. Pressured by business elites competing for scarce government resources, the civil servants fell prey to policy drift and *immobilisme*.

Second, the failure of government policies to produce intended results undermined the legitimacy of the Gowon government among some military officers and such professional elites as teachers and civil servants. Because of government stagnation and policy drift, these elites lost confidence in the military's right to govern. They expected that a civilian government led by moderate northern leaders would better implement the policies originally formulated by the armed forces regime.

Third, military factionalism weakened the government. When in late 1974 General Gowon decided to postpone the restoration of civilian rule, other armed forces officers staged a coup that overthrew him the next year. Generals Mohammed and Obasanjo, who succeeded Gowon, kept their commitment to institute an elected, constitutional government. Other factional conflicts that separated older from younger officers and northerners from southerners also lessened military power and reinforced the trend toward a reconciliation system. Hence, on October 1, 1979, the armed forces abandoned formal government control to elected politicians in Nigeria's second republic.[12]

## The Second Nigerian Republic

Unlike the situation in many Latin American states, the return of elected civilian leaders to power in Nigeria did not produce drastic institutional or policy changes. Under the new reconciliation system, the authoritarian aspects of the former military regime receded somewhat. Social pluralism grew stronger. Several political parties competed at elections. The dispersal of power in many government institutions hindered policy coordination. Yet an oligarchy of senior civil servants, professionals, and private businesspeople still dominated the policy process, even though that oligarchy became more competitive with the addition of elected politicians to decision-making circles. This oligarchy implemented most of the same policies originally initiated by the previous military regime.

### The Fluidity of the Social
### Stratification System

With the establishment of the reconciliation system, social groups regained some political power that they had lost under military rule. Traders, realtors, contractors, and speculators continued to shape public policies. For example, entrepreneurs and contractors, along with university professors, lawyers, physicians, and administrators, drafted the 1979 constitution. Businesspeople and civil servants held most positions in the state assemblies. Merchants and contractors received key contracts, licenses, and jobs from government policies. Neither trade unions nor small farmer associations wielded significant influence over the policy process. Fragmented and disorganized, they faced greater difficulties transforming their policy preferences into government decisions. The 1979 constitution established a secular government, even though courts of appeal in some northern states relied on Islamic law. Especially in the western region, Muslims and Christians competed for converts. Northern states faced conflicts between Muslim elites and more populist Islamic associations appealing to young commoners. Economic development led by Fulani contractors, agribusinesspeople, and merchants alienated urban Muslim youths, who suffered from overcrowded housing, underemployment, and increased inequalities. These young men, who had migrated from rural areas to the northern cities, turned to Muslim sects, such as the Yan Izala, which denounced the northern *nouveaux riches*, promised an end to corruption, and advocated Islamic learning and a behavioral commitment to Islamic law. As indicated by the 1979 electoral returns, ethnic groups exerted less political power than under the first republic. A single ethnic group held a demographic majority in twelve out of nineteen states. Hence, political parties needed to gain support from several ethnic groups to win elections. Minority ethnic groups within the former "Middle Belt" became more politically important, since they could potentially control several state governments.[13] In short, during the second republic social pluralism remained strong. Even though economic inequalities limited the possibilities for upward social mobility, diverse groups had the opportunity to compete for scarce government resources within a fairly fluid social stratification system.

### Government Institutions and
### Dispersed Power

As expected under a reconciliation system, the constitutional arrangements for the Nigerian second republic created a more dispersed power network than had prevailed during military rule. The power of the armed forces and police over opposition groups declined. Even though police banned some public meetings and the government placed some restrictions on press freedom, government coercion remained limited. According to the Freedom House study, which ranked over 160 governments on their commitment to civil liberties and competitive elections, during the 1980–1983 period Nigeria, along with Botswana, practiced the least coercive rule in Africa.

Within the federal framework, the central government and the nineteen state governments shared policymaking powers. Whereas the federal government financed policies, the state governments implemented these decisions. Federal grants to the states stemmed from income taxes, oil export duties, license fees, and taxes on petroleum profits. However great the strength of the national government to supply revenues, state governments retained important powers. Under the proportional representation procedures, civilian government agencies, the armed forces, universities, and political parties had to ensure a "fair share" representation for all nineteen states. Small states held a veto power in the Senate, the upper house of the federal legislature. State governments, along with the federal government, left few activities for local councils to perform. Whereas the federal government usually supplied from 60 percent to 80 percent of council revenues, locally raised taxes accounted for no more than 20 percent of finances. State governors had the authority to dissolve elected local councils. The state government, federal secretariat, or special-purpose agencies handled education, health, housing, and agriculture; council members spent more money on training local civil servants and accountants than on educating personnel for public works, agriculture, and health. Hence, under the federal system, the national and state governments struggled for revenues and for authority over policy implementation.

The dispersed power situation impeded the coordination of government activities. At the federal government level, the president, his cabinet ministers, and senior civil servants had responsibility for unifying the policy process. Because civil servants became dependent on an elected politician (the cabinet minister) for recruitment and promotion, their coordinating power declined. Besides the bureaucracy, other government agencies such as the House of Representatives, the Senate, and the Supreme Court shared decision-making authority. The federal Supreme Court, as well as state high courts, had the authority to review legislative and executive decisions and decide their constitutionality. At the state government level, the governor coordinated the policy process. He promoted civil servants, who then depended on elected government ministers for further advancement. In short, under the new reconciliation system, civil servants played a less dominant coordinating role than under the military regime.[14]

### Political Parties and Social Pluralism

Unlike the situation during military rule, recruitment to government office under the second republic occurred through the electoral process; political parties reflected Nigeria's social pluralism. In the 1979 elections five parties competed for votes: the National Party of Nigeria (NPN), the Unity Party of Nigeria (UPN), the Nigerian People's Party (NPP), the People's Redemption Party (PRP), and the Great Nigeria People's Party (GNPP). The NPN emerged from the election with the greatest power throughout Nigeria. Its candidate, Shehu Shagari, won the presidency, and it also secured the largest number of seats in the House of Representatives, the Senate, and state assemblies. In these four elections the UPN scored second best, the NPP came in third, with the PRP and the GNPP obtaining the fewest votes and government offices.

Both ethnic appeals and policy promises made by the parties shaped electoral behavior. The NPN drew support from people in the Hausa-Fulani emirate (Sokoto) as well as from southern ethnic minorities that resented the Igbo and Yoruba. The Yoruba states (Ogun, Ondo, Oyo, Lagos) supported the UPN and its leader Obafemi Awolowo, who as western government premier during the early 1970s had produced such concrete benefits as paved roads, hospitals, water supplies, and educational services. Similarly, the NPP successfully appealed to the Igbo, who had lost the civil war, and to Plateau ethnic minorities that opposed NPN northern domination and preferred the more generous education and health policies advocated by the NPP. In Kano state, Hausa commoners (small farmers, teachers, other young professionals) backed the PRP, which had earlier split away from the NPN because of its control by the Fulani aristocracy. The GNPP, led by a Kanuri, held a dominating position only in Borno state, where the Kanuri people comprised the ethnic majority.

Even though the three dominant parties—the NPN, UPN, NPP—tried to broaden their group appeals to win national support, they retained certain continuities with the leading parties of the first republic: the NPC, the AG, and the NCNC. Both the AG and the NCNC secured their main backing from Yoruba and Igbo, respectively. Only the NPN managed to extend its control beyond the northern base formerly dominated by the NPC. Nevertheless, the parties in the second republic did downplay ethnic appeals. Faced with competing parties in several states, voters of diverse ethnic groups had the opportunity to vote according to the parties' economic promises. Thus, economic considerations became a more important reason behind electoral behavior than during the first republic.

Most parties never developed a powerful, cohesive organization that mobilized the voters throughout the nation. They operated as electoral machines, not mobilizing agencies. Voters showed little involvement in party activities. Only around one-quarter of registered voters participated in all four 1979 elections; turnouts were especially low among youths and rural residents. One reason for the weak structural base stems from the brief time that parties had to organize their activities; the military regime lifted its ban on political parties in September 1978, only ten months before the four elections that occurred during July and August 1979. Parties hence lacked the time to develop mass roots. Factional rivalries based on issues and personalities also fragmented party cohesion. Moreover, the reconciliation system in the second republic operated as a competitive oligarchy. The government prevented trade unions and student associations from organizing electoral campaigns. All the parties maintained close ties with businesspeople, especially merchants, lawyers, and contractors, who dominated party activities. Because of the economic power wielded by Fulani business executives, Hausa merchants, and Yoruba entrepreneurs, the NPN and the UPN developed the strongest party organizations and emerged with the greatest electoral support.

The issue stands articulated by the parties stressed concrete benefits, not abstract, doctrinaire ideologies. All party candidates promised government contracts for business elites. Electoral appeals to rank-and-file citizens focused on education, housing, health care, jobs, and cheaper food. The NPN adopted the most pro-capitalist orientation, campaigning for private ownership and expanded foreign investment. The GNPP and NPP supported a regulated economy. Further to the "left," the UPN rallied behind a social democratic program that called for free education, free health care, and increased social security benefits. Proclaiming the strongest socialist views, the PRP advocated egalitarian policies (progressive taxes, mass literacy, public health care, rent controls) and public ownership of financial institutions, oil export firms, and heavy industries. Despite these ideological cleavages, electoral campaigns primarily rested on promises to secure material benefits for their supporters.[15]

### The Instrumentalist Political Culture

As revealed by the 1979 elections, political beliefs in the second republic revolved around instrumental concerns—the pursuit of concrete benefits—rather than ideological or theological issues. Citizens expected politicians to deliver such benefits as paved roads, irrigation facilities, fertilizers, expanded schooling, improved health care, and greater employment opportunities. Rather than pursuing these benefits for the individual only, Nigerians sought rewards for the collectivity: family, relatives, and clan. Within this reconciliation context, freedom meant the liberty to gain upward social mobility. As expressed by President Shehu Shagari, political freedom entailed the need to maintain the rule of law and institutional separation of powers, so that no group would gain the opportunity to repress another group's mobility. According to him, political leaders should commit themselves to tolerance and the reconciliation of divergent group interests. Opposed to equal economic rewards, President Shagari nevertheless maintained that government policies should narrow the gap between rich and poor and should expand the opportunities for all people to rise through the social stratification system.[16]

### Public Policies and the Policy Process

The civilian leaders who headed the first republic changed few policies formulated during the 1970s military regimes. Government corporations, both federal and state, controlled communications facilities (newspapers, radio, television), the economic infrastructure, and some industries such as steel, petrochemicals, and armaments production. As under armed forces rule, government policies still promoted banking, insurance, domestic trade, and the general service sector. Federal government expenditures went primarily for defense, police work, general administration, transportation, communication, construction, and education, rather than for agricultural development or manufacturing. Hence, the

237

private Nigerian manufacturing sector remained weak. Nigerian firms mainly processed food, assembled consumer durables (cars, television sets), constructed buildings, and produced leatherwork and clothes. Multinational corporations continued to dominate heavier industry. A 1981 law passed by the Shagari government even gave more favorable incentives to foreign investors than had the 1972 military administration.

However similar the economic policies pursued by the military and civilian governments, economic performance declined during the early 1980s. From 1980 to 1983 the annual rise in consumer prices averaged over 15 percent, and the real gross domestic product declined 2 percent each year. As unemployment grew, Nigerians faced increased income inequalities. What variables explain these economic outcomes? The falling growth rates stemmed mainly from the declining world market oil prices. As these prices began to fall in 1981, the growth rate also nosedived. Because oil products constituted more than 90 percent of all export earnings and financed 85 percent of government revenues, lower world oil prices meant a drop in funds for government projects, such as schools, water supplies, sewage, housing, and transportation. Inflation derived from supply shortages and from an overvalued currency that led to high expenditures for imported goods: food, spare parts, raw materials, capital goods, and luxury consumer goods. As imports increased and exports declined, a balance-of-payments deficit ensued. The transfer of money overseas led to lower economic growth and higher inflation, mainly because the domestic production of goods failed to keep pace with aggregate demand. Rising unemployment derived from the stagnant production and capital-intensive government projects—railways, steel plants, agroindustries—that did not absorb the available labor supply. Most urban workers had to find employment in the informal sector, mainly as traders, smugglers, tailors, and artisans. Small farmers suffered the most from declining agricultural production. When unemployment grew worse, income inequalities became more severe. The groups securing the greatest rewards from civilian government policies included the economic elites: senior civil servants, military officials, police officers, bankers, insurance agents, employees of the multinational corporations, and private Nigerian entrepreneurs, especially traders and contractors. They secured land grants, jobs, import licenses, and government contracts.[17]

Inequalities continued to plague education policy perfomance. Under the second republic a disjunction occurred between the egalitarian ideals and actual results. Normatively, although the Universal Primary Education program promised equal opportunity for all, urban male children in the southern states, especially Bendel, Ondo, Oyo, Imo, and Anambra, secured greater access to educational institutions than did female northern children who lived in the rural areas. A national mass literacy campaign launched by the federal government in 1982 intended to teach all people such cognitive skills as reading and writing. Yet few state governments took actions to implement this campaign. Both urban and particularly rural schools lacked the personnel, books, and equipment to promote cognitive development. Limited funds went for adult education. Because education was a state government responsibility, no national coordinating agency oversaw the literacy campaign. Neither the political parties nor the mass media mobilized efforts behind the literacy drive. Hence, during the mid-1980s the illiteracy rate remained fairly high; among people over fourteen years old, probably no more than one-half the men and one-third the women could read or write. Rural residents faced lower rates. Expanding primary and secondary school enrollments did not lead to upward occupational mobility and a more modernized agricultural sector. The curriculum offered few skills relevant to the expansion of farm production. Instead of securing high-paying office jobs, most school leavers became unemployed. The increase of secondary schools from 1979 through 1981 primarily benefited contractors, district officials, and state legislators—the politicoeconomic elite.[18]

Nigerian government leaders in the second republic gave lower priority to health care than to education. Public health projects, especially preventive programs, received less than 1 percent of the gross domestic product. Minimal federal government grants went to state governments, which implemented the health policies. They took charge of operating urban hospitals, comprehensive health centers in the cities, primary health centers in small towns, and village health clinics. These health facilities, particularly the rural ones, lacked trained staff, medicines, and equipment. Most physicians worked as civil servants but also managed a private practice. Even though these doctors earned a high salary, they increased their income by transferring scarce drugs and equipment from the public health centers to their private offices. Health conditions throughout the nation revealed striking inequalities. Wealthy urban residents—civil servants, senior army officers, business executives, professionals—had access to private for-profit hospitals and also gained the major benefits from government health programs. Rural residents secured the fewest health-care services. Only about a third of the total Nigerian population participated in the public health program. The remaining two-thirds, primarily rural inhabitants, used the services of a traditional healer, an herbalist and diviner, who set bones, provided child care, and helped patients overcome their mental disturbances. As a result of the inadequate public health facilities, the polluted water, and the

239

inoperative sewage disposal systems, infant mortality remained high. In 1985 around 110 infants for every 1000 live births died before reaching one year old. Life expectancy at birth reached only fifty years. Given Nigeria's oil resources, these rates appeared relatively unfavorable, compared with less wealthy African states such as Ghana, Kenya, Lesotho, Morocco, Togo, Zaire, and Zambia.[19]

Civilian political leaders in the second republic used a flexible reconciliation strategy for handling the four basic policy issues. First, motivated by a desire for social advancement, Nigerian policymakers adopted a voluntaristic orientation. Through ambition, hard work, education, and a "get ahead" spirit, they believed in the possibilities for rapid upward mobility. This voluntarist ethos was particularly held by southern leaders who had received a western education and who worked as entrepreneurs.

Second, social spontaneity took precedence over political organization. National government agencies and political parties revealed a weak, faction-ridden base. Business and professional associations played a key role shaping public policies.

Third, public policies brought gradual changes to Nigeria. Under the second republic, change blended with continuity. Traditional leaders facilitated modern changes in the economic and education sectors. Fulani aristocrats became politicians and businesspeople. Yoruba chiefs gained a formal Western education, worked as entrepreneurs, and dominated modern political decision-making. The Igbo, who had valued trade and education in the precolonial period, also excelled at these activities during the second republic.

Fourth, the policy process demonstrated a weak procedural consensus that impeded the peaceful accommodation of conflicts. Government institutions, political parties, and social groups came into conflict. At the federal government level, the two-house National Assembly often challenged the president. State governors competed with federal executive officials for scarce resources available under the revenue-sharing program. Within each state, conflicts emerged between the governor and the assembly. Political party conflicts overwhelmed an agreement on procedures to reconcile the disputes. The dominant party in each state struggled against opposition parties. Within the federal government the NPP first allied with the NPN, but this coalition dissolved in 1981. Besides these interparty rivalries, factional rivalries within the same party shaped policymaking, as divergent personalities and policy orientations struggled for supremacy. Social-group conflicts also affected the policy process. Ethnic groups tried to create new states where they could hold dominant control and secure more government funds. Rural northerners perceived that urban southerners secured more benefits from government policies. Religious conflicts pitted the Islamic north against the more Christianized south, especially in the education policy arena. Finally, economic conflicts grew more severe because public policies brought rewards mainly to the politico-economic elite; unskilled workers and small farmers gained few policy benefits. The absence of a powerful procedural consensus to reconcile all these conflicts partially explains the military coup that occurred in December 1983.[20]

### Restoration of Military Rule

The same conditions that caused the 1966 coup also accounted for the 1983 military overthrow of the elected government. As during the 1960–1966 period, incompetent policy performance and unsatisfactory results weakened support for the civilian regime. Inefficient planning, auditing, and accounting procedures paralyzed the implementation of central government decisions. Because of falling oil prices and low agricultural output, economic growth declined to negative rates. High inflation and unemployment also plagued the country. Trade deficits meant the lack of foreign currency to pay for imported raw materials and spare parts; thus urban unemployment escalated. Growing inequalities, both within urban areas and between cities and the countryside, aggravated hostilities toward the government. As central and state government debts mounted, schools closed and teachers went unpaid. Urban public utilities such as sewage disposal facilities, water supplies, and electricity no longer operated effectively. Medical care remained inadequate. When these problems became more severe, Nigerians blamed the corrupt, immobilist civilian governments. Military leaders who staged the coup promised to institute more honest, efficient policy performance, like that implemented by General Murtala Mohammed during 1975–1976.

The corruption and ineffective policy performance undermined the right to rule of the civilian government, which won neither material nor moral legitimacy. Although corruption had prevailed under all twentieth-century regimes, it became particularly blatant during the Shagari administration. Blurring any distinction between the public good and private economic interests, government officials used public resources for the benefits of their family, relatives, and party supporters. Civil servants, armed forces officers, policemen, and private business executives gained generous rewards from government contracts, import licenses, land, and employment. Bribery, extortion, and embezzlement weakened the civil servants' professional morale, increased administrative costs, and reinforced alienation from civilian rule. Three conditions explain this pervasive corruption. First, under the precolonial political systems, people granted traditional elders gifts so as to win favors from them; similarly, during the civilian regime kin expected that the political leader, the "big man," would supply jobs, educational loans, contracts, and licenses. Second, the British colonial system featured rule by a paternalistic authoritarian government. Nigerian civil servants emulated the British bureaucrats in their pursuit of luxurious homes and automobiles. Third, the expanding oil revenues brought rapid economic growth during the 1970s; hence, government officials had more financial resources to spend on projects that benefited private developers. When the oil boom went bust in 1981, the political leaders advocated austerity for the masses but continued their corrupt practices. Thus support for the civilian government declined. Military officials promised to end corruption and enforce public discipline.

Moral legitimacy based on procedural consensus or an ethical/ideological cause also remained weak under the second republic. Viewing politics as a zero-sum game, Nigerian leaders used their government offices for private benefit and showed a weak commitment to uphold rules that promote fair play. Fraudulent elections indicated this tepid procedural legitimacy. Just as the 1964 and 1965 elections demonstrated irregularities, so the August/September 1983 elections for president, Senate, House of Representatives, and state governors revealed exaggerated rolls, stuffed ballot boxes, false counts, and changed returns. The National Party of Nigeria, which controlled the Federal Electoral Commission, scored the greatest successes. All its candidates won by higher margins than in the 1979 elections; President Shehu Shagari not only gained a plurality in all the states he had won during 1979 but also emerged victorious in Bornu and Plateau. The other parties—the UPN, NPP, PRP, and GNPP—did worse. Particularly in the western region, Yoruba supporters of the UPN reacted violently to the rigged returns. Even though the nationalist sentiment was stronger throughout Nigeria in 1983 than in 1965, most Nigerians still gave their primary loyalties to a subnational group rather than to the nation. Few felt a strong moral commitment to upholding the national community or national government. Religious animosities still divided north from south; some northern Islamic leaders threatened to secede from the federation. When overthrowing the civilian government on December 31, 1983, the military officers announced their intention to strengthen the government's national orientation, reduce violence, and uphold obedience to legal procedures.

Declining moral and material legitimacy signaled a disintegrating power structure. The cohesion of social groups backing civilian rule grew weaker as group particularism overwhelmed commitment to national institutions. Government institutions operated to fulfill the interests of subnational groups, especially economic associations and local communities. When political institutions failed to continue providing concrete benefits, the civilian government fell. Despite factional rivalries based on age, political ideology, and regional attachment, the military developed a stronger cohesive base than the civilian groups and thus could engineer the coup. The Shagari administration was unable to wield effective coercive power or exert consensual power. Lacking a powerful political party and strong legislature, civilian government leaders never achieved control over the police and military, the key coercive agents. Just as the federal coalition between the NPC and the NCNC had dissolved in 1963, so in 1981 the federal alliance linking their successors—the NPN and the NPP—also collapsed. Finally, foreign pressures from the International Monetary Fund and the World Bank undermined the civilians' political power. The high trade deficits impelled the Nigerian government to seek loans from these transnational financial institutions. Receipt of these loans depended on the civilian leaders enacting an austerity program: lower wages for workers, cuts in government subsidies, devaluation of the currency, and reductions of imported goods. Yet by decreasing aggregate demand, these policies led to higher unemployment and hence reinforced antagonism toward the civilian government. Faced with fewer group pressures except from lower-ranking soldiers, the top military officers appeared more willing to impose austerity measures.[21]

With the restoration of military rule, the regime instituted a repressive bureaucratic-authoritarian mode of policymaking. The government of Major-General Mohammed Buhari purged civil servants and state governors, dismissed police officers and high-ranking armed forces personnel, banned political parties, suppressed the National Association of Nigerian Students, and repressed labor unions. Public policies more closely resembled the decisions taken by the Pinochet government than those of the Gowon military administration. Under pressure from the "Kaduna Mafia"—Hausa-Fulani Muslim elites who controlled banks, agribusinesses, cabinet ministries, and the top ranks of the civil service— General Buhari, a resident of Kaduna state, implemented policies that slashed expenditures for health and education, froze wages, raised taxes, and impoverished urban artisans, traders, and shopkeepers who work within the informal economic sector. Aligning itself with the patriarchal northern Muslim emirs, the military government chastised women for their supposed immodesty, threatened to execute them for smuggling heroin into Nigeria, and denied girls the opportunity to receive a formal education. The regime disbanded the Universal Primary Education program initiated by the Gowon administration, a decision that especially hurt rural youths and young women.

243

Despite these repressive austerity policies, the social problems inherited from the Shagari government remained. High unemployment, inflation, low growth rates, trade deficits, severe income inequalities, fraud, extortion, bribery, armed robbery, and urban violence still afflicted Nigeria. Although initially promising to implement policies that would industrialize the nation, the military elites by late 1984 abandoned their plans to increase imported supplies for domestic industries. Merchants regained the right to import whatever goods they wanted, usually luxury consumer items that brought the highest profits. Thus, as under the previous regimes, in the Buhari government the government officials and private merchants once again solidified their alliance. Despite changes in government personnel, the ruling elites remained the same. Public policies promoted commerce rather than industrial or agricultural development.

Plagued by continuing corruption, growing economic inequalities, falling world oil prices, and a rising birth rate, Nigeria in August 1985 experienced another military coup that overthrew General Buhari and installed his army chief of staff, General Ibrahim Babangida, as head of the Armed Forces Ruling Council. Hailing from Niger, a Middle Belt state, General Babangida announced his intention to curtail Hausa-Fulani influence over the policy process, repeal censorship laws, release political prisoners, expand public education programs, and restore civilian rule by 1992. Even though these proposals seemed to imply a reconciliation system, police crackdowns on students, unionists, and journalists as well as military support for a technocratic economy based on a powerful, professionalized armed forces and new defense industries indicated a bias toward bureaucratic-authoritarian ways of processing policy issues.[22]

In conclusion, all Nigerian governments during the twentieth century have faced the tensions between political change and economic continuity. As the political system moves between bureaucratic-authoritarian and more reconciliation modes of decision-making, political leaders change. Yet public policies create only gradual changes in society, not an industrial base or a more productive agriculture sector. The same situation that Karl Marx attributed to nineteenth-century India applies to contemporary Nigeria: "The structure of the fundamental economic elements of society remains untouched by the storms which blow up in the cloudy regions of politics."[23] As we have seen, Nigerians have confronted numerous political storms since gaining political independence. Yet the several military coups and civilian governments have scarcely altered the basic economic structure, one dominated by agriculture, commerce, and oil exports. State bureaucrats, merchant capitalists, and professionals still control the economic and political systems. The high ethnic/regional diversity within the large population impedes the effective functioning of a national political organization that will implement policies securing extensive societal changes. The Nigerian central government has never gained the autonomy from social groups achieved by the Chilean state. Unlike the Vietnamese, Nigerians have never experienced a mobilizing party that wielded power throughout the whole nation. Partly for these reasons, the political storms have brought new leaders to government power but have only modified, rather than fundamentally changed, Nigeria's socioeconomic conditions.

# Notes

1 Chinua Achebe, *Things Fall Apart* (New York: Fawcett Crest, 1959).
2 Joseph Uyanga, "Ethnicity and Regionalism in Nigeria," *Plural Societies* 11 (Autumn 1980): 49–56.
3 See James S. Coleman, *Nigeria: Background to Nationalism* (Berkeley: University of California Press, 1958); James S. Coleman, "The Politics of Sub-Saharan Africa," in *The Politics of the Developing Areas*, ed. Gabriel A. Almond and James S. Coleman (Princeton, N.J.: Princeton University Press, 1960), 252–270; F. C. Okoli, "The Dilemma of Premature Bureaucratization in the New States of Africa: The Case of Nigeria," *African Studies Review* 23 (September 1980): 1–16; Sam Egite Oyovbaire, "Structural Change and Political Processes in Nigeria," *African Affairs* 82 (July 1983): 3–28; Louis J. Munoz, "Traditional Participation in a Modern Political System—the Case of Western Nigeria," *Journal of Modern African Studies* 18 (September 1980): 443-468; Peter B. Clarke, "The Religious Factor in the Developmental Process in Nigeria: A Socio-Historical Analysis," *Genève-Afrique* 17, no. 1 (1979): 45–65; Pierre L. van den Berghe, "Nigeria and Peru: Two Contrasting Cases in Ethnic Pluralism," *International Journal of Comparative Sociology* 20 (March–June 1979): 162–174; Chibuzo S. A. Ogbuagu, "The Nigerian Indigenization Policy: Nationalism or Pragmatism?" *African Affairs* 82 (April 1983): 241–247; J. A. A. Ayoade, "Inter-Government Relations in Nigeria," *Quarterly Journal of Administration* 14 (January 1980): 119–132; Donatus C. I. Okpala, "Municipal Governments and City Planning and Management in Nigeria," *African Studies Review* 22 (December 1979): 15–31; Brian Smith, "Federal-State Relations in Nigeria," *African Affairs* 80 (July 1981): 363; Richard A. Joseph, "Class, State, and Prebendal Politics in Nigeria," *Journal of Commonwealth and Comparative Politics* 21 (November 1983): 23; Haroun Usman Sanusi, *State and Capitalist Development in Nigeria: A Political Economy* (Ph.D. dissertation, Department of Political Science, Northwestern University, 1982), 76–196; Omo Omoruyi, "Nigerian Educational Policy for National Integration: An Examination of the Premises," *Sociologus*, ser. 2, vol. 31, no. 1 (1981): 61–81; Sylvester Ogoh Alubo, *The Political Economy of Health and Medical Care in Nigeria* (Ph.D. dissertation, Department of Sociology, University of Missouri, Columbia, 1983), 102–142; Adeoye Akinsanya, "Multinational Corporations in Nigeria and Issues of Development," *Genève-Afrique* 23, no. 2 (1985): 79–96; Ehiedu E. G. Iweriebor, "Proletarians and Politics in Colonial and Post-Colonial Nigeria: 1912–1964," *Africa* (Roma) 41 (March 1986): 29–47.

4  See Charles F. Andrain, *Political Concepts of African Leaders* (Ph.D. dissertation, Department of Political Science, University of California, Berkeley, 1964), 86–94; Charles F. Andrain, "Democracy and Socialism: Ideologies of African Leaders," in *Ideology and Discontent*, ed. David E. Apter (New York: The Free Press of Glencoe, 1964), 166–169.

5  Larry Diamond, "Class, Ethnicity, and the Democratic State: Nigeria, 1950–1966," *Comparative Studies in Society and History* 25 (July 1983): 457–489; Smith, "Federal-State Relations in Nigeria," 355–357; H. N. Nwosu, "Inter-Governmental Relations in Nigeria: The Increasing Dependency of the State Governments on the Federal Government," *Quarterly Journal of Administration* 14 (January 1980): 197–206; J. Bayo Adekanye, "'Federal Character' Provisions of the 1979 Constitution and Composition of the Nigerian Armed Forces: The Old Quota Idea by New Name," *Plural Societies* 14 (Spring/Summer 1983): 66; Sanusi, *State and Capitalist Development in Nigeria*, 197–246; Omoruyi, "Nigerian Educational Policy for National Integration," 61–81; Alubo, *The Political Economy of Health*, 143–195; Billy Dudley, *An Introduction to Nigerian Government and Politics* (Bloomington: Indiana University Press, 1982), 41–73; Okoli, "The Dilemma of Premature Bureaucratization," 1–16: Godson Onyekwere Nwankwo, "The Bureaucratic Elite in Nigeria," *Philippine Journal of Public Administration* 24 (July 1980): 295–318; David D. Laitin, *Hegemony and Culture: Politics and Religious Change among the Yoruba* (Chicago: University of Chicago Press, 1986).

6  Femi Otubanjo, "Army Size and the Future of Politics in Nigeria," *Plural Societies* 11 (Summer 1980): 25–42.

7  Lawrence P. Frank, "Ideological Competition in Nigeria: Urban Populism Versus Elite Nationalism," *Journal of Modern African Studies* 17 (September 1979): 433–452; René Bénezra, "Nigeria: Le Retour au pouvoir civil, un tournant pour l'Afrique?" *Afrique contemporaine* 18 (March/April 1979): 13; Claude S. Phillips, "Nigeria's New Political Institutions, 1975–9," *Journal of Modern African Studies* 18 (March 1980): 19–22.

8  Phillips, "Nigeria's New Political Institutions," 1–22; Verkijika G. Fanso, "Leadership and National Crisis in Africa: Gowon and the Nigerian Civil War," *Présence africaine*, no. 109 (1979): 29–49; Adekanye, "'Federal Character' Provisions of the 1979 Constitution," 66–69; Marshall Carter and Otwin Marenin, "Police Culture in Nigeria: A Comparative Perspective," *Journal of Asian and African Studies* 15 (July–October 1980): 242–260; Ogbuagu, "The Nigerian Indigenization Policy," 258–259; Eghosa E. Osaghae, "Do Ethnic Minorities Still Exist in Nigeria?" *Journal of Commonwealth and Comparative Politics* 24 (July 1986): 151–168; Uyanga, "Ethnicity and Regionalism in Nigeria," 49–56; Brian C. Smith, "The Powers and Functions of Local Government in Nigeria 1966–1980," *International Review of Administrative Sciences* 47, no. 4 (1981): 325–331; Egite Oyovbaire, "Politicization of the Higher Civil Service in the Nigerian Presidential System of Government," *Quarterly Journal of Administration* 14 (April 1980): 267–283; Lawrence A. Rupley, "Revenue Sharing in the Nigerian Federation," *Journal of Modern African Studies* 19 (June 1981): 257–277; Peter Koehn, "The Role of Public Administrators in Public Policy Making: Practice and Prospects in Nigeria," *Public Administration and Development* 3 (January–March 1983): 1–26; Jinmi Adisa, "Political Risk and Social Obligation: The Demobilisation of the Nigerian Army 1970–1979," *Plural Societies* 15 (June 1984): 97–113; Otwin Marenin, "Policing Nigeria: Control and

Autonomy in the Exercise of Coercion," *African Studies Review* 28 (March 1985): 73–93; Joane Nagel, "Politics and the Organization of Collective Action: The Case of Nigeria, 1960–1975," *Political Behavior* 3, no. 1 (1981): 87–116; C. O. Lerche, "Social Strife in Nigeria, 1971–1978," *Journal of African Studies* 9 (Spring 1982): 2–12; John F. Ohiorhenuan, "The Political Economy of Military Rule in Nigeria," *Review of Radical Political Economics* 16 (Summer/Fall 1984): 21–22; Abel K. Ubeku, *Industrial Relations in Developing Countries: The Case of Nigeria* (London: Macmillan, 1983); Daniel A. Offiong, "Organised Labour in the Second Republic of Nigeria," *Africa* (Roma) 39 (December 1984): 571–593; Paul Francis, "'For the Use and Common Benefit of All Nigerians': Consequences of the 1978 Land Nationalization," *Africa* 54, no. 3 (1984): 5–28; Ebele N. E. Ume-Nwagbo, "Broadcasting in Nigeria: Its Post-Independence Status," *Journalism Quarterly* 61 (Autumn 1984): 585–592; S. Ogoh Alubo, "The Political Economy of Doctors' Strikes in Nigeria: A Marxist Interpretation," *Social Science and Medicine* 22, no. 4 (1986): 474.

9  Michael Adejugbe, "The Myths and Realities of Nigeria's Business Indigenization," *Development and Change* 15 (October 1984): 577–592; Ogbuagu, "The Nigerian Indigenization Policy," 241–266; Ohiorhenuan, "The Political Economy of Military Rule in Nigeria," 1–27; Paul Collins, "The State and Industrial Capitalism in West Africa," *Development and Change* 14 (July 1983): 403–429; Sayre P. Schatz, "The Nigerian Economy since the Great Oil-Price Increases of 1973–74," *Africa Today* 29, no. 3 (1982): 33–42; Sanusi, *State and Capitalist Development in Nigeria*, 197–542; Ikenna Nzimiro, "Militarization in Nigeria: Its Economic and Social Consequences," *International Social Science Journal* 35, no. 1 (1983): 125–139; Jon Kraus, "Nigeria under Shagari," *Current History* 81 (March 1982): 106–108; Tim Wallace, "The Challenge of Food: Nigeria's Approach to Agriculture 1975–80," *Canadian Journal of African Studies* 15, no. 2 (1981): 239–258; Adeyemo Aderinto, "Regional and Social Development Problems in Nigeria," *Quarterly Journal of African Studies* 14 (April 1980): 307–323; Ladun Anise, "Desubsidization: An Alternative Approach to Governmental Cost Containment and Income Redistribution Policy in Nigeria," *African Studies Review* 23 (September 1980): 17–37; B. C. Sullivan, "Structural Dependency: The Nigerian Economy as a Case Study," *Journal of Asian and African Studies* 14 (January–April 1979): 44–55; Koehn, "The Role of Public Administrators in Public Policy Making," 14–19; *International Financial Statistics Yearbook 1986*, vol. 39 (Washington, D.C: International Monetary Fund, 1986), 86–87, 110–111, 152–153; *UNESCO Statistical Yearbook* (Paris: United Nations Educational, Scientific, and Cultural Organization, 1977–1983); Stockholm International Peace Research Institute, *World Armaments and Disarmament: SIPRI Yearbook 1979* (New York: Crane, Russak, 1979), 52–53; *SIPRI Yearbook 1984* (London: Taylor and Francis, 1984), 129; World Bank, *World Development Report 1981* (New York: Oxford University Press, 1981), 134, 136, 180; World Bank, *World Development Report 1986* (New York: Oxford University Press, 1986), 238; Michael J. Watts and Thomas J. Bassett, "Politics, the State and Agrarian Development: A Comparative Study of Nigeria and the Ivory Coast," *Political Geography Quarterly* 5 (April 1986): 106–114; Uyi-Ekpen Ogbeide, *The Expansion of the State and Ethnic Mobilization: The Nigerian Experience* (Ph.D. dissertation, Department of Sociology, Vanderbilt University, 1984), 320–379; Ben E. Aigbokhan, "Size Distribution of Income in Nigeria: Decomposition Analysis," *Scandinavian Journal of Development Alternatives* 5 (December 1986): 25–33;

Ubeku, *Industrial Relations in Developing Countries*, 55; and the following essays in I. William Zartman, ed., *The Political Economy of Nigeria* (New York: Praeger, 1983): Henry Bienen, "Income Distribution and Politics in Nigeria," 85–104; Michael Watts and Paul Lubeck, "The Popular Classes and the Oil Boom: A Political Economy of Rural and Urban Poverty," 105–144; Adeoye A. Akinsanya, "State Strategies toward Nigerian and Foreign Business," 145–184; Thomas J. Biersteker, "Indigenization in Nigeria: Renationalization or Denationalization?" 185–206.

10 Omoruyi, "Nigerian Educational Policy for National Integration," 71–78; Marg Csapo, "Universal Primary Education in Nigeria: Its Problems and Implications," *African Studies Review* 26 (March 1983): 91–106; O. Y. Oyeneye, "Educational Planning and Self-Allocation: An Example from Nigeria," *Comparative Education* 16 (June 1980): 129–137; Emmanuel Chukwuma Anusionwu, "The Determinants of Regional Distribution of Lower Education in Nigeria," *African Studies Review* 23 (April 1980): 51–68; James Urwick, "Politics and Professionalism in Nigerian Educational Planning," *Comparative Education Review* 27 (October 1983): 323–340; Clive Harber, "Schools and National Awareness in Nigeria," *International Journal of Political Education* 5 (April 1982): 83–100; E. J. Chuta, "Free Education in Nigeria: Socioeconomic Implications and Emerging Issues," *Comparative Education Review* 30 (November 1986): 523–531.

11 Alubo, *The Political Economy of Health*, 143–195; Nzimiro, "Militarization in Nigeria," 134–135; Ruth Leger Sivard, *World Military and Social Expenditures 1981* (Leesburg, Va.: World Priorities, 1981), 33.

12 S. E. Finer, "The Retreat to the Barracks: Notes on the Practice and the Theory of Military Withdrawal from the Seats of Power," *Third World Quarterly* 7 (January 1985): 16–30; Jon Kraus, "The Return of Civilian Rule in Nigeria and Ghana," *Current History* 78 (March 1980): 115–118, 128; Dudley, *An Introduction to Nigerian Government*, 79–100.

13 Kraus, "Nigeria under Shagari," 108–110, 136; Paul M. Lubeck, "Islamic Networks and Urban Capitalism: An Instance of Articulation from Northern Nigeria," *Cahiers d'études africaines* 21, nos. 1–3 (1981): 67–78; Dudley, *An Introduction to Nigerian Government*, 159–161; Uyanga, "Ethnicity and Regionalism in Nigeria," 54–55; Patrick J. Ryan, "Islam and Politics in West Africa: Minority and Majority Models," *Muslim World* 77 (January 1987): 1–15; Henry S. Bienen, "Religion and Economic Change in Nigeria," in *Global Economics and Religion*, ed. James Finn (New Brunswick, N.J.: Transaction Books, 1983), 201–227; Henry Bienen, "Religion, Legitimacy, and Conflict in Nigeria," *Annals of the American Academy of Political and Social Science* 483 (January 1986): 50–60.

14 Raymond D. Gastil, *Freedom in the World: Political Rights and Civil Liberties, 1985–1986* (Westport, Conn.: Greenwood Press, 1986), 59–71; L. Adele Jinadu, "The Constitutional Situation of the Nigerian States," *Publius: The Journal of Federalism* 12 (Winter 1983): 155–185; Moses Akpan, "The 1979 Nigerian Constitution and Human Rights," *Universal Human Rights* 2 (April-June 1980): 23–41; Nkeonye Otakpor, "Pluralism and Consociational Democracy in Nigeria," *Il politico* 46 (March-June 1981): 107–125; Smith, "Federal-State Relations in Nigeria," 366–368; Oyovbaire, "Structural Change and Political Processes in Nigeria," 16–28; G. Onyekwere Nwankwo, "Management Problems of the Proliferation of Local Government in Nigeria," *Public Administration*

*and Development* 4 (January-March 1984): 61–78; Dele Olowu, "Local Government Innovation in Nigeria and Brazil: A Comparative Discussion of Innovational Transfers and Intergovernmental Relations," *Public Administration and Development* 2 (October-December 1982): 345–357; Adekanye, "'Federal Character' Provisions of the 1979 Constitution," 70–72; Oyovbaire, "Politicization of the Higher Civil Service in the Nigerian Presidential System of Government," 267–283; Alex Gboyega, "The 'Federal Character' or the Attempt to Create Representative Bureaucracies in Nigeria," *International Review of Administrative Sciences* 50, no. 1 (1984): 17–24; Dudley, *An Introduction to Nigerian Government,* 125–178; Koehn, "The Role of Public Administrators in Public Policy Making," 8–21.

15 Billy J. Dudley, "The Nigerian Elections of 1979: The Voting Decision," *Journal of Commonwealth and Comparative Politics* 19 (November 1981): 276–298; Dudley, *An Introduction to Nigerian Government,* 179–225; P. E. Ollawa, "The Nigerian Elections of 1979: A Further Comment," *Journal of Commonwealth and Comparative Politics* 19 (November 1981): 299–308; Jinadu, "The Constitutional Situation of the Nigerian States," 155–185; Smith, "Federal-State Relations in Nigeria," 373–377; Peter Koehn, "Prelude to Civilian Rule: The Nigerian Elections of 1979," *Africa Today* 28, no. 1 (1981): 17–45; Larry Diamond, "Social Change and Political Conflict in Nigeria's Second Republic," in Zartman, ed., *The Political Economy of Nigeria,* 34–47; Larry Diamond, "Cleavage, Conflict, and Anxiety in the Second Nigerian Republic," *Journal of Modern African Studies* 20 (December 1982): 629–668; Larry Diamond, "Shagari's First Two Years," *Africa Report* 27 (January/February 1982): 4–10; Richard A. Joseph, "Democratization under Military Tutelage: Crisis and Consensus in the Nigerian 1979 Elections," *Comparative Politics* 14 (October 1981): 75–100; Stephen Wright, "Nigeria: A Mid-Term Assessment," *World Today* 38 (March 1982): 105–113; Olatunde J. B. Ojo, "The Impact of Personality and Ethnicity on the Nigerian Elections of 1979," *Africa Today* 28, no. 1 (1981): 47–58; S. W. Tyoden, "Continuity and Change in Nigeria's Political Evolution: The 1979 Elections," *African Review* 8, nos. 3/4 (1978): 77–89.

16 Shehu Shagari, *My Vision of Nigeria,* eds. Aminu Tijjani and David Williams (London: Frank Cass, 1981); Diamond, "Shagari's First Two Years," 4–10.

17 Christopher Stevens, *The Political Economy of Nigeria* (New York: Cambridge University Press, 1984); Quentin Peel, "Nigeria: Economic Options and Political Constraints," *World Today* 40 (June 1984): 226–233; Sayre P. Schatz, "Pirate Capitalism and the Inert Economy of Nigeria," *Journal of Modern African Studies* 22 (March 1984): 45–57; Ogbuagu, "The Nigerian Indigenization Policy," 264–265; Alhaji Ibrahim Gusau, "Nigeria's Green Revolution," *Africa Report* 26 (July/August 1981): 19–22; Peter Koehn, "State Land Allocation and Class Formation in Nigeria," *Journal of Modern African Studies* 21 (September 1983): 461–481; Reginald Herbold Green and Hans Singer, "Sub-Saharan Africa in Depression: The Impact on the Welfare of Children," *World Development* 12 (March 1984): 287–289; *International Financial Statistics Yearbook 1986,* vol. 39, pp. 111, 153; A. 'Sesan Ayodele, "The Conflict in the Growth of the Nigerian Petroleum Industry and the Environmental Quality," *Socio-Economic Planning Sciences* 19, no. 5 (1985): 295–301.

18 George Kelly and Peter Lassa, "The Quality of Learning in Nigerian Primary Education: The UPE Programme 1976–1982," *International Review of Education* 29, no. 2 (1983): 231–243; Michael Omolewa, "The First Year of Nigeria's Mass

Literacy Campaign and New Prospects for the Future," *Convergence*, no. 1 (1984): 55–62; J. Okpako Enaohwo, "Resource Distribution in Nigerian Secondary Schools: Issues of Urban-Rural Inequality," *Educational Review* 35 (February 1983): 25–33; Urwick, "Politics and Professionalism in Nigerian Educational Planning," 323–340; United Nations and Children's Fund, *The State of the World's Children 1987* (New York: Oxford University Press, 1987), 128; Guy Nicolas, "Evolution du système fédéral nigérian," *Le Mois en Afrique* 15 (June/July 1980): 52; C. O. Ikporukpo, "Politics and Regional Policies: The Issue of State Creation in Nigeria," *Political Geography Quarterly* 5 (April 1986): 127–139, esp. 130.

19  Folorunso Abudu, "Planning Priorities and Health Care Delivery in Nigeria," *Social Science and Medicine* 17, no. 24 (1984): 1995–2002; Timothy O. Egunjobi, "Characteristics of Health Care Resource Problems in Nigeria," *Canadian Journal of African Studies* 17, no. 2 (1983): 235–238; Robert Stock, "Health Care for Some: A Nigerian Study of Who Gets What, Where and Why?" *International Journal of Health Services* 15, no. 3 (1985): 469–484; Alubo, "The Political Economy of Doctors' Strikes in Nigeria," 467–477; United Nations Children's Fund, *State of the World's Children 1987*, 128.

20  Kraus, "Nigeria under Shagari," 109–110, 136; Diamond, "Cleavage, Conflict, and Anxiety in the Second Nigerian Republic," 647–649; Stevens, *The Political Economy of Nigeria*, 7.

21  C. S. Whitaker, Jr., "The Unfinished State of Nigeria," *Worldview* 27 (March 1984): 5–8; Richard A. Joseph, "The Overthrow of Nigeria's Second Republic," *Current History* 83 (March 1984): 122–124, 138; Larry Diamond, "Nigeria in Search of Democracy," *Foreign Affairs* 62 (Spring 1984): 905–927; Larry Diamond, "The Coup and the Future," *Africa Report* 29 (March/April 1984): 9–15; Larry Diamond, "A Tarnished Victory for the NPN?" *Africa Report* 28 (November/December 1983): 18–23; Stephen Wright, "Nigeria: The 1983 Elections," *The Round Table*, no. 289 (January 1984): 69–75; Daniel A. Offiong, "The Prevalence and Repercussions of Corruption in Nigeria," *Indian Political Science Review* 18 (January 1984): 59–72; Sola Aina, "Bureaucratic Corruption in Nigeria: The Continuing Search for Causes and Cures," *International Review of Administrative Sciences* 48, no. 1 (1982): 70–76; Dele Olowu, "The Nature of Bureaucratic Corruption in Nigeria," *International Review of Administrative Sciences* 49, no. 3 (1983): 291–296; William N. Brownsberger, "Development and Governmental Corruption: Materialism and Political Fragmentation in Nigeria," *Journal of Modern African Studies* 21 (June 1983): 215–233; O. A. Bamisaye, "Political Parties and National Disintegration in Nigeria 1960–83," *Plural Societies* 15 (June 1984): 114–132; G. Onyekwere Nwankwo, "Political Parties and Their Role in the Electoral Process: The Nigerian Experiment with the Presidential System of Government," *Journal of Constitutional and Parliamentary Studies* 17 (July–December 1983): 300–305; Tom Forrest, "The Political Economy of Civil Rule and the Economic Crisis in Nigeria (1979–84)," *Review of African Political Economy*, no. 35 (May 1986): 4–26.

22  Larry Diamond, "Nigeria between Dictatorship and Democracy," *Current History* 86 (May 1987): 201–204, 222–224; Larry Diamond, "High Stakes for Babangida," *Africa Report* 30 (November/December 1985): 54–57; Jean Blomet, "Nigeria's Military: 'We Will Not Mortgage Our Country,'" *AfricAsia*, no. 4 (April 1984): 40–41; Mary Dixon, "Nigeria Curious Reforms," *AfricAsia*, no. 14 (February 1985): 31–32; Aidan Meehan, "The Nigerian Nightmare," *AfricAsia*,

no. 18 (June 1985): 8–10; Charles T. Powers, "Little Headway Seen in Solving Nigeria's Nagging Problems," *Los Angeles Times*, April 12, 1984, part I-B, pp. 1, 4; Herbert Ekwe-Ekwe, "The Nigerian Plight: Shagari to Buhari," *Third World Quarterly* 7 (July 1985): 610–625; Shehu Othman, "Classes, Crises and Coup: The Demise of Shagari's Regime," *African Affairs* 83 (October 1984): 441–461; Suzanne Cronje, "Nigeria: Army Ushers in Arms City and the IMF," *New Statesman* 110 (September 6, 1985): 20.

23 Karl Marx, *Capital: A Critique of Political Economy*, vol. 1, trans. Ben Fowkes (New York: Vintage Books, 1977), 479.

# 8

## POLITICAL CHANGE IN IRAN

Every people has the right, indeed the duty, to reach towards or return to a Great Civilization. . . . Iran can only be faithful to its ancestral, universalist tradition. This tradition has in fact always sprung from a combination of several different values. To a certain purely Iranian spirit has been added the best which could be assimilated from other civilizations. The people cannot allow themselves to disdain material achievements, nor the inventions and discoveries of other nations.

— Shah Mohammed Reza Pahlavi

The solution of social problems and the relief of human misery require foundations in faith and morals; merely acquiring material power as wealth, conquering nature and space have no effect in this regard. They must be supplemented by, and balanced with, the faith, the conviction, and the morality of Islam in order truly to serve humanity instead of endangering it.

— The Ayatollah Ruhollah Khomeini

During the last sixty years Iran has experienced fundamental sociopolitical changes. Beginning in the 1920s Shah Reza Pahlavi tried to industrialize and secularize the nation. His son Shah Mohammed Reza Pahlavi continued this process when he came to power in 1941. Particularly during the 1950s and 1960s Iran became more urbanized, formally educated, and exposed to Western influences from the United States and Europe. Land distribution policies reduced the power of the traditional aristocrats. Women gained more rights. The Muslim Shia clergy lost their authority over the educational and legal systems. Acting as a modernizing monarch, the Shah played the dominant role in forging these social changes. Yet his modernization efforts sparked a profound cultural reaction. A coalition of motley groups led by the clergy forced the Shah to leave the country in early 1979. Soon thereafter the clergy established a theocratic Islamic republic that implemented fundamental changes.

The sociopolitical changes in Iran stemmed from several profound conflicts. First, a tension between political stagnation and social change plagued the Shah's bureaucratic-authoritarian regime. Headed by a personal ruler who made all the key government decisions, the Pahlavi dynasty proved too simple and inflexible a system for a complex, structurally differentiated society. As Samuel P. Huntington observes, political elites who wish to avert political decay need strong institutions that will control the participation arising from education, rapid urbanization, extension of mass media, and incipient industrialization. Operating as "gatekeepers," strong political institutions, especially political parties with a mass base, assimilate new social groups and thereby secure political order. Only complex and adaptable institutions can enforce the rules for conflict regulation, provide for leadership succession, expand the resources needed to implement public policies, and hence control the general effects of rapid social change.[1] Huntington's insights clearly apply to Iran during the 1970s. By failing to develop flexible and complex institutions dependent on several leaders, not merely one, the Shah prepared the way for the Islamic revolution.

Second, the disintegration of the Pahlavi dynasty derived from the conflict between modernization and traditionalism. Modernization denotes structural differentiation and cultural secularization. In the political sphere, several different structures—government agencies, parties, political associations—perform diverse activities. Economic modernization involves the greater structural specialization that accompanies industrialization. As machine power becomes widespread, large-scale industrial enterprises outside the home produce a variety of goods. Cultural secularization emerges when people differentiate secular and sacred values. Individuals view material improvement in this world as an important goal distinct from spiritual salvation. Civil law becomes separated from religious norms. Educational institutions emphasize a scientific, empirical understanding of the universe. By contrast, a nonmodernized, traditional society features lower structural differentiation and less cultural secularization. One political leader, such as a king, makes all political decisions. Few machines exist to increase economic productivity. Instead, animals and humans work the land. Traders operate small-scale family businesses. Artisans make handicrafts. From the cultural perspective, traditionalism fuses secular and sacred values. Material happiness in this life depends on a commitment to spiritual values. Laws regulating human behavior rest on a religious foundation. Operated by the clergy, schools teach a spiritual interpretation of world events and stress the need for students to uphold sacred principles.

In Iran the Shah governed as a traditional leader, a patrimonial despot, but spearheaded industrialization and cultural secularization; a coalition of diverse groups opposed this blend of political traditionalism and economic-cultural modernization. Rejecting the Shah's absolutist rule, constitutional reformists supported a reconciliation system in which parliament would formulate the crucial decisions, public policies would expand economic opportunities, and cultural values would promote tolerance, that is, a separation of spiritual ends from material means. The socialist Left wanted modernization but a different type than implemented by the Shah. Struggling for the overthrow of the monarchy, it denounced the Shah's policies that brought profits to the multinational corporations but economic misery to the Iranian workers. The socialists saw revolution as the way to attain a more egalitarian society. The traditionalists emerged as the dominant group in the anti-Shah coalition. Composed of the mullahs (*ulama*, Islamic scholars), theology students, bazaar merchants, and the urban dispossessed (*mostazafin*), traditionalists supported political modernization but rejected the cultural-economic modernization associated with the Shah. Politically, they favored the overthrow of the monarchy and the establishment of a republican government based on differentiated institutions. They attacked the Shah's state-directed industrialization policies, which had undermined the economic livelihood of the mullahs, merchants, artisans, and urban dispossessed. According to their cultural orientations, the Shah's Westernization policies brought spiritual decay, moral corruption, and decadence as Iranians sought to imitate the permissive lifestyles in Western Europe and the United States. To overcome this cultural decadence, a leading segment of the mullahs favored a fusion of sacred and secular values in a theocratic regime, where the Shia clergy would not only conduct worship in the mosques but also rule the whole Iranian society.[2]

Third, the conflict between a theocratic folk culture and mobilizing structures propels political change under the Islamic republic. As we saw in Chapter 2, folk systems thrived in nonindustrial societies where people hunted wild game, gathered berries, fished, herded cattle, and grew crops for their subsistence needs. These societies were homogeneous, nondifferentiated, and decentralized. No administrative state maintained political order. Instead, shared sacred values and peer-group pressures supplied social harmony. If some family members became dissatisfied with their life situation, they had the opportunity to move away and form a new folk system. By contrast, Iran is a partially industrialized society with an ethnically diverse, economically heterogeneous population. Under the Shah's rule the state became a powerful, coercive, centralized institution. Islamic, Persian, West European, and North American values competed for influence. In the Islamic republic the theocratic folk culture clashes with elitist mobilization structures. The mobilization agencies — Islamic committees, revolutionary courts, revolutionary guards — reflect an elitist, centralized, and complex power structure, not the populist, decentralized, and simple organizations associated with the folk system. Political dissidents have only limited opportunities to flee from the nation-state and find refuge in another society.

In short, both the monarchical regime and the current theocratic system have suffered from the same incongruity: a tension between a complex society and a rigid, simple political system that cannot meet the irreconcilable pressures from a structurally differentiated society. Whereas the Shah operated through rigid political structures, the mullahs remain committed to inflexible values. For the ruling elites in both systems, government coercion has seemed the most effective way to control social discontent.

## The Bureaucratic Monarchy:
## Political Stagnation versus Social Change

Under the Pahlavi dynasty the power of the state greatly expanded. In 1921 the army officer Reza Khan staged a coup against the Qajar dynasty and declared himself Shah (monarch) in 1925. He centralized government control, established a strong army, created a powerful state bureaucracy, concentrated most public resources on urban development, reduced the power of the Shiite clergy, and stressed a nationalistic but pre-Islamic culture based on the Persian Empire. The mullahs lost control over educational institutions, courts, and their private armies. Westernized reforms in education, law, and women's rights expanded opportunities for urban professionals. State-directed industrialization took priority over agricultural development. The Reza Shah set up several state industries, such as armaments, sugar factories, textile plants, and chemical plants. These economic policies centralized economic development and undermined the influence of traditional merchants and handicraft producers. When Mohammed Reza Pahlavi acquired government power in 1941, he continued his father's policies. Particularly after 1953 monarchical rule became more centralized and coercive. The state wielded a broad scope of power that included literacy promotion, land redistribution, price controls, and the operation of industries.

Despite the fundamental social changes secured by government policies, the monarchical system remained rigid. Perceiving himself as both the symbol of Iranian nationalism and the supreme political decision maker, the Shah coordinated the policy process. The military and bureaucracy became personally dependent upon him for support. Most social groups exerted little independence from government control. Yet the Shah created no political party that maintained a mass base; hence, new groups that emerged with expanded industrialization, formal education, and urbanization had few opportunities to participate in political life. Committed to strengthening the power of state structures and industrializing the society with oil revenues, the Shah failed to articulate political beliefs that would justify the socioeconomic changes and legitimate his personal rule.

### The Pahlavi Power Structure

From 1941 through 1979 Shah Mohammed Reza Pahlavi governed through a patrimonial form of bureaucratic-authoritarian rule. Government coercion prevailed over consensual power. Initially during the 1941–1953 period, however, coercive power remained limited. A quasi-reconciliation system ruled Iran; the royal family, merchants, landlords, and urban professionals constituted a competitive oligarchy that made the key policies. Parliament wielded some autonomous authority. The press enjoyed limited freedoms. Trade unions and the Tudeh (Communist) party organized workers in the oil fields and urban factories. During this era, the Shah governed as a constitutional monarch. After 1953, when the army, backed by the U.S. Central Intelligence Agency, restored the Shah to power, his rule became more oppressive. The armed forces, secret police (Savak, National Information and Security Organization), imperial inspectorate, and Ministry of Interior and Information tried to maintain political order and prevent dissident groups from once again overthrowing the dynasty.

Under the Shah's reign, centralized power wielded by the state bureaucracy, army, and security police grew stronger. The land redistribution policies of the 1960s eroded the control that large landowners and other local leaders (tribal chiefs, village headmen, Shia clergy) used to exert. As roads, railways, radio, television, and telegraph expanded throughout the country, regional autonomy declined. The Shah resisted efforts by non-Persian ethnic groups, especially the Kurds, to claim decision-making authority over their regions.

Only limited social pluralism pervaded the Pahlavi dynasty. Primordial, religious, and economic groups all came under central government control, with the Muslim clergy and bazaar merchants retaining the greatest autonomy. Minority ethnic groups, including Azerbaijanis, Kurds, Baluchis, and Arabs, composed around 50 percent of the Iranian population. They had few opportunities to press their demands on government policymakers. The Persians, the most urbanized, educated, and wealthy ethnic group, dominated the policy process and secured the greatest benefits from government decisions.

Even if ethnic minority groups had only limited power, women improved their position under the Shah's reforms. In 1963 they won the right to vote and to become legislators. As school enrollments rapidly expanded, females benefited from the sexual integration of educational facilities. Growing educational opportunities meant that women secured employment in the government administration, courts, legal profession, medicine, and engineering. By 1978 women constituted nearly half the civil servants. More equality between men and woman emerged in family relations. Legislative decrees banned polygamy, legalized abortion, raised the marriage age for females to eighteen, and made it easier for women to secure a divorce.

Opposed to all these changes that expanded women's rights, the Muslim mullahs saw their political power decline under the Shah. Land redistribution policies reduced the clergy's wealth. The Literacy Corps and secular education eroded their control over education. The Shah's secularization of the legal system dislodged the mullahs' authority over the courts. Despite all these efforts to weaken the mullahs' political power, they still retained more independence than any other social group. Because the Shah repressed unions, professional associations, and political parties, the mosques retained the greatest power to protest his policies. The mullahs' experience in organizing religious processions reinforced their ability to mount street demonstrations against the Shah. Skilled at rhetoric, they could articulate grievances felt by the urban population. Religious taxes and charitable contributions from the bazaar merchants financed the mosques. Thus the urban mullahs had the motives, financial resources, contact with the urban masses, and organizational skills to lead the anti-Shah revolution.

Pursuing a policy of state capitalism, the Shah allowed domestic economic groups only limited political autonomy. The royal family and foreign-owned corporations controlled large-scale industries. Workers in the oil fields, manufacturing firms, and construction industries exerted no independent power; the Shah created official unions that denied workers' demands for higher pay and better working conditions. Although the land redistribution policies eroded the landlords' political and economic power, even the peasants who gained more land lacked access to political organizations that would transform their policy preferences into government decisions. Of all domestic economic groups, the bazaar merchants probably retained the greatest independence from state domination. As devout Moslems allied with the mullahs, they resisted government attempts to control profiteering, prices, retail trade, and the supply of credit.

The bureaucratic-authoritarian mode of policymaking pursued by the Shah reflected a conflict between personal coordination and the expanding scope of government activities. Especially from 1953 through late 1978, the Shah both reigned and ruled as "king of kings." Governing as a patrimonial ruler, he tried to coordinate personally those government activities involving foreign policy, military matters, and oil production. Appointments and promotions within the civil service and armed forces depended on an individual's personal loyalty to the Shah. Yet this tendency toward personal absolutism proved too simple for the complex activities that the government performed. Committed to rapid industrialization, the Shah involved the state in detailed economic decision-making. Central government agencies planned economic development, redistributed land, regulated agribusinesses, promoted foreign investment, supplied credit, supervised trade, and operated diverse public enterprises: steel plants, petrochemical industries, oil companies, electronics industries, textile firms, aluminum companies, railways, ports, telecommunications facilities, and banks. As the scope of government power over the economy increased, the Shah faced greater difficulties unifying the policy process. His indecisiveness, his failure to delegate authority, and overlapping bureaucratic jurisdictions paralyzed government decision-making.[3]

### The Basis of Political Legitimacy

Although the Shah constructed a relatively powerful state edifice, he neglected to develop a set of moral beliefs that legitimated his personal rule and policies. Particularly during the 1970s, when sociopolitical problems began to mount, his legitimacy weakened. Reflecting a bureaucratic-authoritarian ethos, his political beliefs upheld political elitism but downgraded civil liberties. Perceiving himself as the enlightened monarch, the "Light of the Aryans," he advocated a "Shah-people revolution" that originated from the political hierarchy. According to him, the sovereign incarnated Iranian nationalism and brought unity to the nation. Despite his stress on political elitism, he wanted greater income equality and especially greater cultural equality between men and women, including the right of women to vote and hold public office. The Shah's conception of freedom rested on a collectivist foundation. From his perspective, freedom meant the resurgence of Iranian nationalism

258

and state sovereignty rather than civil liberties for such enemies as "communist subversives," "international agitators," and "reactionary" clergy and bazaar merchants.

Political legitimacy rested on collectivist beliefs and on a blend of moral values with material interests. Nationalism and statism took precedence over the expression of individual interests. For the Shah, Iranian nationalism stemmed from pre-Islamic Persian traditions that extended back to Cyrus the Great (600–529 B.C.), the founder of the Persian Empire. Only by synthesizing moral and material beliefs would Iran experience a national resurgence, a "Great Civilization." Thus he tried to synthesize Iran's moral traditions ("Iranian theology") with the material benefits that Western powers such as the United States, Britain, and France could provide—benefits such as science, technology, nuclear power, and economic credits. Through promoting expansionary economic policies, the Shah hoped to improve educational, health, and housing conditions of the Iranian people and thereby win support for his rule.[4]

### Policy Processes

The Shah's strategy for modernization rested on a bureaucratic-authoritarian way of processing policy issues. Voluntarism triumphed over determinism. By exercising his will to surmount all obstacles that blocked the path toward a resurgent nation, the Shah assumed that Iran would quickly become the most powerful country in the Middle East and soon reach European levels of development. According to the Shah, this modernization drive required a powerful state, a competent bureaucracy, and professionalized armed forces that would propel the nation forward. Social groups had little spontaneity to express their opposition to the modernization policies. Fearing anarchy and disorder, the Shah tried to repress all political conflicts and impose a consensus on those participating in the policy process. Loyalty to the Shah's leadership served as the foundation for unifying subordinate elites. As we have seen, the policy process did secure important social changes, such as expanded educational opportunities, some industrialization, and the growth of mass communications facilities. Yet the political system remained inflexible. Faced with this rigid political system dependent on a single ruler, diverse groups coalesced to overthrow the Shah's bureaucratic-authoritarian regime.

# The Disintegration of the Pahlavi Dynasty:
## Modernization versus Traditionalism

Despite the powerful state created by the Shah, the Pahlavi dynasty collapsed in January 1979. Why? The major reason centers on the conflict between modernization and traditionalism. Under the Shah's regime, Iran experienced rapid socioeconomic change. As newspapers, radio, television, and taperecorders became more pervasive, these modern communications media raised popular expectations about government performance and also facilitated the transmission of grievances through-out the nation. Urbanization drew rural young men into the cities such as Tehran, where they sought jobs in the construction industry or in factories manufacturing consumer goods. The expanded education programs heightened national awareness, stimulated political interest, and increased political information. As a result of this modernization process, there emerged several new groups: highly educated professionals, schoolteachers, students, white-collar service employees, skilled factory workers, and unskilled migrants from the rural areas. These groups, along with the mullahs and merchants, became disaffected from the Shah's modernization policies and his patrimonial rule. From their perspective, the Shah denied opportunities for political participation, caused economic suffering, corrupted public morality, and violated Islamic principles. Unlike other Third World states undergoing fundamental political change, Iran experienced neither a mass-based political party nor a secular guerrilla movement that rallied disaffected groups behind the revolutionary campaign. Instead, the traditionalist clergy—ayatollahs (theologians with the sign of God), hojatolislams (religious officials one rank below the ayatollahs), and mullahs—led the coalition against the Shah.

### Ineffective Policy Performance
Ineffective policy performance that stimulated diverse grievances undermined both the power and the legitimacy of the Pahlavi dynasty. The Shah's economic policies assumed that the state would guide the industrialization process. An alliance occurred among state bureaucrats, large-scale private industrialists, and multinational corporation executives. The state operated a vast array of industries, financed investment, regulated trade, controlled credit, and provided some social services. The Pahlavi foundation funded large-scale private industrialists, mainly members of the royal family. Multinational corporations, primarily based in the United States, Britain, and France, invested in oil, chemicals, minerals, metals, machinery, and construction. Bazaar merchants,

artisans, and small shopkeepers felt threatened by the Shah's state-directed industrial development program. Under the agrarian redistribution policies carried out during the 1960s, one-third of the rural population acquired land, around 45 percent became tenant farmers, and one-fifth remained landless peasants. State bureaucrats—urban technocrats, civil servants, army officers, secret police—implemented the agrarian development plan. The Savak distributed wheat and sent farmers to new towns, the *shahraks*. Agribusinesses, which replaced the formerly dominant landlord class, produced food for export, not for domestic consumption. As agriculture became more mechanized and commercialized, small farmers went bankrupt, partly because they received far less credit than agribusiness owners or medium-sized farmers. Although the landless farmers who became agricultural laborers earned high wages, they held insecure jobs, had low status, and could not grow food for their family's needs. Despite their economic deprivation, landless peasants and agricultural wage laborers were geographically dispersed, dependent on landowners, and difficult to organize. Hence, they played a limited role in the Islamic revolution.

Attempting to lessen antagonism to his industrial and agricultural policies, the Shah made frequent policy changes that exacerbated opposition to him. Price controls on retail goods alternated with a commitment to a freer market. After introducing redistributive, egalitarian policies such as expanded social services, wage increases, and higher food subsidies, he switched toward austerity policies demanded by the International Monetary Fund, thereby deflating the economy. By raising and then dashing expectations of government performance, these policy inconsistencies reinforced popular discontent.

During the late 1970s a gap emerged between policy intentions and consequences. Although the Shah hoped that his programs would bring rapid economic growth, lower unemployment, and greater income equality, by 1977 lower growth, higher inflation, rising unemployment, and greater inequality had actually resulted. From 1960 through 1976 the real increase in the gross domestic product averaged nearly 10 percent a year, one of the highest growth rates in the Third World. The growth rate, however, fell 2 percent in 1977 and 5 percent the next year. Iranians faced the "J-curve" formulated by James Davies, who assumed that a revolution most likely emerges when a sharp economic reversal follows an extended period of rapid growth and prosperity. The wide gap between higher expectations engendered by rapid growth and lower satisfaction brought on by the economic decline leads to frustration, which motivates aggrieved groups to stage a revolution against the incumbent government. Certainly, this disjunction emerged in urban Iran just prior to the Shah's overthrow.[5]

The expanding oil revenues that mainly contributed to high growth until 1977 also accelerated inflation. From 1960 through 1972 the yearly inflation rate averaged around 3 percent. Between 1973, the year of soaring world oil prices, and 1978 consumer price increases quintupled to nearly 15 percent a year. The importation of expensive machinery, a shortage of consumer goods, and the expansion of the money supply produced by rising oil revenues caused this price explosion. Poorer rural Iranians who migrated to the cities resented the wealthy urban residents who profited from the price instability by engaging in speculative activities—for example, real estate transactions that raised rental prices.

The high rate of economic growth during the 1960s and early 1970s failed to lower unemployment. Oil corporations employed fewer than 1 percent of the labor force; hence, most Iranians did not gain increased employment opportunities from expanding oil revenues. Government policies promoted capital-intensive urban industries and rural agribusiness corporations. State banks supplied low-interest loans to capital-intensive firms, not to small shopkeepers, artisans, and farmers. As a result, small enterprises went bankrupt. Many small farmers lost their land and migrated to the cities in search of jobs. Yet especially after 1976 employment opportunities became limited; by 1979 the jobless rate exceeded 20 percent.

Income inequalities increased both within the cities and between the urban and rural areas. Whereas bazaar merchants, shopkeepers, artisans, urban underemployed, and landless peasants suffered the greatest losses, the royal family, large-scale industrialists, financiers, agricapitalists, and multinational executives secured the most benefits. As income inequality worsened, regional disparities in access to income, health care, and education became more severe.[6]

Even if the Shah intended to improve educational and health conditions of the Iranian people, his government's policy performance proved ineffective in generating greater support for the monarchical regime. Although school enrollments soared, poor facilities and inadequate libraries plagued the educational system. The Shah's Literacy Corps sent university graduates to rural areas. Rural residents gained higher literacy, but they and university-educated youths felt greater political alienation. The university curriculum stressed social sciences, humanities, and theology, not modern science, agriculture, or technology. Secondary schools offered only limited vocational training. Particularly after 1975 both university and secondary school graduates faced growing unemployment. During 1977 and 1978, students from secondary schools, universities, and theological seminaries most actively participated in staging demonstrations, rallies, marches, and armed violence against the Shah's government. Dedicated to building up the military power of the state, the Shah allocated far more public revenues to armaments than to social development projects. Few rural residents received public health care or other social services. Wealthy urban Iranians had access to private health care. Military personnel and some government civil servants, not the whole population, gained most public health-care benefits. Despite its oil revenues, Iran experienced higher infant mortality and lower life expectancy rates than most other Third World countries with a similar gross national product. In 1978, for example, 112 babies out of 1000 live births died before reaching age one. Life expectancy at birth was only 52 years.[7] These unfavorable educational and health outcomes weakened the Shah's legitimacy among the populace.

### The Decline of Political Legitimacy

Ineffective policy performance undermined the Shah's moral and especially material legitimacy. Unlike the frequent Nigerian coups, the Islamic revolution that overthrew the Pahlavi dynasty in January 1979 represented a populist movement. Although the Shiite clergy led the revolution, other groups rallied behind the clergy to bring about fundamental political changes. Their support for the Shah's downfall stemmed from diverse material and moral grievances. For example, constitutional reformists such as Mehdi Bazargan, Bani Sadr, and other urban professionals opposed the Shah's regime primarily on moral grounds: It violated civil liberties, tortured and imprisoned dissidents, wielded absolutist power, and provided no real opportunities for effective political participation. These reformists sought a nontheocratic constitutional republic that respected human rights, protected civil liberties, promoted multiparty competition, strengthened parliamentary authority, and ensured that professional achievement, not family background or loyalty to the ruler, would guide appointments within the government civil service.

Another group opposed to monarchical regime comprised the socialist Left, which included the Tudeh party, the Mojahedin, and the Fedayin. The pro-Soviet Tudeh (Masses) party rallied oil workers, unionists, some intellectuals, and national ethnic minorities against the Shah. Oil workers demanded higher wages and called strikes in 1978. The Kurdish minority strove for greater regional autonomy. Tudeh intellectuals opposed the Shah's policies of state capitalism and a close alliance with the United States. Students and other bourgeois radicals (government employees, office workers, engineers, young clergy) joined the two urban guerrilla movements: the Mojahedin (Organization of Freedom Fighters of the Iranian People) and the Fedayin (People's Fighters). Whereas the Mojahedin articulated the need for Islamic Marxist policies and a classless society, the Fedayin members proclaimed a more orthodox secular Marxism-Leninism. All three leftist groups advocated greater economic equality, more nationalized industries, and the rupture of Iran's ties with the United States, Britain, and Israel. Strikes, rallies, street demonstrations, and attacks on military barracks, government buildings, and armories signaled the leftist rejection of the Shah's legitimacy.

Led by the mullahs, the traditionalists played the greatest role in the movement to dislodge the Shah from power. Merchants, *mostazafin* (the urban dispossessed), and mullahs formed a powerful alliance. Bazaar merchants and artisans opposed the Shah's decisions to regulate their profits, control prices, expand foreign investment, and establish retail supermarkets that would put them out of business. Sellers of ice cream, lemonade, vegetables, and cloth felt threatened by these state-sponsored supermarkets located outside the bazaar. Large-scale factories that manufactured shoes, furniture, and textiles endangered small handicraft producers. The *mostazafin* — unskilled construction workers, maids, porters, squatters, urban poor — suffered from high unemployment, growing inequality, and soaring price increases for food, consumer goods, and rental housing. As a protest against the Shah, they participated in street demonstrations, attended rallies, and listened in the mosques to tape recordings of the Ayatollah Khomeini, who denounced the corrupt lifestyle of the royal family.

The Shiite mullahs held both material and especially moral grievances against the Pahlavi dynasty. When the government seized control over holy endowments, closed down religious publishing houses, disbanded student religious associations, and arrested, tortured, and executed dissident mullahs during the 1970s, their hostility toward the Shah mounted. Secret police invasions of mosques and shrines failed to deter their opposition. Responding to this political suppression, the mullahs launched a moral crusade against the Shah and accused him of violating Islamic law. From their perspective, his stress on Persian culture, secular values, and ties with the United States and Britain signified illegitimate rule. The Shah's father assumed the royal name Pahlavi, the term for the Iranian language during the Sassanian dynasty, which ruled Persia before Shia Islam became the state religion in 1501. The Shah often identified with Cyrus the Great. In 1976 a new calendar going back to Cyrus the Great replaced the Islamic calendar. The Shah's first marriage to a Sunni Egyptian, his policies that extended rights to women, and laws allowing abortion also offended the Shiite clergy. According to the mullahs, only they, not secular rulers, had the authority to implement Koranic law and govern the society so that Iran would recapture the spiritual purity of the early Islamic order. Mobilizing the masses against

POLITICAL CHANGE IN IRAN

the monarchical regime, the mullahs staged passion plays and other rituals that celebrated the martyrdom of former imams (spiritual leaders) by unjust rulers. Making an analogy between Iran in A.D. 680 and during the 1970s, the clergy equated the Ayatollah Khomeini with the slain Imam Hussein (the Prophet Mohammed's grandson), the Shah with the unjust ruler Yazid, and Tehran with the plains of Kerbala, where Hussein, his family, and supporters were executed by Yazid. Religious activities such as plays, processions and mourning rituals emerged as political events that gave Shiite Muslims the opportunity to express their hostility toward an evil, corrupt, decadent political regime. Through these mobilizing activities that linked sacred traditions to the contemporary political situation, the mullahs weakened the Shah's legitimacy and thereby undermined his power base.[8]

### The Collapse of the Shah's Power Base

The monarchical regime collapsed in January 1979 when the Shah's power base disintegrated. Despite his attempts to construct a powerful bureaucratic state, by the mid-1970s he had failed to form effective group coalitions and deter the opposition by reliance on coercive force. Hence, he lost power to a clergy-led coalition that lacked the extensive military resources controlled by the Shah.

During the late 1970s the Shah's coercive and consensual power began to deteriorate. He could neither wield effective coercion nor form alliances that would strengthen his power. Around 1974 he first learned that he suffered from lymphatic cancer. This illness partly caused his indecisive, vacillating political behavior. Coercive rule by the Savak and military waxed and waned. Martial law and press censorship alternated with more lenient treatment of antigovernment dissidents. Rather than deterring the opposition, this inconsistent use of coercive force strengthened its resolution to overthrow the Shah. As Alexis de Tocqueville pointed out for prerevolutionary France, "When a people which has put up with an oppressive rule over a long period without protest suddenly finds the government relaxing its pressure, it takes up arms against it."[9] Why? Extensive coercion breeds anger and fear. Although people resent oppression, they fear the consequences of revolting against it. When the government adopts a less punitive stance, opponents still feel angry, yet their fear subsides. As coercion declines, the expectations of successful action against a repressive regime increase. This situation occurred both in 1780s France and in Iran after 1976. Under pressure from the U.S. Carter administration, the Shah began to allow greater dissent. The Savak's power to control opposition groups waned. Most top-ranking military officials remained loyal to the Shah until he left Iran on January

16, 1979. After his departure armed forces personnel fled the nation, chose neutrality between the republicans and monarchists, or defected to Khomeini, as did the chairman of the joint chiefs, the air force commander, air cadets, and many army troops. Because the military remained passive and the secret police was faction-ridden, the Khomeini coalition could seize government control less than one month after the Shah left Iran. The Mojahedin and the Fedayin staged some guerrilla attacks on military installations; however, the movement that overthrew the Shah used only minimal violence.

The revolutionaries' success largely stemmed from the Shah's inability to form a broad coalition. Besides top-ranking military officers and the secret police, his main supporters included senior civil servants, technocrats, and the *nouveaux riches* industrialists and financiers. Yet particularly during 1978 they proved unreliable. Many wealthy Iranians took their capital and fled the country. Factional rivalries weakened military and police power. Most technocrats and government employees showed only tepid support for the Shah; during 1978 strikes by civil servants within the Ministry of Finance, Central Bank, Postal Service, Power Organization, and National Iranian Oil Company paralyzed the nation. Deprived of solid elite backing, the Shah never took steps to broaden his base of political support among the masses. No strong political party every mobilized the populace. Although he formed the Rastakhiz party in 1975 and banned all other parties, it never developed close organizational ties with the urban or rural citizens. Hence, the Shah remained too isolated from both the masses and the professional elites, relying instead on military armaments and financial assistance from Western countries (the United States and Britain) to consolidate his power.

By contrast, the opposition constructed a powerful alliance among several urban disaffected groups: constitutional reformists, socialists, and traditionalists (Shiite clergy, seminary students, bazaar merchants, the urban dispossessed). Even though these groups disagreed about specific features of the political system that would replace the Pahlavi dynasty, they all supported the Shah's overthrow, the establishment of a republican government, and the reduction of U.S. influence over Iranian society. With the strongest organization and the most fervent dedication to a moral cause—the redemption of Iran—the Muslim mullahs dominated the anti-Shah coalition and established a new theocratic political system.[10]

## The Creation of the Islamic Theocracy:
## Folk Culture versus Mobilizing Structures

Few theocratic regimes have ever functioned in the Third World, if by "theocracy" we mean political rule by the clergy. Even where established churches exist, religious officials remain subordinate to the government elites. Usually the clergy advise political rulers and try to legitimate the leaders' authority.[11] Thus the Islamic theocracy organized in 1979 represents a unique phenomenon in the contemporary Third World.

The Iranian theocracy blends sacred folk values with elitist mobilization structures. In other Third World mobilization systems such as China and Vietnam, a political party and army organized the masses to overthrow the *ancien régime* and to establish a more egalitarian socialist society. The party-state elite limits the political autonomy of church organizations, so that they concentrate on religious worship rather than on political advocacy. Either material interests triumph over moral-spiritual values in the pursuit of higher growth rates, or else the elites invest rapid industrialization with moral significance. Unlike these other mobilization systems, the Islamic Republic of Iran asserts the primacy of moral-spiritual beliefs (purity, piety, adherence to sacred law) found in folk systems. Yet the structures for organizing power reflect the elitist mobilization model. Revolutionary Guards and revolutionary councils mobilize the masses. Acting as the vanguard of the Islamic revolution, the clergy coordinate government activities. In early 1979 the power of the central government declined. The consolidation of the revolution, however, produced a more centralized state that tolerated little regional autonomy. The clerical elite applied extensive physical, economic, and normative coercion against all "nonbelievers." Like other revolutionary states, the theocratic government came to wield an expanded scope of power even more wide-ranging than under the *ancien régime*. State control over education, family life, and personal behavior increased. In short, the religious elites used mobilization structures to implement their vision of a purified Islamic community. As a result, the regime reshaped dominant political beliefs, structures, policy contents, and ways of processing policy issues.

### The Theocratic Culture

Unlike the Shah, who concentrated on constructing a powerful state structure, the Ayatollah Khomeini has given primary attention to articulating a theocratic political culture. His theological interpretations sketch a vision of an ideal political order that guides public policymaking. As in the folk system, political legitimacy rests on a commitment to

267

moral-spiritual values and to a collectivist ethos. Equality among believers takes precedence over civil liberties for the "non-believers."

According to Khomeini, political legitimacy depends on the leaders' ethical rectitude: their knowledge of the Koranic law and their commitment to practice justice, which he defines as excellence in moral behavior. Whereas the Shah believed that government must promote industrial growth, Khomeini assumes that government functions mainly to implement the divine laws of the Koran and the Prophet Mohammed. Political leaders justify their rule by promoting justice and educating the masses in righteous behavior. From Khomeini's viewpoint, only by restoring the purity and piety of the early Islamic community will Iranian government officials avoid the decadence, corruption, and "Westoxication" that plagued the Shah's regime. Iran has the obligation to demonstrate the spiritual rebirth of Islam to the world.

Both the Shah and the Ayatollah Khomeini assert the dominance of collectivism over individualism. Whereas the Shah upheld nationalism and statism, Khomeini perceives the Islamic community, the *umma*, as the dominant collective entity. Individuals must subordinate their desires to the dictates of the umma. From his perspective, nationalism is a means, not an end in itself. He has stressed the need for the Iranian state officials to work toward a more universal pan-Islamic solidarity that unites Iranians with Arabs, Shiites with Sunni Muslims. Like most other revolutionaries, Khomeini's collectivist ethos blends nationalist and universalist beliefs; Iran functions as a redeemer nation that brings liberation to the Islamic world.

Although Khomeini advocates greater economic equality, he upholds political elitism by the Shiite clergy. Whereas the Shah believed in rule by a monarch, the Ayatollah from 1960 through early 1979 opposed the monarchical state and pressed for a republican government. According to him, only God is sovereign, the true monarch. Khomeini wants the clergy to operate as the key political decision makers. The mullahs, hojatolislams, and ayatollahs are the enlightened ones who operate as a vanguard of the Islamic revolution to create a new, purified society. Because they know Islamic law and practice justice, they best fulfill the requirements for political leadership. They have the duty to awaken, enlighten, and guide the masses, as well as to supervise the government. Khomeini urges government officials to show concern for the dispossessed and minimize income differences. From his perspective, the extensive income inequality under the Shah stimulated class conflict, disorder, and chaos. Thus Iranians should pursue an austere, simple lifestyle.

Even if Khomeini proclaims spiritual equality—the equality of all believers before Allah—he downgrades equality between men and women. Upholding the traditional sexual division of labor, he stresses the need for men to exercise authority over the government civil service and the legal system and for women to concentrate on their domestic duties — rearing children and educating them in Islamic values.

Like the Shah, the Ayatollah Khomeini has shown scant regard for individual civil liberties. He perceives human nature as basically evil. When uneducated by Islamic religious scholars, people give vent to their insatiable passions. Excessive liberty leads to anarchy, disorder, chaos, and general self-indulgence. Hence, social institutions such as the state, family, and especially the Muslim courts must restrain the passions. For Khomeini, the Koranic law must be totalistic — applicable to all aspects of life, including both public and private behavior. Guided by comprehensive Islamic law, government officials should deny freedom to all groups that hold non-Islamic beliefs, such as Islamic Marxists, university professors who teach Western ideas, political parties that act contrary to the people's interests, and members of the Bahai religious sect, which Khomeini regards as an agent of Zionism.

Khomeini's interpretation of freedom reflects his theological monism. Committed to theocratic populism, he upholds the people's will, social harmony, and political unanimity but downgrades diversity. For him, freedom involves a collectivist orientation: liberation from the Shah's oppression, national independence from control by the United States, and the reassertion of an Islamic cultural identity separate from both Western and Eastern blocs. Economic freedom necessitates an economy based on Islamic principles, not on capitalist consumerism or communist atheistic materialism. Although Khomeini wants government officials to preserve the freedom to own private property, he views profiteering and usury as contrary to Islamic law.

Although Khomeini's beliefs emerged as the dominant theology shaping the policy process, other Shiite Muslims who originally participated in the revolutionary movement against the Shah sketched a more pluralistic vision. Whereas Khomeini advocated a one-party state, rule by the Shiite ulama, and the dominance of Islamic values, reformists such as Mehdi Bazargan, the first prime minister in the Islamic republic, and its first president, Bani Sadr, favored diverse political parties, a more secular state, and the synthesis of Islamic values with modern technology based on Western values. Nevertheless, partly because of his charismatic authority and rhetorical appeals, Khomeini and the Shiite clergy who supported him triumphed over their opponents. Hence, the monistic political beliefs of Khomeini became the value system that mobilized the masses to construct a new sociopolitical order.[12]

269

*The Theocratic Power Structure*

To implement the theological principles of the Ayatollah Khomeini, the mullahs quickly established their control over political organizations, both inside and outside the government. Using the mosques as their power base, the clergy dominate nearly all structures: Revolutionary Council, Revolutionary Guards, Foundation for the Dispossessed, Foundation of Martyrs, Crusade for Reconstruction, revolutionary committees (*komitehs*), educational institutions, Islamic courts, legislature, presidency, judiciary, military, Council of Experts, and Council of Guardians, which has veto power over laws passed by the legislature. From these power centers, the mullahs perform comprehensive functions. They distribute ration coupons to buy food (eggs, butter, meat), provide references for employment, approve students' entry into universities, grant building licenses, and supply passports. They also administer courts, implement decrees based on Koranic law, collect taxes, propagate the official ideology, write textbooks, operate schools, supervise the armed forces, and recruit volunteers for the war against Iraq. In short, the Islamic republic operates as a "mullacracy," a more structurally differentiated system than the Shah's bureaucratic-authoritarian patrimonial despotism.

Even though the mullahs claim to rule on behalf of the masses, the theocratic political structures more closely resemble an elitist than a populist mobilization system. The Shiite clergy have become the new ruling elite. Few if any political organizations operate outside clerical domination. Six months after the mullahs seized power, they moved to weaken the influence wielded by workers' councils, or *shuras*, which managed and operated factories. Instead, Islamic associations and elitist managers assumed control over factory operations and demanded compulsory collective prayers during the weekday. In the countryside rural revolutionary committees wield only limited power. Although they regulate land disputes in a few large villages, elsewhere they mainly concentrate on maintaining Islamic legality and faith. Peasants who encounter serious problems consult administrators and the police rather than the revolutionary committees.

As in the typical elitist mobilization system, militarism pervades political life. According to the Islamic Republic constitution, the "fighting clergy" have the duty to wage a "holy war" to "expand the rule of God's law in the world" and "to strike terror into the hearts of the enemies of God." Particularly since the war with Iraq began in 1980, wartime mobilization has strengthened political elitism. Viewing the war as an Islamic crusade, the mullahs rallied youths to fight as soldiers of Islam against the Iraqi President Saddam Hussein. Just as young people had demonstrated their moral zeal against the Shah's monarchical regime, so they were urged to sacrifice themselves as martyrs for the Islamic republic.

The mullahs have wielded more extensive coercion than did even the Shah's repressive bureaucratic-authoritarian regime. Whereas the Shah relied on the Savak to maintain political order, the clerical elite have used several different coercive organizations: Revolutionary Guards, people's militias, secret police (Savama), neighborhood public safety and protection centers, and revolutionary courts. Physical, economic, and normative coercion pervades the society. Physical coercion includes imprisonment of political dissidents, torture, and executions, all justified by appeals to Koranic law and Islamic principles. Flogging, electric shocks, stoning, and amputation of thieves' fingers constitute forms of physical punishment. Manpower renewal and placement committees controlled by the mullahs have purged civil servants, teachers, judges, and high-ranking military officers from their jobs. Those who demonstrate their knowledge of Koranic law and their willingness to practice Islamic justice gain employment in government agencies and schools. Normative coercion appears especially widespread. Whereas the Shah demanded outward conformity to his rule, the Shiite clergy seek attitudinal commitment as well as obedient behavior. The Center for Combating Sin, along with mullah-dominated bureaus in the civil service, armed forces, police, factories, and educational institutions, implements the Islamicization of society, ensuring that all those who deviate from Islamic values face punishment. With this focus on normative coercion, Iran practices the type of "repressive law" that Émile Durkheim associated with folk societies. According to him, a society that views crime as an offense against God inflicts far more severe penalties than do societies perceiving crime as injurious to people. Particularly when a powerful state implements punitive religious laws, restitutive law becomes less important.[13]

Specific targets of physical, economic, and normative coercion comprise supporters as well as opponents of the Shah's regime. The mullahs ordered the executions of numerous high-ranking military officers who served the Shah. Ethnic minorities such as Kurds who demand greater regional autonomy have been repressed. Even members of the original coalition that mobilized the population against the Shah experienced persecution soon after the mullahs gained dominant control. These groups include the constitutional reformists, the pro-Soviet Tudeh party, and the two leftist guerrilla movements, the Fedayin and especially the Mojahedin. Women who participated in the movement to overthrow the Shah but resisted clerical efforts to subordinate them to male patriarchs also came under state repression; one-third of the political dissidents imprisoned during the mid-1980s were women.

271

Wielding extensive political coercion, the mullahs hardly show strong support for social pluralism; primordial, minority religious, and economic groups all fall under clerical control. Under neither the Pahlavi dynasty nor the Islamic republic have minority ethnic groups gained regional autonomy. Like the Shah, the Shiite clergy reject demands for political independence by the Azerbaijanis and especially the Kurds. They, along with the Baluchis and Turks, have gained only limited representation in the parliament.

Women have fared less well under the Islamic republic than under the monarchy. Although women retain the right to vote and hold legislative office, the mullahs have taken steps to reduce their influence over education, employment, marriage, and divorce. Women can no longer attend law schools, and they face difficulties entering scientific and technological universities. The government bars women from serving as court judges and discourages their employment in the civil service. Their major careers revolve around teaching, nursing, and textile production, although many still work in banks, airlines, and government offices. Married women who serve as government employees cannot receive food tokens. The state has closed all government-funded day nurseries, curtailed health benefits and retirement insurance for working women, and paid women lower salaries than men who perform the same job. Husbands can now deny their wives the right to seek employment outside the home. Committed to a patriarchal social order, the theocratic regime has restored male polygamy, lowered the marriage age for females to only thirteen years, forbidden abortions, facilitated the husband's right to gain a divorce, and impeded the opportunity for the wife to divorce her husband. Rather than. actively participating in political life, women primarily concentrate on the role of motherhood. All these policy changes have mainly affected the well-educated urban women who used to work outside the home.

Minority religious groups also experience little political freedom. Members of the Bahai sect, which split away from Islam during the nineteenth century and today constitute less than 1 percent of the Iranian population, face especially severe repressive measures, including execution. Principle 13 of the Islamic Republican Constitution acknowledges Zoroastrians, Jews, and Christians as the only "recognized minorities" free to practice their religion; the Bahais are not even mentioned.

The theocratic system has granted more autonomy to economic groups than to women, ethnic minorities, or minority religious associations. Allied with the clergy, the merchants of the bazaar exert some influence on economic policies. Rural landowners and urban real estate owners have regained some of the political power that they wielded under the monarchy. Factory workers have scored less well in translating their policy preferences into government decisions. Islamic associations dominated by the mullahs have crushed the power of independent unions trying to represent factory and office workers.

As the mullahs consolidated their power over the revolutionary movement, the centralized state expanded its power over local agencies. In 1979 when the Islamic revolutionaries overthrew the Shah, the central government in Tehran temporarily lost control as the power of the armed forces and secret police weakened. Ethnic minorities in such regions as Kurdistan and Azerbaijan reasserted their demands for regional autonomy. Yet in late 1981 and early 1982, the central army, backed by the Revolutionary Guards, crushed the separatist movement in Kurdistan and reestablished central government control over the non-Persian regions. When the revolution became institutionalized during the early 1980s, central government institutions reasserted their authority over the less bureaucratic mobilization organizations. For example, the revolutionary *komitehs* yielded power to the Ministry of Interior. The revolutionary courts came under control of the Supreme Judiciary Council.

The Ayatollah Khomeini and the clergy have coordinated both government and nongovernment agencies, Khomeini has functioned as the representative of the twelfth imam (the Mahdi), who, as perceived by Shiites, went into hiding during the ninth century and will reappear at the end of time to judge the world. Khomeini also has symbolized divine legal authority, has embodied the "people's will," and has made the crucial government decisions. According to the Islamic republic's constitution, he serves as "the exalted religious authority," a "virtuous, well-informed, courageous, efficient administrator and religious jurist, enjoying the confidence of the majority of the people" — in effect, the "Viceroy of God on earth" who rules as a theocratic populist. Unlike the Shah, who concentrated on oil production, defense, and economic development, Khomeini gives primary attention to education and legal/judicial matters. By appointing judges, education administrators, and military officers and by arbitrating disputes among his lieutenants, he has exerted a coordinating role over the policy process. Although he upholds private property and supports greater economic equality, the Ayatollah has taken less interest in economic decision-making. Technocrats and civil servants have retained some independent authority to plan economic development projects and manage the government's economic ministries. As the vanguard elite directing the Islamic revolution, the mullahs have acted as a collective leadership that coordinates specific public policymaking. The top coordinating officials include the nation's president, prime minister, and speaker of the parliament—all Shiite clerics. Below them, in every government agency, mullahs oversee the bureaucrats' adherence to Islamic principles.

Unlike such elitist mobilization systems as Vietnam, North Korea, and Cuba, Iran has no powerful political party that coordinates all government decisions. From 1979 through 1987, the Islamic Republic party (IRP) hardly wielded total control over the policy process. Even though the IRP had representatives in factories, government offices, military bases, and schools, the party did not dominate the mullahs. Instead, the clergy controlled the IRP and the legislative, executive, and judicial agencies. In 1983 only about 50 percent of the national legislators belonged to the IRP; the remaining parliamentarians served as independents. Within the IRP, factionalism weakened party discipline. Thus the IRP wielded indirect influence through the mullahs. Attempts to coordinate the policy process occurred at the mosques, not the party headquarters. Viewing the IRP as functionally unnecessary, the Ayatollah Khomeini disbanded the party in 1987.

The Iranian revolution increased the scope of state power. Under the mullahs, the central government nationalized banks, insurance companies, and large-scale industries, especially those owned by the Pahlavi family. The state established tighter control over foreign trade; approximately four-fifths of imports were channeled through government agencies. Limited land redistribution took place, mainly to the clergy but also to a few small farmers. State farms and government-administered cooperatives now manage production on the publicly owned lands. Along with nongovernment organizations such as the Crusade for Reconstruction, the Foundation of Martyrs, and the Foundation for the Dispossessed, the government provides social services to the poor. Most private ethnic and religious schools have closed. Education and health care have come under closer supervision by mullahs who implement government policies.[14]

### Theocratic Policies and Policy Processes

Because the Ayatollah Khomeini failed to articulate clear economic policy stands, several different factions within the government elite compete for dominance. Particularly from 1979 through 1981 policymakers preferring more egalitarian, state-oriented programs gained the upper hand. Several government and nongovernment agencies seized private property. In the countryside the Foundation for the Dispossessed, the Crusade for Reconstruction, land transfer committees, the Fedayin, and the Revolutionary Guards confiscated land owned by the royal family and high-ranking government officials. In the urban areas the Foundation for Economic Mobilization, the Foundation for the Dispossessed, the Iran

National Industries Organization, the Ministry of Commerce, and the Ministry of Financial and Economic Affairs took control of large-scale private businesses, such as banks, insurance companies, heavy industries, oil refineries, textile firms, department stores, warehouses, cold storage plants, and trucking firms. The Housing Foundation nationalized urban real estate, mainly vacant land and unoccupied land; the Ministry of Housing came to administer this urban property. By 1982 a more conservative faction supported by Khomeini emerged triumphant. The senior ayatollahs, Muslim jurists, government bureaucrats, and the Council of Guardians limited further nationalization of land, urban housing, and foreign trade. They returned some nationalized property to its former private owners and encouraged private investment. Unlike the Nigerian bureaucrats, the Iranian civil servants rejected extensive state ownership, viewing it as too unwieldly for efficient management.

Purges of top-ranking civil servants, the mullahs' inexperience in making economic decisions, factional rivalries within the ruling elite, and the war with Iraq all contributed to rather poor economic performance during the first five years of the Islamic republic. Although the government and revolutionary organizations secured more economic equality than under the Shah's regime, the growth rate declined, inflation rates soared, and unemployment also rose. Whereas the Shah's state-directed economic policies had secured a high growth rate through the mid-1970s, from 1979 through 1985 the real gross domestic product rose only about 1 percent a year. Lower world market oil prices, shortages of spare parts, domestic violence, the war with Iraq, and consequent diversions of resources from industrial development projects partially explain the economic stagnation. The war also produced accelerating inflation rates; between 1979 and 1985, consumer prices increased nearly 16 percent a year. Wage hikes stimulated aggregate demand, but the war effort led to supply shortages. Hence, the prices of consumer necessities, especially housing and nonrationed food, soared.

Along with higher inflation went greater unemployment, which ranged from 20 percent to 30 percent of the labor force. As the agricultural sector continued to stagnate, poor farmers moved to the urban areas. There some young men found employment in the Revolutionary Guards and other nongovernment agencies such as the Crusade for Reconstruction. Educated male youths secured jobs in the ranks of the vastly expanded government civil service. Partly because the industrial sector operated at only two-thirds of its pre-1979 capacity, the supply of new jobs failed to match the urban demand.

Despite the low growth and high unemployment, the theocratic regime achieved slightly more economic equality than prevailed during the

Pahlavi dynasty. By expropriating the property of the royal family and high-ranking government officials loyal to the Shah, the state eroded the wealth of the economic elite. Government bans on interest charges weakened the financiers. The civil service instituted more egalitarian pay scales. Government and revolutionary organizations redistributed some rural land and urban housing to the poor, especially during the 1979–1981 period. Price controls and rationing of food (bread, sugar, vegetables) partly assisted low-income urban dwellers. Mosques and the Reconstruction Crusade provided some health-care services to the disadvantaged.

Yet the actual progress toward real income equality never matched the theological commitment to narrow the gap between rich and poor. Stark contrasts separated the villas in northern Tehran from the slums of southern Tehran. Corruption, bribes, and payoffs enriched many government officials. Urban real estate was sold at market prices to the wealthy rather than distributed to the poor. Landless farmers gained less land than did the mullahs, who now own around one-third of agrarian property. The mullahs and their allies in the private business sector secured import licenses, contracts, and other economic favors from public policymakers. Hence, the religious, governmental, and economic elites, not the urban dispossessed, primarily benefited from public policies. Opponents charged that the Foundation for the Dispossessed had become the "Foundation of Possession Owners."[15]

The education policies pursued by the Islamic republic have stressed the normative, rather than the cognitive, functions of the school system. According to the theocratic elite, all levels of education—primary, secondary, and university—must propagate Islamic principles and purify students contaminated by Western and Soviet influences. Rather than yielding to "Westoxication," the curriculum should uphold the independent, anticolonial traditions associated with Islamic culture. Besides teaching Islamic values and creating an "Islamic personality," schools have the obligation to prepare students for adult roles. Even though universities now emphasize agriculture, engineering, medicine, and the physical sciences (mathematics, physics, computer programming), training a committed Muslim takes precedence over instructing a technical expert who will raise economic productivity. Compared with the normative and role behavior functions, the cognitive model of educational institutions has assumed less importance. Particularly in the humanities and social sciences courses, the information transmitted to the students is heavily value-laden; few teachers place great importance on teaching the abstract cognitive skills that will enable students to transcend theological dogma.

To implement this normative model, educational policymakers have tried to mobilize faculty and students behind the mullahs' theocratic vision. Shiite clergy monitor all educational institutions, making sure that administrators and teachers affirm the correct Islamic beliefs. Instructors must demonstrate their knowledge of Koranic law as well as their technical competence in a particular subject. Criteria for admission to universities include commitment to Islamic philosophy, knowledge of Muslim jurisprudence, and sacrifice in war, as well as performance on national examinations. At the universities the Management Council, dominated by the mullahs, ensures that no one hinders the Islamicization process. Purges have eliminated professors and students who oppose these theocratic educational policies. Those remaining in the humanities, social science, and law programs lack academic freedom. The mullahs have also removed from bookstores and libraries all materials that contradict the principles espoused by the Ayatollah Khomeini. In short, for Khomeini, the educational system serves as a primary center for creating a new Islamic citizen who adheres to his interpretation of the Koran. Like economic decision-making, the educational policy process blends elitist mobilization structures with sacred folk values to achieve this normative vision.[16]

The purification process extends not only to educational policies but also to the health-care sector. After the revolutionaries gained government power in 1979, they announced their intention to cleanse Iran of all physicians who had become contaminated by foreign influences. Hence, many Western-trained medical personnel left the country. Physician shortages continued to plague the rural areas. To remedy this situation, the government recruited doctors from India, Pakistan, Bangladesh, and the Philippines. It sent paramedics and medical students to villages and small towns. Nongovernment revolutionary agencies such as the Crusade for Reconstruction built public baths and health centers throughout the countryside. Mosques and private hospitals provided some health-care services to the poor, especially wounded war veterans. Despite these egalitarian moves, the urban wealthy continued to gain superior health services in private hospitals. Rural Iranians still faced unhealthy living conditions. In 1984 around 110 babies for every 1000 live births died before reaching one year old, a comparatively high infant mortality rate for an upper-middle-income Third World nation. Life expectancy at birth averaged about sixty years, the same figure found in such poorer countries as Egypt, Guatemala, and Honduras. Hence, the war with Iraq, the purges of Western-trained physicians, and the concentration of resources in the cities have impeded the advance toward a healthier population.[17]

In conclusion, the way that Iranian policymakers have handled the four basic issues reflects their attempt to link sacred folk values to elitist mobilization structures. As in the typical mobilization system, revolutionary voluntarism takes primacy over determinism. Compared with the Sunni ulama, the Shiite clergy have greater authority to interpret the will of Allah and lead their followers toward a new social order. In the Islamic Republic of Iran, the Ayatollah Khomeini plays this leadership role. By articulating the will of Allah, he has mobilized his supporters to pursue comprehensive political changes.

The mobilization strategy involves the dominance of clerical organization, not social spontaneity, in the policy process. The mullahs control nearly all social groups. Few voluntary associations have the spontaneous opportunity to assert their policy preferences independent of mullah domination.

The policy process blends consensus with conflict. A commitment to Islamic principles provides the consensus that unites the policymakers. They lead the conflict against all domestic and foreign "enemies" that deviate from the Ayatollah Khomeini's interpretations. The struggle with Iraq, the United States, the Soviet Union, Israeli Zionists, Bahais, Islamic Marxists, secularists, and "decadent materialists" promotes solidarity behind the theocratic regime. Factional policy disputes occur more within the ruling elite circles than in public arenas. Whereas some senior ayatollahs, the Council of Guardians, bazaar merchants, and government civil servants have backed economic policies that uphold private ownership and limits on income equality, more radical factions within the clergy have advocated greater state ownership and economic equality.

The Islamic revolutionary government has implemented policies that brought radical and reactionary changes to Iran.[18] It has symbolically upgraded the status of the urban dispossessed and has tried to secure more economic equality. These efforts represent radical change. A republican form of government, not a monarchy, rules Iran. The parliament plays a greater role in the policy process now than during the Shah's regime. Technologically advanced communications equipment propagates the slogans that mobilize the masses behind government activities to reconstruct the Iranian society, win the war with Iraq, and bring liberation to other oppressed Islamic peoples. Other policy dimensions, however, reflect a reactionary orientation based on a seventh-century Islamic Utopia that never existed. Under the theoretic regime, mullahs exert more political power over public policymaking than ever before in Iranian history. Women enjoy fewer rights than they held during the monarchy. Rejecting secular values, educational policies promote the Islamicization of the schools rather than a synthesis of Western and Islamic principles. The legal system implements such punitive policies as public stoning of prostitutes, public whippings, and the amputation of thieves' fingers. In sum, guided by Islamic folk values, the elitist mobilization system has secured some radical changes while retreating backward into traditionalism.

## Notes

1 See Samuel P. Huntington, *Political Order in Changing Societies* (New Haven, Conn.: Yale University Press, 1968), esp. chs. 1, 3, and 7.
2 David E. Apter, *The Politics of Modernization* (Chicago: University of Chicago Press, 1965), 43–122; Marion J. Levy, Jr., "Modernization Exhumed," *Journal of Developing Societies* 2, no. 1 (1986): 1–11; Donald Eugene Smith, *Religion and Political Development* (Boston: Little, Brown, 1970), 1–32; Andrew C. Janos, *Politics and Paradigms: Changing Theories of Change in Social Science* (Stanford, Ca.: Stanford University Press, 1986), 7–64; Ali Banuazizi, "Social-Psychological Approaches to Political Development," in *Understanding Political Development*, ed. Myron Weiner and Samuel P. Huntington (Boston: Little, Brown, 1987), 281–308; William O. Beeman, *Language, Status, and Power in Iran* (Bloomington: Indiana University Press, 1986), 207–211.
3 Akbar Aghajanian, "Ethnic Inequality in Iran: An Overview," *International Journal of Middle East Studies* 15 (May 1983): 211–224; Zalmay Khalilzad, "The Politics of Ethnicity in Southwest Asia: Political Development or Political Decay?" *Political Science Quarterly* 99 (Winter 1984–85): 671–674; Mangol Bayat, "The Iranian Revolution of 1978–79: Fundamentalist or Modern?" *Middle East Journal* 37 (Winter 1983): 32; Mansoor Moaddel, "The Shi'i Ulama and the State in Iran," *Theory and Society* 15, no. 3 (1986): 519–556; Shahrough Akhavi, "The Ideology and Praxis of Shi'ism in the Iranian Revolution," *Comparative Studies in Society and History* 25 (April 1983): 195–211; Khosrow Fatemi, "Leadership by Distrust: The Shah's *Modus Operandi*," *Middle East Journal* 36 (Winter 1982): 48–61; A. H. H. Abidi, "The Iranian Revolution: Its Origins and Dimensions," *International Studies* 18 (April-June 1979): 129–161; Timothy W. Luke, "Dependent Development and the OPEC States: State Formation in Saudi Arabia and Iran under the International Energy Regime," *Studies in Comparative International Development* 20 (Spring 1985): 31–54; Theda Skocpol, "Rentier State and Shi'a Islam in the Iranian Revolution," *Theory and Society* 11 (May 1982): 265–283; Nikki R. Keddie, "Comments on Skocpol," *Theory and Society* 11 (May 1982): 285–292; Ahmad Ashraf and Ali Banuazizi, "The State, Classes and Modes of Mobilization in the Iranian Revolution," *State, Culture, and Society* 1 (Spring 1985): 3–40; Habib Ladjevardi, "The Origins of U.S. Support for an Autocratic Iran," *International Journal of Middle East Studies* 15 (May 1983): 225–239; Mohammad Hariri-Akbari, *Territorial Politics in a Transitional Society: Towards a New Political Sociology of Iran* (Ph.D. dissertation, Department of Sociology, Maxwell School of Citizenship and Public Affairs, Syracuse University, 1983); Haleh Afshar, "The Legal, Social and Political Position of Women in Iran," *International Journal of the Sociology of Law* 13 (February 1985): 47–60; Haleh Afshar, "Women, State and Ideology in Iran," *Third World Quarterly* 7 (April 1985): 256–278; Guity Nashat, "Women in the Islamic Republic of Iran," *Iranian Studies* 13, nos. 1–4 (1980): 165–190.
4 Mohammad Reza Pahlavi, *The Shah's Story*, trans. Teresa Waugh (London:

Michael Joseph, 1980): Mohammad Reza Pahlavi, *Answer to History* (New York: Stein and Day, 1980); D. Ray Heisey and J. David Trebing, "A Comparison of the Rhetorical Visions and Strategies of the Shah's White Revolution and the Ayatollah's Islamic Revolution," *Communication Monographs* 50 (June 1983): 158–174; David Menashri, "The Shah and Khomeini: Conflicting Nationalisms," *Crossroads*, no. 8 (Winter/Spring 1982): 53–79; Hariri-Akbari, *Territorial Politics in a Transitional Society*, 237.

5 James C. Davies, "Toward a Theory of Revolution," in *Anger, Violence, and Politics: Theories and Research*, ed. Ivo K. Feierabend, Rosalind L. Feierabend, and Ted Robert Gurr (Englewood Cliffs, N.J.: Prentice-Hall, 1972), 67–84; International Monetary Fund, *International Financial Statistics Yearbook 1985*, vol. 38 (Washington, D.C.: International Monetary Fund, 1985), 132–133.

6 M. H. Pesaran, "The System of Dependent Capitalism in Pre- and Post-Revolutionary Iran," *International Journal of Middle East Studies* 14 (November 1982): 501–522; Manoucher Parvin and Amir N. Zamani, "Political Economy of Growth and Destruction: A Statistical Interpretation of the Iranian Case," *Iranian Studies* 12, nos. 1/2 (Winter/Spring 1979): 43–78; James F. Petras and Morris H. Morley, "Development and Revolution: Contradictions in the Advanced Third World Countries—Brazil, South Africa, and Iran," *Studies in Comparative International Development* 16 (Spring 1981): 3–43; Norriss S. Hetherington, "Industrialization and Revolution in Iran: Forced Progress or Unmet Expectation?" *Middle East Journal* 36 (Summer 1982): 362–373; Nikki R. Keddie, "Iranian Revolutions in Comparative Perspective," *American Historical Review* 88 (June 1983): 579–598; Sharif Arani, "Iran: From the Shah's Dictatorship to Khomeini's Demagogic Theocracy," *Dissent* 27 (Winter 1980): 9–26; Yair P. Hirschfeld, "Decline and Fall of the Pahlavis," *Jerusalem Quarterly*, no. 12 (Summer 1979): 20–33; Grace E. Goodell, "How the Shah De-Stabilized Himself," *Policy Review*, no. 16 (Spring 1981): 55–72; International Monetary Fund, *International Financial Statistics Yearbook 1987*, vol. 40 (Washington, D.C.: International Monetary Fund, 1987), 114–115; Cyrus Yeganeh, "The Agrarian Structure of Iran: From Land Reform to Revolution," *State, Culture, and Society* 1 (Spring 1985): 67–84; Fatemeh E. Moghadam, "An Evaluation of the Productive Performance of Agribusinesses: An Iranian Case Study," *Economic Development and Cultural Change* 33 (July 1985): 755–776; Robert E. Looney, "Origins of Pre-Revolutionary Iran's Development Strategy," *Middle Eastern Studies* 22 (January 1986): 104–119; Robert E. Looney, "A Monetarist Interpretation of Inflation in Pre-Revolutionary Iran," *Journal of Social, Political and Economic Studies* 10 (Spring 1985): 87–101; Nasser Momayezi, "Economic Correlates of Political Violence: The Case of Iran," *Middle East Journal* 40 (Winter 1986): 68–81; Misagh Parsa, "Economic Development and Political Transformation: A Comparative Analysis of the United States, Russia, Nicaragua, and Iran," *Theory and Society* 14 (September 1985): 623–675; James G. Scoville, "The Labor Market in Prerevolutionary Iran," *Economic Development and Cultural Change* 34 (October 1985): 143–155.

7 Theodore H. Moran, "Iranian Defense Expenditures and the Social Crisis," *International Security* 3 (Winter 1978/1979): 178–192; Marvin Zonis, "Educational Ambivalence in Iran," *Iranian Studies* 1 (Fall 1968): 133–153; Jerrold D. Green, *Revolution in Iran: The Politics of Countermobilization* (New York: Praeger, 1982), 29; Ruth Leger Sivard, *World Military and Social Expenditures 1981*

(Leesburg, Va.: World Priorities, 1981), 31; Ashraf and Banuazizi, "The State, Classes and Modes of Mobilization in the Iranian Revolution," 25–27, 35.

8 Hetherington, "Industrialization and Revolution in Iran," 362–373; Shahram Chubin, "Leftist Forces in Iran," *Problems of Communism* 29 (July/August 1980): 1–25; Sepehr Zabih, "Iran's Revolutionary Left," *Problems of Communism* 32 (March/April 1983): 79–84; Farhad Kazemi, "Urban Migrants and the Revolution," *Iranian Studies* 13, nos. 1–4 (1980): 257–277; Keddie, "Iranian Revolutions in Comparative Perspective," 579–598; Said Amir Arjomand, "Iran's Islamic Revolution in Comparative Perspective," *World Politics* 38 (April 1986): 383–414; Hirschfeld, "Decline and Fall of the Pahlavis," 20–33; Abidi, "The Iranian Revolution," 129–161; Banuazizi, "Social-Psychological Approaches to Political Development," 300–308; Moaddel, "The Shi'i Ulama and the State in Iran," 539–547; Farideh Farhi, *State Disintegration and Urban-Based Revolutionary Crisis: The Iranian Case* (Ph.D. dissertation, Department of Political Science, University of Colorado at Boulder, 1986); Bernard Hourcade, "La Société iranienne continue sa révolution," *Projet*, no. 193 (May/June 1985): 103–108; Skocpol, "Rentier State and Shi'a Islam in the Iranian Revolution," 265–283; Editorial, "The Fate of the Shah and the Lessons of History," *Civilisations* 29, nos. 1/2 (1979): 2–28; James A. Bill, "Power and Religion in Revolutionary Iran," *Middle East Journal* 36 (Winter 1982): 22–47; L. P. Elwell-Sutton, "The Iranian Revolution," *International Journal* 34 (Summer 1979): 391–407; David Menashri, "Strange Bedfellows: The Khomeini Coalition," *Jerusalem Quarterly*, no. 12 (Summer 1979): 34–48; Said Amir Arjomand, "Shi'ite Islam and the Revolution in Iran," *Government and Opposition* 16 (Summer 1981): 293–316; Akhavi, "The Ideology and Praxis of Shi'ism in the Iranian Revolution," 195–211; Mary Hegland, "Ritual and Revolution in Iran," in *Political Anthropology*, vol. 2: *Culture and Political Change*, ed. Myron J. Arnoff (New Brunswick, N.J.: Transaction Books, 1983), 78–100.

9 Alexis de Tocqueville, *The Old Régime and the French Revolution*, trans. Stuart Gilbert (Garden City, N.Y.: Doubleday Anchor, 1955), 176.

10 Menashri, "Strange Bedfellows," 34–48; Fatemi, "Leadership by Distrust," 48–61; Keddie, "Iranian Revolutions in Comparative Perspective," 579–598; Hirschfeld, "Decline and Fall of the Pahlavis," 20–33; Val Moghadam, "Iran: Development, Revolution and the Problem of Analysis," *Review of Radical Political Economics* 16 (Summer/Fall 1984): 227–240; Walter Laquer, "Why the Shah Fell," *Commentary* 67 (March 1979): 47–55; Abidi, "The Iranian Revolution," 129–161; Richard W. Cottam, "Revolutionary Iran," *Current History* 78 (January 1980): 12–16, 34–35; Arani, "Iran," 9–26; Hooshang Kuklan, "The Administrative System in the Islamic Republic of Iran: New Trends and Directions," *International Review of Administrative Sciences* 47, no. 3 (1981): 281; Green, *Revolution in Iran*, 134–144.

11 Smith, *Religion and Political Development*, 70–75.

12 Imam Khomeini, *Islam and Revolution*, ed. and trans. Hamid Algar (Berkeley, Calif.: Mizan Press, 1981); Ahmad Doost-Mohammadi, *The Line of the Imam* (Ph.D. dissertation, Department of Government, Claremont Graduate School, 1983); Raymond N. Habiby and Fariborz Ghavidel, "Khumayni's Islamic Republic," *Middle East Review* 11 (Summer 1979): 12–20, Norman Calder, "Accommodation and Revolution in Imami Shi'i Jurisprudence: Khumayni and the Classical Tradition," *Middle Eastern Studies* 18 (January 1982): 3–20; Menashri, "The Shah and Khomeini," 53–79; Heisey and Trebing, "A

Comparison of the Rhetorical Visions and Strategies of the Shah's White Revolution and the Ayatollah's Islamic Revolution," 158–174; Amir H. Ferdows, "Khomaini and Fadayan's Society and Politics," *International Journal of Middle East Studies* 15 (May 1983): 241–257; Willem M. Floor, "The Revolutionary Character of the Iranian Ulama: Wishful Thinking or Reality?" *International Journal of Middle East Studies* 12 (December 1980): 501–524; R. K. Ramazani, "Iran's Islamic Revolution and the Persian Gulf," *Current History* 84 (January 1985): 5–8, 40–41; Riaz Hassan, "Iran's Islamic Revolutionaries: Before and After the Revolution," *Third World Quarterly* 6 (July 1984): 678.

13 See Steve Fenton, with Robert Reiner and Ian Hammett, *Durkheim and Modern Sociology* (New York: Cambridge University Press, 1984), 51, 175–201.

14 Bill, "Power and Religion in Revolutionary Iran," 22–47; Hassan, "Iran's Islamic Revolutionaries," 675–686; Barry Rubin, "From Ardor to Apathy in Postrevolutionary Iran," *Asia* 6 (November/December 1983): 38–46; Assef Bayat, "Workers' Control after the Revolution," *Merip Reports* 13 (March/April 1983): 19–23, 33–34; Manijeh Dowlat, Bernard Hourcade, and Odile Puech, "Les Paysans et la Révolution Iranienne," *Peuples méditerranéens*, no. 10 (January-March 1980): 19–42; "Constitution of the Islamic Republic of Iran," *Middle East Journal* 34 (Spring 1980): 184–204; Shahram Chubin, "Waging a War without End," *New Society* 71 (March 21, 1985): 437–439; Sheikh R. Ali, "Holier than Thou: The Iran-Iraq War," *Middle East Review* 17 (Fall 1984): 50–57; Nozar Alaolmolki, "Iranian Opposition to Khomaini and the Islamic Republic," *Australian Outlook* 38 (August 1984): 99–105; Richard Dowden, "In the Terror of Tehran," *New York Review of Books* 31 (February 2, 1984): 8–12; *Amnesty International Report 1986* (London: Amnesty International Publications, 1986), 327–330; *Torture in the Eighties* (London: Amnesty International Publications, 1984), 229–231; Mansour Farhang and John Hossein Motavalli, "Iran: A Great Leap Backward," *Progressive* 48 (August 1984): 19–22; Farhang Jahanpour, "Iran: The Rise and Fall of the Tudeh Party," *World Today* 40 (April 1984): 152–159; Vahe Petrossian, "Iran's Crisis of Leadership," *World Today* 37 (February 1981): 39–44; Ahmad Ashraf, "Bazaar and Mosque in Iran's Revolution," *Merip Reports* 13 (March/April 1983): 16–18; Khalilzad, "The Politics of Ethnicity in Southwest Asia," 671–674; Afshar, "Women, State and Ideology in Iran," 256–278; Nashat, "Women in the Islamic Republic of Iran," 165–190; Patricia J. Higgins, "Women in the Islamic Republic of Iran: Legal, Social, and Ideological Changes," *Signs: Journal of Women in Culture and Society* 10 (Spring 1985): 477–494; "Retrogressive Work Legislation against Women," *Women and Struggle in Iran*, no. 4 (Spring 1985): 43–44, 57; Fred Halliday, "Year IV of the Islamic Republic," *Merip Reports* 13 (March/April 1983): 3–8; Kambiz Afrachteh, "The Predominance and Dilemmas of Theocratic Populism in Contemporary Iran," *Iranian Studies* 14 (Summer/Autumn 1981): 189–213; Shaul Bakhash, *The Reign of the Ayatollahs: Iran and the Islamic Revolution* (New York: Basic Books, 1984), 217–250; Cheryl Benard and Zalmay Khalilzad, *"The Government of God"—Iran's Islamic Republic* (New York: Columbia University Press, 1984), 103–192; Elaine Sciolino, "Iran's Durable Revolution," *Foreign Affairs* 61 (Spring 1983): 893–920; David Menashri, "The Islamic Revolution in Iran: The Consolidation Phase," *Orient* 25 (December 1984): 499–515; Abbas Vali and Sami Zubaida, "Factionalism and Political Discourse in the Islamic Republic of Iran: The Case of the Hujjatiyeh Society: *Economy and Society* 14 (May 1985): 139–173; Marvin Zonis, "The Rule of the Clerics in the Islamic Republic of Iran," *Annals*

of the *American Academy of Political and Social Science* 482 (November 1985): 85–107; Mehdi Mozaffari, "Authority in Islam: From Muhammad to Khomeini," *International Journal of Politics* 16 (Winter 1986/1987): 37–39, 49–51, 97–103; William O. Beeman, "Iran's Religious Regime: What Makes It Tick? Will It Ever Run Down?" *Annals of the American Academy of Political and Social Science* 483 (January 1986): 73–83; William O. Beeman, "Living with Iran," *Ethics and International Affairs* 1 (1987): 87–92.

15 Bakhash, *The Reign of the Ayatollahs*, 166–216; David R. Francis, "Iran's Resilient Economy Takes the Costs of Iraqi War in Stride," *Christian Science Monitor*, July 11, 1985, pp. 19–20; Dowlat, Hourcade, and Puech, "Les Paysans et la Révolution Iranienne," 34–41; Eric Rouleau, "Khomeini's Iran," *Foreign Affairs* 59 (Fall 1980): 16; Yeganeh, "The Agrarian Structure of Iran," 79–83; A. H. H. Abidi, "Iran on the Anvil," *International Studies* 22 (October-December 1985): 337–351; Beeman, "Iran's Religious Regime," 77–78, 82–83; Shahrough Akhavi, "Institutionalizing the New Order in Iran," *Current History* 86 (February 1987): 53–56, 83–84; Menashri, "The Islamic Revolution in Iran," 509; Vali and Zubaida, "Factionalism and Political Discourse in the Islamic Republic of Iran," 142–146, 162–164; Helene Kafi, "Iran's Ticking Time Bomb," *San Francisco Chronicle This World*, September 14, 1986, pp. 7–8; International Monetary Fund, *International Financial Statistics Yearbook 1987*, 115, 161; *International Financial Statistics* 40 (April 1987): 274.

16 Menashri, "The Islamic Revolution in Iran," 506; Zonis, "The Rule of the Clerics in the Islamic Republic of Iran," 104; Khosrow Sobhe, "Education in Revolution: Is Iran Duplicating the Chinese Cultural Revolution?" *Comparative Education* 18, no. 3 (1982): 271–280; Khosrow Sobhe, "Educational Planning for Engineering Schools: A Study of Iran between 1962 and 1982," *Higher Education* 12 (January 1983): 61–76; Farideh Selhoun, "Iran," *Integrated Education* 20 (November 1983): 13–14; Farhang and Motavelli, "Iran," 20; Doost-Mohammadi, *The Line of the Imam*, 71–77.

17 Hossain A. Ronaghy and Harold J. Simon, "Effects of the Islamic Revolution in Iran on Medical Education: The Shiraz University School of Medicine," *American Journal of Public Health* 73 (December 1983): 1400–1401; Emad Ferdows, "The Reconstruction Crusade and Class Conflict in Iran," *Merip Reports* 13 (March/April 1983): 11–15; Sobhe, "Education in Revolution," 277–278; Abidi, "Iran on the Anvil," 345; World Bank, *World Development Report 1986* (New York: Oxford University Press, 1986), 180–181, 232–233.

18 See Fred Halliday, "The Iranian Revolution: Uneven Development and Religious Populism," *Journal of International Affairs* 36 (Fall/Winter 1982/1983): 187–207.

# CONCLUSION

As we bring the state back in to its proper central place in explanations of social change and politics, . . . we need solidly grounded and analytically sharp understandings of the causal regularities that underlie the histories of states, social structures, and transnational relations in the modern world.
— Theda Skocpol

What conclusions can we draw from the analysis of political changes in Vietnam, Cuba, Chile, Nigeria, and Iran? Let us probe the credibility of the five hypotheses formulated in Chapter 3. First, political systems experience the most fundamental between-system change when the state's coercive and consensual power disintegrates and when the opposition movement more effectively manages to wield coercion and form a coalition. Leon Trotsky pointed out in his *History of the Russian Revolution*: "The fate of every revolution at a certain point is decided by a break in the disposition of the army. Against a numerous, disciplined, well-armed and ably led military force, unarmed or almost unarmed masses of the people cannot possibly gain a victory."[1] As the MIRistas and leftist Socialists in Chile discovered to their chagrin, revolutionary rhetoric unaccompanied by a powerful political party or revolutionary army can lead to disaster. Certainly in Chile during the early 1970s, the conservative elite and professional armed forces opposed to the Allende programs were more powerfully organized than Allende's supporters. Similarly, in Vietnam and Cuba the revolutionaries successfully seized government power partly because the Thieu and Batista military forces disintegrated, overwhelmed by the revolutionary armies. Nigeria's civilian leaders never developed sufficiently powerful organizations, such as a political party or a government agency, that would restrain military coups.

Despite the importance of coercive power in explaining system disintegration, the use of military resources, not their magnitude, wields the more crucial impact. In Cuba the Rebel Army led by Fidel Castro and in Vietnam the People's Liberation Armed Forces and the People's Army of

Vietnam had neither the troops nor the advanced weapons controlled by the incumbent government. Nevertheless, they triumphed because they more skillfully used their military resources than did their opponents. The Cuban revolutionaries also formed a more cohesive alliance of powerful social groups. Similarly, in Iran the Shah, with assistance from the United States, had established a modernized, professionalized military, yet it proved unable to prevent the largely unarmed Islamic revolutionaries from overthrowing the Pahlavi dynasty. After the Shah left Iran during January 1979, the armed forces and police remained leaderless, unwilling to continue repressing mullahs, students, merchants, and the urban dispossessed who wanted to institute a new political system. Particularly during 1977, 1978, and early 1979, the social groups supporting the Shah no longer rallied around him; however, the mullahs successfully developed a broad-based group coalition behind their revolutionary movement. Hence, however limited their magnitude of coercive power, they emerged victorious against the numerically superior forces employed by the Shah.

Second, the actions taken by such foreign nations as the United States and the Soviet Union exert an indirect, not a direct, impact on between-system change. The two superpowers mainly affect political change by strengthening or weakening domestic conditions. For instance, the Nixon administration undermined Salvador Allende by imposing economic sanctions against Chile and by increasing military assistance to the armed forces. Yet it did not directly cause the coup but rather exploited the internal weaknesses of the Unidad Popular. Even without U.S. assistance, the Chilean opposition to the Allende government controlled powerful organizations that engineered the *golpe de estado*. The U.S. government certainly gave far more human and material assistance to the South Vietnamese government than the U.S.S.R. or China ever offered the North Vietnamese. Yet because of domestic vulnerabilities, both cultural and structural, the Saigon government finally collapsed in 1975. Cuba geographically resides in the U.S. sphere of influence. Despite the U.S. blockade of Cuba and the extensive aid to anti-Castro rebels from 1960 to 1974, no American administration dislodged Castro from power during this period. True, he relied partly on Soviet assistance to maintain his regime, but a more important reason for his continuation in power revolved around the effective ways that he mobilized the Cuban population. Although the U.S. government during the 1970s gave extensive military assistance to the Shah's regime and tried to make it the dominant military power in the Middle East, the coalition led by the Shiite clergy still managed to overthrow the Shah, largely because of his domestic weaknesses. The Shah's political behavior, not the human rights ideals articulated by Carter administration officials, mainly caused the disintegration of the Pahlavi dynasty. Despite the geographical proximity of the U.S.S.R. to Iran, the Soviet government scarcely engineered the Islamic revolution, however great its support for the Tudeh party. Instead, a coalition of clergy, students, merchants, professionals, and the urban poor, rather than the Soviet Union or the Tudeh party, played the leading role in toppling the Shah from government power. Nigeria remains largely outside the orbit of superpower rivalries; thus, neither the United States nor the Soviet Union influenced the various military coups and the civilian return to government office.

Third, political beliefs contribute to between-system change by undermining the power of the established regime and by portraying a vision of a new political system. In all five countries, the incumbent governments faced declining legitimacy; powerful social groups (Cuba, Chile, Iran) and the military (Vietnam, Chile, Nigeria) no longer believed that the ruling elites had the right to govern the society. Committed to a cause that blended concrete needs with more abstract ideological goals, opposition leaders in Vietnam, Cuba, Chile, and Iran demonstrated stronger morale than did the incumbent government officials. Particularly in Vietnam and Iran the revolutionaries' dedication to ideological or theological principles—Vietnamese Marxism-Leninism and Shiite Islam—motivated them to endure the repressive treatment imposed by ruling elites and to continue working for a new political system.[2]

Except in Nigeria, the vision of a reconstructed political system contributed to fundamental sociopolitical changes. Ideologues and theocrats sketched a vision of a transformed political regime. Through political education and mobilization, they tried to convince people to share their political vision: a socialist society in Cuba and Vietnam, an Islamic theocracy in Iran, and in Chile an anti-Marxist system that blended Hispanic autocracy with free-market economic policies. This vision of an alternative political system served as a magnet that pulled alienated individuals away from the established government and toward the opposition that promised to rectify the policy failures of the previous regime. In Nigeria, however, neither the civilian politicians nor the military officers had the ideological vision and organizational means to implement public policies that would realize fundamental sociopolitical changes. Oriented toward the pursuit of concrete benefits, not abstract moral-spiritual goals, they sought government power mainly to reward the elite rather than to transform society.

Fourth, ineffective policy performance by itself does not necessarily produce between-system change; only when policy failures combine with the disintegration of state power and declining regime legitimacy does the opposition gain the opportunity to overthrow the established government. For example, between 1975 and 1986 the southern region in Vietnam suffered from high inflation and high unemployment rates. Yet the Vietnamese Communist elite still remained in political power. During the late 1960s and mid-1980s, Cuban leaders were unable to realize high economic growth rates. Shortages of consumer goods caused disenchantment among the Cuban population; however, Castro continued to dominate the political system.

After the 1973 Chilean coup, high unemployment, growing income inequality, and erratic growth plagued the society. The economic growth rate declined around 13 to 14 percent in 1975 and 1982, compared with the 5.6 percent drop in the real gross domestic product in 1973. From 1974 through 1985 Chileans experienced double-digit unemployment rates. During the Unidad Popular regime, however, the joblessness rate never exceeded 5 percent. Despite these different policy impacts, the Allende reconciliation system was overthrown, whereas the bureaucratic-authoritarian system dominated by President Pinochet survived a far longer time.

The Islamic revolutionaries governing Iran since early 1979 have secured less favorable economic results than did the Shah in the 1960s and early 1970s. Inflation and unemployment remain high. The manufacturing sector has declined. Only oil exports contribute to economic growth. Although the gap between rich and poor has lessened somewhat, the urban poor still suffer from food shortages, scarce housing, and ineffective health care. Yet so long as the theocratic regime maintains tight control over social groups and government agencies, especially the police and the armed forces, the opposition seems unlikely to emerge victorious.

After the Nigerian military overthrew the civilian government in late 1983, it scarcely produced impressive policy results. As under the Shagari administration, corruption, inflation, unemployment, and severe income inequalities remained. The major change was that a more repressive bureaucratic-authoritarian regime tried to stifle dissidents such as students, trade unionists, and journalists who protested policy malfeasance.

Fifth, folk, reconciliation, and mobilization systems are fragile regimes in the contemporary Third World. Folk systems cannot withstand challenges by more centralized political agencies. Even though the folk values of communal solidarity, moral purity, and social equality remain alive in the Iranian theocracy, the decentralized structures associated with the folk system have collapsed, as Vietnam, Iran, and Nigeria show. Reconciliation systems also remain weak. After gaining independence in 1960, Nigerians lived under a reconciliation regime from 1960 to 1965 and from

1979 to 1983. A military dictatorship governed during the other periods. Before the 1973 coup Chileans enjoyed a more democratic heritage than most other Latin Americans. Yet when the Unidad Popular tried to realize fundamental politico-economic changes during the early 1970s, the armed forces overthrew the reconciliation system.

Leaders who want to create a populist mobilization system in a reconciliation context face overwhelming difficulties, as demonstrated in Chile. Because the government encourages civil liberties and operates under pluralistic arrangements, the mobilizers cannot easily gain the sufficient power needed to smash the state. Mobilization from below meets opposition from both the reconciliation leaders and more conservative bureaucratic forces. Hence, populist mobilization movements usually fail to consolidate their gains.

Elitist mobilization systems also appear fairly transitory, as illustrated by the Vietnamese, Cuban, and Iranian cases. Most often, elitist mobilization systems become bureaucratized when disenchantment with the ideological cause grows and the masses no longer show great enthusiasm about participating in mobilization activities. After an initial burst of enthusiasm that surrounds the revolutionary seizure of government power, pressures arise for greater order, efficiency, and concrete demonstrations of regime effectiveness. At this point, the latent bureaucratic strains of an elitist mobilization system become more manifest. This trend has appeared not only in Vietnam and Cuba but also in Iran. Widespread popular belief in the theocratic vision has waned. Urban citizens no longer seem so enthusiastic about participating in elections and mass demonstrations. Government bureaucracies have begun to supplant the Islamic revolutionary committees that wielded the greatest power immediately after the revolutionaries seized government control in early 1979. Only the war of attrition with Iraq keeps the populace mobilized behind the regime. Iraqi President Saddam Hussein has replaced the Shah as the evil Yazid against whom the theocratic elite mobilize the faithful.

Sixth, during the twentieth century, the bureaucratic-authoritarian political system has become the dominant type throughout the Third World. Despite their different policies, ideologies, and social stratification patterns, bureaucratic officials — technocrats, managers, administrators, planners, engineers — wield crucial power over the policy process in Vietnam, Cuba, Chile, Nigeria, and Iran. Since the current leaders seized power, the state has grown stronger. The armed forces play a powerful role. All five nations have experienced centralized, hierarchical, coercive rule. Political organization assumes primacy over social-group spontaneity. Even the political beliefs of the Vietnamese Communists, Castro,

Pinochet, Khomeini, and the Nigerian military officers show a few similarities, such as their common commitment to political loyalty, order, hard work, and labor discipline.

The pervasiveness of the bureaucratic-authoritarian system stems from political, economic, and cultural reasons. The growth in political participation, combined with mounting demands for government decisions that will benefit the claimants, sensitizes political elites to the need for order, a special concern of bureaucratic officials. When the state assumes an increasingly wide range of responsibilities, bureaucratic expertise becomes essential. Under the policies pursued by Vietnamese, Cuban, Nigerian, and Iranian leaders, the state manages the economy. Although voicing a "free-market" monetarist policy, Chilean policymakers delegate major economic tasks to civilian technocrats, military officers, heads of Chilean concentrated industries, and executives who manage the multinational corporations—all elites with a bureaucratic orientation. Upholding the need for technical expertise, efficiency, hierarchy, order, and specialization, these bureaucratic elites articulate cultural values that reinforce the trend toward bureaucratic-authoritarian systems as the dominant type for implementing political change in the Third World.

## Notes

1 Leon Trotsky, *The Basic Writings of Trotsky*, ed. Irving Howe (New York: Schocken Books, 1976), 97.
2 James DeNardo, *Power in Numbers: The Political Strategy of Protest and Rebellion* (Princeton, N.J.: Princeton University Press, 1985), 154–187.

# ABOUT THE AUTHOR

Charles F. Andrain is professor of political science at San Diego State University. Since receiving his Ph.D. from the University of California at Berkeley in 1964, he has written several books about crossnational public policy and political change. These include *Social Policies in Western Industrial Societies* (1985), *Foundations of Comparative Politics: A Policy Perspective* (1983), and *Political Life and Social Change* (1975).

# INDEX

Afghanistan 33
Africa 1, 30–1, 66
Alessandri, Jorge 155, 159, 177
Alessandri, President Arturo 67
Allende, President Salvador 6, 53, 68–9,
  71–3, 151–5, 157, 159, 161, 163–6,
  170–2, 174, 176–7, 179–82, 184–5,
  187, 192, 195, 201, 285
  administration 157, 160, 166–70, 172–3,
    175–82, 186, 188–90, 192, 196,
    198–200, 203, 284, 287
  see also Chile, Unidad Popular
Angola 72, 132, 225
Argentina 23, 34, 37, 68, 157
Asia 1, 30–1, 33–4, 66
Awolowo, Obafemi 221, 235
Azikiwe, President Nnamdi 71, 221

Babangida, President Ibrahim 72, 244
Balewa, Prime Minister Abubakar Tafawa
  221
Bangladesh 277
Batista, Fulgencio 7, 67, 69, 121–2, 124–7,
  129, 144, 153
  regime 121–7, 130–2, 136, 140, 153, 284
  bureaucratic-authoritarian system 124
Bazargan, Medhi 263, 269
between-system changes 10–11, 54, 58–69
Biafra 72
Bolivia, reconciliation system 37
Botswana 234
Brazil 23, 32–3, 37, 157
Britain 22, 30, 68–9, 71, 259–60
  imperialism 66, 71–2, 215, 217–21, 242
  influence in Iran 264, 266
Buddhism 67, 79–80, 90, 93–5, 104, 110
Buhari, President Mohammed 72, 243–4
bureaucratic-authoritarian systems 7–8, 10,
  13, 22–30, 32, 42, 46, 49, 53, 55–6, 60,
  62, 64–9, 90, 97, 121, 126–7, 163,
  172–3, 182–203, 219, 244, 253, 259,
  265, 271, 287–9
  agrarian 8–9, 21–9, 38, 42
  between-system change 60–2, 64
  industrial 8–9, 23–9
  within-system change 56

Cambodia 83
Castro, Fidel 6–7, 53, 58, 67, 69–70, 71–3,
  119–21, 123–9, 131–8, 140, 142–4,
  152–3, 177, 182, 284–5, 287–8
  regime 121–2, 127–44
Catholicism 14, 34, 93, 95, 104, 110, 122
  see also named countries
Champa Empire 76, 81
Chile 3, 52–3, 67–70, 151–203, 245, 284,
  286, 288–9
  agrarian reform 159, 166, 168–70, 176, 180
  armed forces 53, 71, 153–4, 176
  bureaucratic-authoritarian system 7, 53,
    69, 182–203
  Catholic influence 158–9, 164, 171, 177,
    184, 187–9, 192, 199, 201
  Christian Democrats 155, 158–61, 163–5,
    171–2, 174–6, 178, 180–1, 186–90, 200
  civil liberties 154–5, 184, 186
  Communists 152, 160–1, 165, 170–2, 175,
    177, 187, 189–90
  Congress 161, 163–5, 168, 176, 178
  economic
    growth 165–7, 179, 184, 196–7
    policies 151, 158, 166, 168–9, 183, 185,
      191, 197, 200–1, 289
  education policies 170–2, 192
  foreign influence, see USA
  golpe of the generals 174–82, 201, 285
  health policies 171–2
  Hispanic influence 184, 200, 286
  income inequalities 165–6, 169, 179, 184,
    196, 198
  industrial output 167–8, 195
  inflation 165–9, 175, 179–80, 184, 195–8
  military coup 33, 49, 53, 68–9, 71, 152–3,
    155, 174, 177–9, 287
  military regime 183–92, 194
    economic policies 192–4, 197–8
    education policies 199–200
    health policies 200–1
    public policies 187–8, 192–203
  mobilization systems 7, 48–9, 71, 163, 173
  Movement of the Revolutionary Left
    (MIR) 7, 71, 152, 157, 160, 170, 173,
    178–81, 190, 284

291

Chile—*continued*
Movement of United Popular Action (MAPU) 158, 160, 170, 172–3, 175, 177, 180, 189–90
National party 155, 158–9, 161, 163–4, 173, 175–8, 180–1, 189–90
political changes 13, 151–203, 284
political parties 157–63
Popular Democratic Movement 189, 200
Popular Front government 155, 157
public policies 165–74
Radical party 165, 170–1, 177, 190
reconciliation systems 7, 31, 34, 53, 69, 154, 156–7, 163, 172, 178–9, 181
Social Democrats 177, 190
social services 165, 171, 198
social stratification system 155–6, 158, 182–3
Socialists 160–1, 163, 165, 170–3, 175, 180–1, 187, 189–90, 284
unemployment 165–7, 169–70, 179, 187, 195–6, 198
Unidad Popular (UP) 7, 69, 72, 152, 155, 157–61, 163–6, 169–72, 174–81, 186, 188, 190, 195–6, 199, 200–1, 285, 287–8
economic policies 169
reconciliation system 155–74, 182–3, 185
*see also* Allende, Frei, Pinochet
China 6, 81, 89, 99, 120, 131, 267
bureaucratic-authoritarian system 26
folk system 26
influence in Vietnam 71, 76–7, 80–1, 99–100, 107, 110, 112, 120, 285
mobilization system 48
civil liberties 33, 37–8, 68, 101
*see also* named countries
colonialism 6, 23, 30, 33, 42–3, 46, 66
Confucianism 67, 76, 79–80, 82–4, 91–3, 112, 120
Costa Rica 5, 32, 201
Cuba 52–3, 67–70, 73, 106, 119–44, 151–3, 182–3, 186, 188, 193, 201, 203, 274, 284–6, 288–9
bureaucratic-authoritarian system 7, 53, 69, 121
Catholic church 122, 124, 135
civil liberties 53, 124
Committees for the Defense of the Revolution (CDRs) 70, 127, 130–1, 133, 136, 139, 141
Communist party 70, 121, 125, 127–35, 140, 142–3
economic
growth 137, 287

policies 120–1, 124, 129–30, 136–8
stratification system 130
education policies 119, 129–30, 139–41
ethnic groups 122
Federation of Cuban Women 135, 139, 142
foreign influence in, see Spain, USA, USSR
health policies 120, 141–2
mass associations 127, 132, 134–6
mobilization systems 48, 53, 69, 119, 121, 127, 132–3, 135, 142, 144
overseas programs 132, 139
political
change 13, 119–44, 284
organizations 124–6, 131–6
Popular Socialist Party (PSP) 121, 152
public policies 136–44
Rebel Army 123–7, 131, 153, 284
reconciliation system 7
revolution 121–7, 134
Revolutionary Armed Forces (FAR) 127, 131–2, 134
social
services 130
stratification systems 129–31
unemployment 138–9
women's roles 129–30
*see also* Batista, Castro

Danjuma, Theophilus General 215
Diem, President 91, 93–4
Dien Bien Phu (1954) 87, 90
Dominican Republic 33
Durkheim, Emile 15–16, 79, 271

economic policies 4, 10
*see also* named countries
education policies 4, 10, 30, 32
*see also* named countries
Egypt 22, 33, 277
El Salvador, reconciliation system 37
ethnic groups, *see* named countries

folk systems 7–8, 10, 13, 15–22, 26, 43, 54–6, 60–1, 64, 66–7, 267, 287
agricultural 8–9, 16–18, 20–1, 54
between-system change 60–1, 63, 65
hunting-gathering 8–9, 16–20
political beliefs 17, 19, 21
religious values 19–20
role specialization 15–21
theocratic 62, 67–8, 70
within-system changes 55–6
France 30, 87–8, 120, 158, 259–60, 265
colonialism 62, 66, 82–90, 102–3, 217, 219

influence in Vietnam 67, 69, 76, 82–9,
102–3, 217, 219
Frei, President Eduardo 157, 159, 171, 177,
185, 187, 192, 195, 201, 203
government 160, 166, 169, 171

Ghana 240
Gowon, General Yakubu 225, 232, 243
Guatemala 33, 277
reconciliation system 37
Guevara, Ernesto "Che" 128, 135, 140, 143

Haiphong 83, 104
Haiti 186
Hanoi 83–4, 89, 103
Havana 53, 123, 126, 136, 139
health policies 4, 10
*see also* named countries
Henriquez, Cardinal Raul Silva 187
Ho Chi Minh, President 3, 58, 88, 90–2, 96,
99, 109, 120
Honduras 277
Hussein, President Saddam 270, 288

Ibanez, General Carlos 67
India 277
reconciliation system 31, 34
individualism 80, 101, 119–20, 128, 151,
184, 268
Indonesia 32
industrialization 1, 22, 29–30, 34, 42–3, 46,
48, 70, 107
Inter-American Development Bank 193,
197
International Monetary Fund 14, 63, 107,
193, 243, 261
Iran 3, 5, 52, 67–8, 70, 252–79, 285–9
anti-Shah coalition 254, 260, 266, 285
bureaucratic-authoritarian system 53
education policy 54
ethnic groups 256–7, 263
Fedayin 263–4, 266
folk culture 254–5
foreign influence, *see* Britain, Israel,
USA, USSR
Islamic Republic 3, 5, 67, 253–5, 264,
267–74, 277
civil liberties 267–9
constitution 270, 272–3
Council of Guardians 270, 275, 278
creation of 267–79
Crusade for Reconstruction 270, 274–7
economic growth 275, 287
economic policies 268, 271–2, 274–6,
278, 287
education policies 274, 276–7

ethnic groups 268, 271–3
folk system 267
Foundation for the Dispossessed 270,
274, 276
Foundation of Martyrs 270, 274
health policies 274, 276–7, 287
land redistribution 274, 276
mobilization systems 270, 278–9
muslim clergy 260, 265, 268–78
muslims 268–9, 274–7
nationalization policy 274–5
policy processes 274–9
religious freedom 269, 272
revolutionary committees 53, 67, 270,
288
revolutionary courts 271, 273
Revolutionary Guards 53, 67, 270–1,
273–5
theocratic policies 267–70, 274–9
unemployment 275, 287
war with Iraq 54, 270, 275, 277–8, 288
women's rights 269, 271–2, 278
military coup 255
Mojahedin 263, 266, 271
monarchical system 255–6
mostazafin 254, 264
Muslim clergy 73, 252, 254–5, 260, 264–6,
285
nationalism 256, 258–9
political change in 13, 252–79, 284
Rastakhiz party 266
reconciliation system 256
Savak 53, 256, 261, 265, 271
secret police 256, 261, 264, 266, 271
Shiite muslims 54, 67, 70, 73, 255, 263–4,
266, 268–70, 272–3, 277–8, 285–6
Tudeh party 256, 263, 271, 286
*see also* Khomeini, Pahlavi regime
Iraq 54, 270, 275, 277–8, 288
Islamic Republic, *see* Iran
Islamic revolution 53, 62, 67, 71–2, 253,
263, 267–8, 273, 285, 287
Israel
influence in Iran 264
US influence in 33
Italy 53, 157–8

Japan 33, 67, 87, 138, 194
influence in Vietnam 67, 76, 87

Kenya 240
Khmer Empire 76, 81, 113
Khmer Rouge 100, 107, 110, 112
Khomeini, Ayatollah Ruhollah 3, 5, 53, 67,
72, 252, 264–70, 273–5, 277–8, 289
Ky, General 93

Lagos 217, 219, 226, 230
Laos 83
Latin America 1, 22, 69
  reconciliation systems 31, 34
Le Doc Tho 110, 112
Le Duan 112
Lebanon 5
Leninism 70, 120, 154, 156, 178, 185
Lesotho 240

Machado, General Gerardo 153
Marx, Karl 52, 181, 244
Marxism 76, 151, 154, 156, 160, 174–5,
  177–8, 182–9, 199, 201
Marxist-Leninism 6, 33, 48, 52, 67, 73,
  91–2, 96, 101, 109–10, 112–13, 120,
  126, 140, 143, 151, 156, 177, 264
Mexico 158
Middle East, reconciliation systems 31
military coups 33, 286
  see also named countries
mobilization systems 7–8, 10, 13, 41–9, 53,
  55, 57, 60, 64, 66–9, 71, 73, 119, 121,
  127, 132–3, 135, 142, 144, 163, 172–3,
  182, 267, 270, 278–9
  between-system change 60, 62, 64–5
  elitist 8–9, 43–9, 57, 64–5, 67, 97, 100,
    103, 110, 113, 119, 203, 270, 274, 288
  leaders 42–3, 47–8, 58
  populist 8–9, 43–9, 64, 163, 173, 288
  within-system changes 57–8
Mohammed, General Murtala 225, 232, 241
monetarism 3, 183, 194, 289
Mongolia 33, 105–6
  mobilization system 48
Morocco 240
multinational corporations 23, 26–7, 29,
  33–4, 63, 153, 167, 180, 183, 228, 238,
  260

Nauru, reconciliation system 31
Ngo Dinh Diem, President 90–1
Nguyen Cao Ky, General 90
Nguyen Hien 109
Nguyen Khac Vien 76
Nguyen Van Thieu, General 90
Nigeria 6, 52–3, 67–9, 71–3, 215–16, 275,
  284, 286, 288–9
  Action Group 223, 236
  agrarian folk system 20
  British colonial rule 71–2, 215, 217–21,
    242
    bureaucratic-authoritarian system
    68–9, 219
  civil war 53, 72, 226

economic
  growth 242
  policies 244, 287
  stratification system 218
education program 230–1, 238, 243
ethnic groups 215, 217, 219, 222–4, 227,
  235–6, 240, 242
First Republic 220–4
  education policy 223–4
  ethnic groups 222
  federal government 221, 223–4
  occupational pluralism 222–3
  overthrow of 224
  political structures 221–4
  reconciliation system 221–2
  regional government 221–4
foreign influence 72, 217–18
Fulani 217, 222, 233, 236, 240
Great Nigeria People's Party (GNPP)
  235–7, 242
Hausa 218, 222, 227, 231, 236
Hausa–Fulani 218, 222–3, 227, 235, 243–4
Igbo 20, 215–17, 219, 222–7, 230, 235–6,
  240
land tenure system 218
military coups 53, 69, 225, 241, 244
military regime 225–6
  bureaucratic-authoritarian system 225
  economic policies 227, 229–30
  education policies 230–1
  ethnic groups in 227
  health policies 231–2
  indiginization program 228
  institutional changes 226–8
  policy changes 228–32
  restoration of civilian rule 232
  unemployment 229–30
National Convention of Nigerian
  Citizens (NCNC) 223–4, 236, 243
National Party of Nigeria (NPN) 235,
  237, 240, 242–3
Northern People's Congress party
  (NPC) 223–4, 236, 243
People's Party (NPP) 235–7, 240, 242–3
People's Redemption Party (PRP) 235–7,
  242
political change in 13, 215–45, 284
reconciliation system 53, 68–9, 232
religious groups 217–18, 222, 233, 241,
  243
Second Republic 233–45
  civil liberties 234
  economic performance 238, 241
  education policy 230–1, 238–9, 243
  federal government 237
  health policies 239–40

overthrow of 241
policy process 237–41
political parties 235–7
power network 234–5
reconciliation system 233, 236
social pluralism 235–7
social stratification system 233–4, 237
unemployment 238, 241
unemployment 229–30, 244, 287
Unity Party of Nigeria (UPN) 235–7, 242
Universal Primary Education Program
    (UPE) 230–1, 238, 243
see also Gowon, Shagari
North Korea 6, 33, 105, 108, 188, 274
mobilization system 48

Obasanjo, Lieutenant General Olusegun
    225, 232
Ottoman empire 22

Pahlavi, Shah Mohammed Reza 53, 67,
    70–1, 252–4, 256–60, 264–70, 272–3,
    275, 285–8
dynasty 252–3, 255–9, 272, 276, 285
regime 70–1, 255–6
    armed forces 256, 258–9, 266
    bureaucratic-authoritarian system 253,
        259, 265, 271
    civil liberties 258–9, 263
    collapse of 260–6, 285–6
    economic growth 261–2
    economic policies 257–60, 262–3
    educational policies 257–9, 261–4, 268,
        287
    ethnic groups 256–7, 263
    folk system 254–5
    foreign influence in, see USA
    health policies 259, 262–3
    industrialization 259–61
    land redistribution policies 256–8, 261
    Literacy Corps 257, 262
    modernization 254, 259–60
    Moslems 256–8
    policy performance 259–63
    political legitimacy 258–9, 263–5
    political policy 258
    unemployment 261–2, 264, 287
    women's rights 257–8, 264
Pakistan 33, 277
Persian Empire 255, 259
Peru, reconciliation system 37
Pham Van Dong 110
Philippines 33, 277
Pinochet, President Augusto 151, 182,
    188–9, 191, 195, 199, 201, 287, 289
    administration 183, 189–90, 243

ideology 183–5
regime 183–92
police 26–7, 29, 34, 47–8, 56, 63, 67–8, 84
    see also named countries
policy performance 64–5, 286–7
    see also named countries
political
    beliefs 13–14, 24, 35, 44
    change 1–11
        see also named countries
    legitimacy 61–2, 286
    power 63, 103
    stagnation 30, 41, 64
    systems, models of 7–9, 13–51
Prats, General Carlos 186

Qajar dynasty 255

reconciliation systems 7–8, 10, 13, 30–42,
    49, 53, 55, 60, 64, 66–9, 154–7, 163,
    172–3, 178–9, 181, 216, 221–2, 232,
    244, 256, 287–8
    between-system change 60, 62, 64–5
    competitive oligarchy 8–9, 34–8, 40–1,
        46, 68, 236
    pluralist democracy 8–9, 30, 34–42, 56,
        157, 181
    within-system change 56–7
religious groups 26, 29, 34–5, 39–40, 46–8
    see also named countries
revolution 41–2, 67, 119, 121–2, 128, 284
    see also named countries
role specialization 15–16, 19–21, 34, 43, 47

Sadr, Bani 263, 269
Saigon 52, 67, 70, 83, 87, 89–91, 93–4, 103,
    108
Santiago 163–4, 169, 176, 190, 196, 201
Sassanian dynasty 264
Shagari, President Shehu 215, 235, 237, 242
    administration 238, 241, 243–4, 287
Shah of Iran, see Pahlavi
social stratification systems 10–11, 16, 29,
    37, 41, 48, 57, 85–8, 95, 129–31,
    155–6, 158, 182–3, 288
    see also named countries
South Africa 72
South Korea, bureaucratic-authoritarian
    system 32
Spain 22, 154, 157–8
    influence in Cuba 153, 217
Sri Lanka, reconciliation system 31
Syrian empire 22

Taiwan 23, 33
    bureaucratic-authoritarian system 32

Tehran 260, 265, 273, 276
Thieu, General 52, 69, 93, 99
    regime 98, 101–3, 108, 112, 284
Third World political systems, models of
    13–51
Tito, Marshal 177
Tomic, Radomiro 155
Trotsky, Leon 284
Truong Chinh 110
Truong Nhu Tang 96

Unidad Popular, see Chile
Uruguay 23, 68
    reconciliation system 31, 34, 37
USA 23, 31, 63, 67, 126, 128, 133, 183, 185,
    194, 259–60, 265, 285–6
    influence in
        Chile 33, 71–2, 122, 125, 153, 167,
            179–80, 285
        Cuba 70–1, 120, 122, 125, 135, 137–8,
            142, 153, 285
        Iran 71–2, 256, 264–6, 285
        Nigeria 72
        Third World 33, 71
        Vietnam 52, 70–1, 76, 89–90, 94–9,
            102–3, 107, 110, 285
USSR 23, 63, 67, 119–21, 131, 183, 285–6
    influence in
        Cuba 33, 71–2, 120, 136–8, 142–3
        Iran 72, 286
        Third World 33, 71
        Vietnam 33, 71, 89, 99–100, 106–7, 285

Venezuela, reconciliation system 31
Vietnam 3, 7, 52, 66–70, 83–4, 90, 119–20,
    127, 131, 134, 182, 188, 245, 267, 274,
    284, 286–9
    bureaucratic–authoritarian system 7, 26,
        52, 66, 69, 77, 82
    civil war 90–100
    Communist Party (VCP) 3, 52, 66–7, 69,
        72, 76, 80, 88, 90–2, 100–1, 103–5,
        110, 119–21, 125–6, 182, 287–8
    Democratic Republic of (DRV) 69, 87–8,
        90, 97, 120
        foreign support 99–100
        land redistribution program 95
    folk system 7, 26, 66–7, 69, 77
    foreign influence in 94, 99–100
        see also China, France, Japan, USA,
            USSR
    French colonial rule 82–90, 102–3, 217,
        219
    land reform 94

Lao Dong party 90, 95–6, 98, 120
Marxists 100, 286
mobilization system 52, 67, 69
monarchy 77–84, 285
    bureaucratic–authoritarian agrarian
        system 80–2
    folk system 80–2
    political beliefs 78–80
    political structures 80–2
    religious beliefs 79–80
    social stratification 77–8
National Liberation Front (NLF) 69, 71,
    90–9, 103
People's Army of 52, 101–3, 113, 120,
    125, 284
People's Liberation Armed Forces
    (PLAF) 92–3, 97, 99, 103, 125, 284
People's Revolutionary Party 95, 97–8,
    103
political
    change in 13, 76–118, 284
    power in 91–100
Republic of 90, 93–9, 285
revolution 62, 76–7
social stratification 77–8, 82
Socialist Republic of (SRV) 52–3, 90,
    100–13
    economic growth rate 106–7, 112
    economic policies 105–8
    education policies 109–10
    foreign influence 100, 106–7, 110, 112,
        120
    health policies 110
    military police 101
    political organizations 101–5
    public policies 105–13
    religious policies 104, 110
    unemployment 108
Viet Cong (Vietnam Cong San) 90
Viet Minh 87–90, 93, 285
voluntarism 29, 48–9, 56–7, 65, 142, 180,
    201, 240, 259, 278
voluntary associations 39–41

West Europe 33, 194
West Indies, reconciliation systems 31
within-system changes 10–11, 54–8
women, political role 47, 80, 104, 130
World Bank 63, 193, 197, 243

Zaire 240
Zambia 240
Zedong, Mao 177